EMOTION, EVOLUTION, AND RATIONALITY

EMOTION, EVOLUTION, AND RATIONALITY

Edited by

DYLAN EVANS

*Faculty of Computing, Engineering and Mathematical Sciences,
University of the West of England,
Bristol*

PIERRE CRUSE

*Centre de Philosophie des Sciences,
Université Catholique de Louvain,
Louvain-la-Neuve*

OXFORD
UNIVERSITY PRESS

OXFORD
UNIVERSITY PRESS

Great Clarendon Street, Oxford OX2 6DP

Oxford University Press is a department of the University of Oxford.
It furthers the University's objective of excellence in research, scholarship,
and education by publishing worldwide in

Oxford New York

Auckland Cape Town Dar es Salaam Hong Kong Karachi
Kuala Lumpur Madrid Melbourne Mexico City Nairobi
New Delhi Shanghai Taipei Toronto

With offices in

Argentina Austria Brazil Chile Czech Republic France Greece
Guatemala Hungary Italy Japan South Korea Poland Portugal
Singapore Switzerland Thailand Turkey Ukraine Vietnam

Published in the United States
by Oxford University Press Inc., New York

First published 2004
Reprinted 2005 (twice), 2006

A catalogue record for this title is available from the British Library

ISBN   0 19 852897 3 (Hbk)
         0 19 852898 1 (Pbk)

10 9 8 7 6 5 4

Typeset by Cepha Imaging Pvt Ltd
Printed in Great Britain
on acid-free paper by
Biddles Ltd., King's Lynn, Norfolk

P8

ACKNOWLEDGEMENTS

The conference from which this book evolved was organized with the support of a grant from the AHRB to Professors Mark Sainsbury and David Papineau at King's College London for a research project entitled 'The function of the emotions: an investigation into their evolutionary role and an exploration of the philosophical consequences'. More information about the project, which ran for three years, from 1999–2002, can be found at:

   http://www.kcl.ac.uk/depsta/philosophy/project/emotions/

   The editors wish to thank all the invited speakers whose contributions appear in this volume, and Martin Baum at Oxford University Press. Thanks are also due to Oxford University Press for permission to reprint 'The search hypothesis of emotion', by Dylan Evans, which originally appeared in the *British Journal for the Philosophy of Science*, vol. 53 (4), 2002, pp. 497–509.

CONTENTS

Contributors *ix*

Introduction *xi*

Part I: Neuroscientific foundations

1. William James and the modern neurobiology of emotion *3*
   Antonio R. Damasio

2. Homologizing human emotions *15*
   Andrew D. Lawrence and Andrew J. Calder

Part II: Emotion, belief, and appraisal

3. Emotional behaviour and the scope of belief-desire explanation *51*
   Finn Spicer

4. Which emotions are basic? *69*
   Jesse Prinz

5. Towards a 'Machiavellian' theory of emotional appraisal *89*
   Paul E. Griffiths

6. Unpicking reasonable emotions *107*
   Brian Parkinson

Part III: Evolution and the rationality of emotion

7. Evolution, culture, and the irrationality of the emotions *133*
   Chandra Sekhar Sripada and Stephen Stich

8. The role of emotions in ecological and practical rationality *159*
   Matteo Mameli

9. The search hypothesis of emotion *179*
   Dylan Evans

10. Adaptive illusions: optimism, control, and human rationality *193*
    Daniel Nettle

11. Emotion versus reason as a genetic conflict *209*
     Christopher Badcock

Part IV: Philosophical perspectives

12. Conscience and conflict: Darwin, Freud, and the origins of human aggression *225*
     Jim Hopkins

13. Emotion, reason, and virtue *249*
     Peter Goldie

Index *269*

CONTRIBUTORS

Christopher Badcock
Department of Sociology, London
School of Economics and Political
Science, Houghton Street,
London WC2A 2AE.

Andrew J. Calder
MRC Cognition and Brain Sciences
Unit, Cambridge, 15 Chancer Road,
Cambridge CB2 2EF.

Pierre Cruse
Centre de Philosophie des Sciences,
Université Catholique de Louvain,
College Mercier, Place du Cardinal
Mercier 14, B-1348
Louvain-la-Neuve, Belgium.

Antonio R. Damasio
Department of Neurology,
University of Iowa College of
Medicine, 200 Hawkins Drive,
Iowa City, Iowa 522242, USA.

Dylan Evans
Faculty of Computing, Engineering
and Mathematical Sciences,
University of the West of England,
Bristol BS16 1QY.

Peter Goldie
Department of Philosophy, King's
College London, Strand, London
WC2R 2LS.

Paul Griffiths
Department of History and
Philosophy of Science, University of
Pittsburgh, Pittsburgh,
Philadelphia 15260, USA.

Jim Hopkins
Department of Philosophy, King's
College London, Strand,
London WC2R 2LS.

Andrew D. Lawrence
MRC Cognition and Brain Sciences
Unit, Cambridge, 15 Chancer Road,
Cambridge CB2 2EF.

Gianmatteo Mameli
Centre for Philosophy of Natural
and Social Science, London School
of Economics and Political Science,
Houghton Street,
London WC2A, 2AE.

Daniel Nettle
Departments of Psychology and
Biological Sciences, Open
University, Walton Hall,
Milton Keynes MK7 6AA.

Brian Parkinson
Department of Experimental
Psychology, University of Oxford,
South Parks Road,
Oxford OXI 3UD.

Jesse Prinz
Department of Philosophy,
University of North Carolina at
Chapel Hill, Chapel Hill,
North Carolina 27599, USA.

Finn Spicer,
Department of Philosophy,
University of Bristol, 9 Woodlands
Road, Clifton, Bristol BS8 ITB.

Chandra Sekhar Sripada
Department of Philosophy and
Centre for Cognitive Science,
Rutgers University, 26 Nichol
Avenue, New Brunswick,
New Jersey 08901-1411, USA.

Stephen Stich
Department of Philosophy and
Centre for Cognitive Science,
Rutgers University, 26 Nichol
Avenue, New Brunswick,
New Jersey 08901-1411, USA.

INTRODUCTION

It is an exciting time for emotion research. After almost a century of relative neglect by scientists, the emotions are reclaiming the scientific attention that they enjoyed at the end of the nineteenth century. Charles Darwin (Darwin 1872), William James (James 1884) and Sigmund Freud (Freud 1915) all regarded the study of emotion as a key part of psychological enquiry, but with advent of behaviourism in the 1920s, attention turned away from mental processes to phenomena that could be described purely in terms of stimulus-response. The rise of cognitivism in the late 1950s restored scientific legitimacy to discussions of mental processes, but the computational theory of mind did not appear to lend itself easily to modelling emotions, and so, with one or two notable exceptions (Abelson 1963), emotional phenomena remained outside cognitive theories of the mind. For much of the twentieth century, then, the emotions received scant attention in science, with only a few neuroscientists (Cannon 1927, Maclean 1970, Panksepp 1982) and anthropologists bucking the trend.

It was only in the last decade of the twentieth century that emotions began to return to the centre stage of psychological enquiry. Evolutionary psychologists played a leading role in this renaissance (Tooby and Cosmides 1990), along with neuroscientists like Antonio Damasio and Joseph LeDoux, who were also keen to stress the evolutionary origins of emotional mechanisms (Damasio 1994, LeDoux 1998). Now, at the beginning of the twenty-first century, emotions are once again a hot topic for scientific research. Cognitive psychologists, anthropologists, philosophers, and researchers in artificial intelligence have joined in the debate, and a new journal entitled simply *Emotion* was launched in 2001.

To reflect the increasingly interdisciplinary nature of the current resurgence of interest in the emotions, the Philosophy Department at King's College London organized an international conference in April 2002 at which some of the leading lights in emotion research gathered to exchange ideas. Neuroscientists and psychologists rubbed shoulders with philosophers and researchers in artificial intelligence in what turned out to be a very fruitful meeting. This book brings together some of the most stimulating papers from that conference so that the ideas they put forward may reach a wider audience. It is our hope that, by publishing these papers together in book form, the intellectual momentum generated by the conference may not be lost.

The theme of this book

As the title suggests, the central theme of this book (and of the conference from which it springs) is the connection between evolution, emotion and rationality. The role that emotions play in 'rational' thought and decision-making is an increasingly important topic in contemporary psychology and philosophy. For many researchers, however, this topic cannot be properly addressed without setting it in the context of evolutionary biology. The Cornell economist Robert Frank, for example, has argued that many emotional responses that appear to be irrational when one considers only short-term losses and gains reveal a kind of 'global rationality' when considered from an evolutionary perspective (Frank 1988).

For thousands of years, it was almost universally assumed by Western thinkers that emotions were, at best, harmless luxuries, and at worst outright obstacles to intelligent action. One of the central ideas to emerge from the recent renaissance of interest in the emotions, however, is that this 'negative view of emotion' cannot be correct. A consensus is appearing among scientists from a range of disciplines that emotions are in fact vital to intelligent action. To draw on a metaphor from science fiction, a being like Spock from *Star Trek*, who lacked the capacity for emotion, would not be more rational than us, but less rational and less intelligent (Evans 2001).

Evolutionary considerations have played a vital role in this shift to a more positive view of emotion. Emotions are the result of complex neural mechanisms that show all the hallmarks of special design. They are, in other words, adaptations designed by natural selection. But natural selection does not build adaptations unless they serve some useful function. So emotions cannot be harmless but useless luxuries; still less can they be 'sand in the machinery of action', to use Jon Elster's evocative phrase (Elster 1999). Rather, they must have some vital function. Opinions differ as to the exact nature of the function or functions that emotions serve, but many emotion researchers now agree that, whatever they may be, these functions are so important that a creature that lacked all emotional capacities simply could not survive. To return to the Star Trek metaphor, it is not just that a being like Spock would be less rational than us; such a creature could not even evolve (Evans 2001).

The central theme of this book, then, is the role that evolutionary considerations can play in helping us to answer the age-old question of whether emotions are helpful or detrimental to rational thought and decision-making. How should we understand the evolutionary role of emotions? And can this explain the relationship between emotions and rationality?

Neuroscientific foundations

In the first chapter **Antonio Damasio** introduces some of the key ideas that are taken up throughout the book. Damasio highlights the general resurgence in interest in the emotions in neuroscience, and situates some of the key findings from that research in the context of William James' classic theory of emotions. He argues that the research largely vindicates James, and relates this to his own theory of emotions as somatic markers.

In the second paper, **Andrew Lawrence** and **Andy Calder** present further neurological evidence relating to the role of emotions in individual psychology. Lawrence and Calder contrast accounts of the neural structure of emotional systems that posit a general purpose 'limbic' system which subserves all our emotional capacities, and those that posit distinct specialized systems which subserve distinct 'affect programs'. The authors present data from neuroimaging studies that suggest there are distinct neural systems for responding to signals of fear and disgust and other emotions.

Emotion, belief and appraisal

In the second section, the papers turn to related questions concerning the way in which emotions respond to states of the environment—questions related to 'appraisal'—and the way in which they interact with rational thought. An influential idea linking these questions is that both are to be explained with reference to the idea that emotions involve, or are in some way closely related to *beliefs*—they respond to the environment through involving beliefs that represent the environment as instantiating features that concern us, and they interact with rational thought in the same way as ordinary beliefs, as explained by common-sense belief-desire psychology.

The idea that the role of emotions in individual psychology is to be explained by their relation to beliefs is investigated in the third paper by **Finn Spicer**. Spicer notes that an influential view in the philosophy of psychology is the 'Humean' claim that the rational production and control of action is entirely to be explained with reference to the beliefs and desires of the individual subject. Emotions raise a problem for this view since they appear to be highly relevant to the production of action, but don't obviously fall into the categories of belief or desire. Spicer investigates three solutions to this problem, which each involve the claim that emotions are in some way intimately linked to beliefs. Spicer argues that while the only view that has been proposed in the literature along these lines—the claim that emotions are constituted of beliefs—is untenable, there are two more promising solutions for the Humean—that emotions can either be treated as beliefs, or that they are nomologically connected with beliefs. However, Spicer raises two problems for these claims. One is that in certain important cases they lead to clumsy explanations of action involving implausible belief attributions. Another is that the link they postulate between emotions and beliefs and desires raises a demand for explanation that is unlikely to be satisfied without an appeal to some form of intentional explanation general enough to subsume belief–desire explanations of action as a special case. Spicer therefore argues that consideration of the way emotions feature in action explanation make it likely that the scope of Humean-style action explanation is smaller than Humeans often suppose.

In the fourth chapter, **Jesse Prinz** proposes a way to reconcile traditional 'cognitive' theories of emotion, which assign a central role to beliefs or other cognitive states such as appraisals, with evolutionary accounts that emphasize the involvement of the body. Prinz's 'embodied appraisal' theory holds that emotions are simple perceptions of bodily changes (as William James argued), but also that the patterns of bodily response themselves can be culturally informed. Thus, emotions can be both embodied and socially constructed, so there is some truth in the views of both evolutionary psychologists and social constructionists. In aguing for this reconciliation, Prinz also contests the claims put forward by some researchers, such as Paul Griffiths, that there are fundamentally different types of emotion. According to Prinz, all emotions are fundamentally alike.

The idea that emotions are *appraisals*—that is, responses to features of the environment that concern us—is also taken up by **Paul Griffiths** in the fifth chapter. Griffiths argues that neurological and experimental psychological evidence point to the conclusion that emotional appraisal takes place on at least two different levels—appraisals can involve complex judgements about the environment, but can also take place at a 'lower' level at which they completely bypass cognitive mechanisms, and often conflict with cognitions. However, Griffiths argues against Prinz's claim in the last chapter, that the relationship between lower-level emotions and higher-level cognitions cannot be explained on the grounds of the intentional content of those states since the impoverished inferential role of lower-level states suggests it is inappropriate to attribute conceptual content to them at all. Instead, Griffiths argues that the relationship between lower and higher level appraisals is better understood in terms of the fact that they both track features of concern to organisms in their environment, and in particular 'affordances'—or possibilities for action. As Griffiths notes this suggests the conclusion that emotions are in fact 'strategic' or 'Machiavellian', in that they respond not only to the immediate state of the environment, but also the likely consequences of the emotion's being triggered in that environment.

In the sixth chapter **Brian Parkinson** also takes up the question of appraisal and belief. Parkinson notes that standard appraisal theory holds that different emotions have evolved independently to occur when the environment presents certain functional demands to organisms. This view suggests that emotions are 'preparations for action' which occur when an organism perceives the environment as instantiating certain specific features of concern. However, Parkinson claims that psychological evidence and evolutionary considerations both suggest that this view cannot account for the flexibility with which emotions unfold in real-time transactions, both in respect of the situations in which they are triggered, and the behaviour to which they lead. Parkinson claims that it is more plausible to see emotional responses as determined largely by processes of socialization, rather than as evolutionarily selected responses to determinate situations, and that it is the capacity to develop emotional strategies on the basis of experience that is evolutionarily determined rather than the emotions themselves.

Evolution and the rationality of the emotions

So far, all the contributions agree that emotions (or at least the developmental processes that give rise to them) have been designed by natural selection, and that this ensures that emotions will play a positive role in rational decision-making. In chapter seven, however, **Chandra Sripada** and **Stephen Stich** cast doubt on whether emotions really are rational in this sense. Sripada and Stich argue that emotions are intrinsically linked to mentally represented sets of goals values and standards that they call a 'value structure'. They claim that there are reasons to think that the contents of value structures will often be maladaptive, and that when they are the emotions and behaviour that they lead to are irrational. Thus there is good reason to think that emotions will sometimes fail to be conducive to rational action.

In chapter eight **Matteo Mameli** also considers the question of whether emotions are conducive or destructive of rationality. Mameli notes that while there is a developing consensus that emotions are advantageous to 'ecological' rationality—the ability of an organism to cope successfully with its environment (though this consensus is not universally shared, as demonstrated by the last chapter) it is often thought that emotions remain destructive of 'practical' rationality—an organism's ability to make correct decisions about how to act. Mameli attempts to query the latter conclusion, appealing to Antonio Damasio's 'somatic marker hypothesis', on which emotions are feelings that represent certain somatic states, and on which the ability to instantiate such states is seen as essential to rational decision-making. However, Mameli argues that Damasio's explanation of how somatic markers contribute to decision making is inadequate, and puts forward an alternative explanation on which emotions are even more crucial to practical rationality than Damasio proposes.

In chapter nine **Dylan Evans** considers a further proposal that promises to rehabilitate the role of emotions in deliberative rationality, which he calls the 'search hypothesis of emotion'. Rooted in a model of decision-making derived from artificial intelligence, the search hypothesis characterizes emotions as psychological devices that restrict agents' attention to a small subset of the possible consequences of any action. On this view emotions are essential catalysts in the production of rational action, as they prevent agents from having to consider the potentially infinite number of possible consequences that an action may lead to. Evans argues that while the search hypothesis is not viable as a definition of emotions, it may prove to be a good account of what emotions typically do.

In chapter ten **Daniel Nettle** also considers the relationship between emotions and deliberative rationality. Nettle argues that there are evolutionary reasons to think that emotions are in some cases likely systematically to skew rationality. Standard models of rationality assume that the mind is able to come to accurate assessments of the probability of future contingencies. However, robust evidence shows that people systematically overestimate the probability of positive future contingencies, and underestimate the probability of negative ones—only those who are depressed or dysphoric come to accurate assessments. Nettle argues that there are good evolutionary reasons why this should be the case, since there is an asymmetric pattern of costs and benefits from getting motivational judgements wrong.

In chapter eleven, **Christopher Badcock** argues that there are genetic reasons for postulating a conflict between rationality and emotion in human decision-making. Badcock puts forward evidence that genes that build the limbic system are expressed only when inherited from the father, and those that construct the cortex only when they come from the mother. He argues that this suggests that conflicts between rationality and emotion in social and sexual behaviour can be explained as a conflict between the interests of maternal and paternal genes.

Philosophical perspectives

In Chapter twelve **Jim Hopkins** argues that evolutionary considerations can be combined with psychoanalytic insights to explain the way in which humans acquire a range of emotional dispositions related to the way they direct aggression towards others—perhaps a paradigm of 'irrational' emotion. Hopkins argues that Darwinian insights coincide with Freudian theories of identification and projection to show that aggression towards out-group members is a necessary concomitant of the development of 'conscientious' or moral emotions towards ingroup members relating to blame, punishment and guilt, which are essential to group cohesion, and confer substantial selective advantages. Hopkins shows that Darwinian and Freudian theories both trace the roots of these emotions to the competition for resources between mother and child in early infancy, and in particular the child's response to its initial development of a concept of its mother as a distinct continuing individual.

In the final chapter, **Peter Goldie** looks at the issue of the rationality of the emotions from a slightly different angle, focusing on the relationship between emotions and *epistemic* rationality. Goldie observes that emotions seem capable both of helping and hindering our ability to gain knowledge of the world. On the one hand emotions offer insights that would not be available in their absence, as suggested by the fact that the capacity for emotion seems to be an evolutionary adaptation. However at other times emotions *skew the epistemic landscape*, that is, predispose us to adopt certain beliefs in the absence of epistemic justification and distort our ability to see things as they are. Goldie argues that these phenomena suggest that it is critical to our ability to be epistemically virtuous, that we also have virtuous prudential and moral emotional dispositions. Moreover, since we may not be able, at least introspectively, to *know* whether and how our emotions are affecting our reason, the requirement for epistemic virtue is simply that we *be* prudentially and morally virtuous, independent of whether we know, or intend, that this is so. Goldie suggests that this casts doubt on the claim that we can only be praised or blamed for what is within our direct voluntary control, since while it is only the intention to have virtuous emotional dispositions we can have control over, our practice is to attach praise and blame to those dispositions themselves.

The evolutionary rationality of emotion

One conclusion that emerges from several of the contributions to this volume is that the stark dichotomy between the 'negative' and 'positive' views of emotion is too simplistic. Certainly, emotions are not merely obstacles to intelligent action, but nor are they unambiguous aids to rational decision making. If they were, the negative view of emotion would probably never have got off the ground to begin with. Emotions can both help and hinder rational thought.

To those used to adopting an evolutionary perspective, this should really come as no surprise. Like any other product of natural selection, emotions are not flawless mechanisms, honed to perfection by Darwinian optimization. Evolutionary psychology has nothing to do with a Panglossian view of organisms, according to which 'all is for the best in this best of all possible worlds'. Mental adaptations like emotions are rarely optimal in some abstract sense. Rather, they are *good enough* to have enabled those of our ancestors that possessed them to outcompete those of our ancestors that didn't. The evolutionary perspective on emotion enables us to reconcile the adaptive and the maladaptive aspects of emotion within a single coherent theoretical framework that explains when emotions help rational decision-making and when they hinder it.

Dylan Evans
University of the West of England

Pierre Cruse
Université Catholique de Louvain

July 2003

References

Abelson, R. P. (1963). Computer simulation of 'hot' cognition. *Computer Simulations of Personality*. S. S. Tomkins and S. Messinck. New York, Wiley.

Cannon, W. B. (1927). The James-Lange theory of emotion. *The Nature of Emotion*. M. B. Arnold. Harmondsworth, Penguin. 1968: 43–52.

Damasio, A. R. (1994). *Descartes' Error: Emotion, Reason and Human Brain*. London, Papermac.

Darwin, C. (1872). *The Expression of the Emotions in Man and Animals*. Chicago, University of Chicago Press, 1965.

Elster, J. (1999). *Alchemies of the Mind: Rationality and the Emotions*. Cambridge, Cambridge University Press.

Evans, D. (2001). *Emotion: the Science of Sentiment*. Oxford & New York, Oxford University Press.

Frank, R. H. (1998). *Passions within Reason: the Strategic Role of the Emotions*. New York, Norton.

Freud, S. (1915). Mourning and melancholia. *The Standard Edition of the Complete Psychological Works of Sigmund Freud*. J. Strachey. London, Hogarth Press. **14**, 239–290.

James, W. (1884). What is an emotion? *The Nature of Emotion*. M. B. Arnold. Harmondsworth, Penguin, 1968: 17–36.

LeDoux, J. (1998). *The Emotional Brain: The Mysterious Underpinnings of Emotional Life*. London, Weidenfeld & Nicholson.

Maclean, P. D. (1970). The triune brain, emotion and scientific bias. *The Neurosciences: Second Study Program*. F. O. Schmitt. New York, Rockefeller University Press: 336–348.

Panksepp, J. (1982). Towards a general psychological theory of emotion. *Behavioral and Brain Sciences*, **5**, 407–67.

Tooby, J. and Cosmides, L. (1990). The past explains the present: emotional adaptations and the structure of ancestral environments. *Ethology and Sociology*, **11**, 375–424.

PART I
NEUROSCIENTIFIC FOUNDATIONS

WILLIAM JAMES AND THE MODERN NEUROBIOLOGY OF EMOTION

ANTONIO R. DAMASIO

After a long period of neglect neuroscience has turned its attention to the elucidation of emotion. A substantial number of new findings have been gathered over the past decade and in spite of the manifest difficulties of the problem few would doubt that a rich neurobiological account of the emotions is now a possibility.

In an attempt to make sense of the data currently available, a reference to William James and to his view of the emotions is inevitable. Notwithstanding his forerunners, as well as the evidence gathered in the century that followed him, James' proposal remains a controversial standard against which modern interpretations are judged. There are those who believe William James' account of the emotions was adequate, even brilliantly so. There are those who believe James' account was hopelessly incorrect. One claims allegiance to James or one marks one's distance to him, and one is praised or pilloried, accordingly, by Jamesian partisans or detractors. In this chapter essay I attempt to define my current position on the debate.

James on emotion

The details of William James' proposal were presented in a text entitled 'What is an Emotion?' published in 1884 (James, 1884; see also James, 1890). They are well known and need not be repeated here other than in summary. James believed that the perception of certain objects (the famous bear, for example) would lead the brain to instigate a certain specific kind of a reaction. The reaction would modify the body and produce some useful behavior (running away from the bear, for example). Both visceral and vascular changes would occur prominently. Subsequently, these bodily changes would be represented mentally, thus giving rise to the feeling of the emotion.

Of note to the present discussion is the fact that James did not make a systematic distinction between emotion and feeling. James does make a reference to the feeling of emotional changes, but when he describes the end result of perceiving bodily changes he uses the term emotion and feeling interchangeably. Also of note, in James' account the *actual* body is a necessary partner in the process of emotion.

James' views were strongly supported by those of Carl Lange (James and Lange, 1885). Lange's account is largely the same but somewhat narrower in the sense that he gives visceral changes an even greater role than that accorded by James. In the Lange account emotions become coextensive with visceral activity, whereas James also factored in muscular activity. It should be noted that neither James nor Lange made any reference to the hormonal changes that are now known to be a part of emotional states and which had not been described in their time.

A contemporary account of the emotions from a neurobiological perspective

In order to define my position regarding William James' views I will begin by outlining my own account of the emotions (see Damasio, 1994; 1999; 2003, for details). I chose my own account as a basis for the comparison, not because I believe that mine is the most representative among the current neurobiological treatments of emotion, but because it has, on occasion, been praised or vilified in terms of its proximity to James', thus exemplifying the state of affairs to which I referred above. The account applies to a broad compass of emotions—from the background emotions to the social emotions—but as far as the contrast with James is concerned it need only apply to those emotions about which there is a near universal agreement on their status as emotions, namely, primary emotions such as fear, anger, sadness, and happiness. The key points of this account are as follows.

1. Emotions are not exclusively human. They have a long evolutionary past and are part of the natural behavior of many other species.

2. Emotions constitute a particular set of complex regulatory behaviors aimed, directly or indirectly, at the maintenance of homeostasis. Accordingly, emotions are conducive to survival. Emotions are also conducive, directly or indirectly, to well-being. This is because the set point of homeostasis toward which emotions work is located in the positive range of the affective spectrum rather than being neutral.

3. In my account, I establish a principled distinction between the process of emotion and the process of feeling. The process of emotion encompasses a number of physiological steps. The first step pertains to the evaluation or appraisal of the *emotionally-competent stimulus* (the latter is an object or situation which can reliably evoke a specific kind of emotion). The second step consists in triggering or inducing the emotion. The third step is the execution of the emotion. The fourth step is the emotional state itself.

The achievement of the emotional state is accompanied and followed by yet another step: the feeling of the emotion. Feeling consists of the *joint perception* of (a) the *causative* object; (b) the ensuing *emotional state*; and (c) the cognitive mode and *related thoughts that may follow*. Thus the intentionality of the emotions—the sense of what they are *about*—arises early in this physiological cycle with the perceptual definition of the emotionally-competent stimulus, and is completed in the feeling stage whose unfolding remains pointed to the emotionally-competent stimulus.

The intentionality issue is important because it is often misunderstood. A typical criticism of the position I articulate here comes in the form of saying that when we feel sad or joyful our feelings are about the external cause of the respective emotions and not about our own body. The criticism is not valid, however. Our feelings are no doubt about the causative external objects; but feelings are, in and of themselves, largely constituted by perceptions of bodily changes. The two sets of phenomena—images of causative objects *and* images of body change—are entirely compatible.

My distinction between emotion and feeling is part of a research strategy. I am well aware of the fact that the border between emotion and feeling is difficult to determine, in practical terms, given the rapidity with which the changes described in the steps leading to an emotion are perceived and thus become feeling. But the fact that the border between emotion and feeling is difficult to define introspectively and difficult to measure physiologically does not deny the existence of a distinction between emotion and feeling. At the very least, the beginning and conclusion of the emotion-feeling cycle, as described above, can be easily separated. We have shown this experimentally in studies in which psychophysiological changes clearly preceded the instants in which the feeling of an emotion began (Damasio *et al.*, 2000).

From the above perspective an emotion is a largely automated and unlearned set of reactions to certain classes of stimuli. The automation is compatible with the fact that the reactions can be modulated by the cognitive context and thus vary slightly, from instantiation to instantiation, for example, in terms of intensity and duration. The perspective is also compatible with the fact that emotionally-competent stimuli can be actually present or be recalled from memory, and also, that the stimuli may have been prescribed evolution-arily or may have been acquired by learning, in each organism, as a result of prior cognitive and emotional experiences.

4. The emotional reactions I envision are played out in one or both of *two* arenas: in the body itself, within a variety of physiological compartments; *and* in a number of regions in the central nervous system in which the structure and numerous parameters of the state of the body are continu-ously mapped.

The body's physiological compartments encompass not just the musculo-skeletal and visceral systems but also the internal milieu (the multifarious patterns of chemistries continuously realized in the blood stream and the intercellular spaces).

The body-related regions of the central nervous system encompass nuclei in the brain stem and in the hypothalamus, as well as the somatosensory cortices (such as the insula, SII, and SI and related association cortices, in the lateral and medial parietal lobe), and the cingulate cortex.

5. The curious existence of a 'double-body'—the actual body-proper, on the one hand, and its detailed dynamic map in the somatosensory regions, on the other—opens the way for a physiological possibility not envisaged at the time of William James. It concerns the somatosensory regions and the hypothesis that they can be made to *simulate* body states that are not actually occurring. I advanced this hypothesis over a decade ago, under the designation of 'as-if-body-loop'. I suggested that, in numerous circum-stances, our emotions are played out, at least in part, in the central nerv-ous system rather than peripherally in the body-proper (my designation for the mechanism involving the body-proper was 'the body loop'). The 'as-if-body loop' permitted remarkable economies of energy consumption and time.

At the time the hypothesis was formulated, the possibility of centrally manufactured simulations of body state was made plausible by the existence of neuroanatomical pathways arising in prefrontal regions and capable of influencing the state of the somatosensory regions. In the intervening years, however, there has been mounting evidence that the maps of body state can indeed be thus affected, as shown, for example in animal and human studies involving 'mirror neurons' (Gallese and Goodman, 1998; Haari, 1998). The investigation of the neural correlates of movement is also showing the extent to which a dynamic model of the body is available in the human brain (Berthoz, 2000; see also Churchland, 2002, for a review of evidence of neural emulators). Moreover, there is also additional evidence for the fact that signals from the body, which are being conveyed to the brain, can be modified in transit, as, for example, when nociceptive signals are suppressed or enhanced under the influence of neurons in the periaqueductal gray (Bandler, Shipley, 1994; Behbehani, 1995; see Damasio (2003) Chapter 3 for review). In brief, it is possible to generate an emotional state in the body-proper, in the full Jamesian sense. But it is also possible to simulate an emotional state in the brain's body maps, partially or completely. The curious fact is that the simulation is not made from whole cloth, as it were, but rather from the *shaping* of signals pertaining to whatever ongoing body state is being mapped at any given time. The simulation does not play out on an empty, passive screen. Rather the simulation arises from a certain degree of physiological conflict with the actual body state as mapped. That actual body state introduces an element of unpredictability in the process and makes it more likely that the result is not stereotyped.

It is reasonable to ask to what degree is the above account of emotion and feeling Jamesian? The answer is fairly clear to me: it is Jamesian in the sense that it conforms to William James' insight, i.e., that, in a general sense, body changes constitute the essence of an emotion and the basis for feeling; yet it is *not* Jamesian on a number of grounds. Importantly, in the above account, the emotional changes can occur in body maps, be simulated as it were, rather than being necessarily the result of an actual body change. The actual body intervenes as a contributor to the emotional body map, but the context of the body's contribution may not be the one that would arise from a specific emotion being directly enacted in the body. This is not what James had in mind.

The account is also non-Jamesian in the sense that the parameters used to construct a body state, either faithful to reality or simulated, are far more numerous than William James envisaged. As I see it, the relative value of those parameters is also different from that envisaged by James and Lange.

The role accorded to the process of evaluating or appraising the cause of an emotion, that is, the process of defining an emotionally-competent stimulus, is given a greater play in my account than in James'. James moves too rapidly from causative stimulus to emotional reaction and requires very little interposed processing in either the cognitive or the neural senses. While this abbreviated mechanism may work in circumstances in which emotions are triggered not just rapidly and automatically but even unconsciously, the mechanism is not likely to obtain for most circumstances. I regard James' mechanism as too stereotyped and inflexible. It leaves little or no room for the cognitive context to play a significant role in the unfolding of an emotion and feeling, and the neural undergirding it calls for is oversimplified.

Finally, James did not insist on a distinction between emotion and feeling, something that came back to haunt him in the criticisms of his detractors.

How right or wrong was William James?

From the foregoing it is apparent that I regard James as more right than wrong. One can say that James was wrong in not carving a greater role for the appraisal phase of emotion, and that he was wrong in assuming that actual body changes caused by a specific stimulus always played a role in emotion. In my view, however, James was certainly not wrong in linking emotion and feeling to body signals, provided 'the body' also can be taken to refer to the integrated set of varied internal maps which model the body in the central nervous system. As far as giving a comprehensive view of the body-related signals involved in emotion, James was incomplete, inevitably so, given the limited amount of knowledge available in his time, but he was not wrong. And he was also incomplete rather than wrong when he failed to separate emotion and feeling consistently.

While other neurobiologists working on emotion share this largely positive assessment of William James (e.g. LeDoux, 1996, Iversen et al., 2000), the common judgment is often negative. The negative judgment rests on philosophical and neuroscientific arguments. Addressing the philosophical arguments is outside the scope of this brief essay but I will address some of the neuroscientific arguments.

General criticisms

In essence, the general argument against James states that inputs from the body are not relevant to feelings. This idea was probably based on the false notion that, if James were correct, tetraplegic patients with spinal cord transection caused by injury should not be able to emote or feel. However, the critics said and still say, those patients, seem to be able to emote and feel. This general criticism overlooks the fact that only a part of the body input relevant for feelings travels in the spinal cord. The following facts should be noted:

(a) a considerable part of the information relevant for feelings actually travels in the vagus nerve, which exits and enters the brain at the level of the brain stem, above the highest level of the spinal cord that can be possibly damaged in an accident;

(b) only a part of the enactment of emotions depends on the spinal cord; a large proportion of the process is mediated by cranial nerves at brain stem level—e.g., those nerves which can act on the face—and by other brain stem nuclei which can act directly on the brain located even higher than their level;

(c) a significant part of body input actually does not travel in nerves at all but rather via the bloodstream; this too reaches the central nervous system at the level of brain stem, at the area postrema, or higher, again well above the level of spinal cord damage;

(d) the surveys of patients with spinal cord damage, including those surveys biased to discover an impairment of feeling and those biased to discover that feelings were intact, have revealed some degree of impaired feeling; this is as should have been expected given that the spinal cord is only a *partial* conduit for relevant body input;

(e) an important fact emerged from the studies alluded to in (d), namely, that the higher the placement of damage in the spinal cord, the more impaired feeling turns out to be. This is relevant because the higher the section made in the spinal cord, the less is the input from the body that will reach the brain. Higher sections should correlate with less feeling, lower sections with more. The finding would be difficult to explain were it not for the fact that some body input is precluded by spinal cord damage;

(f) spinal cord transections are hardly ever complete, thus allowing for escape pathways into the central nervous system;

(g) these general criticisms conceptualized the body as that part of the organism that sits below the neck; the head was forgotten; however, the face and skull, as well as the oral cavity, tongue, pharynx, and larynx, whose combination constitutes the upper portion of the respiratory and digestive tracts as well as most of the vocal system, provide a massive input into the brain. This input also penetrates the brain at brain stem level, again at a level higher than that of any spinal cord injury. Since most of the emotions express themselves prominently in changes of the facial musculature, in changes of the musculature of the throat, and in autonomic changes of the skin in the face and scalp, the mapping of those changes in the brain does not require the spinal cord at all. The mapping is available as a base for feelings even in patients with the most *complete* forms of spinal cord transection.

In brief, we normally use the spinal cord for two purposes: to enact a *part* of some emotions and to bring back to the brain signals about *part* of the enactment of those emotions. Even the most complete section of the spinal cord would fail to disrupt the two-way signals required for emotion and feeling.

That some defect is actually found in cases of spinal cord injury adds support to the notion that body input is relevant to the experience of emotion.

Another general criticism suggested that visceral changes were insufficiently differentiated to provide a specific basis for different emotions. The experimental support for this notion is inexistent, however. The probes used to measure visceral changes continue to be extremely limited—they are usually confined to measures of heart rhythm, respiration, skin conductance and temperature, and blood pressure. This is a meager sample of all the subtle and not-so-subtle changes that can rapidly occur in the viscera, not to mention the internal milieu. Neither have yet been sampled in a comprehensive way. To the poverty of experimental evidence to support this criticism, we must add the fact that it runs counter to one's subjective and intuitive findings. We know for certain that the mental differences we can appreciate when we feel fear, grief, or experience an orgasm are defined by remarkably different perceptions of our body states. Finally, we should not overlook the fact that the varied body states which define different emotions are also based on muscular patterns whose probing also has been experimentally insufficient (largely confined to EMG measures).

Criticisms based on experimental evidence

Most of the experimental arguments against James stem from the work of two leading neuroscientists of the earlier part of the 20th century, namely, Charles Sherrington and Walter Cannon. Most of their objections are presented succinctly in Cannon's 'Bodily Changes in Pain, Hunger, Fear and Rage', published in 1929 (Cannon, 1929; see also Cannon, 1927). The centerpiece of their attack is based on a misinterpretation of their results. The most challenging of the experiments they described consisted of the combined section of the vagus nerve and of the spinal cord of the animals, resulting in a profound block of body signaling to the brain. As noted in the previous section, however, such a block was by no means complete because it left the entire range of inputs from the head free to travel to the central nervous system, not to mention that the chemical route of body signaling remained untouched.

The critical procedure in those experiments consisted of successfully evoking emotions in the animals. The emotions were caused, for example, by showing a cat to a surgically-deafferented dog. The presence of emotion was seen as a denial of the James theory of emotion.

This interpretation of the results is, first of all, an example of the confusions which result from not distinguishing emotion from feeling. A dog or a cat in whom the vagus nerve and spinal cord have been severed should not have a complete loss of emotional display, as these researchers predicted. Severing the vagus nerve and the spinal cord does not interfere with the neural pathways necessary to alter the face of the animal, such that it will display rage, fear, or surprise. Those responses arise from the brain stem and are mediated by cranial nerves which were never compromised in Sherrington's or Cannon's experiments. Thus resulting emotional facial expressions remained intact, after combined sections of the vagus and of the spinal cord, as they should. Dogs responded angrily when shown cats and vice versa, even if they could not move their bodies, which were paralyzed below the neck. Incidentally, had those animals been stimulated electrically in the septal region, they would have shown the phenomenon known as 'sham rage,' a display of unmotivated expressions of anger.

The animals' feelings could not be tested, but based on the account described, those feelings were probably altered only in part. The animals would receive signals from their facial expressions and would have intact signaling from brain stem nuclei, both of which would form a base for feeling. However, the animals would not receive visceral input via the vagus nerve and the spinal cord. Imprudently, Cannon suggested that when there was so much of an emotional display feelings could not be possibly far behind. He took the presence of emotion as a sign that feelings should be present too. The error is attributable to the lack of a principled distinction between emotion and feeling, and also to the lack of a clear conceptualization of the likely sequence of physiological events, from the emotionally-competent stimulus, to the triggering and execution of emotion, to the mapping of emotional changes, to feeling itself.

Other evidence

One of the most intriguing, albeit indirect, lines of evidence for the importance of body input in the generation of feelings comes from the 'locked-in syndrome', a tragic neurological condition which occurs when a part of the brain stem such as the pons or midbrain is damaged in its ventral aspect (anteriorly), rather than, in its dorsal aspect (posteriorly). The motor pathways which convey movement command signals to the skeletal muscles are thus destroyed and only the pathways which control vertical movement of the eyes and blinking are spared, sometimes incompletely.

The lesions that cause 'locked-in syndrome' are present directly in front of the area whose lesions cause coma or persistent vegetative state, and because of this locked-in patients have an intact consciousness. They cannot move any muscle in their face, limbs, or trunk, and their communication ability is largely limited to vertical movements of the eyes. Yet they remain awake, alert, and conscious of their mental activity. The voluntary blinking in these patients is their sole means of communication with the world. Using a blink to signify a letter of the alphabet is the laborious technique with which locked-in patients compose words and sentences to those around them.

A remarkable aspect of this condition is that although patients are thrown, fully conscious, into a state of nearly complete mechanical imprisonment, they do not experience the anguish and turmoil that their horrifying situation would lead observers to expect. They have a considerable range of feelings, from sadness to joy. From several detailed accounts the patients may even experience a strange tranquility. They are aware of the tragedy of their situation, and they can report an intellectual sense of sadness or frustration with their virtual imprisonment. What they do not report is the terror that one imagines would arise in their horrible circumstances (Bauby, 1997; Mozersky, 1996).

I explain this surprising set of findings as follows. Blinking and vertical eye movements aside, the damage in 'locked-in syndrome' precludes any motion, either voluntary or enacted by emotional responses, of any part of the body. Facial expression and bodily gestures in response to a deliberate command or to an emotion are thus precluded (tears can be produced although the motor accompaniments of crying are missing). Any mental process which would normally induce an actual 'bodily' emotion fails to do so through the 'body loop' mechanism. Nonetheless, the brain can still activate emotion-induction sites in the basal forebrain, hypothalamus, and brain stem, and generate some of the internal brain changes on which feelings depend. Moreover, since most signaling systems from the body to the brain are entirely patent, the brain can receive direct neural and chemical signals from the varied organism profiles that conform to background emotions. Those profiles are related to basic regulatory aspects of the internal milieu and are largely uncoupled from the patient's mental state because of brain stem damage (only the bloodstream chemical routes remain open both ways). I have suggested that some of the internal milieu states are perceived as calm and pleasant. Also, these patients do register pain. For example, they report feeling stiff and cramped when they are not moved by their nurses for a long time. Importantly, the suffering that usually follows pain seems to be blunted, probably because suffering is caused by an emotion, and emotion can no longer be fully produced in the body and is thus restricted to the 'as if body' mechanism. Be that as it may, these findings give the lie to Cannon's notion that signaling from the body to the brain, independently of the cognitive set that would cause an emotion, would *not* cause feelings. They clearly do.

Cannon's notion that the viscera are not especially sensitive components of our body, and are thus not likely to contribute to emotion is undermined by the above facts as well as by everyday experience. If the viscera were insensitive we would never have discovered what it is to be anxious—in the heart, in the chest, in one's throat—and we would never have experienced gut feelings.

Concluding remarks

I believe that modern neurobiology is quite supportive of William James. At the very least, his was a seminal insight into the nature and workings of emotion. We can agree that the account was incomplete, simplified, and even narrow. But the account's main idea remains unchallenged.

References

Bandler, R. and Shipley, M. T. (1994). Columnar organization in the rat midbrain peri-aqueductal gray: modules for emotional expression? *Trends in Neurosciences*, **17**, 379–89.

Bauby, J.-D. (1997). *Le scaphandre et le papillon*. Editions Robert Laffont, Paris.

Behbehani, M. M. (1995). Functional characteristics of the midbrain periaqueductal gray. *Progress in Neurobiology*, **46**, 575–605.

Berthoz, A. (2000). *The brain's sense of movement*. Harvard University Press, Cambridge.

Cannon, W. B. (1927). The James-Lange theory of emotions: A critical examination and an alternative theory. *American Journal of Psychology*, **39**, 106–24.

Cannon, W. B. (1929). *Bodily changes in pain, hunger, fear and rage*. Appleton, New York.

Churchland, P. S. (2002). *Brain-wise*. MIT Press, Cambridge.

Damasio, A. R. (1994). *Descartes error: emotion, reason, and the human brain*. Grosset/Putnam, New York.

Damasio, A. R. (1999). *The feeling of what happens: body and emotion in the making of con-sciousness*. Harcourt, New York.

Damasio, A. R., Grabowski T. J., Bechara, A., Damasio, H., Ponto L. L., Parvizi, J., and Hichwa, R. D. (2000). Subcortical and cortical brain activity during the feeling of self-generated emotions. *Nature Neuroscience*, **3**, 1049–1056.

Damasio, A. R. (2003). *Looking for Spinoza: joy, sorrow, and the feeling brain*. Harcourt, New York.

Gallese, V. and Goodman, A. (1998). Mirror neurons and the simulation theory of mind-reading. *Trends in Cognitive Sciences*, **2** (12), 493–501.

Haari, R., Forss, N., Avikainen, S., Kirveskari, E., Salenius, S., and Rizzolatti, G. (1998). Activation of human primary motor cortex during action observation: a neuromagnetic study. *Proceedings of the National Academy of Sciences*, **95**, 15061–5.

James, W. (1884). What is an Emotion? *Mind*, 1884. See also James, W (1890). *Principles of Psychology*, Vol. 2. Dover Publications, 1950.

James, W. and Lange, C. (1885). *The Emotions.* Williams and Wilkins, Baltimore, 1922.

Iversen, S., Kupfermann, I., and Kandel, ER. (2000). Emotional states and feelings. In *Principles of neural science*, 4th edition. (ed. E. R. Kandel, J. H. Schwartz and T. M. Jessell).

LeDoux, J. (1996). *The emotional brain.* Simon and Shuster, New York.

Mozersky, J. (1996). *Locked in: a young woman's battle with stroke.* The Golden Dog Press, Toronto.

CHAPTER 2

HOMOLOGIZING HUMAN EMOTIONS

ANDREW D. LAWRENCE AND ANDREW J. CALDER

The term 'limbic system' is still frequently used to refer to the emotion circuits of the brain. The limbic system theory postulated that emotion is mediated by a specialized group of structures, acting as an integrated neural system (Maclean 1955). Despite its continuing survival as a view of how the brain mediates emotion, the limbic system is problematic, both as an anatomical concept (Reiner 1990, LeDoux 1991) and as a theory of the neural substrate of the emotions (Calder *et al.* 2001).

The shortcomings of the limbic system concept do not, however, discredit the more general notion that the brain contains a unitary, integrated emotion system (LeDoux 1991). In our own research, we have set out to examine this thesis using techniques established in the field of cognitive neuropsychology. According to Bub (1994), 'The general methodological problem for neuropsychology is how evidence, in the form of patterns of cognitive deficits, bears on theory, in the form of rival functional architectures'. In collecting evidence, neuropsychologists design experiments to elicit dissociations in task performance. Dissocations can be single (task A normal, task B abnormal), or multiple (Tasks A, B normal, tasks C, D abnormal). Double dissociations are obtained when task A is normal, task B abnormal in patient group P1; task B normal, task A abnormal in patient group P2 (Teuber 1955). Double dissociation evidence is perhaps the most compelling of all. This is because partial lesions allow dissociations to arise from 'resource artefacts', as one task demands more of some computational resource of a processing component than another (Shallice 1988, Bub 1994). It is generally considered that resource artefacts can be ruled out by double dissociations (Shallice 1988), and that only systems that contain a high degree of functionally specialized subsystems can produce strong double dissociations. For this argument to hold, two relatively uncontroversial assumptions must be made: (a) the 'subtraction' assumption: impaired processing is explicable in terms of the same model as normal processing, except that certain parameters of the model are changed (i.e. processes are not fundamentally re-organized following damage) and (b) the 'monotonicity' assumption: task performance is a monotone-increasing function of the computational resource of any module activated in performing the task (Shallice 1988, Bub 1994).

The aim of neuropsychological work (De Sousa (1987) calls it 'cutting and snipping') is primarily to dissociate functional models and not to impute functions to particular structures in the brain (decomposition versus localization—Bechtel and Richardson (1993)). The problem of imputing function to structure on the basis of the effects of brain lesions requires that multiple sources of information be integrated, including, for example, data from functional neuroimaging and neuroanatomy (Young *et al.* 2000).

We have begun to develop a systematic research program seeking to discover evidence for dissociable emotion systems following brain injury (and other manipulations), with the ultimate ambition of helping to develop a non-arbitrary, biologically based taxonomy of emotions (or at least some of the things that are subsumed by the term 'emotions') (Scherer 1993). Like many researchers, we believe that an evolutionary approach to the emotions has great potential. In particular, we are interested in explaining human emotions in a causal framework that subsumes other species as well (Lang *et al.* 2002); a position advocated for some time by Panksepp (1991, 2000).

A major problem for certain evolutionary accounts of emotion, such as for example, the evolutionary psychology approach of Tooby and Cosmides (1990), is that their primary focus seems to be on what are clearly uniquely human emotions (much is made of jealousy, for example). By neglecting the comparative perspective, such theories are based on a rather limited data set (sample size of one), and hence make it impossible to embed our notion of human emotions within a wider set of traits found in other species (Lang *et al.*, 2002). The comparative, phylogenetic approach has a unique and invaluable role to play in the study of the evolution of behavior (Griffiths 1997, 2001, Robson-Brown 1999, Heyes 2000, Iwaniuk and Whishaw 2000, Preuss 2000). A phylogenetic perspective 'looks for emotion systems in humans that are elaborations of mechanisms seen in other species and which therefore may have existed in a common ancestor' (Griffiths 1997). Such an approach has already been fruitfully applied to our understanding of the nature and evolution of primate facial expressions of emotion (Darwin 1872/1965, Ekman 1973, Preuschoft and van Hooff 1995).

Two philosophers, Griffiths (1990, 1997, 2001) and, more recently, Matthen (1998), have championed the role of homology in emotion (see also Wise and Bozarth (1987) for an application of the homology concept to motivational systems). An evolutionary taxonomy identifies elements as the same across species when they are homologous, that is, when they have a common evolutionary origin, rather than because they share a common function (Streidter and Northcutt 1991, Burton 1998, Butler and Saidel 2000, Streidter 2002). Griffiths (in press) has succinctly stated this approach: 'Suppose that two animals have psychological traits that are homologous—the basic emotion of fear in humans and fear in chimpanzees, for example. We can predict that, even if the function of fear has been subtly altered by the different meaning of "danger" for humans and for chimps, the computational methods used to process danger-related information will be very similar and the neural structures that implement them will be very similar indeed'.

In addition to emphasizing the role of homology in emotion, Griffiths (1990) has argued for a view of emotion that is 'response' or 'action' focused (see also Frijda 1986). That is, the identity of an emotion depends on the character of the response, not on the nature of the stimuli antecedent to the response. The antecedents of an emotion will vary enormously not only across species, but also within species, in response to local culture and individual learning (although, as we will argue below, there may be some way to rescue a very broad notion of 'universal antecedents' or 'core relational themes' (Lazarus 1994) for at least some emotions). By focusing on elements of emotion that are pan-cultural, it is possible to discern what is common to emotions in all humans, and also related species (Griffiths, 1990).

Whilst agreeing with Griffiths on this point, we feel that there is at least one class of emotional 'inputs' that is appropriate for study in an evolutionary approach: the facial expressions of one's conspecifics. Facial expressions are pan-cultural responses, with clear homologies in other mammals, including primates and rodents, and are likely to have cognitive and neural systems dedicated to their processing. Perhaps as a result of their ubiquity and reliable presence in the environment, especially in the relationship between infant and primary care giver, the facial expressions of one's conspecifics are also likely to be important antecedents for eliciting one's own emotions. That is, facial expressions are pan-cultural emotion stimuli, capable of evoking (the same) emotion in the viewer. Hence the study of the neural systems involved in processing the facial expressions of others is likely to provide insights not just into the systems involved in recognizing emotion, but the nature of emotion systems more generally.

The general link between expression and response (and experience; Ekman (1977) considers experience a form of emotional response) in emotion has been criticized by the so-called 'behavioral ecology' or 'paralanguage' approach, associated particularly with Fridlund (1997). According to this view, facial expressions are signals (facial displays) by which an individual communicates certain behavioral intentions to his/her social interactants. They do not express emotions. In contrast to Fridlund's views, results from game theoretic models suggest that honest, veridical expressions can in fact be evolutionarily stable under a broad range of conditions (Silk *et al.* 2000). Also, many experiments support coherence between expressive and experiential systems in emotion in the absence of 'display rules' (e.g. Rosenberg and Ekman 1994, Jakobs *et al.* 1999). It seems reasonable to suppose that expressions of emotion can serve many functions, ranging from the purely expressive to the purely strategic. As Hinde (1985) has argued, signals lie on a continuum, from those that are entirely expressive to those involving almost pure 'negotiation' (with negotiation emphasizing interaction between individuals, not necessarily manipulation). In any case, the empirical data support a rather strong coupling between the experience of an emotion and the recognition of that same emotion in others, at least for certain emotions.

Below, we summarize the results of our own and others' neuropsychological investigations of emotion processing. We detail findings of selective impairments in humans in the recognition and experience (broadly defined) of three emotions: fear, disgust and anger, together with strong evidence of homology in mammalian emotion systems. Finally, we discuss the implications of findings of dissociable emotion systems for current emotion theories, and how the neuropsychological data demonstrate the utility of an approach to emotion based on the phylogenetic, comparative method.

The amygdala, fear responses and fear recognition

Mammals react to a host of life-threatening dangers encountered in their natural environment, for example from predators or threatening physical environmental features, with a variety of defensive responses. The most intensely investigated of these defensive responses are flight/avoidance, freezing, potentiated startle response, hypoalgesia and the defensive attack pattern seen in the context of a discrete, very close, threat stimulus such as a predator or an approaching shock prod (Blanchard and Blanchard 1989a,b). These behaviors can, in fact, be quite flexible, and are strongly influenced by features of both the threat stimulus and the situation in which it is encountered. Thus, for example, flight is dominant when an escape route is available, but freezing is seen when escape is blocked, etc. These defensive behaviors tend to be similar across mammalian species, in both their form and effect, for the threatening stimulus or situation. Likewise, the specific stimuli and situations eliciting and modulating particular defensive behaviors are similar across various mammalian groups. Indeed, it has been suggested that the patterning of these defensive behaviors is homologous across mammals, including humans (Blanchard *et al.* 2001a). The term 'fear' is used to refer to the activation of the mammalian defensive behavioral system that gives rise to this constellation of reactions to threatening stimuli.

Fear responses are also evoked by arbitrary stimuli that reliably predict the occurrence of such dangers (so-called 'conditioned fear'). Conditioned fear cues recruit defensive responses in anticipation of danger, with the nature of the conditioned response being related to the nature of the predictive signal (Hollis 1997). Learning is enhanced if the conditioned and unconditioned stimuli 'belong' together (Garcia *et al.* 1983, Rozin and Schull, 1988, Hollis 1997), and there appear to be 'predispositions' (Rozin and Schull 1988) to learn that certain things are frightening (Mineka, 1992; Öhman and Mineka, 2001).

The finding that fear responses, amongst other things, were severely reduced following damage to rather large regions of the temporal lobes and related structures (Brown and Schafer 1888, Klüver and Bucy 1937) was vital in the development of the concept of a limbic system (LeDoux 1991). From quite early on, however, there was evidence to suggest that the amygdala was the critical site for the production of fear responses in primates (Delgado *et al.* 1956). A vast corpus of data now indicates that the amygdala plays a critical role in the development and expression of fear responses. Thus, in the rodent at least, lesions of the amygdala disrupt several components of fear, including various autonomic and hormonal measures (heart rate, blood pressure, respiration, corticosterone release, etc.), various motor behaviors (freezing, reflex facilitation), high-frequency vocalizations, and hypoalgesia (Blanchard and Blanchard 1972, LeDoux 1991, Fendt and Fanselow 1999, Davis 2000).

Similar findings have also been demonstrated in nonhuman primates, using selective excitotoxins sparing fibers of passage coursing through the amygdala. Thus, such lesions impair defensive responses, especially freezing, and increase approach responses to predators (snakes) and unfamiliar inanimate objects (Meunier *et al.* 1999, Kalin *et al.* 2001, Emery *et al.* 2001, Prather *et al.* 2001). Amygdala lesions, however, seem to spare responses to human intruders (Kalin *et al.* 2001). The relevance of human threat paradigms to fear in primates has, however, been challenged (Barros and Tomaz 2002). It is significant that lesions to the amygdala, at least in juvenile macaque monkeys, actually lead to increases in fear grimaces and screams relative to controls during dyadic social interactions (Thompson *et al.* 1969, Prather *et al.* 2001)

Although the majority of this work has been carried out in mammals (particularly rodents and macaque monkeys), lesions in regions homologous to the mammalian amygdala, in both birds and lizards, lead to reduced fear responses (Davis 2000, Davies *et al.* 2002).

In humans, several studies have now confirmed that the amygdala is critical for the acquisition and expression of fear responses (Bechara *et al.* 1995, LaBar *et al.* 1995, Funayama *et al.* 2001, Peper *et al.* 2001), a finding supported by functional neuroimaging experiments (Calder *et al.* 2001). Significantly, damage to the amygdala does not impair declarative memories of the fear learning protocol, but only the affective consequences of such learning. There appear to be interesting differences between the left and right amygdalae (Calder *et al.* 2001, Funayama *et al.* 2001), but the interpretation of these data is unclear. There is also some debate as to whether or not the role of the amygdala in fear processing is time limited, although it appears probable that the amygdala is the actual site of storage of fear 'memories' (Davis 2000). As with primates and rodents, amygdala lesions in humans also alter responses to unfamiliar physical objects and environments (Adolphs and Tranel 1999a). It is important to note that the amygdala does not appear to be involved in the voluntary production of, e.g., facial expressions of fear (Anderson and Phelps 2002), which is unsurprising given the well-known double dissociation between voluntary and passive or reflexive facial expressions of emotion (Rinn 1984).

Building on the findings of the role of the amygdala in fear processing in a number of species, Adolphs and colleagues (Adolphs *et al.* 1994, 1995) addressed the question of whether the human amygdala is involved in the recognition of fearful facial expressions. Their initial study included a patient (SM) with complete and largely selective bilateral lesions to the amygdala resulting from Urbach–Wiethe disease and six patients with unilateral damage to the left or right amygdala. Participants rated examples of six facial expressions of emotion (happiness, sadness, anger, fear, disgust and surprise) plus neutral expressions on several emotion scales. In comparison to controls with or without neurological damage to areas excluding the amygdala, SM showed abnormal ratings of facial expressions of fear, and to a lesser extent, anger and surprise. In contrast, patients with damage to the right amygdala showed no significant impairments, whereas patients with damage to the left amygdala showed some evidence of abnormal performance, but not for fear. Additional studies in SM have revealed that, across several repetitions of Adolphs' rating task, the most consistent impairment is in processing facial expressions of fear (Adolphs and Tranel 2000). In recent work, Anderson *et al.* (2000) have used an adapted version of Adolphs' task and found significant impairments in a larger group of patients with unilateral antero-medial temporal lobectomies, encompassing the right, but not left, amygdala. These patients showed abnormal processing of faces expressing fear, sadness, disgust and happiness.

Adolphs' rating task has been used in several other investigations, including a larger study of nine patients with amygdala damage due to various aetiologies. This study (Adolphs *et al.* 1999b) found that, when analyzed as a group, fear processing was most affected in these nine patients, but not all of them showed obvious impairments for fear. In fact, an earlier study by Hamann and colleagues (Hamann *et al.* 1996) had reported that two of these patients, with complete bilateral damage to the amygdala following herpes simplex encephalitis, showed no significant impairment for any emotion on Adolphs's task. In the light of differences between the patients in Hamann's study and patient SM, Hamman *et al.* suggested that a fear recognition impairment might be contingent on acquiring amygdala damage early in life. Subsequent evidence of impaired fear recognition from patients who do not satisfy this criterion, however, has made this explanation untenable (Calder *et al.* 2001). The puzzle of the negative findings of Hamann *et al.* (1996) has recently been resolved, however, by Schmolck and Squire (2001), who found that a different method of analyzing these patients' ratings revealed impaired performance. Impairments were also found on two further tests of facial-expression recognition, particularly for fear and sadness. One of these additional tasks used a forced-choice labeling procedure, a format used widely in facial-expression research (see Frank and Stennett (2001) for a response to criticisms of the forced-choice paradigm). This task was one of the two used originally by Calder *et al.* (1996) with two patients with bilateral amygdala lesions: DR, whose lesions were a result of a series of stereotaxic operations for intractable epilepsy, and SE, whose lesions were a result of encephalitis. The second task involved morphed (blended) facial expressions, and is illustrated in Calder *et al.* (2001).

Across the two facial expression labeling tasks, both DR and SE showed impaired identification of fear, and to a lesser extent, anger, thus complementing the original findings of Adolphs and colleagues. Reports of further patients with bilateral amygdala damage have since shown similar fear-recognition impairments on the same forced-choice tasks (Broks *et al.* 1998). In certain cases, these can be highly selective for fearful expressions (Sprengelmeyer *et al.* 1999).

An important issue concerns the extent to which the role of the amygdala is restricted to processing facial expressions of emotion, especially fear, or whether it is involved in processing expressions and signals of emotion from other sensory modalities. In several mammalian species, auditory stimuli are powerful elicitors of amygdala neuronal firing. For example, in squirrel monkeys amygdala activity is seen in response to conspecific calls, in particular isolation and alarm peeps and snake calls (Kling *et al.* 1987), all of which are related to predator defense. In the cat, amygdala neurons respond to salient auditory stimuli, such as cat howls and vocal threats by the experimenter (Jacobs and McGinty 1972). Further, as detailed above, there is strong evidence for the critical involvement of the amygdala in auditory fear conditioning.

In human neuropsychological data, support for the poly-modal hypothesis comes primarily from two bilateral amygdala patients—DR and NM. DR showed impaired recognition of fear and anger from both facial and vocal cues, whereas NM's deficits with facial, vocal and body posture cues were restricted to fear. These deficits were seen both in tests requiring recognition of fear conveyed by non-verbal sound patterns (e.g. screams) and fear conveyed by prosodic features (Scott *et al.* 1997, Sprengelmeyer *et al.* 1999). In contrast, Adolphs and Tranel (1999b) found that SM and a second bilateral amygdala patient, RH, showed no deficit on a vocal variant (emotional prosody) of Adolphs's facial expression rating task, despite both showing deficits on the original facial expression task. Further, SM can recognize fear signaled by bimodal stimuli: fearful facial expressions accompanied by prosodic fear stimuli (Adolphs and Tranel 2000). However, one method of analyzing the vocal data (Anderson and Tranel 2000) indicated that RH experienced some difficulty with vocal cues of fear and sadness. Anderson and Phelps (1998) have reported intact recognition of vocal (non-verbal sounds and prosody) but not facial expressions of fear in patient SP, who has bilateral amygdala damage. However, SP's recognition of other vocal expressions, including surprise and disgust is impaired.

The data on auditory fear stimuli are thus less compelling than the face processing data. Three patients with bilateral amygdala damage (DR, NM and RH) show impaired auditory fear recognition, two (SM, SP) do not. Anatomical and lesion data (Kemble *et al.* 1990, Steffanaci and Amaral 2000) show that there are sensory-specific domains within the amygdala, and therefore one possibility is that in patients with spared auditory fear recognition, these regions are intact. SM does appear to have rather complete amygdala damage, however, reducing the plausibility of this argument. Nevertheless, we tend to favor the notion that the amygdala is involved in processing fear signals across multiple modalities (see also Calder *et al.* 2001 for a review of supporting evidence from the neuroimaging literature).

One particularly controversial topic is the role of the amygdala in the 'conscious' experience of fear. This issue is complicated somewhat by the idea that there are multiple varieties of emotional experience (Lambie and Marcel 2002), not all of them available to self-report. Nevertheless, patient NM (Sprengelmeyer *et al.* 1999) shows reduced self-report levels of fear as measured by the Fear survey schedule (Brown and Crawford 1988), and is extremely fond of dangerous activities, in which he reports feeling no fear— for example, hanging on a rope under a helicopter whilst hunting for deer in Siberia! Patient SM also seems to experience (or at least report) reduced levels of fear. For example, she reports not feeling afraid when shown film clips that normally elicit fear (e.g. 'The Shining' and 'The Silence of the Lambs'), but does seem to experience other emotions, such as anger, strongly (Adolphs and Tranel 2000). Further, when the amygdala is stimulated during surgery in humans, fear is commonly evoked (Halgren 1992). In contrast, in a recent report, Anderson and Phelps (2002) found that SP, a bilateral lesions of amygdala reported no significant differences in the magnitude and frequency of fear as measured by the PANAS (positive and negative affect) scales (Watson *et al.* 1988), when asked to rate her feelings at the end of each day over the course of one month.

In general then, the human amygdala seems to be involved in the production of fearful responses, the recognition of fear in others (particularly as expressed by the face), and in the experience of fear, as measured by self-report.

There is an important caveat that should be raised at this point. Dissociations in processing of an emotion can occur, not because processing of the emotion relies on processing in an isolable subsystem, but because of resource artefacts, i.e. processing of fear faces may simply be differentially sensitive to neurological disease (Shallice 1988). In fact, Rapcsak *et al.* (2000) found that in a group of patients with various focal lesions, the recognition of fearful facial expressions was disproportionately impaired relative to other emotions, regardless of whether the damage included the amygdala or not. They attributed these findings to the fact that neurologically intact controls find fear more difficult to recognize than other emotions, and the marked fear recognition impairments were simply an effect of difficulty level. Similarly, greater activation to fear stimuli in the amygdala, relative to other emotions, does not necessarily imply that the amygdala is specialized for fear processing (Duncan and Owen 2000). The strongest argument for isolable emotion subsystems is to find evidence for a classical double dissociation between fear and another emotion, which can apply not only to patient-based lesion approaches but also to functional neuroimaging data (Duncan and Owen 2000).

The gustatory insular and globus pallidus, disgust responses and disgust recognition

In a series of important papers, Garcia has argued for a fundamental duality between two isolable mammalian defense systems: 'external' and 'internal' (Garcia 1989, 1990, Garcia et al. 1974, 1983). Telereceptor (auditory and visual) and cutaneous stimuli activate the external or 'skin' defense system. It serves to protect the external body surface from injury, and has evolved under the natural selective pressure of predation. According to Garcia and colleagues, the standard experimental fear conditioning protocol of loud noise followed by a cutaneous shock is an ideal stimulus combination to activate this defense system, mimicking as it does the footsteps and bite of a predator (Garcia et al. 1983). Activation of this external, skin or telereceptor-cutaneous defense system is associated with the fear responses described earlier (Garcia et al. 1983).

In contrast, in mammals, taste and emetic toxins impinge upon an 'internal' or 'gut' defense system evolved under the pressure of plants and animals that employ toxins to fend off foragers and predators. According to Garcia the standard taste aversion learning protocol of taste followed by internal malaise is the ideal stimulus combination to activate this system, mimicking the consequences of eating and absorbing poisonous plant foods in the natural environment. Distaste reactions are associated with activation of the internal or gut defense system (Garcia et al. 1983).

Intriguingly, olfaction can be both an 'internal' and an 'external' sense, associated with distaste and fear reactions, respectively (Garcia et al. 1983, Rozin 1982). Odor alone acts as an external signal. However, when odor is compounded with taste in acquisition, odor alone acts like taste, an internal cue (Garcia et al. 1983).

Garcia et al. (1983) have argued that rats given taste-illness pairings develop more than simply an avoidance to that substance; the taste actually undergoes a hedonic or palatability shift such that it becomes distasteful. An index of distaste or unpalatability in the rat is the taste reactivity test of Grill and Norgren (1978). In this test, distaste is reflected by stereotyped responses such as gaping, fluid expulsion, head shaking and forelimb flailing in response to intraoral infusion of fluids (curiously, rats do not vomit (Smith et al. 2001)). It has been suggested that gaping represents the most sensitive measure of distaste in rats, as the muscular movements involved in gaping mimic those seen in species capable of emetic reactions (Travers and Norgren 1986, see also Steiner et al. 2001 for evidence of homology in mammalian distaste reactions).

In contrast to their effects on fear responses, lesions of the rodent amygdala leave intact the distaste response, whilst impairing other forms of food defense, including fear responses such as food neophobia (Dunn and Everitt 1988,

Bermudez-Rattoni and McGaugh 1991, Galaverna *et al.* 1993). Instead damage to the gustatory neocortex of the rat, located in the agranular insular cortex, impairs the distaste reaction. For example, Kiefer and Orr (1992) have shown that although agranular insular lesioned rats can learn to avoid a taste paired with illness, albeit at a much slower rate than control rats, lesioned rats do not appear to experience the hedonic shift in taste when it is accompanied by illness, as measured by aversive reactivity (gapes, especially) tested in the taste reactivity test. Intriguingly, agranular insular lesioned rats do show some aversive responses (e.g. gapes) to a strong quinine HCl solution, although they do show reduced head shaking and forelimb flailing relative to control rats. Taste aversions also appear to be disturbed by lesions to the globus pallidus, an output nucleus of the basal ganglia, which is linked to the gustatory neocortex (Hernádi *et al.* 1997). In humans, lesions to the presumably homologous area of the gustatory insula (Sewards and Sewards 2001) impair reactions to bitter tastes, including quinine HCl and citric acid (Pritchard *et al.* 1999).

Following Darwin (1872/1965), Rozin and colleagues (Rozin and Fallon 1987, Rozin *et al.* 1997, 2000) have proposed that the human emotion disgust evolved from the mammalian distaste response. In particular, the disgust response originates in the gape response described above. Rozin suggests that a 'core' disgust system is constructed from the distaste food rejection system, via a process akin to evolutionary preadaptation (but see Shelley (1999) for some problems with Rozin's use of the term preadaptation) in which the disgust response is attached successively to a variety of things that are offensive within any particular culture. So, according to Rozin, the major event in the cultural evolution of disgust is the expansion or replacement of meanings and elicitors, with the output side of disgust largely intact. Some of these elicitors, like faeces, and perhaps contact with death, are likely to be pan-cultural, but many are not (see Curtis and Biran 2001). According to Rozin and colleagues (Rozin *et al.* 1997, 2000), the principal elicitors of core disgust are animals and animal products in a food context. In both individual and cultural evolution, the core disgust system is expanded to include animal nature reminders. Parenthetically, we would prefer to consider what Rozin calls 'core' disgust as the human homologue of the mammalian distaste response, without recourse to the notion of preadaptation.

Rozin *et al.* posit two further domains of disgust elicitors: interpersonal disgust, related to contact with undesirable persons, and moral disgust, related to violations of moral 'purity' (Rozin *et al.* 1997, 2000). They have no suggestion as to an ordering of these two domains, either in individual development or in cultural evolution. In Rozin and colleagues' theory, disgust becomes the means by which cultures can internalize rejection of an offensive object, behavior, or thought. The phenomenon of contagion, originally linked to core disgust, becomes an important component of reactions to the wider range of disgust elicitors, again, according to Rozin by a process of preadaptation (but see Shelley 1999).

Evidence that disgust might be associated with a particular neural substrate came initially from an investigation of people with manifest Huntington's disease (HD), an autosomal dominant neurogenetic disorder. Participants in this study (Sprengelmeyer *et al.* 1996) were shown the same facial-expression identification tests that were used with several of the bilateral amygdala patients (see earlier). The patients with HD showed problems in recognizing several emotions, but a disproportionately severe impairment was found for disgust expressions. Similar findings were found in recognizing vocal (prosodic) expressions of disgust (see also Sprengelmeyer *et al.* 1997). Further evidence that HD particularly affects the recognition of disgust came from an investigation of face processing (including facial expression recognition) in people at risk of carrying the mutation associated with HD (Gray *et al.* 1997). Participants that were subsequently identified as gene carriers (AR+) were compared with participants that did not carry the gene (AR−). A comparison of the scores revealed just one significant difference for recognition of emotion—the AR+ group made significantly more errors in recognizing facial expressions of disgust than did the AR− group.

Impairments in disgust recognition (and to a lesser extent anger) have also been reported in patients with Obsessive Compulsive Disorder (OCD) and in patients with Tourette's syndrome who show co-morbid OCD (Sprengelmeyer *et al.* 1998). Although HD, OCD and Tourette's syndrome are not characterized by focal neuropathology, both HD and OCD patients show pathology in regions of the globus pallidus and insula presumably homologous to the regions associated with the distaste response in rats (Rauch *et al.* 1998, Thieben *et al.* 2002).

The strongest evidence for a selective impairment in disgust recognition, however, comes from the study of an individual, NK (Calder *et al.*, 2000b). The damage to NK's brain was lateralized to the left hemisphere and included the insula, putamen, internal capsule, globus pallidus and, to a lesser extent, the head of the caudate nucleus. On tests of facial expression recognition and vocal expression recognition (both prosody and non-verbal sounds, such as retching for disgust), NK showed a highly selective deficit for disgust in the context of predominantly preserved recognition of other emotions. Again, these data strongly suggest a link between regions involved in the distaste reaction and regions involved in processing disgust facial expressions.

Data from functional imaging experiments also support a role for the insula and globus pallidus in disgust recognition (Calder *et al.* 2001).

In addition to a selective disgust recognition impairment, NK also showed abnormal performance on a questionnaire tapping his experience of disgust, whereas his scores for comparable questionnaires assessing his experience of anger and fear were normal. The disgust questionnaire was based on Rozin's theory of disgust, and measures disgust sensitivity in several domains relevant to that theory (Haidt *et al.* 1994). The scale comprises eight subscales, and NK showed a significant or borderline reduction in his scores for five of these, scoring at or near the minimum on the categories of food, animals, body products, body envelope violation and death, but not on the hygiene, sex or magical (disgust by connotation) categories. This result is potentially extremely important, as it suggests that NK's disgust impairments relate more to Rozin's core/animal nature disgust domain (with the exception of hygiene), rather than the interpersonal or moral disgust domains, and does not support the disease protection/hygiene theory of disgust (Curtis and Biran 2001). Before we posit a strong fractionation between different categories of disgust, however, further data are clearly required. Patients with HD have also been administered the disgust scale, and show impairments on the body products, sex, hygiene and magical scales (Sprengelmeyer *et al.* 1996, 1997) (with different HD patients showing different patterns of impairment), raising interesting issues about potential differences between their disgust impairment and that seen in NK.

The data from NK, in particular, point to a strong link between the recognition of the facial expression of disgust in others, and in the experience of disgust (especially core disgusts), similar to that seen in the case of fear. Tomkins (1963) argued that primary disgusts are frequently induced by the display of disgust in others, i.e. that disgust faces are a pan-cultural disgust stimulus. The data from NK, in particular, would support such a proposal.

The data we have presented thus point to a double dissociation between fear and disgust impairments. As discussed in the introduction, only systems that contain a high degree of functionally specialized subsystems can produce strong double dissociations of the type seen between fear and disgust. These data thus argue strongly against the notion of a unitary emotion system. The data also point to strong homologies in the mammalian neural systems involved in fear and disgust. In reviewing the neuropsychological literature on facial expression processing, Adolphs (2002) has argued that 'it would make sense to suppose that fear and disgust are the only two emotions for whose recognition there evolved relatively specialized circuitry given the ecological relevance and phylogenetic ubiquity of these two emotions'. We believe, however, that a phylogenetic perspective on emotion would predict otherwise, and we present data to show that, based on predictions from comparative data, selective deficits in the recognition of other emotions can in fact be found.

Dopamine, aggression and anger recognition

At least in mammals, aggression may be considered a heterogeneous phenomenon as far as motivations, context, behavioral patterns of attack and presumed functions are concerned (Parmigiani *et al.* 1998). It is possible to distinguish between at least two broad categories of aggression: one concerned with competition for, and defense of, valued resources—which has been referred to as 'appetitive' aggression or 'property defense' (Rasa 1976) (where property is used to denote resources such as territory, a mate, or a place in a rank order), 'competitive' aggression (Parmigiani *et al.* 1998), or 'offensive' aggression (Blanchard and Blanchard 1984, 1989a,b); and the other concerned with protection of the animal's own body—referred to as 'self-protective' (Parmigiani *et al.* 1998), or 'self-defensive' aggression (Rasa 1976, Blanchard and Blanchard 1984, 1989a,b). Whilst self-defensive aggression appears to rely on the same amygdala-centered system as other types of fear-related behaviors (Blanchard and Takahashi 1988), appetitive/ competitive/offensive aggression relies on a distinct motivational system. The action patterns associated with this form of aggression (offense) have much in common across various mammalian species. Indeed, it has been suggested that the patterning of these aggressive behaviors is homologous across mammals, including humans (Adams 1981, Blanchard and Blanchard 1984, 1989a,b, Blanchard *et al.* 2001b), and that the human emotion of anger is related to activation of this system (Blanchard and Blanchard 1984).

The dopamine system (Smeets and González 2000) has been implicated in the production of offensive responses and in the processing of conspecific aggression signals in social-agonistic encounters in a wide variety of species. For example, in vivo microdialysis experiments in rats have shown that dopamine levels are elevated during social-agonistic encounters (Louilot *et al.* 1986, van Erp and Miczek 2000), and ex vivo dissection experiments in mice show altered dopamine levels following aggressive behavior (Hadfield 1983). This latter study also found increases of dopamine in mice witnessing fighting but prevented from participating, raising a number of intriguing questions (Johnstone 2001). Furthermore, acute administration of dopamine antagonists, especially those of the D2 receptor, such as sulpiride, selectively impairs responses to agonistic encounters in rodents (Simon *et al.* 1989, Redolat *et al.* 1991, Manzaneque and Navarro 1999). In cynomolgous monkeys there is an increase in dopamine D2 receptor numbers or availability in individuals who achieve social dominance and who display marked increases in their levels of aggression relative to subordinates (Morgan *et al.* 2002; see Winberg and Nilsson 1992 for similar findings in Arctic charr). In humans, we have shown that dopamine levels are increased when playing a competitive-aggressive video game (Koepp *et al.* 1998) and there are data to suggest that increased dopamine levels in humans are associated with heightened feelings of anger (Goodwin *et al.* 1970). Homologous systems in lizards respond to conspecific aggression signals (Korzan *et al.* 2001). Dopamine systems even appear to be involved in the production of offensive aggressive responses towards conspecifics in species such as weakly electric fish (Maler and Ellis 1987) and ants (Kostowski *et al.* 1975) suggesting a remarkable degree of conservation in this system.

Given the role of dopamine systems in the production of aggressive behaviors and in the processing of conspecific aggression signals, together with the suggestion that prototypical facial expressions of anger in humans signal offensive aggression (Öhman 1986) and that a challenging conspecific should elicit some motivation or tendency toward offensive attack (Blanchard and Blanchard 1984), we hypothesized that acute dopaminergic blockade, produced by the administration of sulpiride (a D2 receptor antagonist), would produce a selective disruption in the recognition of anger displayed in the face, but leave intact the recognition of other facial expressions, and facial identity processing. This prediction was confirmed in a within subject, double blind, placebo controlled crossover experiment (Lawrence *et al.* 2002). Thus, acute dopamine blockade led to a selective impairment in recognizing angry faces, but spared the recognition of other facial expressions (including fear and disgust) and facial identity processing. A remarkably deep homology appears to exist in the neural systems involved in processing conspecific aggression signals, in both mammals and non-mammalian species.

As was the case with fear and disgust deficits, our finding of a role for the dopamine system in anger recognition further supports an intimate link between the recognition of anger in others, in aggressive responses, and in the experience of anger.

It is also noteworthy that, in many species, dopamine has long been implicated in the processing of foods, water, mating opportunities and novel environments, and stimuli that reliably predict them (Schultz 1998). All of these stimuli can be considered as valued (fitness enhancing) resources, from an evolutionary perspective. Given that competitive/appetitive/offensive aggression occurs in the context of competition for such resources, and is increased by successful utilization or defense of resources or dominance, such as sexual activity or prior residence in the fighting arena (Blanchard and Blanchard 1989a,b), we have suggested that, at least in certain species, dopamine may play a general role in processing signals and coordinating responses relevant to the acquisition and protection of valued resources, including aggressive responses (Lawrence *et al.* 2002).

Implications for evolutionary approaches to emotions

We have presented evidence for a triple dissociation between systems involved in recognizing facial expressions of fear, disgust, and anger in humans. Furthermore, these same manipulations affect not just the recognition of emotion from the face and other channels, but also the emotional responses themselves and, in some cases, the feelings (as indexed by self-report, at least) of those same emotions. What implications do these data have for theories of the emotions, and in particular, for evolutionary theories of the emotions?

The finding of dissociations between different emotions argues strongly against the notion of a unitary emotion system. As discussed in the introduction, it is widely agreed that only systems that contain a high degree of functionally specialized subsystems can produce strong (triple) dissociations of the type seen here. Although neuropsychological dissociations are used primarily to dissociate functional models and not to impute functions to particular structures in the brain, when taken together with the functional imaging data (Calder *et al.* 2001, Murphy, Nimmo-Smith and Lawrence, in press) and other sources of evidence, they are also problematic for the limbic system neural model of the emotions. Of course, the core set of 'limbic' structures has been in flux since its very origin (LeDoux 1991) and some have suggested that it includes regions such as the insula, basal ganglia, and brainstem neuromodulatory systems. But the criteria for including these structures would mean placing structures at every level of the neuraxis, from the spinal cord to the neocortex in the limbic system (LeDoux 1991), which just shows how broad, vague, and unproductive the limbic system concept has become.

Some researchers have argued that, although emotions can be dissociated at the neural level, the limbic system model nevertheless retains a positive heuristic value (e.g. Damasio 1998, Panksepp 2000). We would argue, however, that retaining the notion of a limbic system is likely to have a negative heuristic value. We believe the notion of a unitary limbic system has helped to reinforce the assumption of a unitary emotion system (at both neural and psychological levels, even though one does not necessarily imply the other, of course) as well as other unproductive ideas (e.g. that emotion is a natural kind), and has hindered both the collection of empirical data on the differences between different emotions and the possibility of theoretical developments.

There are, of course, a number of neuropsychological theories of emotion that are not single system models. The data we have presented, however, provide considerable difficulties for a number of such theories. For example, the finding of a double dissociation between anger and fear recognition argues against the idea that there is a neural system specialized for the processing of highly arousing, unpleasant emotions, of which fear and anger are two exemplars (Adolphs *et al.* 1999a). The data also prove difficult for theories positing that the fundamental distinction between the neural substrates of emotion is based on systems (or states) coding a small number (usually two) of dimensions, such as valence and arousal (e.g. Bradley and Lang 2000) or approach and avoidance (Davidson 1994, Cacioppo *et al.* 1999, Mendoza and Ruys 2001), which again would not predict the pattern of dissociations we have described. Panksepp (1991, 2000) who has pioneered the affective neuroscience approach, posits a more plausible multi-system model of emotions. The data we present on the role of dopamine systems in certain forms of aggression and anger recognition are problematic for his theory, however, since according to Panksepp (1991, 2000) dopamine mediates a 'seeking' system linked to exploratory activity and feelings of curiosity, which is distinct from a 'rage' system mediating aggressive responses.

A recurring finding has been that deficits in the recognition of emotion co-occur with impairments in emotional responses. What might this be telling us? One possibility is that facial expressions of emotion act as unconditional emotional stimuli, evoking (the same) emotion in the viewer (Mineka 1992, Owren and Rendell 1997). This would be consistent, with Tomkins' (1963) idea that, in humans, disgust faces are the 'primary' disgust stimulus, but on a much wider scale. At least for fear and disgust, it would be extremely advantageous to be able to learn what is frightening or disgusting in the environment by using information provided by a reliable feature of that environment: the facial expressions of the primary care giver (Griffiths 1990). To the extent that juveniles can use the expressions of adults to assess the significance of events in the current environment, they should be able to reduce the costs of independent learning by trial and error. Indeed, across mammals, this appears to be a common occurrence (Coomes *et al.* 1980, Klinnert *et al.* 1983, Mineka 1992, Yoerg and Shier 1997, Öhman and Mineka

2001, Galef 2002, Gerull and Rapee 2002, Snowdon and Boe 2003). A learning mechanism with certain predispositions could 'combine both flexibility in the face of environmental variation with the advantage of inheriting the experience of previous generations' (Griffiths 1997). A similar argument could be made for anger, although there is little data on this (but see Malamuth and Addison 2001). It could be argued (as has been done by Goldie 1999) that there is little reason for anger expressions to induce the same state in the viewer, as opposed to say, fear, especially in juveniles, who seem, at least in some contexts, to respond to angry expressions with fear (Balaban 1995). This may be the case, however, in only some contexts, and there are data suggesting a link between viewing others' aggression and the probability of aggression in the viewer (Malamuth and Addison 2001); and, as with fear and disgust, this may be one way to learn the relevant targets for aggressive responding. Also, in many circumstances, a challenging conspecific should elicit some motivation or tendency toward offensive attack (Blanchard and Blanchard 1984).

In humans, in particular, having the face as a pan-cultural emotional input provides an evolutionary model consistent with the large cultural variation seen in emotion elicitors (Wierzbicka 1986, see also Mallon and Stich 2000). Stimuli that reliably predict the production of an emotional expression in the primary caregiver can become the stimuli that elicit the same reaction in the infant. In the introduction, we raised the issue about whether evolutionary theories could be usefully applied to emotional inputs, and whether we could say anything about pan-cultural antecedents to emotion (Lazarus 1994). To the extent that facial expressions in parents can be reliably associated pan-culturally with certain kinds of situations, together with certain (minimal) learning predispositions, this provides a potential route to pan-cultural emotional antecedents.

It may also be possible to infer something about the general classes of stimuli that elicit homologous fear, disgust and anger responses across related species. Data reviewed do suggest the specific stimuli and situations eliciting and modulating particular emotional responses have much in common across various mammalian species. For example, the property that all eliciting situations for fear have in common, and which are affected by damage to the amygdala, is the abstract property that they may cause harm to the external surface of the body, and are perceived by the distal or telereceptor (visual, auditory, sometimes olfactory) and cutaneous senses. The thing that all eliciting situations for disgust have in common is that they may cause harm to internal regions of the body, especially the gut and related systems, and are perceived as distasteful. Anger (at least one form of anger—competitive/appetitive/

offensive) occurs in the context of conspecific challenge and threat to the acquisition and protection of valued biological resources. Therefore fear, disgust and anger could be considered, in some sense, to be defense motivational systems or 'defense system' emotions.

This does not mean, however, that we would want to identify human emotions with the functions of protecting the external body surface in the case of fear, the internal body in the case of disgust, and the acquisition and protection of valued resources in the case of anger. Such a functional classification (see e.g. Izard 1979, Plutchik 1980, 2001, McNaughton 1989, Nesse 1990, Tooby and Cosmides 1990, Lazarus 1991, Frijda 1994, Cacioppo *et al.* 1999, Damasio 1999, Keltner and Haidt 2001 for exemplars of evolutionarily-inspired theories of emotion based on functional considerations), or an ecological level classification, rather than a historical classification (one based on homology) (Griffiths 1997, Matthen 1998) suffers from the problem that different species may have evolved different solutions to the same or similar ecological problems (homoplasy or analogy) (see e.g. Kavaliers *et al.* (2001) for the range of mechanisms that have evolved to cope with protecting the external body surface and Garcia *et al.* (1983) for the range of evolved poison avoidance mechanisms). Hence an ecological classification of human emotions in terms of particular functions, although of potential value for certain projects (for example, building a robot—Frijda 1995) is of little utility in identifying, the nature of the particular pattern of responses (including non-functional responses), such as facial expressions, associated with, or the neural implementation of, human emotions. We agree with Griffiths (1990, 1997, 2001) and Matthen (1998) that, at least for neuropsychology, a historical approach, is likely to prove more fruitful than a functional/ecological approach. The human emotions of fear, disgust and anger may represent homologies of mechanisms that, although potentially evolved in response to certain classes of ecological threat, were realized only by a particular lineage of organisms, and hence, only for organisms with a particular evolutionary history will be associated with certain neural systems, etc. (Griffiths 1997). Their functions may also have altered over the course of their evolutionary history. As eloquently argued by Griffiths (1997) 'generalizations about the effects of particular ecological factors are likely to be richer and more reliable when confined within taxonomic groups that approach the 'problem' with a common inheritance'.

The co-occurrence of emotion recognition and emotional response deficits may also be telling us something interesting about the mechanism of emotion recognition itself. A number of theorists have proposed some kind of a link between the production of emotional behaviors, and the recognition of those emotions in others. Lipps (1903, 1907) proposed that mimicry leads—via a feedback process—to shared affect, which in turn facilitates emotion recognition. This theory, and others (Hess *et al.* 1999), generally suppose that (a) some kind of motor mimicry or facial feedback is necessary for this process; and there is good evidence both for imitation in facial recognition, even when the expressions to be recognized are presented subliminally (Hess *et al.* 1999, Dimberg *et al.* 2000); (b) and emotions are 'contagious' or 'infectious' (Hatfield *et al.* 1994, Wild *et al.* 2001). Facial mimicry per se, however, is unlikely to be necessary for facial expression recognition, as individuals with congenital facial paralysis (Möbius syndrome) show spared facial expression recognition (Calder *et al.* 2000a).

An alternative is a simulation-like theory of expression recognition. According to simulation theory, other people's mental states are represented by adopting their perspective: by 'tracking or matching their states with resonant states of one's own' (Gallese and Goldman 1998). This might suggest that either some internal model of the facial expression (Adolphs 2002) could be generated and compared to the to-be-recognized emotion, or, as we favor, the facial expression of the other induces (or 'affords') shared affect (or shared action tendency (Frijda 1986)) in the viewer; and via some central process, not requiring mimicry, this emotional state is used to label the others' expression. Such a mechanism could account for some of the well-known emotion-congruency effects in perception (Niedenthal *et al.* in press; see Goldie 1999 for a critical appraisal of simulation theories).

It could also be argued that for each emotion system, recognition and responses have co-evolved, and as a purely contingent historical matter, the two capacities are co-localized—thus explaining conjoint deficits in emotion recognition and emotion responses. While accepting this possibility, the data we present are at least supportive of a simulation-based account. In fact, we think our finding that the administration of a pharmacological agent known to block aggressive responses results in the impairment of anger recognition, is the strongest evidence to date for a simulation-based account of emotion recognition.

Conclusions

To conclude, the data presented here provide strong evidence for homology in at least three emotion systems across mammals: fear, disgust and anger. Thus, across all mammalian species investigated (admittedly, rather few— we agree with Preuss (2000) that emotion neuroscientists need to carry out an explicitly comparative agenda, of the kind pioneered by the Blanchards and Garcia), the amygdala is required for fear responses, in humans also. In humans, the amygdala is involved in the recognition of fear in other people, at least in the face, and probably the voice and other channels. In addition, there appears to be some evidence to suggest that the experience of fear (or self-report, at any rate) is reduced following lesions to the amygdala in humans. The homologies appear to extend beyond mammals: the homologue of the amygdala in reptiles also appears to mediate certain fear responses.

Likewise, the gustatory insula, and possibly globus pallidus, in humans is involved in the distaste response, in the recognition of disgust in others, and also in the experience of (at least some components of) disgust. The homologous region in rodents mediates the distaste response. Finally, the dopamine system in humans is involved in the recognition of facial expressions of anger, in certain forms of aggression, and in feelings of anger. The homologous system in mammals is also implicated in the processing of conspecific aggression signals and in aggressive behaviours. Again, the homologies appear to run deep: homologous systems in reptiles and other species are involved in the processing of conspecific aggression signals. The data thus powerfully vindicate the phylogenetic perspective on emotion advocated by Griffiths (1990, 1997, 2001) and others.

We are not suggesting, of course, that the data we have described demonstrate that there are 'fear', 'disgust' and 'anger' centers in the brain, corresponding to the (English-language) folk-psychological categories of fear, disgust and anger. The fractures we have described do not occur along the 'fault lines' carved out by the English emotion lexicon. Rather, only some instances of what the English language describes as 'fear' are impaired following lesions to the amygdala, and similarly for 'disgust' impairments following gustatory insula and pallidal lesions and 'anger' following acute dopaminergic blockade. These instances appear to be extremely similar to the fear, anger and disgust 'affect programs' described by Ekman (1977, 1980). According to Ekman, affect programs direct emotional responses that are brief, often quick, complex, organized and difficult to control. The term 'affect program' refers to a (neural) mechanism that stores the patterns for these complex organized responses, and which then triggers their occurrence. Griffiths (1990, 1997) suggests that the system that produces an affect program has the properties of a modular system.

While this account may turn out to be substantially correct, we would caution against interpreting our data as strong support for a modular affect program theory for several reasons. For a start, the necessary and sufficient conditions for a system's being modular have not been clearly specified (Fodor 2000, Lyons 2000, Flombaum *et al.* 2002, Geary and Huffman 2002). Further, the features used to define modularity (for example informational encapsulation) are not themselves well understood. We feel that Lyons (2001) notion of a 'system' might be usefully applied to the results here, where systems are defined (roughly) as being isolable, specialized, and internally cohesive. These ideas are similar to those of Shallice (1988), and bear some similarities with the ethological notion of a 'behavior system' (Shettleworth 1994, Prescott *et al.* 1999). We think the neuropsychological data point to there being particular 'emotion' systems, with the properties of being isolable, specialized and internally cohesive. These systems are involved in (but not necessarily systems solely for) recognizing fear, anger and disgust in others and in certain fear, disgust and anger responses. Whether these systems turn out to be isomorphic with, for example, Ekman's affect programs is as yet unclear. It may well be that the systems we describe may be further fractionated. There do seem to be hints (e.g. Prather *et al.* 2001) that not even all fear responses that would be included in Ekman's notion of an affect program for fear are impaired following amygdala lesions, and there is not enough data on disgust and anger impairments to draw any firm conclusions as to whether disgust and anger systems might be further fractionated. We must also be careful not to generalize from fear, disgust and anger to the other affect program emotions. Indeed, there are hints from the functional neuroimaging literature that sadness and happiness may be interestingly different from fear, disgust and anger, at least in their neural instantiation (Murphy, Nimmo-Smith and Lawrence, in press). Only future empirical research will enable us to determine what the granularity (Sterelny and Griffiths 1999, Sterelny 2000) of emotion systems really is.

Whatever the level at which emotion systems ultimately prove fractionable, we would argue, echoing Panksepp (1991), that 'affective neuropsychology' has the potential to be as fruitful in understanding the nature of emotion systems as cognitive neuropsychology has been in understanding the nature of cognitive systems, and, in the domain of evolutionary psychology, by adopting a genuinely comparative agenda, possibly even more so.

Acknowledgements

The UK Medical Research Council (MRC) supports our work. Thanks to Sekhar Chandra Sripada for comments on the manuscript.

References

Adams, D. B. (1981). Motivational systems of social behavior in male rats and monkeys— are they homologous? *Aggressive Behavior*, 7, 5–18.

Adolphs, R. (2002). Recognizing emotion from facial expressions: psychological and neurological mechanisms. *Behavioral and Cognitive Neuroscience Reviews*, 1, 21–62.

Adolphs, R. and Tranel, D. (1999a). Preferences for visual stimuli following amygdala damage. *Journal of Cognitive Neuroscience*, 11, 610–16.

Adolphs, R. and Tranel, D. (1999b). Intact recognition of emotional prosody following amygdala damage. *Neuropsychologia*, 37, 1285–92.

Adolphs, R. and Tranel, D. (2000). Emotion recognition and the human amygdala. In *The amygdala: a functional analysis*, 2nd edition (ed. J. P. Aggleton), pp. 587–630. Oxford University Press, Oxford.

Adolphs, R., Russell, J. A., and Tranel, D. (1999a). A role for the human amygdala in recognizing emotional arousal from unpleasant stimuli. *Psychological Science*, 10, 167–71.

Adolphs, R., Tranel, D., Damasio, H., and Damasio, A. (1994). Impaired recognition of emotion in facial expressions following bilateral damage to the human amygdala. *Nature*, 372, 669–72.

Adolphs, R., Tranel, D., Damasio, H., and Damasio, A. (1995). Fear and the human amygdala. *Journal of Neuroscience*, 15, 5879–91.

Adolphs, R., Tranel, D., Hamann, S., et al. (1999b). Recognition of facial emotion in nine individuals with bilateral amygdala damage. *Neuropsychologia*, 37, 1111–7.

Anderson, A. K. and Phelps, E. A. (1998). Intact recognition of vocal expressions of fear following bilateral lesions of the human amygdala. *NeuroReport*, 9, 3607–13.

Anderson, A. K. and Phelps, E. A. (2000). Expression without recognition: contributions of the human amygdala to emotional communication. *Psychological Science*, 11, 106–11.

Anderson, A. K. and Phelps, E. A. (2002). Is the human amygdala critical for the subjective experience of emotion? Evidence of intact dispositional affect in patients with amygdala lesions. *Journal of Cognitive Neuroscience*, 14, 709–20.

Anderson, A. K., Spencer, D. D., Fulbright, R. K., and Phelps, E. A. (2000). Contribution of the anteromedial temporal lobes to the evaluation of facial emotion. *Neuropsychology*, 14, 526–36.

Balaban, M. T. (1995). Affective influences on startle in five-month-old infants: reactions to facial expressions of emotion. *Child Development*, 66, 28–36.

Barros, M. and Tomaz, C. (2002). Non-human primate models for investigating fear and anxiety. *Neuroscience and Biobehavioral Reviews*, 26, 187–2001.

Bechara, A., Tranel, D., Damasio, H., Adolphs, R., Rockland, C., and Damasio, A. R. (1995). Double dissociation of conditioning and declarative knowledge relative to the amygdala and hippocampus in humans. *Science*, 269, 1115–8.

Bechtel, W. and Richardson, R. (1993). *Discovering complexity: decomposition and localization as strategies in scientific research*. Princeton University Press, Princeton, New Jersey.

Bermudez-Rattoni, F. and McGaugh, J. L. (1991). Insular cortex and amygdala lesions differentially affect acquisition on inhibitory avoidance and conditioned taste aversion. *Brain Research*, 549, 165–70.

Blanchard, D. C. and Blanchard, R. J. (1972) Innate and conditioned reactions to threat in rats with amygdaloid lesions. *Journal of Comparative and Physiological Psychology*, 81, 281–90.

Blanchard, D. C. and Blanchard, R. J. (1984). Affect and aggression: an animal model applied to human behavior. In *Advances in the study of aggression*, Vol. 1 (ed. R. J. Blanchard and D. C. Blanchard), pp. 1–62. Academic Press, Orlando.

Blanchard, D. C. and Blanchard, R. J. (1989a). Experimental animal models of aggression: what do they say about human behaviour? In *Human aggression: naturalistic approaches*, (ed. J. Archer and K. Browne), pp. 94–121. Routledge, London.

Blanchard, D. C., Hynd, A. L., Minke, K. A., Minemoto, T., and Blanchard, R. J. (2001a). Human defensive behaviors to threat scenarios show parallels to fear and anxiety-related defense patterns of non-human mammals. *Neuroscience and Biobehavioral Reviews*, 25, 761–70.

Blanchard, D. C. and Takahashi, S. N. (1988). No change in intermale aggression after amygdala lesions which reduce freezing. *Physiology & Behavior*, 42, 613–16.

Blanchard, R. J. and Blanchard, D. C. (1989b). Attack and defense in rodents as ethoexperimental models for the study of emotion. *Progress in Neuro-Psychopharmacology and Biological Psychiatry*, 13, S3–S14.

Blanchard, R. J., Ohl, F., van Kampen, M., Blanchard, D. C., and Fuchs, E. (2001b). Attack and defense in conspecific fighting in tree shrews (*Tupaia belangeri*). *Aggressive Behaviour*, 27, 139–48.

Bradley, M. M. and Lang, P. J. (2000). Measuring emotion: behavior, feeling and physiology. In *Cognitive neuroscience of emotion* (ed. R. D. Lane and L. Nadel), pp. 242–76. Oxford University Press, New York.

Broks, P., Young, A. W., and Maratos, E. J., et al. (1998). Face processing impairments after encephalitis: amygdala damage and recognition of fear. *Neuropsychologia*, 36, 59–70.

Brown, A. M. and Crawford, H. J. (1988). Fear survey schedule-III: oblique and orthogonal factorial structures in an American college population. *Personality and Individual Differences*, 9, 401–10.

Brown, S. and Schafer, A. (1888). An investigation into the functions of the occipital and temporal lobes of the monkey's brain. *Philosophical Transaction of the Royal Society of London (Series B: Biology)*, 179, 303–27.

Bubb, J. (1994). Testing models of cognition through the analysis of brain-damaged performance. *British Journal for Philosophy of Science*, 45, 837–55.

Burton, G. (1998). Homology. In *Comparative psychology: a handbook* (ed. G. Greenberg and M. M. Haraway), pp. 128–33. Garland, New York.

Butler, A. B. and Saidel, W. M. (2000). Defining sameness: historical, biological, and generative homology. *BioEssays*, 22, 846–53.

Cacioppo, J. T., Gardner, W. L., and Bernston, G. G. (1999). The affect system has parallel and integrative processing components: form follows function. *Journal of Personality and Social Psychology*, 76, 839–55.

Calder, A. J., Young, A. W., Rowland, D., Perrett, D. I., Hodges, J. R., and Etcoff, N. L. (1996). Facial emotion recognition after bilateral amygdala damage: differentially severe impairment of fear. *Cognitive Neuropsychology*, 13, 699–745.

Calder, A. J., Keane, J., Cole, J., Campbell, R., and Young, A. W. (2000a). Facial expression recognition by people with Möbius syndrome. *Cognitive Neuropsychology*, 17, 73–87.

Calder, A. J., Keane, J., Manes, F., Antoun, N., and Young, A. W. (2000b). Impaired recognition and experience of disgust following brain injury. *Nature Neuroscience*, 3, 1077–8.

Calder, A. J., Lawrence, A. D., and Young, A. W. (2001). Neuropsychology of fear and loathing. *Nature Reviews Neuroscience*, **2**, 352–63.

Coombes, S., Revusky, S., and Lett, B. T. (1980). Long-delay taste aversion learning in an unpoisoned rat: exposure to a poisoned rat as the unconditioned stimulus. *Learning and Motivation*, **11**, 256–66.

Curtis, V. and Biran, A. (2001). Dirt, disgust and disease. *Perspectives in Biology and Medicine*, **44**, 17–31.

Damasio, A. R. (1998). Emotion in the perspective of an integrated nervous system. *Brain Research Reviews*, **26**, 83–6.

Damasio, A. R. (1999). *The feeling of what happens: body, emotion and the making of consciousness.* Vintage, London.

Darwin (1872/1965). *The expressions of emotion in man and animal.* Chigaco University Press, Chicago.

Davidson, R. J. (1994). Complexities in the search for emotion-specific physiology. In *The nature of emotion: fundamental questions* (ed. P. Ekman and R. J. Davidson), pp. 237–42. Oxford University Press, New York.

Davis, M. (2000). The role of the amygdala in conditioned and unconditioned fear and anxiety. In *The amygdala: a functional analysis*, 2nd edition (ed. J. P. Aggleton), pp. 213–87. Oxford University Press, Oxford.

Davies, D. C., Martínez-García, F., Lanuza, E., and Novejarque, A. (2002). Striato-amygdaloid transition area lesions reduce the duration of tonic immobility in the lizard *Podarcis hispanica. Brain Research Bulletin*, **57**, 537–41.

Delgado, J. M. R., Rosvold, H. E., and Looney, E. (1956). Evoking conditioned fear by electrical stimulation of subcortical structures in the monkey brain. *Journal of Comparative and Physiological Psychology*, **49**, 373–80.

Dimberg, U., Thunberg, M., and Elmehed, K. (2000). Unconscious facial reactions to emotional facial expressions. *Psychological Science*, **11**, 86–9.

Duncan, J. and Owen, A. M. (2000). Dissociative methods in the study of frontal lobe function. In *Control of cognitive processes: Attention and Performance XVIII* (ed. S. Monsell and J. Driver), pp. 567–76. MIT Press, Cambridge MA.

Dunn, L. T. and Everitt, B. J. (1988). Double dissociations of the effects of amygdala and insular cortex lesions on conditioned taste aversion, passive avoidance, and neophobia in the rat using the excitotoxin ibotenic acid. *Behavioral Neuroscience*, **102**, 3–23.

Ekman, P. (ed.) (1973). *Darwin and facial expression: a century of research in review.* Academic Press, New York.

Ekman, P. (1977). Biological and cultural contributions to body and facial movement. In *The anthropology of the body* (ed. J. Blacking), pp. 39–84. Academic Press, London.

Ekman, P. (1980). Biological and cultural contributions to body and facial movements in the expression of emotions. In *Explaining emotions* (ed. A. O. Rorty), pp. 73–101. University of California Press, Berkeley.

Emery, N. J., Capitanio, J. P., Mason, W. A., Machado, C. J., Mendoza, S. P., and Amaral, D. G. (2001). The effects of bilateral lesions of the amygdala on dyadic social interactions in rhesus *monkeys (Macaca mulatta). Behavioral Neuroscience*, **115**, 515–44.

van Erp, A. M. M. and Miczek, K. A. (2000). Aggressive behavior, increased accumbal dopamine, and decreased cortical serotonin in rats. *Journal of Neuroscience*, **20**, 9320–25.

Fendt, M. and Fanselow, M. S. (1999). The neuroanatomical and neurochemical basis of conditioned fear. *Neuroscience and Biobehavioral Reviews*, **23**, 743–60.

Flombaum, J. I., Santos, L. R., and Hauser, M. D. (2002). Neuroecology and psychological modularity. *Trends in Cognitive Science*, **6**, 106–8.

Fodor, J. A. (2000). *The mind doesn't work that way: the scope and limits of computational psychology.* MIT Press, Cambridge MA.

Frank, M. G. and Stennett, J. (2001). The forced-choice paradigm and the perception of facial expressions of emotion. *Journal of Personality and Social Psychology*, **80**, 75–85.

Frijda, N. H. (1986). *The emotions.* Cambridge University Press, Cambridge.

Frijda, N. H. (1994). Emotions are functional, most of the time. In *The nature of emotion*, (ed. P. Ekman and R. J. Davidson), pp. 112–22. Oxford University Press, New York.

Frijda, N. H. (1995). Emotions in robots. In *Comparative approaches to cognitive science* (ed. H. L. Roitblat and J.-A. Meyer), pp. 501–16. MIT Press, Cambridge MA.

Fridlund, A. J. (1997). The new ethology of human facial expressions. In *The psychology of facial expression* (ed. J. A Russell and J. M. Fernández-Dols), pp. 103–29. Cambridge University Press, Cambridge.

Funayama, E. S., Grillon, C., Davis, M., and Phelps, E. A. (2001). A double dissociation in the affective modulation of startle in humans: effects of unilateral temporal lobectomy. *Journal of Cognitive Neuroscience*, **13**, 721–29.

Galaverna, O. G., Seeley, R. J., Berridge, K. C., Grill, H. J., Epstein, A. N., and Schulkin, J. (1993). Lesions of the central nucleus of the amygdala I: effects on taste reactivity, taste aversion learning and sodium appetite. *Behavioral Brain Research*, **59**, 11–7.

Galef, B. G. (2002). Social influences on food choices of Norway rats and mate choices of Japanese quail. *Appetite*, **39**, 179–80.

Gallese, V. and Goldman, A. (1998). Mirror neurons and the simulation theory of mind-reading. *Trends in Cognitive Science*, **2**, 493–501.

Garcia, J. (1989). Food for Tolman: cognition and cathexis in concert. In *Aversion, avoidance and anxiety* (ed. T. Archer and L.-G. Nilson), pp. 45–85. Lawrence Erlbaum Associates, Hillsdale, New Jersey.

Garcia, J. (1990). Learning without memory. *Journal of Cognitive Neuroscience*, **2**, 287–305.

Garcia, J., Hankins, W. G., and Rusiniak, K. W. (1974). Behavioral regulation of the milieu interne in man and rat. *Science*, **185**, 824–31.

Garcia, J., Quick, D. F., and White, B. (1983). Conditioned disgust and fear from mollusk to monkey. In *Primary neural substrates of learning and behavioral change* (ed. D. L. Alkon and J. Farley), pp. 47–61. Cambridge University Press, Cambridge.

Geary, D. C. and Huffman, K. J. (2002). Brain and cognitive evolution: forms of modularity and functions of mind. *Psychological Bulletin*, **128**, 667–98.

Gerull, F. C. and Rapee, R. M. (2002). Mother knows best: effects of maternal modelling on the acquisition of fear and avoidance behaviours in toddlers. *Behaviour Research and Therapy*, **40**, 279–87.

Goldie, P. (1999). How we think of others' emotions. *Mind and Language*, **14**, 394–423.

Goodwin, F. K., Murphy, D. L., Brodie, H. K. H. and Bunney, W. E., Jr. (1970). L-Dopa, catecholamines and behavior: a clinical and biochemical study in depressed patients. *Biological Psychiatry*, **2**, 341–66.

Gray, J. M., Young, A. W., Barker, W. A., Curtis, A., and Gibson, D. (1997). Impaired recognition of disgust in Huntington's disease gene carriers. *Brain*, **120**, 2029–38.

Grill, H. J. and Norgren, R. (1978). The taste reactivity test I. Mimetic responses to gustatory stimuli in neurologically normal rats. *Brain Research*, **143**, 263–79.

Griffiths, P. E. (1990). Modularity, and the psychoevolutionary theory of emotion. *Biology and Philosophy*, **5**, 175–96.

Griffiths, P. E. (1997). *What emotions really are: the problem of psychological categories.* Chicago University Press, Chicago.

Griffiths, P. E. (2001). From adaptive heuristic to phylogenetic perspective: some lessons from the evolutionary psychology of emotion. In *Conceptual challenges in evolutionary psychology* (ed. H. R. Holcomb III), pp. 309–25. Kluwer, Dordrecht.

Griffiths, P. E. (in press). Evo-devo meets the mind: towards a developmental evolutionary psychology. In *Integrating evolution and development* (ed. R. Brandon and R. Sansom), Cambridge University Press, Cambridge.

Hadfield, M. G. (1983). Dopamine: mesocortical vs. nigrostriatal uptake in isolated fighting mice and controls. *Behavioral Brain Research*, **7**, 269–81.

Haidt, J., McCauley, C., and Rozin, P. (1994) Individual differences in sensitivity to disgust: a scale sampling seven domains of disgust elicitors. *Personality and Individual Differences*, **16**, 701–13.

Halgren, E. (1992). Emotional neurophysiology of the amygdala within the context of human cognition. In *The amygdala: neurobiological aspects of emotion, memory, and mental dysfunction* (ed. J.P. Aggleton), pp. 191–228. Wiley-Liss, New York.

Hamann, S. B., Stefanacci, L., and Squire, L. R., et al. (1996). Recognizing facial emotion. *Nature*, **379**, 497.

Hatfield, E., Cacioppo, J. T., and Rapson, R. L. (1994). *Emotional contagion.* Cambridge University Press, Cambridge.

Hernádi, I., Karádi, Z., Faludi, B., and Lénárd, L. (1997). Disturbances of neophobia and taste-aversion learning after bilateral kainate microlesions in the rat pallidum. *Behavioral Neuroscience*, **111**, 137–46.

Hess, U., Philippot, P., and Blairy, S. (1999). Mimicry: facts and fiction. In *The social context of nonverbal behavior*, (ed. P Philippot, RS Feldman, and EJ Coats), pp. 213–41. Cambridge University Press, Cambridge.

Heyes, C. M. (2000). Evolutionary psychology in the round. In *The evolution of cognition*, (ed. C. M. Heyes and L. Huber), pp. 3–22. MIT Press, Cambridge, MA.

Hinde, R. A. (1985). Was 'The expression of the emotions' a misleading phrase? *Animal Behavior*, **33**, 985–92.

Hollis, K. L. (1997). Contemporary research on Pavlovian conditioning. *American Psychologist*, **52**, 956–65.

Izard, C. E. (1979). Emotions as motivations: an evolutionary-developmental perspective. In *Nebraska symposium on motivation, Vol. 26*, (ed. R. A. Dienstbier), pp. 163–200. University of Nebraska Press, Nebraska.

Iwaniuk, A. N. and Whishaw, I. Q. (2000). On the origin of skilled forelimb movements. *Trends in Neurosciences*, **23**, 372–76.

Jacobs, B. L. and McGinty, D. J. (1972). Participation of the amygdala in complex stimulus recognition and behavioral inhibition: evidence from unit studies. *Brain Research*, **36**, 431–36.

Jakobs, E., Manstead, A. S. R., and Fischer, A. H. (1999). Social motives and emotional feelings as determinants of facial displays: the case of smiling. *Personality and Social Psychology Bulletin*, 25, 424–35.

Johnstone, R. A. (2001). Eavesdropping and animal conflict. *Proceedings of the National Academy of Sciences, USA*, 98, 9177–80.

Kalin, N. H., Shelton, S. E., Davidson, R. J., and Kelley, A. E. (2001). The primate amygdala mediates acute fear but not the behavioral and physiological components of anxious temperament. *Journal of Neuroscience*, 21, 2067–74.

Kavaliers, M. and Choleris, E. (2001). Antipredator responses and defensive behavior: ecological and ethological approaches for the neurosciences. *Neuroscience and Biobehavioral Reviews*, 25, 577–86.

Keltner, D. and Haidt, J. (2001). Social functions of emotion. In *Emotions: current issues and future directions* (ed. T. J. Mayne and G. A. Bonanno), pp. 192–213. Guilford Press, New York.

Kemble, E. D., Blanchard, D. C., and Blanchard, R. J. (1990). Effects of regional amygdaloid lesions on flight and defensive behaviors of wild black rats (*Rattus rattus*). *Physiology & Behavior*, 48, 1–5.

Kiefer, S. W. and Orr, M. R. (1992). Taste avoidance, but not aversion, learning in rats lacking gustatory cortex. *Behavioral Neuroscience*, 106, 140–6.

Kling, A. S., Lloyd, R. L., and Perryman, K. M. (1987). Slow wave changes in amygdala to visual, auditory and social stimuli following lesions of the inferior temporal cortex in squirrel monkey (*S. sciureus*). *Behavioral and Neural Biology*, 4, 54–72.

Klinnert, M., Campos, J., Sorce, J., Emde, R., and Svejda, M. (1983). Emotions as behavior regulators: social referencing in infancy. In *Emotion: theory, research and experience* (ed. R. Plutchik, H. Kellerman), pp. 57–86. Academic Press, New York.

Klüver, H. and Bucy, P. C. (1937). 'Psychic blindness' and other symptoms following bilateral temporal lobectomy in rhesus monkeys. *American Journal of Physiology*, 119, 352–3.

Koepp, M. J., Gunn, R. N., and Lawrence, A. D., et al. (1998). Evidence for striatal dopamine release during a videogame. *Nature*, 393, 266–68.

Kostowski, W., Tarchalska, B., and Wañchowicz, B. (1975). Brain catecholamines, spontaneous bioelectrical activity and aggressive behavior in ants (*Formica rufa*). *Pharmacology, Biochemistry and Behavior*, 3, 337–42.

Korzan, W. J., Summers, T. R., Ronan, P. J., Renner, K. J., and Summers, C. H. (2001). The role of monoaminergic nuclei during aggression and sympathetic social signaling. *Brain Behavior and Evolution*, 57, 317–27.

LaBar, K. S., LeDoux, J. E., Spencer, D. D., and Phelps, E. A. (1995). Impaired fear conditioning following unilateral temporal lobectomy in humans. *Journal of Neuroscience*, 15, 6846–54.

Lambie, J. A. and Marcel, A. J. (2002). Consciousness and the varieties of emotion experience: a theoretical framework. *Psychological Review*, 109, 219–59.

Lang, C., Sober, E., and Strier, K. (2002). Are human beings part of the rest of nature? *Biology and Philosophy*, 17, 661–671.

Lawrence, A. D., Calder, A. J., McGowan, S. M., and Grasby, P. M. (2002). Selective disruption of the recognition of facial expressions of anger. *NeuroReport*, 13, 881–4.

Lazarus, R. (1991). *Emotion and adaptation*. Oxford University Press, New York.

Lazarus, R. (1994). Universal antecedents of the emotions. In *The nature of emotion: fundamental questions* (ed. P. Ekman, R. J. Davidson), pp. 163–71. Oxford University Press, New York.

LeDoux, J. E. (1991). Emotion and the limbic system complex. *Concepts in Neuroscience*, 2, 169–99.

Lipps, T. (1903). Einfühlung, innere nachahmung und organempfindung. *Archiv für die Gesamte Psychologie*, 1, 465–519.

Lipps, T. (1907). Das wissen von fremden ichen. In *Psychologische untersuchungen, Band I*, (ed. T. Lipps), pp. 694–722. Engelmann, Leipzig.

Louilot, A., LeMoal, M., and Simon, H. (1986). Differential reactivity of dopaminergic neurons in the nucleus accumbens in response to different behavioral situations. An in vivo voltammetric study in freely moving rats. *Brain Research*, 397, 395–400.

Lyons, J. C. (2001). Carving the mind at its (not necessarily modular) joints. *British Journal for Philosophy of Science*, 52, 277–302.

Maclean, P. D. (1955). The limbic system ('visceral brain') and emotional behavior. Archives of Neurology and Psychiatry, 73, 130–4.

Malamuth, N. M. and Addison, T. (2001). Integrating social psychological research on aggression within an evolutionary-based framework. In *Blackwell handbook of social psychology: interpersonal processes* (ed. G. J. O. Fletcher and M. S. Clark), pp. 129–61. Blackwell, Oxford.

Maler, L. and Ellis, W. G. (1987). Inter-male aggressive signals in weakly electric fish are modulated by monoamines. *Behavioral Brain Research*, 25, 75–81.

Mallon, R. and Stich, S. P. (2000). The odd couple: the compatibility of social construction and evolutionary psychology. *Philosophy of Science*, 67, 133–54.

Matthen, M. (1998). Biological universals and the nature of fear. *Journal of Philosophy*, XCV, 105–32.

Manzaneque, J. M. and Navarro, J. F. (1999). Behavioral profile of amisulpiride in agonistic encounters between male mice. *Aggressive Behavior*, 25, 225–32.

McNaughton, N. (1989). *Biology and emotion*. Cambridge University Press, Cambridge.

Mendoza, S. P. and Ruys, J. D. (2001). The beginning of an alternative view of the neurobiology of emotion. *Social Science Information*, 40, 39–60.

Meunier, M., Bachevalier, J., Murray, E. A., Málková, L., and Mishkin, M. (1999). Effects of aspiration versus neurotoxic lesions of the amygdala on emotional responses in monkeys. *European Journal of Neuroscience*, 11, 4403–18.

Mineka, S. (1992). Evolutionary memories, emotional processing, and the emotional disorders. *Psychology of Learning and Motivation*, 28, 161–206.

Morgan, D., Grant, K. A., Gage, D., et al. (2002). Social dominance in monkeys: dopamine D2 receptors and cocaine self-administration. *Nature Neuroscience*, 5, 169–74.

Murphy, F. C., Nimmo-Smith, I. and Lawrence, A. D. (in press). Functional neuroanatomy of emotions: a meta-analysis. Cognitive, Affective, and Behavioral Neuroscience.

Nesse, R. M. (1990). Evolutionary explanations of emotions. *Human Nature*, 1, 261–89.

Niedenthal, P. M., Ric, F., and Krauth-Gruber, S. (2002). Explaining emotion congruence (and its absence) in terms of perceptual simulation. *Psychological Inquiry*, 13, 80–83.

Öhman, A. (1986). Face the beast and fear the face: animal and social fears as prototypes for evolutionary analyses of emotion. *Psychophysiology*, **23**, 123–45.

Öhman, A. and Mineka, S. (2001). Fears, phobias and preparedness: toward an evolved module of fear and fear learning. *Psychological Review*, **108**, 483–522.

Owren, M. J. and Rendall, D. (1997). An affect-conditioning model of nonhuman primate vocal signaling. In *Perspectives in ethology: Communication*, Vol. 12. (ed. D. H. Owings, M. D. Beecher, and N. S. Thompson), pp. 299–346. Plenum Press, New York.

Panksepp, J. (1991). Affective neuroscience: a conceptual framework for the neurobiological study of emotions. In *International review of studies on emotion*, Vol. 1 (ed. K. T. Strongman), pp. 59–99. John Wiley & Sons, Chichester.

Panksepp, J. (2000). Emotions as natural kinds within the mammalian brain. In *Handbook of emotions*, 2nd edition (ed. M. Lewis and J. M. Haviland-Jones), pp. 137–56. Guilford, New York.

Parmigiani, S., Ferrari, P. F., and Palanza, P. (1998). An evolutionary approach to behavioral pharmacology: using drugs to understand proximate and ultimate mechanisms of different forms of aggression in mice. *Neuroscience and Biobehavioral Reviews*, **23**, 143–53.

Peper, M., Karcher, S., Wohlfarth, R., Reinshagen, G., and LeDoux, J. (2001). Aversive learning in patients with unilateral lesions of the amygdala and hippocampus. *Biological Psychology*, **58**, 1–23.

Plutchik, R. (1980). *Emotion: a psychoevolutionary synthesis*. Harper & Row, New York.

Plutchik, R. (2001). The nature of emotions. *American Scientist*, **89**, 344–50.

Prather, M. D., Lavenex, P., and Mauldin-Jourdain, M. L., et al. (2001). Increased social fear and decreased fear of objects in monkeys with neonatal amygdala lesions. *Neuroscience*, **106**, 653–58.

Prescott, T. J., Redgrave, P., and Gurney, K. (1999). Layered control architectures in robots and vertebrates. *Adaptive Behavior*, **7**, 99–127.

Preuschoft, S., van Hooff J. A. R. A. M. (1995). Homologizing primate facial displays: A critical review of methods. *Folia Primatologica*, **65**, 121–37.

Preuss, T. M. (2000). Taking the measure of diversity: comparative alternatives to the model-animal paradigm in cortical neuroscience. *Brain Behavior Evolution*, **55**, 287–99.

Pritchard, T. C., Macaluso, D. A., and Eslinger, P. J. (1999). Taste perception in patients with insular cortex lesions. *Behavioral Neuroscience*, **113**, 663–71.

Rapcsak, S. Z., Galper, S. R., and Comer, J. F., et al. (2000). Fear recognition deficits after focal brain damage—a cautionary note. *Neurology*, **54**, 575–81.

Rasa, O. A. E. (1976). Aggression: appetite or aversion?—an ethologist's view. *Aggressive Behavior*, **2**, 213–22.

Rauch, S. L., Dougherty, D. D., and Shin, L. M., et al. (1998). Neural correlates of factor-analyzed OCD symptom dimensions: a PET study. *CNS Spectrums*, **3**, 37–43.

Redolat, R., Brain, P. F., and Simón, V. M. (1991). Sulpiride has an antiaggressive effect in mice without markedly depressing motor activity. *Neuropsychopharmacology*, **30**, 41–6.

Reiner, A. (1990). Review of the triune brain in evolution—role in paleocerebral functions—Maclean, PD. *Science*, **250**, 303–5.

Rinn, W. E. (1984). The neuropsychology of facial expression: a review of the neurological and psychological mechanisms for producing facial expressions. *Psychological Bulletin*, **95**, 52–77.

Robson-Brown, K. (1999). Cladistics as a tool in comparative analysis. In *Comparative primate socioecology* (ed. P. C. Lee), pp. 23–43. Cambridge University Press, Cambridge.

Rosenberg, E. L. and Ekman, P. (1994). Coherence between expressive and experiential systems in emotion. *Cognition and Emotion*, **8**, 201–29.

Rozin, P. (1982). 'Taste-smell confusions' and the duality of the olfactory sense. *Perception and Psychophysics*, **31**, 397–401.

Rozin, P. and Fallon, A. E. (1987). A perspective on disgust. *Psychological Review*, **94**, 23–41.

Rozin, P., Haidt, J., McCauley, C., and Imada, S. (1997) Disgust: preadaptation and the cultural evolution of a food-based emotion. In *Food preferences and tastes: continuity and change*, (ed. H. Macbeth), pp. 65–82. Berghahn, Oxford.

Rozin, P., Haidt, J., and McCauley, C. R. (2000). Disgust. In *Handbook of emotions*, 2nd edition (ed. M. Lewis and M. Haviland-Jones), pp. 637–53. Guilford Press, New York.

Rozin, P. and Schull, J. (1988). The adaptive-evolutionary point of view in experimental psychology. In *Stevens' handbook of experimental psychology, perception and motivation*, 2nd edition, Vol. 1 (ed. R. C. Atkinson, R. J. Hernstein, G. Lindzey, and R. D. Luce), pp. 503–46. Wiley, New York.

Scherer, K. (1993). Neuroscience projections to current debates in emotion psychology. *Cognition and Emotion*, **7**, 1–41.

Schmolck, H. and Squire, L. R. (2001). Impaired perception of facial emotions following bilateral damage to the anterior temporal lobe. *Neuropsychology*, **15**, 30–8.

Schultz, W. (1998). Predictive reward signal of dopamine neurons. *Journal of Neurophysiology*, **80**, 1–27.

Scott, S. K., Young, A. W., Calder, A. J., Hellawell, D. J., Aggleton, J. P., and Johnson, M. (1997). Impaired auditory recognition of fear and anger following bilateral amygdala lesions. *Nature*, **385**, 254–7.

Seward, T. V. and Seward, M. A. (2001). Cortical association areas in the gustatory system. *Neuroscience and Biobehavioral Reviews*, **25**, 395–407.

Shallice, T. (1998). *From neuropsychology to mental structure*. Cambridge University Press, Cambridge.

Shelley, C. (1999). Preadaptation and the explanation of human evolution. *Biology and Philosophy*, **14**, 65–82.

Shettleworth, S. J. (1994). What are behavior systems and what use are they? *Psychonomic Bulletin and Review*, **1**, 451–6.

Silk, J. B., Kaldor, E., and Boyd, R. (2000). Cheap talk when interests conflict. *Animal Behavior*, **59**, 423–32.

Simon, V., Minarro, J., Redolat, R., Garmendia, L. (1989). An ethopharmacological study of the effects of three neuroleptics (haloperidol, clozapine and sulpiride) on aggressive encounters in male mice. In *Ethoexperimental approaches to the study of Behavior* (ed. R. J. Blanchard, P. F. Brain, D. C. Blanchard, and S. Parmigiani), pp. 474–83. Kluwer, Doredrecht.

Smeets, W. J. A. J. and González, A. (2000). Catecholamine systems in the brain of vertebrates: new perspectives through a comparative approach. *Brain Research Reviews*, **33**, 308–79.

Smith, J. E., Friedman, M. I., and Andrews, P. L. R. (2001). Conditioned food aversion in *Suncus murinus* (house musk shrew)—a new model for the study of nausea in a species with an emetic reflex. *Physiology & Behavior*, **73**, 593–8.

Snowdon, C. T. and Boe, C. Y. (2003). Social communication about unpalatable foods in tamarins (Saguinus oedipus). *Journal of Comparative Psychology,* 117, 142–148.

de Sousa, R. (1987). *The rationality of emotion.* MIT Press, Cambridge, MA.

Sprengelmeyer, R., Young, A. W., and Calder, A. J., et al. (1996). Loss of disgust: perception of faces and emotions in Huntington's disease. *Brain,* 119, 1647–65.

Sprengelmeyer, R., Young, A. W., and Sprengelmeyer, A., et al. (1997). Recognition of facial expressions: selective impairment of specific emotions in Huntington's disease. *Cognitive Neuropsychology,* 14, 839–79.

Sprengelmeyer, R., Young, A. W., and Pundt, I., et al. (1998). Disgust implicated in obsessive-compulsive disorder. *Proceedings of the Royal Society of London (Series B: Biology),* 264, 1767–73.

Sprengelmeyer, R., Young, A. W., and Schroeder, U., et al. (1999). Knowing no fear. *Proceedings of the Royal Society of London (Series B: Biology),* 266, 2451–6.

Stefanacci, L. and Amaral, D. G. (2000). Topographic organization of cortical inputs to the lateral nucleus of the macaque monkey amygdala: a retrograde tracing study. *Journal of Comparative Neurology,* 421, 52–79.

Steiner, J. E., Glaser, D., Hawilo, M. E., and Berridge, K. C. (2001). Comparative expression of hedonic impact: affective reactions to taste by human infants and other primates. *Neuroscience and Biobehavioral Reviews,* 25, 53–74.

Sterelny, K. (2000). Development, evolution, and adaptation. *Philosophy of Science,* 67 (Proceedings), S369–S387.

Sterelny, K. and Griffiths, P. E. (1999). *Sex and death: an introduction to philosophy of biology.* Chicago University Press, Chicago.

Streidter, G. F. (2002). Brain homology and function: an uneasy alliance. *Brain Research Bulletin,* 57, 239–42.

Streidter, G. F. and Northcutt, R. G. (1991). Biological hierarchies and the concept of homology. *Brain Behavior Evolution,* 38, 177–89.

Teuber, H. L. (1955). Physiological psychology. *Annual Review of Psychology,* 9, 267–96.

Thieben, M. J., Duggins, A. J., Good, C. D., et al. (2002). The distribution of structural neuropathology in pre-clinical Huntington's disease. *Brain,* 125, 1815–28.

Thompson, C. I., Schwartzbaum, J. S., and Harlow, H. F. (1969). Development of social fear after amygdalectomy in infant rhesus monkeys. *Physiology & Behavior,* 4, 249–54.

Tomkins, S. S. (1963). *Affect, imagery, consciousness: The negative affects,* Vol. 2. Springer, New York.

Tooby, J. and Cosmides, L. (1990). The past explains the present: emotional adaptations and the structure of ancestral environments. *Ethology and Sociobiology,* 11, 375–424.

Travers, J. B. and Norgren, R. (1986). Electromyographic analysis of the ingestion and rejection of sapid stimuli in the rat. *Behavioral Neuroscience,* 100, 544–55.

Watson, D., Clark, L. A., and Tellegen, A. (1988). Development and validation of brief measures of positive and negative affect: the PANAS scales. *Journal of Personality and Social Psychology,* 54, 1063–70.

Wierzbicka, A. (1986). Human emotions: universal or culture-specific? *American Anthropologist,* 88, 584–94.

Wild, B., Erb, M., and Bartels, M. (2001). Are emotions contagious? Evoked emotions while viewing emotionally expressive faces: quality, quantity, time course and gender differences. *Psychiatry Research,* 102, 109–24.

Winberg, S. and Nilsson, G. E. (1992). Induction of social dominance by L-dopa treatment in Arctic charr. *NeuroReport*, **3**, 243–46.

Wise, R. A. and Bozarth, M. A. (1987). A psychomotor stimulant theory of addiction. *Psychological Review*, **94**, 469–92.

Yoerg, S. I. and Shier, D. M. (1997). Maternal presence and rearing conditions affect responses to a live predator in Kangaroo rats (*Dipodomys heermanni arenae*). *Journal of Comparative Psychology*, **111**, 362–69.

Young, M. P., Hilgetag, C.-C., and Scannell, J. W. (2000). On imputing function to structure from the behavioural effects of brain lesions. *Philosophical Transactions of the Royal Society of London (Series B, Biology)*, **355**, 147–61.

PART II
EMOTION, BELIEF, AND APPRAISAL

EMOTIONAL BEHAVIOUR AND THE SCOPE OF BELIEF–DESIRE EXPLANATION

FINN SPICER

I

In our everyday psychologizing, emotions figure largely. When we are trying to explain and predict what a person says and does, that person's emotions are very much among the objects of our thoughts. Despite this, emotions do not figure largely in our philosophical reconstruction of everyday psychological practice—in philosophical accounts of the rational production and control of behaviour. Barry Smith has noted this point:

> We frequently mention people's emotional states when assessing how they behave, when trying to understand why they say and do the things they say and do, and when deciding how to deal with them. A large part of our awareness of others and our ability to make sense of them depends on their emotional make-up and our appreciation of how this affects their thoughts and actions. All of this is missing from the standard accounts of folk psychology, and the key question is why? (Smith, 2002: 111-2)

Before beginning to answer Smith's question, I want to say more to characterize the approach in philosophical psychology which he is questioning. There are many detailed philosophical accounts of the rational production and control of behaviour. My aim here is not to examine these details, but to characterize a certain species of philosophical psychology—one which holds that one can explain the rational production and control of behaviour in terms of a narrow set of mental state types: belief, desire (and perhaps a few others: perception or intention). Hence my label for this species: 'Humean psychology'.

The orthodox Humean view is that rational agency can be explained adequately by appeal to the agent's beliefs and desires. So, to borrow an example from Davidson (1978), we can explain a person's adding salt to the stew by citing her belief that if she adds salt then the stew will taste better, and in doing so we rationalize her action—show it to be rational. Two aspects of the cited belief and desire are important for the explanation and rationalization of the behaviour: the content and their attitude-type. One must cite the content of the belief to explain why she added salt to the stew, rather than anything else. But, as Davidson points out, the two contents *if she adds salt then the stew will taste better and the stew will taste better* alone neither explain nor rationalize. But if we further specify the directions of fit that her mental states have, then both explanation and rationalization are achieved. When we know that the state with content *if she adds salt then the stew will taste better* is world-guided, but the state with content *the stew will taste better* is world-guiding, then we know enough to explain and rationalize. These two directions of fit characterize the two attitudes which figure in the explanations of Humean psychology—beliefs and desires respectively. I will call explanations in terms of the attitude and content of beliefs and desires 'rational explanations'; these are the explanations of Humean psychology.

Smith himself has a suggestion as to why Humean psychology has excluded emotion, with its focus on belief and desire:

> The most likely explanation for the exclusion of the emotions from accounts of rational psychology is that they are seen as mere distractions from rational agency: noise in the system, which at best serve as accompaniments to the real explanatory factors at work in agency and, at worse, interfere with the workings of reason guided action. (Smith 2002: 112)

I want to take this thought as my point of departure in this paper, for Smith's answer contains an important point. The point is that in so far as the production and control of behaviour is rational, emotions are absent, and when emotions are present and playing a role, then the production and control of behaviour is less than fully rational. Emotions are here seen as mere hindrances to the proper workings of the rational mind—as 'sand in the system' one might say, changing Smith's metaphor a little. Recently the attitude towards emotion represented by the sand-in-the-system view has been challenged by theorists who have begun to claim that emotion, rather than being an unwelcome interruption to reason, is often essential to the proper working of reason (for example, Nussbaum 2001, Damasio 1994 and Mameli, this volume, Chapter 8). We might say that they are moving to view emotions as the oil in the system of reason.

There is more to this debate than just whether emotions are good or bad for reason. The issue is not just the evaluation of the outcome of the interaction of emotions with reasoning, but concerns the details of how the emotions interact with reason—how they serve (or interfere with) the rational processes which produce and guide behaviour. It is here that I propose we should look to find an answer to our question of why Humean psychology neglects emotion and trades only in belief and desire.

II

It is sometimes claimed (e.g. Frijda 1994) that moods differ from emotions in that whereas emotions have non-global effects on cognition, moods have only global effects on cognition. For example, one's good mood has the global effect on deliberation of leading one to overestimate the probable success of a course of action. There is one species of non-global effect in particular that emotions have, which is important for our project, and is related to the other difference that is often cited between emotions and moods: the difference that emotions have intentional content, whereas moods lack intentional content. These are that non-global effects emotions have by virtue of their having the intentional content they do.

To illustrate the intentional and non-intentional effects of emotion, let us take a sudden, eruptive emotion as an example. Suppose that, reading in bed, alone, a woman is gripped with fear upon hearing something downstairs in the night. When gripped with fear, there are a variety of bodily changes which occur rapidly together, some on the surface, like a change in facial expression, others within. Among these changes are changes in circulation: an increase in the person's heart rate and diversion of blood away from her stomach to the muscles. This change will affect the performance of any number of strenuous behaviours (though it might be fighting and fleeing in particular which it is these changes' function to affect). Also in her terror there is a global change in her attention: she becomes sensitive to the slightest noises. This change too will have effects on behaviour, because the change in attention will alter the quantity and nature of the incoming information which informs that behaviour. These two are relatively global effects of the fear on behaviour, and in characterizing these effects, I did not need to mention any *intentional* property of the fear, such as that she is afraid of an intruder.

Emotions have intentional effects too. Returning to our woman, still terrified upstairs, the thought comes to her that there is an intruder downstairs. She cannot shake this thought, both in the sense of not being able to think about anything else, and in the sense that she is convinced it is true. It occupies her mind as an *idée fixe*, to use Peter Goldie's expression, and skews her epistemic landscape so that all the evidence points towards it (Goldie, this volume, Chapter 13).[1] The evidential force of considerations which support it are heightened, and the force of the evidence which would undermine her *idée fixe* is diminished. Minutes before becoming afraid (had she considered it) she would have found the following argument sound:

1. If there were an intruder downstairs the alarm would have gone off.

2. The alarm has not gone off.

3. Therefore there is no intruder downstairs.

Now, in her fear, her epistemic landscape is skewed against 3 and the epistemic force of the argument is reversed so as to weigh against 1. Furthermore, her mind 'goes looking' (Goldie's phrase again) for reasons to doubt this premise: perhaps the man who sold her the system was a crook ..., perhaps she forgot to switch the alarm on ..., and so on. These effects of her fear are intentional effects; they depend on the intentional properties of the fear. It is not the evidential force of all her beliefs which is enhanced, only the force of some of them—such as her belief that the alarm salesman was crooked and her belief that the back door is easy to force open. And in specifying which beliefs are so enhanced by the fear, one must appeal to relations between the intentional content of those beliefs to the content of her fear.

Examples such as these are familiar; in our everyday psychology we acknowledge that emotions play complex roles such as these in a person's mind (however well or badly folk psychology furnishes us with a theory which explains these roles). I do not need to argue here for the claim that emotions have effects such as these on our thought and behaviour, rather my point is that these effects are part of the data which Humean psychology must accommodate. The question is: how does a Humean psychology, using only belief and desire, accommodate the effects of emotion on behaviour?

Of the various effects of emotions, it is the intentional effects which present a challenge to one giving an answer to the above question. For if emotions are like beliefs and desires in having intentional effects on behaviour, then surely we need to cite emotions in our explanations of behaviour just as we cite beliefs and desires? And if not by citing emotions alongside beliefs and desires, then how else can a belief–desire psychology account for the intentional effects of emotions on behaviour?

---

1 The landscape metaphor comes from Nussbaum (2001).

III

I want to answer the question with which I ended the previous section by offering the following strategy to Humean psychology: Humean psychology can accommodate the complex, non-global causal roles of emotions by keeping its focus on belief and desire, and arguing that the way emotions have intentional effects on thought and behaviour is always via belief and desire. I will offer three versions of this strategy; of the three only the first has been explicitly taken up by defenders of Humean psychology, but the second and third are viable.

Beliefs and desires themselves, of course, have intentional effects on thought and behaviour. My belief that the man in the coat is a spy does not affect all my other beliefs equally (though if epistemic holism is true, it may affect all my other beliefs). In spelling out the effects of this belief, one must specify (amongst other things) relations between the content of this belief and the contents of the states with which it causally interacts (such as my belief about whether he has a gun, and my desire to expose all spies as traitors).

The three strategies I will outline all explain the intentional effects that emotions have on the production and control of behaviour as parasitic on the effects that beliefs and desires have within the rational production and control of behaviour, hooking emotions to beliefs and desires in three different ways. The first strategy I will give is now (rightly) no longer popular, but it serves a useful role providing a contrast with which to define the other two.

The first strategy is to claim that emotions are made of beliefs and desires, perhaps together with other, non-intentional ingredients—call them 'feelings'. I call this the 'hybrid view of emotion' (following Paul Griffiths 1997, ch. 2); Peter Goldie calls this view 'the add-on view of emotion' (2000a, and this volume, Chapter 13). Philosophers who have endorsed the hybrid view of emotion were offering a reductive theory, analyzing emotions (often from the armchair) into composites of a belief, a desire and a feeling (or multiples of these ingredients). So, for example, a hybrid theory might conclude that a certain kind of righteous anger is a composite of: a bad feeling of a certain sort, a negative evaluative belief that there has been an offence, a belief that someone is blameworthy, together with a desire to punish that someone (cf. Solomon 1977, 226–9). Using the hybrid theory, one can account for both the intentional and the non-intentional effects of anger on thought and behaviour. One can account for the non-intentional effects by identifying them as effects either of the constituent non-intentional feeling, or of the non-intentional properties of a constituent propositional attitude, such as the strength of the desire (Marks 1982). And one can account for the intentional effects of the anger by identifying these effects as the constituent belief and desire playing their usual role in driving and guiding action.

The second and third options for Humean psychology are the heirs to the hybrid view of emotion, each in different ways. I call the second option 'the umbrella view'. The umbrella view differs from the hybrid view in this respect: it claims not that an emotion is a composite of a belief, a desire, and a feeling, but that one can treat an emotion as a belief, or as a desire in one's account of how the emotion figures as part of the production and control of behaviour. We can introduce umbrella terms 'belief-like' and 'desire-like' to capture the roles beliefs and desires respectively play in combining to produce and guide behaviour. In these terms we can state two claims which are important for the umbrella view—the first is the central claim of the umbrella view; the second is a claim which must be true if the umbrella view is to be a worthwhile strategy for integrating emotions into Humean psychology.

The central claim of the umbrella view is that beliefs are not the only belief-like states and desires are not the only desire-like states, and that, in particular, sometimes emotions are belief-like and sometimes emotions are desire-like. To claim that a state is belief-like is to say it has the kind of propositional content which beliefs have and it has the belief direction of fit, so the central claim is that emotions sometimes have propositional content and a world-guided direction of fit, and similarly for desire.

The claim which the umbrella view requires to be true in order to be a successful strategy is that not only are emotions sometimes belief-like and sometimes desire-like but that almost every time emotions are among the intentional causes of behaviour, they are so in virtue of being belief-like or being desire-like. The umbrella view does not need to capture those cases where emotions have non-intentional effects on behaviour; these can be relegated outside the proper scope of psychological explanation and explained physiologically. But it can only tolerate a few cases where emotions have intentional effects which are not in virtue of the emotion's being belief-like or desire-like. For it is the intentional effects of emotions for which we want to give a psychological explanation, so to the extent that the umbrella view fails to capture the intentional effects of emotion as belief-like or desire-like, Humean psychology fails to capture psychological explanation.

The third option for Humean psychology is again an heir to the hybrid view; I call this view 'the nomological view', for reasons soon to become clear. The hybrid view was that emotions are beliefs and desires; the umbrella view that emotions behave like beliefs and desires; the nomological view is that emotions carry beliefs and desires with them, as companions as it were. Recall the analysis of a particular kind of anger given above to illustrate the hybrid view—anger involves: a bad feeling, a negative evaluative belief that there has been an offence, a belief that someone is blameworthy, together with a desire to punish that someone. On the nomological view, the right way to read this claim is not as a constitutive claim about what anger is, but rather as a generalization about anger—as the empirical claim that anger generally comes with these items. Recognizing the empirical status of this claim is essential to understanding the nomological view.

The nomological view is committed to the truth of conditionals such as 'if one is angry at X, then ceteris paribus, one believes that X is responsible for an offence' and it uses these conditionals to build explanations from emotion to behaviour. Furthermore it is committed to these conditionals being lawlike generalizations, otherwise these conditionals will not help build explanatory connections from emotions to behaviour. But note that these generalizations are not laws of Humean psychology, for to say that a person is angry at X is not to say that she has a reason to believe that X is responsible for an offence. Rather, generalizations of this kind lie outside the domain of rational explanation (I will have more to say about what kind of laws these are later). But Humean psychology can use these laws, as entry and exit rules, in and out of the domain within which its explanations operate.

In this way the nomological view allows behaviour out of emotion to be accommodated into Humean psychology, while preserving the purity of Humean psychology as employing only belief–desire explanations. A person's behaviour out of emotion can be given an explanation which is both a belief–desire explanation and mentions the emotion as an intentional cause of the behaviour. But the explanation will have two parts. The first part lies outside the domain of rational explanation, and explains the person's beliefs and desires in terms of her emotional state. This serves as an entry rule for the second part, which is a rational explanation of her behaviour in the light of her beliefs and desires.

An analogy with perception is helpful here to illustrate entry and exit rules. Perceptual states give rise to beliefs: ceteris paribus, if I see that there is a banana on the desk, then seeing this causes me to believe that there is a banana on the desk. And this is a robust generalization connecting perception to belief. Followers of McDowell (McDowell 1994, Brewer 1999) will place this connection within the scope of rational explanation, saying that my perceptual state gives me a reason to believe this.[2] Those who are not followers

---

2 This McDowellean account of perceptual states as providing reasons for belief suggests another strategy for giving rational explanations of behaviour out of emotion: the strategy of elevating emotions into the space of reasons. Then rational explanations will not appeal

will disagree and will maintain instead that this generalisation is merely a law of some other kind. Their position with respect to the relation between perception and belief will be analogous to the nomological theorist's position with respect to the relation between emotion and belief and desire. Continuing this analogy, a non-McDowellean explanation of what I do when I eat the banana will have two parts. There will be a rational explanation of my action in terms of my beliefs and desires, and (should anyone demand an explanation of why I have these beliefs and desires) there will be a different kind of explanation of my belief that there is a banana within reach—invoking my perceptual state together with the law that ceteris paribus, people believe what they see. In this way non-McDowelleans maintain the purity of the explanations of Humean psychology as belief–desire explanations, by committing themselves to another level of explanation where perceptual states are robustly connected to belief.

IV

The question with which I began this paper asked why Humean psychology appeals only to an agent's beliefs and desires in its explanations when it is a commonsense truth that people sometimes act out of emotion. My answer has been that, despite the fact that we sometimes act out of emotion, Humean psychologists feel that they do not need to include emotion-terms into their explanatory vocabulary, because they have strategies for successfully explaining such actions in terms of belief and desire alone. In the hybrid view, the umbrella view and the nomological view, I have offered three such strategies. In this section I put the hybrid view to one side as a bad strategy; in the next section I bring the umbrella and nomological strategies under a single heading— 'the non-reductive view'. The rest of the paper then begins to explore the merits and limits of non-reductive Humean explanation of emotional behaviour.

The hybrid view of emotion has been a well-occupied position in the philosophy of emotion (Kenny 1963, Solomon 1977, Marks 1982, Taylor 1984, Lyons 1980, Oakley 1992), but it has (to my mind) been decisively criticized, the best of this criticism coming from Paul Griffiths (Griffiths 1997, ch. 2,

....

to just two kinds of attitude (or three)–belief, desire (and perception)–but more, for there will also be *emotional attitudes* too. And the conditional connecting emotion to belief will not be an entry rule *into* the rational, but will *express* a rational connection between emotions and belief and desire. I want to put this possibility aside, because such an extended rational psychology would not be a species of Humean psychology as I am discussing it here. It also looks like an implausible view, using a notion of *reason* far from the intuitive notion. Does my disgust give me a *reason* to want to spit out the food? Does my anger give me a *reason* to believe that his comment was offensive? The answer seems to be 'no'.

see also Goldie 2000a, ch. 2, Goldie and Spicer 2002). One of Griffiths' criticisms targets the a prioristic methodology behind the hybrid view, pointing out that, with its basis in bad philosophy of language, the hybrid view was wrong in its attempt to deliver an account of the referents of emotion-terms from data consisting of folk-theory held by users of emotion-terms. So, with respect to the above example, to the extent that it strikes us as necessary that if one is angry at a person, one desires to punish that person, we should only conclude that it is implicit in our folk-conception of anger that when one is angry, one typically desires this. We cannot conclude that anger is a composite of this desire and some other ingredients. Even to the extent it is true that when one is angry, one typically desires this, the folk have only captured an empirical truth about this kind of anger, not a conceptual one.

The umbrella view is not subject to this criticism. To say that an emotion falls under the desire-umbrella as a desire to punish a person, is to make a claim about the role that this anger can play in the production and control of behaviour, not about what anger is. Furthermore, the umbrella view's claim about roles is consistent with the theory Griffiths offers about how the referents of emotion-terms are determined. Griffiths' view (which is also mine for the purposes of this paper) is that a particular emotion-type should be individuated as that natural kind (if there is one) underlying certain measurable features associated with the emotion-term. These observable features include distinctive facial expression, emotion-typical action, measurable autonomic and other bodily changes, and distinctive phenomenology (Griffiths 1997). Similarly with the nomological view: the claim that an emotion is nomologically related to a desire is not a claim about what the emotion is, and is a claim consistent with Griffiths' view that the emotion is the kind underlying a certain syndrome of changes.

V

The umbrella and the nomological views seem close cousins, one claiming that emotions behave like beliefs and desires, the other that emotions causally co-occur with beliefs and desires. In fact, the two are species of a more general view which I shall call 'the non-reductive view'. We can state the central claim of the non-reductive view by saying that emotions robustly co-occur with states which behave like beliefs and desires. Put this way, the nomological view is the non-reductive view plus the claim that the relation of robust co-occurrence is a causal relation between distinct states. And the umbrella view is the non-reductive view plus the claim that the relation of robust co-occurrence is the identity relation.

The non-reductive view contrasts clearly with the (reductive) hybrid view. The heart of the non-reductive view is the claim that there is a body of true conditionals robustly connecting belief and desire to emotion, and that these conditionals have the status of empirical truths about the way emotions and cognitive states interact in minds like ours, rather than the status of a reduction of emotions to belief and desire.[3] The large literature which the hybrid view has generated over the years (see especially Solomon 1997, Kenny 1963, Marks 1982, and Gordon 1987) is full of generalizations connecting emotions to beliefs, desires and non-intentional states which, although they are in this literature offered as analyses of emotions, can be adopted by non-reductivists as empirical hypotheses. If these generalizations prove to be robust, then the non-reductive view is well placed to furnish Humean explanation with the beliefs and desires it needs to explain action out of emotion an emotional behaviour.

Are these explanations robust? In the case of generalizations connecting the basic emotions (such as anger, fear, and separation distress[4]) to non-intentional (sometimes bodily) states, we have a science to hand to supply robustness. Neuroscience is giving the beginnings of accounts of how emotions give rise to and interact with autonomic nervous system changes, changes in facial and vocal expression and other bodily changes. Although I suspect that neuroscience is not the place to hope to find generalizations connecting emotions with the intentional states belief and desire, let us assume, for the purposes of the rest of this paper, that there are robust generalizations connecting these states (in the next section I will give the name 'intentional psychology' to the theory which includes these generalizations).

The non-reductive view of emotion, armed with this body of generalizations, can set itself to defend the purity of Humean psychology as belief–desire explanation, while acknowledging that some of our behaviour is done out of emotion. The hope for the success of this project will be that for any emotional behaviour, it will fall into one of two categories. Either the behaviour can be

....

3 So evidence that it is possible for emotions to occur in the absence of the relevant beliefs and desires will not threaten the non-reductive view, while this possibility is fatal to the hybrid view. Whether there is such evidence is another matter: Zajonc' work showing that there can be emotional appraisal without cognitive appraisal (meaning verbal report) only supports this possibility if reportability is necessary for possession of beliefs and desires (Zajonc 1980). Arguments from the observation that infants and animals have the capacity to exhibit emotions while lacking the conceptual abilities to have the relevant beliefs and desires look stronger.

4 The question as to which are the basic emotions I leave aside, but see Ekman and Davidson 1994, ch. 1.

assimilated to the bodily changes involved in emotional episodes such as change in facial expression or heart rate, or alternatively the behaviour can be explained in belief–desire terms. If this hope comes good then all of the behaviour out of emotion which is not mere bodily change will receive an explanation within Humean psychology; if the hope does not come good, then there will be behaviours for which we want to give a psychological explanation (for they are not mere bodily changes), but for which we cannot give a belief–desire explanation. The non-intentional effects of emotions on behaviour pose no threat to this hope; we are happy to think of them as bodily changes. It is the intentional effects of emotions which pose a threat. In the next section I will give some examples of intentional effects of emotions which look hard to explain in belief–desire terms.

VI

There is a spectrum of ways that emotions give rise to behaviour (see Goldie 2000b). At one end there are those actions which are amenable to belief–desire explanation, and we have been examining how a Humean psychology which trades in belief–desire explanations can accommodate such actions sometimes being done out of emotion. At the other end of the spectrum are those behaviours which can be regarded as mere bodily changes, to be explained in physiological terms.

Peter Goldie finds the middle ground of this spectrum interesting, locating within this space a range of what he calls 'expressive behaviours' (Goldie 2000b). Expressive behaviours themselves form a spectrum: toward the bodily-change end are behaviours more like changes in facial expression—behaviours which are more closely tied to the specific emotion, and which involve fewer other intentional states in their production. In the middle and toward the other end (closer to those behaviours that are clearly belief–desire explicable) are behaviours which are intentional effects of emotions, but which fit awkwardly into the belief–desire mould.

Goldie discusses an example of such a behaviour: of a person who, out of anger at a person, gouges at the eyes in that person's photograph (Goldie 2000b, 27). This piece of (bad) behaviour—the gouging—fits badly into either category of being like a bodily change or being belief–desire explicable. It is too disanalogous to facial expressions to fit the first category: her gouging was something that this woman did, which she was in control of, and this control was mediated by other intentional states such as her perception of the photo and her beliefs about it. But her gouging is difficult to give a satisfactory belief–desire explanation either: if one tries to force it into the belief–desire mould, one has to posit unlikely beliefs and desires to yield an explanation (does she desire to injure anything that looks like her enemy, or does she believe that by gouging she is injuring her enemy?).[5]

Other problematic cases of emotional behaviour occupying the middle ground are what Craig DeLancey calls 'postfunctional' behaviours (DeLancey 2002). DeLancey argues that emotions are sometimes postfunctional in that they continue to drive behaviour after all the relevant desires are satisfied (and are believed to be satisfied). He gives an example of a person who is enraged at a dog which has attacked his child, and who takes his gun, goes out, and shoots the dog (DeLancey 2002, 53). As described so far, the person's shooting can be described in belief–desire terms. He wanted to kill the dog, and believed that shooting it would achieve this. And the shooting can be explanatorily connected to the man's anger by giving an entry rule showing how anger gives rise to desires of this sort. But the man's behaviour, as DeLancey goes on to describe it, is postfunctional: after the dog is dead (palpably dead—the man knows that the dog is dead) he continues to shoot more bullets into the carcass. He continues to fire out of his anger, but this is postfunctional behaviour and in driving this behaviour, the emotion is not playing the desire-role, DeLancey argues. The emotion is driving the behaviour in a way which cannot be explained by citing the any simple desire such as the desire to kill the dog, because any such desire, combined with the man's beliefs, would not drive behaviour the way the emotion does drive it (DeLancey 2002, ch. 3).

Both expressive behaviours and postfunctional behaviours challenge the adequacy of explaining emotional behaviour in terms of belief and desire alone. A third kind of case which poses a challenge are the effects of emotion on a person's epistemic landscape (as I described it earlier). For example, when a person is jealous, his jealousy skews his epistemic landscape. We can imagine a case in which two 'twins'—duplicates in all the relevant epistemic respects—who each come to suspect from a half overheard comment that their wife is being unfaithful. In one twin this suspicion arouses a gnawing jealousy; in the other twin the suspicion is untroubling. The untroubled twin considers the evidence—his wife's recent behaviour, her weekend business trips, and so on—and concludes that, all told, it points to his suspicion's being false. The jealous twin goes over the very same evidence in his mind, but his jealousy has skewed his epistemic landscape: he sees the evidence in a different light. For him, everything seems to point to his wife's unfaithfulness. In a case

---

5 Goldie's own solution is to argue that belief-desire explanation is not sufficient to explain the gouging ; one must appeal to particular species of desire-like state which is produced by the anger: a species he calls 'wishing'.

like this we naturally want to explain the difference in the way the two twins treat the evidence; in particular we want to explain how the jealous twin reasons by citing his jealousy. But, one kind of explanation—the most natural explanation—is ruled out if one is a Humean: that explanation which describes the twins as alike in what they believe and desire, but as reasoning differently because of their different emotional states. This explanation is ruled out because any Humean account of the difference in the twins' reasoning must go via citing a new belief or desire in the jealous twin which results from his jealousy; but any such new belief or desire would create the difference in beliefs and desires which, in describing the scenario, we have stipulated is absent.

The existence of these three problematic cases is not fatal to the non-reductive Humean view; they all depend on careful description to be problematic. In the last epistemic case, the Humean can bite the bullet and deny the possibility of two twins who think alike but conclude differently. Likewise the Humean can explain expressive behaviours and postfunctional behaviours by biting the bullet and admitting that these agents have bizarre beliefs and desires (perhaps, in the gouging case, the woman desires to harm an image of her enemy and, in the shooting case, the man desires to harm the carcass of the dog).

There will be a certain clumsiness in the Humean strategy of positing bizarre beliefs or desires to give belief–desire explanations of expressive and postfunctional behaviours. The success of this strategy depends on how well the emotional behaviour (expressive or postfunctional) is explained as rational in the light of the agent's bizarre beliefs and desires. And the success of the strategy also depends on how well a second explanation can be given. This is the explanation of why, given the person's emotional state, the person has the bizarre beliefs and desires she does. The very bizarreness of the beliefs and desires to which the first explanation appeals increases the demand for the second explanation, and so increases the extent to which the overall success of the Humean strategy depends on the strength of the second explanation. And so the strength of a Humean explanation of a piece of expressive or postfunctional behaviour is partially dependent on the strength of the explanation of the agent's bizarre beliefs and desires.

VII

Some bizarre desires can be explained in terms of other bizarre desires. For example, let us suppose we explain the angry woman's gouging the photograph by appeal to her desire to gouge her enemy's photograph; now the demand is to explain why she desires this. If we give this explanation in belief–desire terms, citing her desire to harm something which resembles her enemy (together with her beliefs that the photo resembles her enemy and that gouging it will harm the photo), then the same question can be asked again: 'why does she desire this?'; we will have a chain of why-questions, and a chain of bizarre desires. The point is not only that the buck has to stop somewhere, but that it should stop with what is clearly an important factor in the woman's behaving as she does: her anger. After all, her anger is precisely what we would think of when commonsense psychologizing: we might think 'well, she might well want to do that, given how angry she is'.

For the Humean, the umbrella view and the nomological view offer the two non-reductive ways to get anger into the picture. The umbrella theorist will say that at some point in specifying a chain of desires, one does mention the anger, for the anger realizes the role of one of these desires. Unfortunately, the demand for explanations will not stop here for the umbrella theorist, since we can ask what it is about this anger which makes it desire-like in the right respect. This demand goes beyond the commonsense asking of 'why?' but rather this particular question about this token of anger is an instance of a more general demand for explanation which we can aim at the umbrella view. We can demand that the umbrella theorist explain how it can be that emotions can play the role of belief and desire in the production and control of behaviour. The answer to this will require a level of explanation which ascribes to emotions both intentional and non-intentional properties. At this level of explanation, the effects of a token emotion are explained by appeal to these properties, citing generalizations which connect possession of these properties to playing a certain causal role. So the umbrella-Humean's account of the angry woman explains what she did by first explaining why the anger was desire-like (in terms of its having the intentional and non-intentional properties required to be desire-like in this way), and then rationally explaining what she did (in terms of her beliefs and desires).

A nomological theorist will answer the demand for an explanation of why this woman desires what she does in a similar way. The nomological theorist will say that there is an entry rule which describes a causal relation between emotion and desire. But, once again, in saying this the nomological theorist commits himself to a level of explanation distinct from rational explanation— a level of causal explanation at which the connections between emotions and beliefs and desires are explained. At this level of explanation, the effects of a token emotion are explained by appeal to their intentional and non-intentional properties, citing generalisations which connect the state's having these properties to its causing the tokening of certain beliefs and desires.

So the nomological-Humean's account of the angry woman explains what she did by first explaining why the anger caused her desire (in terms of the anger's having the intentional and non-intentional properties which typically cause that desire), and then rationally explaining what she did (in terms of her beliefs and desires).

So, whichever form it takes, the non-reductive view needs to appeal to explanations outside the scope of Humean psychology to explain why emotional agents have the beliefs and desires they do. We can call this level of explanation 'intentional psychology'. I already have mentioned intentional psychology as that theory which contains the robust generalizations connecting emotions to beliefs and desires which the non-reductive Humean view requires. So the present point is that this body of robust generalizations is needed to do explanatory work—precisely the work Humean psychology alone cannot do in these difficult cases.

As I have introduced it here, the term 'intentional psychology' is just a place-holder for that theory which contains robust generalizations connecting emotions and perceptual states to beliefs and desires; the term is meant to be neutral on the details which would positively characterize this theory. However, I have committed myself to this much in positive characterization of intentional psychology: intentional psychology posits a set of properties, which intentional states such as emotions, beliefs and desires possess, and in terms of which the causal relations between these states are explained (Fodor 1987). Because the causal relations to be explained at the level of intentional psychology include the intentional effects of emotions on beliefs and desires (which, like the effects of perceptual states on beliefs, are specified in terms of their content) the causally relevant properties include intentional properties. Hence the label 'intentional psychology'.

Various research programs fall under the label of intentional psychology as I use it here, varying in their views as to what intentional properties are. But there could be an intentional psychology which, if explanatorily powerful enough, could legitimately remain neutral on what intentional properties are and leave them as primitives within the theory (Segal 2000).

Intentional psychology gives causal, intentional explanations of cognitive processes. The variety of these processes and explanations is not restricted to the belief–desire interactions treated by Humean psychology; it is in this respect that intentional psychology and Humean psychology differ. The kind of Humean psychology I am discussing in this paper might want distance itself from intentional psychology, in particular refusing to admit that Humean psychology reduces to intentional psychology (Davidson 1970). But we have seen in this section is that it is to intentional psychology that

Humean psychology must turn if it is to explain (by the non-reductive route) how emotions give rise to beliefs and desires, and hence is to explain emotional behaviour.

VIII

In this last section I want to ask whether the price which Humean psychology must pay to preserve belief–desire explanation is worth paying. Or rather I want to suggest that, if one has the currency to pay this price, belief–desire explanation might not be the way to spend it. The currency is intentional psychology; with this currency Humean psychology can buy rational explanations of emotional behaviour. But if one has the causal-explanatory framework of intentional psychology already, could one not use this framework directly to explain actions out of emotion? One would then have a single, unified explanatory framework for the explanation of (emotional and unemotional) behaviour. This is a guiding ambition of the cognitive science research program. Of course, there is not space here to evaluate this program's prospects of success; rather, my aim in this paper has been to show that the ambition of keeping emotional behaviour within the scope of Humean psychology brings with it a commitment to a level of causal explanation powerful enough to explain the intentional effects of emotions on belief and desire. But then the present thought is that this level of explanation alone may be powerful enough to explain emotional behaviour directly. Having a uniform level of explanation is a methodological virtue, so if Humean psychology needs intentional psychology, but not vice-versa, this is a point against Humean psychology. We should prefer the uniform to the mixed-level explanation, so perhaps we should do away with and do without Humean psychology?

Doing without Humean psychology might mean either discarding belief–desire explanation, or subsuming it—by thinking of belief–desire interactions as just one kind of causal-intentional process, and thinking of belief–desire explanation as just one kind of causal-intentional explanation. The former is eliminativism about belief and desire, and nothing in this paper supports this eliminativism. The little I have said positively about intentional psychology is perfectly compatible with intentional psychology's including beliefs and desires in its ontology, so adopting intentional psychology as a unified framework for explaining emotional and unemotional behaviour is compatible with some of these explanations' being belief–desire explanations. The second option of subsumption is supported by the considerations of this paper.

Subsumption has the virtue of allowing the possibility of choice: sometimes the effects of emotions on behaviour might go via beliefs and desires, and sometimes they might not. In some cases the best explanation of a piece of expressive behaviour might be a belief- and desire-invoking explanation; for example one might explain the woman's gouging the photograph in terms of her desiring to harm an image of her enemy, just as the Humean did. But, after subsumption, this belief–desire explanation would be a fragment of a larger explanation which also explains her desire in terms of her anger. In other cases the best explanation of a piece of expressive behaviour might not mention beliefs and desires, but might merely appeal to the intentional properties of other mental states: perceptual states and emotions, say. For a particular piece of emotional behaviour, how will we decide whether beliefs and desires are involved? This seems an empirical issue (LeDoux's work on the multiple pathways of informational processing in fear looks like the kind of empirical work which might allow us to settle this behaviour by behaviour—LeDoux 1994), and it is a virtue of subsuming beliefs and desires into intentional psychology that we are left free to decide it empirically, rather than have it decided by our commitment to an explanatory framework.

Reflection on the clumsiness of Humean explanations of postfunctional and expressive behaviours, and of emotionally skewed inferences, leads me to conjecture that once freed in this way, we might find that our best intentional explanations invoke fewer beliefs and desires than present Humean explanations do. Humean explanations might sometimes capture the real causal pattern by which action arises out of emotion, but there is a (perhaps large) body of 'middle' cases of emotional behaviour where the structure of the causes is not captured by the Humean pattern. Such cases neither are cases of bodily change resulting from emotion, nor are they cases of behaviour explicable in terms of beliefs and desires which in turn are explicable as resulting from emotion. The scope of belief–desire explanation, I suggest, is smaller than as Humeans we presently recognize.

Acknowledgements

Thanks to Jessica Brown, Peter Goldie, Guy Longworth, Matteo Mameli, David Papineau, and Barry C. Smith for helpful comments on earlier drafts of this paper. Thanks also to Aaron Sloman and Lisa Bortolotti for their questions at the *Emotions, Evolution and Rationality* conference at King's College London.

References

Anscombe, E. (1957). *Intention*. Blackwell, Oxford.

Brewer, B. (1999). *Perception and reason*. Oxford University Press, Oxford.

Damasio, A. (1994). *Descartes' error*. Macmillan, London.

Davidson, D. (1970). 'Mental events', reprinted in Davidson 1970, pp. 207–24.

Davidson, D. (1978). 'Intending' reprinted in Davidson 1970, pp. 83–102.

Davidson, D. (1970). *Essays on action and events*. Oxford University Press, Oxford.

DeLancey, C. (2002). *Passionate engines*. Oxford University Press, New York.

Ekman, P. and Davidson, R. J. (1994). *The nature of emotion, fundamental questions*. Oxford University Press, New York.

Fodor, J. (1987). *Psychosemantics*. MIT Press, Cambridge MA.

Frijda, N. (1994). *Varieties of affect: emotions and episodes, moods and sentiments*, in Ekman and Davidson 1994.

Goldie, P. (2000a). *The emotions: a philosophical exploration*. Oxford University Press, Oxford.

Goldie, P. (2000b). Explaining expressions of emotion. *Mind*, **109**, pp. 25–38.

Goldie, P. (2002). *Understanding emotions: minds and morals*. Ashgate Publishing, Aldershot.

Goldie, P. and Spicer, F. (2002). Introduction, in Goldie 2002, pp. 1–22.

Gordon, G. (1987). *The structure of emotion*. Cambridge University Press, Cambridge.

Griffiths, P. (1997). *What emotions really are*. Chicago University Press, Chicago.

Kenny, A. (1963). *Action, emotion and will*. Routledge, London.

LeDoux, J. (1998). *The emotional brain*. Orion Books,London.

Lyons, W. (1980). *Emotion*. Cambridge University Press, Cambridge.

Marks, J. (1982). A Theory of emotions. *Philosophical Studies*, **42**, pp. 227–42.

McDowell, J. (1994). *Mind and world*. Harvard University Press, Cambridge MA.

Nussbaum, M. (2001). *Upheavals of thought*. Cambridge University Press, Cambridge.

Oakley, J. (1992). *Morality and the emotions*. Routledge, London.

Panksepp, J. (1998). *Affective neuroscience*. Oxford University Press, New York.

Segal, G. (2000). *A slim book about narrow content*. MIT Press, Cambridge MA.

Smith, B. (2002). Keeping emotions in mind, in Goldie 2002, pp. 111–22.

Solomon, R. (1977). *The passions*. Hackett, Indianapolis.

Velleman, D. (1992). The Guise of the Good, *Nous* 26, pp. 3–26.

Wollheim, R. (1999). *On the emotions*. Yale University Press, New Haven.

Zajonc, R. B. (1980). Feeling & thinking: preferences need no inferences. *American Psychologist*, **35**, pp. 151–75.

CHAPTER 4

WHICH EMOTIONS ARE BASIC?

JESSE PRINZ

There are two major perspectives on the origin of emotions. According to one, emotions are the products of natural selection. They are evolved adaptations, best understood using the explanatory tools of evolutionary psychology. According to the other, emotions are socially constructed, and they vary across cultural boundaries. There is evidence supporting both perspectives. In light of this, some have argued that both approaches are right. The standard strategy for compromise is to say that some emotions are evolved and others are constructed. The evolved emotions are sometimes given the label 'basic,' and there is considerable agreement about a handful of emotions in this category.

My goal here is to challenge all of these perspectives. I don't think we should adopt a globally evolutionary approach, nor indulge in the radical view that emotions derive entirely from us. I am equally dissatisfied with approaches that attempt to please Darwinians and constructivists by dividing emotions into two separate classes. I will defend another kind of ecumenicalism. Every emotion that we have a name for is the product of both nature and nurture. Emotions are evolved and constructed. The dichotomy between the two approaches cannot be maintained. This thesis will require making some claims that would be regarded as surprising to many emotion researchers. First, while there is a difference between basic emotions and nonbasic emotions, it is not a structural difference. All emotions are fundamentally alike. Second, the standard list of basic emotions, thought by many to be universal across cultures, are not basic after all. We don't have names for the basic emotions. All emotions that we talk about are culturally informed. And finally, this concession to constructivism does not imply that emotions are cognitive in any sense. Emotions are perceptual and embodied. They are gut reactions, and they are not unique to our species. To defend these heresies I will have to present a theory of what the emotions really are.

Two perspectives

Evolutionary psychology

Evolutionary psychologists claim that emotions are adaptations. They are species-typical psychological responses that evolved to cope with various challenges faced by our ancestors. Some defenders of this view restrict their claims to a small set of emotions. The most famous of these are the Big Six, used in Paul Ekman's research on pancultural recognition of emotional expressions (Ekman *et al.*, 1969). The Big Six emotions are happiness, sadness, fear, surprise, anger, and disgust. These have become the most widely accepted candidates for basic emotions. They are considered to be basic in two ways: psychological and biological. They do not contain other emotions as parts, and they are innate. More ambitious evolutionary psychologists argue that many more emotions are biologically based. Ekman (1999) has now expanded his basic emotion list to include: amusement, contempt, contentment, embarrassment, excitement, guilt, pride in achievement, relief, satisfaction, sensory pleasure, and shame. I will refer to the theories that restrict evolved emotions to a small set as modest. Immodest theories are ones that try to accommodate many emotions (see, e.g., Ekman, 1999; Frank, 1988; Pinker, 1997). The most immodest theories claim that every emotion is part of our bioprogram. None is in any sense learned.

Defenders of the evolutionary approach have brought various kinds of evidence to bear. One strategy is to establish that certain emotions are universal. While universality does not entail innateness, it can certainly provide some support. The fact that people universally believe that the sun is warm is not evidence for the innateness of that belief. The sun is warm across the globe. General-purpose learning abilities together with this shared feature of the environment are sufficient to explain the universal belief that that the sun is warm. Contrast this with the fact that people across different cultures have similar responses to music. Many cultures isolated from each other have musical systems organized around octaves, and, across the globe, tonal music tends to be more prevalent than atonal music. Octaves and tonal preferences can even be observed in macaque monkeys (Wright *et al.*, 2000). No shared feature of the environment can be used to explain this pattern. Likewise for colors. People who live in deserts, forests, and arctic plains seem to partition color-space in similar ways, despite the fact that color boundaries find no obvious analogues in the physical world.

It is natural to compare the evidence for emotion universals to the evidence for universals in color perception and music. Some emotions seem to be found pan-culturally, despite significant environmental variations.

Ekman *et al.* (1969) found that an isolated preliterate tribe in New Guinea, the Fore, tended to associate facial expressions of the Big Six emotions with the same kinds of situations with which we associate them in the West. For example, most Fore respondents paired a disgust face with a scenario describing rotten food, they paired the anger face with an insult, and the sadness face with the loss of a child. Ekman *et al.* conclude that the Big Six emotions are universal and biologically basic.

One can add further support to the evolutionary view by raising questions of learnability. The belief that the sun is warm can be learned given a general capacity for belief formation. We acquire this belief on the basis of evidence. Contrast this with sneezing. We do not learn to sneeze by weighing evidence or drawing inferences. Sneezing is an involuntary response. We can fake sneezes, but real sneezes are out of our control. Sneezing is not something that can be learned. Likewise for emotions. Emotions are not like beliefs, so they cannot be aquired by weighing evidence. They are also passive, like sneezes, and outside of voluntary control. They don't seem to be learnable.

Like sneezes, emotions have a lot to do with the body. Emotions are associated with patterns of bodily change, and the brain structures underlying emotion are associated with the perception and production of bodily response (Damasio, 1999). These brain structures are phylogenetically ancient. Reptiles are thought to have homologues of some of the structures that have been implicated in human emotions (Maclean, 1993). The connection between emotions and the body is central to the theory of emotions defended by William James (1884) and Carl Lange (1885). According to them, an emotion is a perception of a patterned change in the body. We sometimes perceive our hearts racing, our lungs inhaling, and our muscles tensing. The perception of these and other changes can be identified with fear. If the James–Lange theory is right, emotions are quite rudimentary from a biological point of view. They involve bodily responses that we share with much simpler animals. The evidence favoring the link between emotions and the body can, therefore, be seen as supporting the evolutionary view.

The bodily response associated with fear is no accident. It prepares an organism for flight. This fact has been used to provide another argument for evolutionary psychology. The evidence adduced so far supports the thesis that emotions are biologically based, but I have said nothing about the thesis that emotions are adaptations. Evolutionary psychologists are committed to this. Fear, they say, has evolved to cope with dangers (Plutchik 1980). When we are afraid, we flee or fight. Both of these responses allow us to cope with potential threats. Danger poses a major survival challenge, so psychological mechanisms that lead us to cope with danger effectively are the kind of behaviors that evolution would have selected for. The adaptiveness of fear lends support to the claim that fear is the product of evolution.

Adaptive explanations are a powerful tool in promoting the evolutionary approach to emotions. By demonstrating the survival value of emotions, evolutionary psychologists can establish the thesis that emotions would have been favored by natural selection. This strategy is obviously applicable to the Big Six emotions, such as fear, anger, and disgust, because all of these arise in contexts where life is potentially at stake. But adaptationist explanations can also be offered to explain more advanced emotions that have no counterparts in non-human animals. Why do we feel guilty? The evolutionary psychologist says that, without guilt, the temptation to cheat others would be much greater. We would take advantage of people whenever we anticipated a personal gain and little risk. Cheating others, however, can be disadvantageous in the long run. If we cheat and get caught, we may reduce prospects for future reciprocal exchanges of resources. If we have the capacity for guilt, others will be more likely to cooperate with us, because they will know that we are unlikely to cheat. If we are caught cheating, and show signs of guilt, others may forgive us and cooperate with us in the future. Guilt, therefore, can be regarded as a mechanism that promotes the kind of behavior that maximizes prospects of reciprocal exchange.

This conception of guilt emerged from the work of Trivers (1971) and was extended by Frank (1988). Frank offers a similar analysis of love. It is advantageous to form long-term bonds with romantic partners. Two people can share the burden of raising a child better than one. Two people can help each other procure food resources, and they can care for each other when they become old. But people are vulnerable to temptation. Short-term payoffs are easier to conceptualize than long-term payoffs, and therefore we have a tendency to abandon future projects in favor of present rewards. So, once we have invested in a long-term relationship, we run the risk of destroying the pair-bond to find gratification in extra-pair coupling. This risk is exacerbated by the fact that there are many fish in the sea. If a person chooses to commit to someone now, there is always the possibility that a better partner will appear down the line. Short-term temptation problems and the many fish problem are serious impediments to the commitment seekers. If I know that you are likely to be unfaithful to me, and you know that I am unlikely to be faithful to you, then there is no reason for us to make a long-term commitment, even though such a commitment would be very advantageous down the line. If things worked out this way, we would often forego what's best for us, for fear of infidelity. According to Frank, love solves this commitment problem. If I love you, and you love me, then we will be more likely to remain committed, at least for a while.

Love blinds us to commitment risks ('We are meant for each other'), and it makes us jump into situations that have uncertain long-term prospects ('True love lasts forever'). Couples do not necessarily stay together forever, in Frank's view, but love gives them the reassurance (or the foolish idea) that they need to get together in the first place. This account explains why love might have evolved.

A related evolutionary story has been developed to explain romantic jealousy—love's unlovely counterpart. Love allows us to make romantic commitments, and jealousy helps prevent our partners from breaking those commitments. Buss *et al.* (1992) argue that men and women face different challenges when it comes to fidelity. When a woman has a baby, she knows, thereby, that it is hers. Driven by selfish genes, she will invest in her baby's well-being. Men can never be certain about their paternity. When a man's lover gives birth, the offspring could belong to another father. Selfish genes do not want to waste energy caring for other people's babies. So male genes promote behaviors designed to reduce the prospects of cuckoldry. Male genes make men jealous, often violently so, and men become especially jealous when their female partners are found to be having sex with other men. If a man's female partner has become romantically involved with someone else but remains sexually faithful, that is better, from the gene's point of view, than if she has sex with someone else and remains romantically faithful. In the former scenario, but not the latter, the man runs a risk of investing resources to care for a baby that belongs to another father. Women never have to worry about investing in someone else's baby, but they face another challenge. It is difficult to raise a baby alone, and women take on special burdens of childcare when their babies are young. It is hard for women to forage when they must dedicate constant attention to their young. For women, then, the most important thing they can get from male partners after insemination is support. Women need men to provide for them. If a woman's male partner has sex with other women, but remains romantically faithful, then he will continue to provide for her. If the man has fallen in love with another woman, however, that support may be lost. Buss *et al.* (1992) reason that, if this evolutionary story is correct, women should be more perturbed to hear that their male partners have fallen in love with someone else than to hear that their male partners are having sex with someone else. Men should be more perturbed by sexual infidelity. This is exactly what they find. The prediction made by the hypothesis that jealousy is an evolved solution to a commitment problem is confirmed.

These examples, guilt, love, and jealousy, illustrate how evolutionary thinking can explain some of our most advanced emotions. Evolutionary psychologists have argued that our innate affective endowment extends beyond the Big Six, and encompasses emotions that may be uniquely human. Frank and Buss defend an immodest view about the evolutionary origins of our emotions, and views of this kind are gaining ground. It has become increasingly popular to suppose that all of our emotions are adaptations.

Social constructionism

Not everyone wants to jump on the Darwinian bandwagon. Critics of evolutionary psychology argue that emotions are products of nurture rather than nature. They argue that emotions are socially constructed. This approach has fewer supporters these days than it has had in the past, but it would be a mistake to think constructionism is moribund. Like evolutionary psychology, the constructionist approach is supported by some powerful lines of evidence.

Constructionists often begin their critique of Darwinian approaches by claiming that evolutionary psychologists have an incorrect theory of what the emotions are. I said that evolutionary psychology fits naturally with a James–Lange theory of the emotions, according to which emotions are fleeting perceptions of involuntary, patterned bodily changes designed to prepare an organism for adaptive behavioral responses. Constructionists typically reject this picture. They argue that emotions are neither fleeting, nor involuntary, nor bodily. This view is nicely represented in the work of Averill (1980). According to Averill, emotions are construed as cognitive appraisals nested in behavioral scripts. An appraisal is a judgment about how one's situation bears on well-being. Appraisals represent situations as matters of concern. Scripts are instructions about what to do when something of concern transpires. Each emotion script dictates a different range of actions, and these actions may be quite complex and protracted. Appraisals and scripts are enculturated. They reflect the values and convictions of a cultural group. When we act out an emotion script, we engage in behavior and decision making that has been prescribed by our culture. In so doing, we are usually exercising our capacity to choose. We could break from the script, and we could form different appraisals. But, according to constructionists, we view these choices as involuntary. Emotions, says Averill (1980), are disclaimed actions: they are voluntary choices that we dupe ourselves into treating as involuntary. Averill also says that emotions need not involve any perturbations of the body. We can have an emotion without a racing heart. The tendency to associate emotions with bodily states is related to the tendency to see emotions as passive. We pretend that they are like animal instincts, rather than cognitive plots.

Social constructionists sometimes defend their position by pointing to examples of emotions that are not highly associated with bodily states. Some examples have already been mentioned. Advanced emotions, such as guilt and love have no obvious bodily correlates. Where fear and anger have identifiable expressions, there is, it seems, no facial visage of love, no grimace of guilt. It seems these emotions can occur without any perturbation of the body. And they can also last a long time. We can be in love or plagued by guilt for years. In addition, these emotions seem to be associated with complex patterns of behavior, indicative of social scripts, rather than immediate gut reactions. When we are guilty, we seek to make amends, by apologizing or improving our behavior. When we are in love, we engage in various forms of courtship. We believe in love at first sight, and we vow to stay with our loved ones forever. These very facts were at the heart of Frank's evolutionary theory, but, on closer examination, they can be interpreted as signs of enculturation. Love and guilt are much more elaborate than, say, the startle response one feels when one trips. Moreover, the kinds of judgments and decisions we are led to when in love or guilty are much more amenable to cognitive influence. The complex ways that love and guilt unfold seem much more voluntary than the shock that follows a trip or tumble. The same can be said of jealousy, with its attendant bouts of paranoid ideation and fantasies of revenge.

The constructionist approach can be extended to subsume emotions that seem biologically grounded. We often presume that anger is an emotion that we share with other creatures: an involuntary disposition to aggression. But this may be a convenient illusion. We sometimes use anger strategically, as when we stage a bout of outrage while returning a defective item at a shop (Greenspan, 2000). It is possible all bouts of anger are strategic choices (Solomon, 1980). Anger, after all, seems to involve a fairly complex conceptualization of the world. Constructionists argue that, to be angry, we need to construe something as an offense, which requires the deployment of subtle, culturally informed moral judgments. Anger is not an animal reflex, but a sophisticated moral attitude.

The primary source of evidence for constructionism is cultural variation. Emotions apparently vary across borders. Anger is, again, a case in point. We regard anger as an irrepressible basic emotion. In Inuit culture, signs of anger are rarely seen (Briggs, 1970). Aggressive responses would be too risky in a small homogeneous culture living in harsh conditions. In Malaysia, there are analogues of anger, but they take on different forms. The Malay language has no exact synonym for 'anger.' The closest term is 'marah,' which is associated with sullen brooding, rather than aggression (Goddard, 1996). Malay also has the term 'amok,' which refers to a violent frenzy. We have imported this term, losing, perhaps, some of its culturally specific meaning.

There are other emotions that have no clear analogue in the West. Consider *amae*, a Japanese term for what has been characterized as an indulgent feeling of dependency, akin to what a child feels towards a mother (Doi, 1973).

Westerners may recognize something like *amae* in children but they rarely attribute anything of that kind to adults. Infantile feelings of dependency are disvalued in our autonomous culture. Japanese also has a term *oime* for a feeling of indebtedness and *fureai*, which refers to a feeling of connectedness (Markus and Kitayama, 1991). This rich vocabulary of interdependence is evidence of a collectivist orientation in Japan. Constructionists believe that this orientation leads the Japanese to have emotions that we would find alien. The diversity and cultural specificity of emotion terms certainly gives one pause. In this light, emotions begin to look less like biological universals and more like enculturated scripts.

Hybrid theories

There is evidence for evolutionary psychology and for constructionism. Both approaches enjoy support. This presents a puzzle for the emotion researcher. How does one choose between such radically different alternatives? One strategy is to avoid the choice. Perhaps both approaches are right, but they apply to different emotions. We can divide and conquer emotions by saying that some are evolved and some are constructed.

Such a hybrid has been defended by Griffiths (1997). He argues that emotions are not a natural kind. He defines Ekman's Big Six as affect programs: modular, automatic, response patterns, which have homologues in nonhuman animals. These can be understood in evolutionary terms. Griffiths also thinks we can extend the evolutionary approach to emotions such as guilt and jealousy, but, he argues, these are not modular or phylogenetically ancient. In contrast to evolved emotions, both ancient and modern, Griffiths allows space for emotions that bear the marks of culture. *Amae* and some culture-bound emotional disorders, such as running amok, may fall into this class.

Another hybrid theory is defended by Oatley and Johnson-Laird (1987). They begin with a subset of Ekman's Big Six (dropping off surprise), and argue that these are basic. Each emotion on this list, they say, can be identified with a distinctive mode of informational processing, built into our cognitive architecture. Other emotions are cognitive elaborations. They are basic emotions plus appraisal judgments. Thus, nonbasic emotions and basic emotions have a different structure. Nonbasic emotions comprise basic emotion processing modes, along with cognitive representations. Because of their cognitive component, nonbasic emotions are amendable to cultural influence. Thus, a Darwinian story can be told about the basic emotions, and a (partially) constructionist story can be told about nonbasic emotions.

I will not offer a full assessment of these hybrid theories. I will simply say that a unified theory, that treats all emotions as structurally alike, would be preferable. I offer three reasons for that assessment. First, emotions have a great deal in common. All emotions are typically (if not always) accompanied by expressive behavior and bodily responses, all are motivating, all are eruptive, all are valenced, and all can affect attention and memory. All emotions also seem to involve overlapping brain structures, and all can be affected by the same clinical conditions (e.g., psychopaths have dampened Big Six emotions as well as dampened social emotions). These commonalities are especially problematic for Griffiths' hybrid, because he argues that emotions form disjoint subclasses. Oatley and Johnson-Laird can explain the similarities because they believe that all emotions contain the same basic parts. But their theory is threatened by a second problem. Hybrid theories cannot easily explain the fact that our emotion terms cut across highly cognitive and highly noncognitive episodes. Anger can be stirred-up by a glare or by a chain of high-level moral reasoning. Fear can be triggered by a sudden loss of support, or by reading the latest election returns. Does this mean we should distinguish two forms of fear and two forms of anger? Should we say that 'fear' is ambiguous between a basic and a nonbasic emotion? Or, should we instead, resist Oatley and Johnson-Laird's suggestion that emotions can be classified by their degree of cognitive elaboration. I think the latter option should be the default. Our emotion vocabulary does not draw a neat line between emotions that are primitive and emotions that are cognitively sophisticated. One and the same emotion can be elicited in numerous ways, both simple and complex. Attempts to put different emotions into different categories violate folk taxonomy. Revision of folk categories may be inevitable in the end, but should be avoided if possible. Ordinary emotion talk recognizes something similar across episodes of anger that are caused perceptually and cognitively. It would be nice to have a unified theory of emotions to capture the sense in which these episodes are alike.

The third point against hybrid views is closely related to the second. If some emotions are socially constructed and others are evolved, we need to decide which are which. The difficulty is that evolutionary psychologists and social constructionists often try to explain the exact same emotions. We have seen, for example, that both camps try to explain love and anger. It would be easier to adopt a hybrid strategy if there was a clear indication of which emotions are cultural and which are biologically based. If the boundary is unclear, the major motive for adopting a hybrid view is lost.

I think we should aim for a unified theory of the emotions. But which kind of theory should we adopt? Should we be immodest evolutionary psychologists or immodest cultural constructionists? I will argue that neither approach is satisfying. We must find another route to unity.

Assessing evolutionary psychology and social constructionism

To adjudicate between competing approaches to the emotions, we must weigh the evidence introduced in the first section. Which side of the Darwin–Culture divide has the better arguments?

Let's begin with evolutionary psychology. First, what are we to make of the claim that certain emotions are universal? This conclusion is based on cross-cultural research on facial expressions. This research is quite compelling at first blush, but it begins to unravel under scrutiny (see Russell, 1994, for a trenchant critical review). In the Ekman *et al.* (1969) study of the Fore, only 44% of respondents correctly identified the facial expression of disgust, and only 50% recognized anger. In some cases, the Fore respondents' modal responses did not match up with a Western control sample. Approximately 45% of the Fore associated the surprise face with fear, rather than surprise. A startling 56% associated the sadness face with what Westerners call anger. This latter finding may support the constructionist hypothesis that small homogenous groups respond to offense with something akin to sulking. Russell (1994) has argued that the correlation between Fore and Western responses may also be seriously inflated due to problems with Ekman *et al.*'s methodology. The Fore were given forced choice test, choosing between sets of three faces, and associating them with scenarios and words that had been picked by the experimenters. In an open-choice paradigm where, say, respondents had to simply name a face, the correlations would have dropped considerably. Thus, the Ekman *et al.* results really don't demonstrate emotion universals. They show, that a significant number of Fore respondents will associate four of six specially selected emotion expressions with words or scenarios that match the responses of Westerners, when given few response options to choose from. Indeed, even if they associated the faces with scenarios and words in the same way as Westerners, we could not be sure that their emotions are exactly like ours. Fore emotions could be similar to ours expressively, but subtly different conceptually, behaviorally, cognitively, phenomenologically, and so forth. Ekman himself (1999) now talks about universal emotion families, rather than universal emotions, indicating that cultures may customize our innate affective stock in different ways. This is consistent with the constructionist conjecture that there are multiple species of anger.

One can also raise objections to the adaptationist tales told by evolutionary psychologists. To show that an emotion is adaptive does not entail that it is a biological adaptation. Adaptive responses can be discovered by individuals or tailored by cultures. The species of anger illustrate the possibility of cultural adaptations. To show that something is an adaptation, one should show that there is no other explanation for it that does not add needless code to our bioprogram. Consider jealousy. Immodest evolutionary psychologists say that jealousy is innate. Here is another possibility. Imagine that jealousy is a blend of several more basic emotions: sadness, fear, anger, and disgust. When someone is unfaithful to you, it causes sadness; you may lose your partner. It also causes anger, because you have been violated, and fear, because you may have to face life alone or compete with another suitor. Finally, infidelity may cause disgust because you feel that your lover's body has been contaminated. So, we have independent reason to think that infidelity will trigger a blend of negative emotions. Jealousy may be a name for this blend. We do not need to postulate a special innate emotion beyond members of the Big Six. Evolutionary psychologists try to establish that jealousy is innate by pointing to gender differences, but these are easy to explain on a cultural model. Women are more concerned about emotional infidelity because, historically, they have been dependent on men for material resources. Losing a man, meant losing the resources essential to life. Thus, woman's jealousy may reflect a pattern of reasoning that woman can make, or it may reflect a learned pattern inculcated within the culture in which women have been systematically disadvantaged. Men, for their part, may disvalue sexual infidelity over romantic infidelity because they have been enculturated to regard women as property. If women are objectified in this way, their preferences and affections are not salient to men. What matters is their behaviour. Men want to control their property; they don't care about the feelings of their property. Other explanations are easy to devise. For example, men may care more about sexual infidelity because they are more preoccupied with sex. We can tell an evolutionary account of male sex drive without supposing that male jealousy is innate. It may be an inevitable by-product. If gender differences in jealousy were genetically based, we might expect little cultural variation. That is not what we find. In some countries, such as the Netherlands and Germany, male and female responses are more alike, with both preferring sexual infidelity to romantic infidelity (Buunk *et al.*, 1996). This can be explained by appeal to cultural differences in male domination and liberal attitudes towards sex.

Similar points can be made about love. Frank suggests that love is a biological program to ensure pair-bonding for the purposes of raising children. This sounds uncomfortably close to Western ideals. It is hard to reconcile with cultural variation. Some cultures have arranged marriages, and some have avunculate arrangements, where mothers raise offspring with their uncles. In some cultures, and in chimpazees, offspring are raised with the assistance of larger groups, so the integrity of a pair-bond is not especially important.

We can only speculate about how children were raised and how relationships were structured in the Pleistocene. To postulate a genetic explanation for the kinds of relationships that we currently value in the West is a bit like postulating an innate basis for capitalism or health spas. We cannot assume that our institutions and preferences have always been the norm.

Despite these concerns about adaptationist explanations, evolutionary psychology still enjoys considerable support. First, there is overwhelming evidence that emotions are associated with basic bodily responses and ancient brain structures. All emotions are accompanied by changes in our autonomic nervous systems, and these changes are very difficult to control. Emotions have obvious analogues in other creatures, and some appear early in development before there has been much time for cultural learning. Putting the question of how any *specific* emotion is acquired, we can safely assume that having emotions, *in general*, depends on our biology.

Where does this leave social constructionism? First, constructionists may be mistaken to assume that emotions can be disembodied. The claim that some emotions, such as guilt and love, are not associated with bodily perturbations has not been fully investigated. But existing functional imaging studies of these two emotions tell against the constructionist conjecture. Shin *et al.* (2000) found activation in the anterior cingulate cortex and the insula when subjects recalled episodes of guilt. Bartels and Zeki (2000) found similar activations when subjects viewed photographs of their lovers. These structures show up in all imaging studies of the emotions, and they are known to play a role in perception and regulation of the body (Damasio, 1999). Of course, one can be in love or guilty for years without having a constant state of arousal or indigestion. This only shows that 'love' and 'guilt' can be used to name dispositional states. A person can be disgusted by peanut butter for a lifetime, without feeling disgust at every moment. But someone who reported being disgusted by peanut butter would be accused of dishonesty if she were not disposed to have a somatic reaction when she came into contact with peanut butter. Likewise, we would distrust the apologies of a defendant who showed no signs of embodied distress when confronted with the victims of her crime. Equally, we would distrust the person who claimed to love someone romatically but never showed the slightest signs of passion.

Constructionists also go too far in emphasizing the role of cognitions in emotion. Emotions can certainly be triggered by complex acts of deliberation, but they can also be set off without any thought at all. Fear can be triggered by seeing a snake, before the image has even reached the neocortex (LeDoux, 1996). Perhaps a man's jealousy can be set off by smelling foreign cologne on his lover's blouse. Emotions need not involve any judgments. Nor need they involve protracted patterns of scripted behavior. An emotion can be very short-lived. When more protracted patterns of behavior do arise, they need not bear on the identity of the emotions. Constructionists have an unfortunate habit of inferring cultural variation in the emotions from variation in emotional behaviors. If love leads to marriage in one culture and to a steamy extramarital liaison in another, we need not say there are two forms of love. The same emotion can have different effects. A change in script is not necessarily a change in emotions. If it were, we would expect to see our emotion vocabulary change as new attitudes about how we ought to behave emerged. It should sound *conceptually* strained to say that love and marriage can come apart.

Despite these complaints against social constructionism, I think the program has much to recommend it. As I said above, evolutionary psychologists have not been able to establish that emotions are exactly the same across cultures. The same situation can be associated with different responses. The variability in facial response, in emotion vocabulary, and in culture-bound emotional disorders provides circumstantial evidence for variation in emotions. Culture can certainly influence when and whether an emotion arises, as well as the valence of our emotional reactions. What one culture finds outrageous, another may find rewarding (consider variable attitudes towards cannibalism). These differences do not entail that cultures have distinct emotions, but they raise that possibility. Constructionists can do an admirable job of relating particular emotional responses to cultural factors. They can explain why *amae* is valued in Japan, and why *amok* is prevalent in Malaysia.

This leaves us in a serious predicament. If what I have been arguing is correct, evolutionary psychologists underestimate the contributions of culture and learning. They offer a flawed theory of how emotions arise. Social constructionists over-emphasize the cognitive and underestimate the centrality of bodily responses. They offer a flawed theory of what emotions, in essence, are. Emotions are neither fixed bioprograms, nor cognitively mediated scripts.

Escaping the predicament

Embodied appraisal theory

We need a theory of emotions that can steer between the extremes of evolutionary psychology and social constructionism. In this section, I will outline such a theory. For a full defense, see Prinz (2004).

The theory has two central tenets. The first tenet concerns the *form* of emotions, i.e., their representational format. I said that emotions bear an intimate relation to the body. More concretely, I think James and Lange were right to identify emotions with perceptions of bodily changes. This approach has recently been defended on neurobiological grounds by Antonio Damasio (1994). The brain centers associated with emotion are also associated with perception and regulation of the body. If body perception is impaired, emotions wane. If the body is stimulated through drugs or through feedback from facial expressions, emotions are felt.

The second tenet concerns the *content* of emotions. James and Lange had little to say about what emotions represent. Their bodily theory gives the impression that emotions are primarily in the business of telling us about our blood pressure, muscle tension, and vasculature. This makes little sense of the role that emotions play in decision making and action. We run when we are afraid. Why? It's certainly not because our hearts are racing. Fear makes us run because fear represents danger. Sadness represents loss, anger represents offenses, and so on.

Many emotion researchers think that such conclusions about what emotions represent can be maintained only if we define emotions as cognitive. To represent danger, fear must contain the judgment that 'I am in danger,' they suppose. I think this is wrongheaded. According to leading theories of intentionality, mental states are represented by functional covariation, not by description (Dretske, 1988). A mental state represents danger if (a) it reliably occurs when danger occurs, and (b) it was acquired for that purpose. Now suppose, with James and Lange, that fear is a perception of a patterned change in the body. If that change reliably arises when we are in danger, and if it was acquired for coping with danger, then the same can be said about our perception of that change. A perception of a patterned bodily response can represent danger in virtue of the fact that it has the function of serving as a danger detector. In other words, emotions are like smoke alarms. A tone in a smoke alarm represents fire because it is set up to be set off by fire. And perceptions of patterned changes in our body represent danger (and loss, and offense, etc.), because they are set up to be set off by danger (and loss, and offense, etc.).

For this to work, there must be a psychological mechanism in place that sustains the link between dangers and perceived bodily responses, just as there is a mechanism in a smoke alarm that gets the tone to go off when fires draw near. Consider how this works in a typical case. You hear a loud sudden noise. That auditory state sets your body into a patterned response. The response is perceived. The perception of that your response is your fear. Loud noises are not the only fear trigger, however. A sudden loss of support, a snake, or an infelicitous election return can all have the same impact. Our mental representations of all these fear elicitors group together into a mental file. When any item in the elicitation file is activated, fear results. Fear represents danger by virtue of the fact that, collectively, the items in the elicitation file calibrate fear to danger, and they have the function of doing so. Danger is what unites all the disparate contents of the elicitation file. Fear represents danger because it has the function of occurring when danger occurs, and it obtains that function via an elicitation file filled with a wide range of perceptions and judgments.

It might be tempting to identify fear with the representations in the elicitation file, rather than the perception of the bodily response. That would be a mistake. The file contents are too varied, and too variable over time. Moreover, an episode of fear can outlast the duration of an active representation in its elicitation file. A loud noise ends before the fear that it causes even begins.

In sum, I think emotions are perceptions of bodily changes that represent such things as dangers, losses, and offenses, because they are set up to be set off by such things. I call this the embodied appraisal theory (Prinz, 2004). Emotions are embodied because they are perceptions of bodily changes, and they are appraisals because they represent matters of concern.

How can culture influence emotions?

If emotions are embodied appraisals, then new emotions can be acquired in various ways. In some cases, new emotions can be acquired by simply combining together existing embodied appraisals to suit situations that have complex emotional significance. Jealousy is an example of that. Cultural factors will determine how intensely this emotion is felt by affecting attitudes towards sexuality and the material consequences of infidelity. In other cases, culture may have an even greater impact. Culture can exert an influence on how our bodies react. For example, we can train ourselves to suppress facial expressions or control breathing. Ekman talks about the cultural influence on facial expressions, and he argues that such influences do not affect the emotions themselves. This is untenable if emotions are perceptions of bodily changes. A change in 'display rules' alters the bodily basis of the emotion. More dramatically, culture may encourage people to act out molar behaviors that reshape our bodily responses. In Malaysia, the behavioral pattern of running amok establishes a distinctive bodily pattern, which is much more active than ordinary Western anger.

Culture can also affect the content of emotions. Content depends on what the emotion is set up to be set off by. Emotions are set off with the help of elicitation files. Some of these files may be biologically based, but, in the course of life, our mental files can grow, and new files can be established. The establishment of new elicitation files has not been investigated, but the process may be relatively simple. Items are added to an existing file by association, and then clusters of new items that are closely related take on a functional autonomy that allows them to trigger the emotion without the aid of anything in the original file. Culture can help to re-calibrate existing emotions to new eliciting conditions in this way. Imagine a sadistic culture that encourages people to take joy in the suffering of others. The file that sustains the relationship between joy and the world will be expanded, under cultural influence, to include representations of people in distress. Thus, *Schadenfruede* is born. *Amae* emerges when cultural factors in Japan lead people to have a warm feeling in the context of dependency relations. Patriotism emerges when joy is recalibrated to national symbols and the accomplishments of fellow citizens. Guilt emerges when sadness gets re-calibrated to personal transgressions.

If these considerations are correct, culture can affect the intensity, incidence, form, and content of our emotions. This is a surprising discovery because it is sometimes assumed that the James–Lange approach to emotions is incompatible with a constructionist approach. I have just shown how emotions can be both embodied and culturally informed. This account presupposes that some emotions are biologically basic, however. Culture reshapes existing bodily responses and re-calibrates existing emotions. What, then, are the emotions that exist prior to cultural influence?

Which emotions are basic?

Rethinking the Big Six

To find emotions that are biologically basic, we need to look for body patterns that are responsive to concerns in the absence of learning. For example, there is evidence that we are phyiscally perturbed by seeing snakes even if we have never been harmed by a snake. This response may need to be triggered under the right environmental conditions, but it does not require inference, induction, sustained conditioning, or other learning processes. It looks like an innate form of fear. But is it really fear? Should we conclude that fear is an innate emotion?

I am inclined towards a negative answer. First, the negative response to snakes is more specific than fear. It is not a representation of danger-in-general. We may have an innate elicitation file containing other causes of the same bodily response (loss of support, darkness, looming objects, loud noises), but these do not add up to a generalized danger detector. Second, even in adulthood, fear may not correspond to a single pattern of response. Emotion researchers distinguish two subspecies, which are given the technical terms worry (associated with future dangers) and panic (associated with present dangers). These may be more basic than fear.

A similar fragmentation may occur for other entries on the Big Six list. Each may begin with a set of responses tuned to highly specific elicitors, and some may have several component subspecies. Happiness, for example, may sub-divide into sensory pleasures, satisfaction associated with goal attainment, and joy from play. Surprise may subdivide into a positive sense of interest or wonder and a negative state that cannot be fully differentiated from low-intensity panic. Anger may emerge as a blend of something like goal frustration and aggressiveness. Sadness and disgust probably don't divide into subspecies, but they may begin life as much narrower emotions than their adult analogues. Sadness may begin as separation distress and then expand to encompass other forms of loss through learning and enculturation. Disgust may begin as a form of physical revulsion that ultimately gets expanded to subsume moral aberrations.

If these speculations are right, then the Big Six emotions may not be innate. They may be outgrowths and byproducts of more fundamental emotions. This fits with the observation that the Big Six are not exactly the same across cultures. Each culture may adapt the primitive stock of biologically basic emotions in distinctive ways. If so, then the emotions that we have words for may all be culturally informed. If this is true of the Big Six, it is almost certainly true of our more advanced emotions. Ordinary emotion words do not name the highly restricted and narrow emotional responses programmed by our genes, but extensions of these that emerge in a cultural setting.

Conclusions

We are now in a position to take stock and find our way out of the predica-ment. I said that social constructionists are wrong about the nature of emo-tions, because they emphasize cognitively mediated cultural scripts, rather than bodily responses. Evolutionary psychology is inadequate because it does not do justice to the contributions of learning and culture. The embodied appraisal reconciles these problems. Emotions are simple perceptions of bodi-ly changes, but they carry information by being calibrated to matters of con-cern. They get calibrated through elicitation files that can be culturally informed, and culture can also alter our patterns of bodily response. Thus, emotions can be both embodied and socially constructed.

On this approach, every emotion that we have a word for bears the mark of both nature and nurture. Each is built up from a biologically basic emotion, but its conditions of elicitation, and hence its content, is influenced by learn-ing. No lexicalized emotion is *biologically* basic. But there is a sense in which all lexicalized emotions are *psychologically* basic. No emotion contains other emotions as component parts. Each is structurally analogous. Each is simply a perception of a patterned bodily change. Even emotions that we acquire by blending have this simple structure. They are simply perceptions of blended bodily patterns. Some emotions are attained by adding conceptually sophisticated judgments to our elicitation files, but this does not alter their structure. Elicitation files are content-determining causes of our emotions, not constituent parts. And all emotions have elicitation files that can contain judgments, as well as perceptual representations. Thus, hybrid theories are wrong. All named emotions are very much alike. All have the same internal structure, and all bear the marks of both nature and nurture.

In sum, everybody is wrong and everybody is right. Contra Evolutionary Psychology, familiar emotions (including the Big Six) show the marks of learning. Contra social constructionism, emotions are embodied states, not cognitive scripts. Contra, hybrid views, all named emotions are very much alike. By the same token, evolutionists are right to think that emotions originate in our genes, constructionists are right to emphasize enculturation, and defenders of hybrid views are right that we can have it both ways.

References

Averill, J. R. (1980). A constructivist view of emotion. In *Emotion: Theory, research and experience: Vol. I. Theories of emotion*, (ed. R. Plutchik and H. Kellerman), pp. 305–339. Academic Press, New York, NY.

Bartels, A. and Zeki, S. (2000). The neural basis of romantic love. *Neuroreport*, 11, 829–834.

Briggs, J. L. (1970). *Never in anger: Portrait of an Eskimo family*. Harvard University Press, Cambridge, MA.

Buss, D. M., Larsen, R. J., Westen, D., and Semmelroth, J. (1992). Sex differences in jealousy: Evolution, physiology, and psychology. *Psychological Science*, 3, 251–255.

Buunk, B., Angleitner, A., Oubaid, V., and Buss, D. (1996). Sex differences in jealousy in evolutionary and cultural perspective: Tests from the Netherlands, Germany, and the United States. *Psychological Science*, 7, 359–363.

Damasio, A. R. (1994). *Descartes' error: Emotion, reason and the human brain*. Gossett/Putnam, New York, NY.

Damasio, A. R. (1999) *The feeling of what happens: Body and emotion in the making of consciousness*. Harcourt Brace & Company, New York, NY.

Doi, T. (1973). *The anatomy of dependence*. Kodansha International, New York, NY.

Dretske, F. (1988). *Explaining behavior*. MIT Press, Cambridge, MA.

Ekman, P. (1999) Basic emotions. In *The handbook of cognition and emotion* (ed. T. Dalgleish and T. Power), pp. 45–60. John Wiley & Sons, New York.

Ekman, P., Sorenson, E. R., and Friesen. W. V. (1969). Pan-cultural elements in facial displays of emotions. *Science*, 164, 86–88.

Frank, R. (1988). *Passions within reason: The strategic role of the emotions*. Norton, New York, NY.

Goddard, C. (1996). The "social emotions" of Malay (Bahasa Melayu). *Ethos*, 24, 426–464.

Greenspan, P. (2000). Emotional strategies and rationality. *Ethics*, 110, 469–87.

Griffiths, P. (1997). *What emotions really are.* University of Chicago Press, Chicago, IL.

James, W. (1884). What is an emotion? *Mind,* **9**, 188–205.

Lange, C. G. (1885). *Om sindsbevaegelser: et psyko-fysiologisk studie.* Kjbenhavn: Jacob Lunds. Reprinted in *The emotions* (ed. C. G. Lange and W. James), I. A. Haupt (trans.) Williams & Wilkins Company 1922, Baltimore.

LeDoux J. E. (1996). *The emotional brain.* Simon & Schuster, New York, NY.

MacLean, P. D. (1993). Cerebral evolution of emotion. In *Handbook of emotions* (ed. M. Lewis and J. M. Haviland), pp. 67–83. Guilford Press, New York, NY.

Markus, H. R. and Kitayama, S. (1991). Culture and the self: Implications for cognition, emotion, and motivation. *Psychological Review,* **98**, 224–253.

Oatley, K. and Johnson-Laird, P. (1987). Towards a cognitive theory of emotions. *Cognition & Emotion,* **1**, 29–50.

Pinker, S. (1997). *How the mind works.* Norton, New York, NY.

Plutchik, R. (1980). *Emotion: A psychoevolutionary analysis.* Harper & Row, New York, NY.

Prinz, J. J. (2004). *Gut reactions: A perceptual theory of emotion.* Oxford University Press, New York, NY.

Russell, J. A. (1994). Is there universal recognition of emotion from facial expression? *Psychological Bulletin,* **95**, 102–141.

Shin, L. M., Dougherty, D., Macklin, M. L., Orr, S. P., Pitman, R. K., Rauch, S. L. (2000). Activation of anterior paralimbic structures during guilt-related script-driven imagery. *Biological Psychiatry,* **48**, 43–50.

Solomon, R. (1980). Emotions and choice. In *Explaining emotions* (ed. A. Rorty), pp. 251–271. University of California Press, Berkeley, CA.

Trivers, R. L. (1971). The evolution of reciprocal altruism. *Quarterly Review of Biology,* **46**, 35–57.

Wright, A. A., Rivera, J. J., Hulse, S. H., Shyan, M. and Neiworth, J.J. (2000). Music perception and octave generalization in rhesus monkeys. *Journal Experimental Psychology General,* **129**, 291–307.

CHAPTER 5

TOWARDS A 'MACHIAVELLIAN' THEORY OF EMOTIONAL APPRAISAL[1]

PAUL E. GRIFFITHS

Emotional appraisal

The aim of appraisal theory in the psychology of emotion is to identify the features of the emotion-eliciting situation that lead to the production of one emotion rather than another.[1] A model of emotional appraisal takes the form of a set of dimensions against which potentially emotion-eliciting situations are assessed. The dimensions of the emotion hyperspace might include, for example, whether the eliciting situation fulfills or frustrates the subject's goals or whether an actor in the eliciting situation has violated a norm. Richard Lazarus's well-known model of emotional appraisal has six dimensions, and the regions of the resulting hyperspace that correspond to particular emotions are summarized by Lazarus as the 'core relational themes' of those emotions. Anger, for example, is elicited by the core relational theme 'a demeaning offence against me and mine', sadness by 'having experienced an irrevocable loss' and guilt by 'having transgressed a moral imperative' (Lazarus 1991).

Dimensional appraisal models have traditionally been tested by asking people who have experienced a particular emotion to report on the appraisal process, or even by asking people to report on the relevance of certain dimensions of

---

1 For a review of appraisal theories, see Scherer (1999).

evaluation to certain emotions. It has therefore been alleged that appraisal theories are based, not on the reality of emotion processes, but rather on the image of those processes recorded in folk-wisdom. As the leading appraisal theorist Klaus Scherer puts it, some supposedly *psychological* studies may in fact 'do little more than explicate the implicational semantic structures of our emotion vocabulary' (Scherer 1999, 655). This challenge to appraisal theory can be met in a number of ways, including prospective studies that manipulate situational factors relevant to the dimensions of appraisal and predict the resultant change in emotion, and studies that rely on objective measures of emotional behavior and physiology rather than on self-report.

The ongoing effort to test appraisal theories as theories of emotion, rather than as elucidations of folk wisdom, has led to a consensus that emotions do not walk in step with cognitive evaluation of the stimulus unless the notion of 'cognitive evaluation' is broadened to include sub-personal processes (Teasdale 1999). Many appraisal theorists have come to accept that even such apparently conceptually complex appraisals as Lazarus's core relational themes can be assessed: 1. Without the information evaluated being available to other cognitive processes, 2. Before perceptual processing of the stimulus has been completed, and 3. Using only simple, sensory cues to define where the eliciting situation falls on the dimensions.

The existence of 'low-level' appraisal is demonstrated when emotional responses are independent of or conflict with explicit, reportable, action-guiding evaluations; when people are afraid of things that they know are not dangerous or disgusted by things they know to be healthy. Robert Zajonc's findings about 'affective primacy' are well known. He showed that subjects can form preferences for stimuli to which they have been have been exposed subliminally so that their ability to identify those stimuli remains at chance levels (Zajonc 1980). Many results have since been obtained which confirm and extend this phenomenon. Arne Öhman and his collaborators have conditioned subjects to dislike angry faces and subsequently elicited the conditioned emotional response when those angry faces were masked by neutral faces so that subjects reported no conscious experience of the angry faces (Esteves and Öhman 1993, Öhman 1986). In another study, subjects were exposed to subliminal images of snakes, spiders, flowers and mushrooms. Although the subjects were unable to identify better than chance the stimuli they had been exposed to, subjects with pre-existing snake phobia showed elevated skin conductance responses to the snake images and subjects with spider phobia showed this response to the spider images (Öhman and Soares 1994)[2].

----

2 For a brief overview, see (Öhman, 2002).

The original controversy aroused by Zajonc's concept of affective primacy concerned whether emotions involve a 'cognitive evaluation of the stimulus' (Lazarus *et al.* 1984, Zajonc 1984a, 1984b). It has become clear that this was not a helpful formulation, and that what is really at issue is whether the information processing that leads to an emotional response is separate from that which leads to paradigmatically cognitive processes such as conscious report and recall, and whether the two informational processes are different in kind. It is not necessary to deny, as Zajonc did, that low-level appraisal is a cognitive process. If emotional appraisal proceeds on several different *cognitive* levels, then traditional views about appraisal will still have to be very significantly modified. The traditional view, expressed here by Robert Solomon, is just too simple:

> all emotions presuppose or have as their preconditions, certain sorts of cognitions—an awareness of danger in fear, recognition of an offense in anger, appreciation of someone or something as lovable in love. Even the most hard-headed neurological or behavioral theory must take account of the fact that no matter what the neurology or the behavior, if a person is demonstrably ignorant of a certain state of affairs or facts, he or she cannot have certain emotions (Solomon 1993, 11)

The concept of 'multi level appraisal' combines the recognition (1) that emotions are elicited by information about certain aspects of the environment and that the emotional response is, in some sense, directed at those aspects of the environment and (2) that these states can occur at many cognitive levels, and an appraisal that leads to an emotion can be separate from, and can contradict, the appraisal of the same stimulus that is verbally reportable and integrated with the organism's other beliefs. The phobic subjects in the study just discussed were, in this sense, 'demonstrably ignorant' of the state of affairs that was the object of their emotional response. Often, of course, high-level appraisal and low-level appraisal march in step with one another, but this is not always the case, and the early advocates of affective primacy were fundamentally correct that even under normal conditions there are two (or more) processes going on. Paul Ekman embodies these ideas in his concept of an 'automatic appraisal mechanism'—a cognitive subsystem that is dedicated to determining whether a stimulus will elicit a basic emotion, and which is able to operate independently of the cognitive systems that lead to conscious, verbally reportable appraisals of the same stimulus (Ekman 1980, Griffiths 1990).

The multi-level approach to appraisal has been solidly confirmed in the case of fear by the neuroscientist Joseph LeDoux (LeDoux 1993, 1996). LeDoux distinguishes between 'cognitive computations' which yield information about stimuli and the relations between them, and 'affective computations' which yield information about the significance of stimuli for the organism and lead to physiological and behavioral responses appropriate to that significance. In fear, and possibly anger, key aspects of affective computation occur in the amygdala. The emotional evaluation of a stimulus can be driven by inputs at various levels of analysis. At a very early stage of perceptual processing, minimally processed data from thalamic sensory relay structures follows the 'low road' to the amygdala. This is the ultimate 'quick and dirty' route to rapid emotional response. Meanwhile, perceptual information follows a slower 'high road' to the visual, auditory, somatosensory, gustatory and olfactory cortices, projections from which to the amygdala allow responses to stimuli in a single, sensory modality. Lesions to these pathways inhibit emotional responses to stimulus features in the corresponding modalities. Finally, the amygdala receives inputs from brain regions associated with full-blown, poly-modal, perceptual representations of the stimulus situation and with memory, allowing the emotional response to be triggered by complex, contextual features of the stimulus. However it is triggered, it is the final response in the amygdala that is associated with fear conditioning, and conditioned fear responses to simple sensory-perceptual stimuli have been shown to be resist-ant to extinction.

Appraisal and the philosophy of emotion

Appraisal theories are the closest scientific equivalents to the theories that have dominated philosophy of emotion since the 1960s. Philosophers have analyzed emotions in terms of the states of affairs appropriate to them (their 'formal objects') (Kenny 1963), as evaluative judgments (Solomon 1976), as evaluative judgments that cause bodily arousal (Lyons 1980), as feelings of comfort or discomfort directed towards an evaluative thought (Greenspan 1988) and as the results of either true belief or uncertainty about emotion-inducing situa-tions (Gordon 1987). For these and many other authors, the central aim of a philosophical theory of emotion is to identify the content of an emotion—the actual or imagined state of affairs in the world to which the emotion has a semantic relationship. In her recent book *Upheavals of Thought: The intelligence of emotions*, Martha Nussbaum uses appraisal theory to capture the idea that emotions are 'intelligent responses to the perception of value' (Nussbaum 2001, 1). She describes Richard Lazarus's appraisal theory as 'in all essentials the view of emotions I have defended in Chapter 1' (Nussbaum 2001, 109). Nussbaum's treatment of the emotions in children and animals also makes use of some-thing like multi-level appraisal. Animals as well as humans make the evaluative judgments that constitute emotions according to Nussbaum's theory, but they do so without self-conscious awareness and in such a way that the content of their judgments cannot be rendered in language without distortion. Nevertheless, she argues, emotion remains primarily an intentional phenomenon. Despite the existence of these low-level appraisals that cannot be expressed in language, '... emotions include in their content judgments that can be true or false, and good or bad guides to ethical choice' (Nussbaum 2001, 6406, 1).

> What we need, in short, is a multifaceted notion of cognitive interpretation or seeing-as, accompanied by a flexible notion of intentionality that allows us to ascribe to a creature more or less precise, vaguer or more demarcated, ways of intending an object and marking it as salient (Nussbaum 2001, 129).

Nussbaum's description of what is needed for an adequate account of emotional cognition is compelling, but levels of appraisal do not just differ *between* organisms. They also differ *within* a single organism. Multi-level models of emotional appraisal suggest that the same stimulus can be represented in several places in the human brain by different representations. Hence it is vital to understand not only what these multiple appraisals have in common, but also how they *differ* and how they *interact*. The existence of multiple representations in a 'hierarchical' emotional architecture (DeLancey 2001) violates a key assumption of most philosophical reasoning about emotion, which is that emotional cognition manipulates emotional representations on the basis of their content, and thus that emotional processes can be explored via the semantic 'logic' of emotions. Multi-level models imply that how emotional and other representations interact, if they interact at all, depends on details of cognitive architecture as well as on the content of the representations. This architecture, of course, cannot be determined by studying the conceptual relations between the contents of emotional representations. Phobias and affective primacy phenomena reveal the architecture of the emotion system by showing what happens when one level of appraisal operates without the others. They reveal that certain information, such as partially analyzed visual data, is available to one level of appraisal and not to another. Another insight is provided by people with 'flattened affect', who are apparently able to carry out high-level appraisal but not low-level appraisal and so do not experience the physiological components of normal emotional response. The possibility of flattened affect without intellectual impairment reveals that only low-level appraisal has direct connections to the effector systems for the automated components of rapid emotional response.

Normal human emotion involves several subsystems that interact; and interact with other cognitive subsystems, in ways that reflect the particular cognitive architecture in which they are embedded. This renders the idea that emotions are intentional states whose identity is determined by their representational

content seriously incomplete, since the same state of affairs is multiply represented. If low-level emotional appraisals are not merely separate from high-
level appraisals but different in kind, that idea becomes still more inadequate.
Nussbaum (127–8) notes that our language may not adequately express the
content of appraisal processes in animals and perhaps also those of infants.
I would add adult low-level appraisal processes to this list. Many of the fine-
grained semantic distinctions we make in ascribing content to thoughts may
fail to get a grip on representational states with more coarse-grained semantics. Neither 'aerial predator' nor 'dark thing overhead of such-and-such
apparent size and moving thusly' should really be taken as a literal rendition of
the 'what the crow thinks' before exhibiting aerial predator-avoidance behavior, although both point to something meaningful (see below). Nussbaum
suggests that we can cope with this phenomenon using a 'flexible notion of
intentionality'. Since this is supposed to allow us to identify what is in common between animal and human emotion her idea is presumably that there is
some degree of isomorphism between the way in which high-level representations relate to one another on the basis of their content and the way in which
low-level representations relate to one another of the basis of their 'content'.
The next two points suggest that this hope may not be borne out.

There are likely to be radical differences between the representational states
involved in low-level and high-level appraisals. Ruth Millikan has suggested
that mental representations in simple organisms may unite the functions of
beliefs and desires in a single, undifferentiated functional role. Low-level
appraisal in humans seems to manifest the same 'collapse of the attitudes'.
Consider the low-level appraisal of the core relational theme 'a demeaning
offence to me and mine' that presumably occurs when a soccer player is
dribbling the ball down the field, another player grabs his jersey causing him
to lose the ball, and the first player turns *angrily* towards the second. I suggest
that it is misleading to say that the relevant brain region *believes* that the
core relational theme has been instantiated. Beliefs are mental states that
represent how things are and which produce action in conjunction
with desires—representations of how the world should be. But in low-level
appraisal for anger there is no question as to what action will be taken. The
frustrated player in our example will orient to the stimulus, produce the pan-
cultural facial expression of anger and undergo physiological changes to
prepare them for aggressive action. The 'affective computation' in this
example is simultaneously the belief that the world is a particular way and the
intention to act in a particular way. Likewise for the better understood case of
affective computing of fear in the amygdala, and, presumably, for any emotion
that has a clear behavioral signature and can be induced to exhibit affective

primacy. I suggest that it is simply misleading to describe low-level appraisal as evaluative judgment, or using any other locution derived from a psychology that presumes a fundamental distinction between data and goals. Instead, low-level emotional appraisal seems to involve action-oriented representation. I discuss below the possibility of capturing the content of such representations using the notion of 'affordances'.

Another way in which low-level emotional appraisal may differ from high-level is in terms of the narrow inferential role imposed on low-level representations by the task-specific architecture in which they occur. The inferential role of these representations is impoverished in three ways. First, low-level appraisal processes do not have access to most of what is represented elsewhere in the brain, which is why knowledge that the cockroach in my drink has been completely sterilized does not eliminate the disgust response. Hence many inferences that would seem to follow from the content we ascribe to this low-level appraisal—in Lazarus's theory, something like 'I am taking in or being too close to an indigestible object'—do not actually follow for subjects because they cannot recombine that content appropriately with their other contentful states. Secondly, the actual processes of affective computing (as opposed to their final output) are not available for inspection by other cognitive sub-systems. Once again, architectural barriers to information flow block inferences that follow from what otherwise seems the natural content to ascribe to those states. Finally, the inferential principles used in affective computing are not truth-preserving, but heuristically survival-enhancing. It simply does not follow from the fact that I have been poked hard and unexpectedly in the small of my back that I have suffered 'a demeaning offence to me and mine' but the automatic appraisal mechanism for anger will reliably draw that conclusion.[3]

There is no scientific puzzle about the nature of information processing in affective computing. The forms of inferential impoverishment I have described all make good psychological and evolutionary sense. But there is a considerable philosophical puzzle about how to ascribe conceptual content to representational states in an isolated cognitive subsystem of this kind. If the concepts that figure in the content ascribed to a representation do not have their usual inferential role, then what is meant by attributing that content? The very idea that the state has conceptual content is thereby called into

---

3 Some Evolutionary Psychologists would say that the appraisal mechanism has innate knowledge that this cue reliably predicts conspecific aggression, or did so in some ancestral environment (Tooby and Cosmides, 1992). I take this to be only rhetorically different from the claim that the appraisal mechanism consistently makes certain logically invalid inferences.

question.[4] The actual role of the representations involved in low-level appraisal and the inferential role of the content-sentences with which we describe those appraisals throws strongly suggests that, in this role at least, appraisal theories simply are not theories of cognitive content.

What is appraisal theory a theory of?

The idea that a low-level appraisal and a high-level appraisal can be the *same appraisal* poses the question of what these two processes have in common. According to multi-level appraisal theories, what they have in common is expressed by the single appraisal that can be made at the various levels, an appraisal such as 'There has been a demeaning offence to me and mine'. I have argued that this shared appraisal cannot be understood as the shared conceptual content of the various appraisal processes, because it is problematic say in what sense low-level appraisal has conceptual content at all. Given the collapse of the attitudes and the impoverishment of inferential roles of representational states in low-level appraisal it makes sense to describe those appraisal processes as 'sub-conceptual'. Instead, I suggest that multi-level appraisal theories are essentially *ecological* theories—theories of the significance of the environment for the organism. An appraisal hyperspace identifies the aspects of the environment that the organism tracks in order to produce adaptive behavior in that environment. The relationship between the concepts that figure in the appraisal theory's representation of the environment and the way the organism actually tracks those aspects of the environment may be very indirect. Lazarus describes the appraisal associated with shame as 'I have failed to live up to an ego-ideal' but low-level appraisal leading to shame may be driven by simple cues that indicate my social standing relative to the person with whom I am interacting.[5] The fact that different appraisal levels are using different surrogates to track the same ecologically significant aspects of the environment helps explain why the different levels sometimes fail to coincide on a common appraisal.

----

4 Gareth Evans famously argued that for a state to have conceptual content its elements must be able to be recombined appropriately with all the other conceptual elements in representational states of the same organism (the 'generality constraint') (Evans 1982). See also Stephen Stich's discussion of 'sub-doxastic' mental representations. The 'beliefs' of low-level appraisal mechanisms resemble those of Stich's 'Mrs T', who remembered that President McKinley was assassinated but was unsure if he was alive or dead (Stich 1983).

5 Anthropologist Daniel Fessler has argued that shame is built out of an ancient behavioral system that leads to aversive feelings in social interactions where one's low relative social status is made salient and that this basic system continues to operate alongside forms of shame that tie the emotion to concepts of responsibility and norm-violation (Fessler 1999).

There is an important sense in which a particular account of the content of emotional appraisal can live a double life, first as a general ecological theory applicable to all appraisal levels and second as a theory of the actual conceptual content of the representational states being processed in high-level appraisal. An appraisal theory can fulfill the first role very well whilst failing in the second role. In fact, abstracting away from the details of any particular psychological process in order to better fulfill the first role is likely to produce a worse theory of the actual psychological process of high-level appraisal. But if an appraisal theory is not primarily treated as a theory of 'what the person is thinking' then it becomes possible to recognize that even high-level appraisal may not present the stimulus to the subject under the concepts that figure in the best theoretical representation of the appraisal hyperspace. For example, if high-level appraisal for shame involves moral concepts from the local cultural milieu, such as 'dishonor', whilst low-level appraisal uses simple cues to assess relative social status (see fn. 4), then the core relational theme 'I have failed to live up to an ego-ideal' is not an accurate rendition of either the conceptual content of the high-level appraisal or the 'content' of the low-level appraisal. It may, however, capture a common aspect of eliciting situations that can be tracked at many levels. In earlier work on philosophical theories of the content of emotions I discussed the problem of relating the very abstract 'analyses' of emotions like fear, anger and envy found in the philosophical literature to the concrete thoughts about particular objects that are present in an individual's consciousness on a particular occasion of emotion (Griffiths 1989, 1997, 38–43). The present suggestion is that greater psychological realism about the conceptual content of high-level appraisal processes can be achieved by recognizing that the general gloss put on such thoughts in an appraisal theory is an ecological description of the significance of the aspects of the environment that the organism is tracking and not necessarily a description of how the organism represents those aspects of the environment to itself.

The idea that appraisal theories are ecological theories of the significance of the environment to the organism immediately suggests a teleosemantic treatment of the content of emotional appraisals, a treatment that, hopefully would explain how appraisals at all levels could have the same conceptual content.[6] The idea would be that appraisals at all levels for, e.g. fear, have the same content—namely, 'I am facing an immediate, concrete, and overwhelming physical danger'—because they have all evolved to be triggered by that

6 For teleosemantic accounts of mental content, see (Dretske 1988, Millikan 1984, Papineau 1987). Jesse Prinz has a specific discussion of teleosemantics and the emotions, but his immediate concern is with what affective feelings represent to the organism (Prinz Forthcoming).

circumstance. But this proposal does not take the idea of assigning conceptual content to a mental representation seriously enough. Teleosemantic programs for naturalistic semantics view the fact that some biological systems have the evolutionary function of responding to a state of the environment as the fundamental way in which 'aboutness' becomes a part of the natural world. The sort of genuine intentionality that characterizes human thought and language is something that can be explained as a sophisticated evolutionary development of this fundamental phenomenon. But that does not mean that any biological system with a broadly representational function is comparable to those distinctive biological systems like the human mind that achieve full-blown intentional representation. As I suggested above, low-level appraisal resembles just those sorts of proto-intentional representational processes that have been the main focus of the teleosemantics literature to date—processes like that by which a frog detects a passing fly and strikes at it (Lettvin *et al.* 1959). The idea that all levels of appraisal have the same 'teleocontent' comes down to nothing more than what has been already argued about, namely, that a multi-level appraisal theory describes the ecological significance of the aspects of the environment that the organism is tracking by varied cognitive means.

Treating appraisal theory as an ecological theory, as opposed to a theory of teleocontent, has the advantage that it does not lump together the biological functions of the various appraisal levels for an emotion as 'representing the core relational theme', as if they were redundant ways to perform the same task. It should be clear that low-level appraisal systems are not merely a hangover from the evolutionary past, performing the same functions in primitive ways. Rather, the ways in which low-level appraisal conflicts with high-level appraisal is part of the normal functioning of these systems. Low-level appraisal ensures that fundamental adaptive action and action preparedness is engaged early and with a low rate of false-negative appraisals. High-level appraisal makes fuller use of human cognitive abilities to make an accurate appraisal that will engage flexible, longer-term coping strategies. So, rather than being redundant mechanisms performing the same function, low-level appraisal and high-level appraisal perform separate and complimentary functions in relation to the same ecologically significant aspects of its environment—dangers, conspecific challenges, and so forth. It is useful to see what low-level and high-level appraisal have in common, but they are not the same thing.

Appraisal and affordance

I have argued that low-level appraisal involves 'action oriented' representations in which the functional roles of belief and desire are not distinct. This makes it natural to describe the ecologically significant features of the environment that the appraisal process is tracking as 'action affordances'—the fact that the environment offers a certain opportunity for action. This approach may perhaps be useful for high-level appraisal as well as low-level appraisal. Nico Frijda has argued that the result of emotional appraisal is a set of 'action tendencies'—the emotion presents the environment to the subject as affording certain possibilities for action (Frijda 1986).

The concept of an affordance derives from J.J. Gibson's theory of, 'ecological perception'. Philosophical discussion of Gibson has focused on his 'direct realism' and rejection of perceptual representations. The concept of an affordance, however, is logically independent of direct realism. In a recent paper Andrea Scarantino has presented an analysis of the affordance concept and pointed out the theoretical value of considering affordances as objects of perception, independent of any particular theory of the perceptual process (Scarantino In Press). Affordances are organism-relative dispositional properties of the environment. The surface of water, for example, affords mosquito larvae the possibility of hanging from it so as to keep their breathing tube exposed to the air. If the mosquito larva acts appropriately, then this disposition will be realized in an act of hanging from the surface. The disposition arises from a conjunction of properties of the larvae and their environment. Water does not afford this possibility to human infants. Adding petrol to the water reduces the surface tension and destroys the disposition.

Scarantino makes two important, orthogonal distinctions between types of affordances. In some cases the eliciting condition guarantees the manifestation of the disposition, while in others it only makes it probable. First, therefore, he distinguishes deterministic ('surefire') affordances from probablistic affordances. Secondly, Scarantino distinguishes 'goal-affordances' and 'happening affordances'. Goal-affordances are manifested by an organism successfully performing a goal-directed behavior—the environment affords the performance of that behavior. A member of the opposite sex, for example, offers a probabilistic goal-affordance of mating. Happening-affordances are manifested by the organism undergoing a passive change. A branch of dubious strength presents an orang-utang with a probabilistic happening-affordance of falling. These distinctions can both be applied to the properties detected in emotional appraisal processes.

Standard presentations of appraisal make emotions appear primarily perceptual. An emotion is the recognition that the world is a certain way. Representing the content of appraisals as affordances brings out the action-oriented nature of emotion. Shame for example, has the core relational theme that 'I have failed to live up to an ego ideal'. But shame also has a characteristic set of behaviors that serve a vital social-communicative function (Darwin 1872, Fessler 1999). Arguably, the fact that the environment is shaming to the subject is a goal-affordance—the environment affords acceptance of the other's dominance as a social-interaction strategy. In some cases, the action-oriented nature of emotion is already present in the 'coping' dimensions of appraisal models and is simply not highlighted in the usual summaries of those models. The core relational theme of anger, for instance, is 'a demeaning offence against me and mine', but what this actually means in Lazarus's model includes the organism's recognition that aggression is a viable coping strategy and that aggression may help achieve the organism's goals (Lazarus 1991). In anger, therefore, what we detect is a goal-affordance for angry behavior. Conceiving of anger in these terms makes sense of an intriguing result from a retrospective self-report study of the causes of emotion by Nancy Stein and colleagues. They found that an important factor in predicting the occurrence of anger rather than sadness as the response to a loss was the possibility of obtaining restitution or compensation for the loss (Stein, Trabasso, and Liwag 1993). Sadness, from this perspective, is an unusual emotion, since, if the sore relational theme really is 'I have experienced an irrevocable loss' then sadness is a deterministic happening-affordance, or something about which nothing can be done! This poses an obvious question about the adaptive utility of the emotion.

Machiavellian appraisal?

In a recent paper I raised the possibility that some aspects of the appraisal process might be 'strategic' or 'Machiavellian' (Griffiths 2003). Organisms may be evaluating not just the significance of what has happened, but also the likely outcome of responding to that occurrence with one emotion or another. The concept of 'Machiavellian intelligence' has moved to the center stage in recent discussions of the evolution of human cognition (Byrne and Whiten 1988, Whiten and Byrne 1997). Human intelligence is 'Machiavellian' to the extent that the evolutionary forces which shaped it arose from social competition within primate groups. Machiavellian intelligence is the result of an intra-species arms race in which increased intelligence at the level of the population merely raises the bar for success at the individual level. Like more traditional conceptions of intelligence, emotional intelligence is Machiavellian in a general sense simply to the extent that it has evolved to mediate social competition.

It seems to be common ground that the *expression* of emotion is strategic, and so, if it has an evolutionary history, is Machiavellian in the above sense. The role of social context in determining emotional expression has long been recognized through Paul Ekman's concept of a 'display rule' (Ekman 1971,

1972) and has been more heavily emphasized by recent 'transactionalist' accounts of emotion (Fridlund 1994, Russell and Fernández-Dols 1997). The contextual factors that predict whether an emotion is expressed are of the sort that are likely to have been significant in human evolution—factors such as conformity to group standards and the status of the individual in the group— and so the sensitivity of emotional expression to such factors is very plausibly part of our evolved social competence. This need not imply, of course, that the specific rules to which individuals conform to in one culture or another can be explained in evolutionary terms. Evolution can be equally relevant when the task is to understand how cultures generate their patterns of difference from a shared developmental system. The generic fact that there are display rules, for example, is very likely to have an evolutionary explanation even if these rules differ radically across cultures.

If the Machiavellian expression of emotions is common ground amongst evolutionary theorists of emotion, the idea that the actual production of emotion is influenced by 'strategic' considerations remains more controversial (Ekman 1997). I have embodied this idea in the '*Machiavellian Emotion Hypothesis*', which suggests that emotional appraisal is sensitive to cues that predict the value to the emotional agent of responding to the situation with a particular emotion, as well as cues that indicate the significance of the stimulus situation to the agent independently of the agent's response (Griffiths 2003). Put in the language of appraisal theories, the hypothesis is that the appraisal hyperspace has 'strategic' dimensions. The organism evaluates the stimulus situation not only along multiple dimensions that assess the significance of what has happened, but along dimensions that assess the significance of what will likely happen if the emotion is produced. In current appraisal models, some strategic considerations are embodied in 'coping' related dimensions. Putting the hypothesis in terms of affordances, it states that emotional appraisal detects goal-affordances.

There is some suggestive evidence of Machiavellian appraisal in primates. The neural connectivity of the amygdala in primates is consistent with the hypothesis that its activity is facilitated or inhibited by the perception of social contextual cues (Emery and Amaral 2000, 167). Behavioral studies of primates also support the idea that adults assess the likely outcome of the emotional interaction when producing emotional behavior. William Mason reports that rhesus macaques deprived of social contact as infants produce grossly normal facial behaviors expressive of fear (grimace), friendliness (lipsmacking) and threat (threat face) (Mason 1985). What seems to be lacking in these animals is an ability to utilize these facial expressions to manage their relationships with other monkeys. They are, as it were, emotionally clumsy. Mason explains these results in terms of the role of social experience in elaborating complex eliciting conditions for emotional behavior. Infant monkeys begin by producing these behaviors in response to relatively simple, context independent stimuli. Later on, 'As a result of functional elaborations, refinements, and transformations of the schemata [*of elicitors for expressive behavior*] present in early infancy, experience creates new sources of social order, new possibilities for the regulation and control of social life' (Mason 1985, 147). The monkeys, in other words, learn to produce the same emotional behaviors in response to subtler aspects of social context, and by doing so are able to manage their social interactions with other animals. It is possible to argue that these findings are accounted for purely by evolved mechanisms for the Machiavellian *expression* of emotions—subordinate Rhesus monkeys feel angry when dominant monkeys search their cheek pouches for food, but never display this anger. I would argue, however, that that this hypothesis adds an unnecessary layer of complexity to account for the behavior.

What would a Machiavellian theory of human emotions look like? Numerous emotion theorists have suggested that emotions may be self-serving, occurring not when the situation objectively warrants the judgment embodied in the emotional appraisal, but rather when it suits the agent to interpret the situation in this light. Jean Paul Sartre famously takes this view (Sartre 1962). According to Sartre, for example, anger ascribes to a person the property of being hateful precisely because he stands between the agent and the satisfaction of her desires. That is the difference between the emotion of anger and rational coping with the conflicting needs of others. Emotions as Sartre describes them are intrinsically pathological—a form of bad faith in which people reject reality out of mental weakness. But the central insight of his theory is independent of this value-judgment. It is simply that people can use emotions to view the world in a light that is psychologically more rewarding to us than other possible interpretations. Highly adaptive versions of this process are described in the literature on 'emotional intelligence', such as using an emotional reinterpretation of the situation to motivate oneself (Salovey, Bedell, Detweiler, and Mayer 2000). From the perspective of the emotional intelligence literature, Sartre's work seems like an insightful account of human psychology marred by the French philosopher's penchant for calling a spade a conspiracy against the soil.

Conclusion

Emotional appraisal happens at more than one level. Low-level appraisals involve representations that are semantically coarse-grained, fuse the functional roles of belief and desire and have impoverished inferential roles, making it best to think of them as sub-conceptual. Multi-level theories of emotional appraisal are thus best conceived, not as theories of the actual conceptual content of emotional appraisals, but as ecological theories that identify the aspects of the environment that appraisal processes are tracking using diverse cognitive means. These aspects of the environment are what the environment 'affords' the organism. Some of these affordances are 'goal-affordances'—possibilities for future action. This perspective on emotional appraisal lends support to the idea that emotional appraisal is in part 'Machiavellian' or 'strategic'. Organisms take into account the payoffs resulting from an emotional response when determining whether the eliciting situation 'warrants' that emotion.

Acknowledgments

In preparing this paper I am indebted to feedback from the audience at the April 2002 King's College London conference on *Emotion, Evolution and Rationality*, and to the comments of Andrea Scarantino on an earlier draft.

References

Byrne, R. W. and Whiten, A. E. (1988). *Machiavellian intelligence.* Oxford University Press, Oxford, New York.

Darwin, C. (1872). *The expressions of emotions in man & animals,* 1st edition. Philosophical Library, New York.

DeLancey, C. (2001). *Passionate engines: what emotions reveal about mind and artificial intelligence.* Oxford University Press, New York, Oxford.

Dretske, F. (1988). *Explaining behaviour.* Bradford/MIT, Cambridge, MA.

Ekman, P. (1971). Universals and cultural differences in facial expressions of emotion. In *Nebraska Symposium on Motivation* 4 (ed. J.K. Cole), pp. 207–83. University of Nebraska Press, Lincoln, Nebraska.

Ekman, P. (1972). *Emotions in the human face.* Pergamon Press, New York.

Ekman, P. (1980). Biological & cultural contributions to body & facial movement in the expression of emotions. In *Explaining* Emotions (ed. A.O. Rorty), University of California Press, Berkeley.

Ekman, P. (1997). Expression or communication about emotion. In *Genetic, ethological and evolutionary perspectives on human development: essays in honor of Dr Daniel G. Freedman* (ed. N. Segal, G. L. Weisfeld, and C. C. Weisfeld). American Psychiatric Association, Washington, D.C.

Emery, N. J. and Amaral, D. G. (2000). The role of the amygdala in primate social cognition. In *The cognitive neuroscience of emotion* (ed. R. Lane and L. Nadel), pp. 156–91. Oxford University Press, New York.

Esteves, F. and Öhman, A. (1993). Masking the face: recognition of emotional facial expression as a function of the parameters of backward masking. *Scandinavian Journal of Psychology,* **34**, 1–18.

Evans, G. (1982). *The varieties of reference.* Oxford University Press, Oxford.

Fessler, D. M. (1999). Toward an understanding of the universality of second-order emotions. In *Biocultural approaches to emotions* (ed. A. L. Hinton), pp. 74–116. Cambridge University Press, Cambridge.

Fridlund, A. (1994). *Human facial expression: an evolutionary view.* Academic Press, San Diego.

Frijda, N. H. (1986). *The Emotions.* Cambridge University Press, Cambridge.

Gordon, R. M. (1987). *The structure of emotions.* Cambridge University Press, Cambridge.

Greenspan, P. (1988). *Emotions and reasons: an inquiry into emotional justification.* Routledge, New York.

Griffiths, P. E. (1989). The degeneration of the cognitive theory of emotion. *Philosophical Psychology,* 2(3), 297–313.

Griffiths, P. E. (1990). Modularity & the psychoevolutionary theory of emotion. *Biology & Philosophy,* 5, 175–96.

Griffiths, P. E. (1997). *What emotions really are: the problem of psychological categories.* University of Chicago Press, Chicago.

Griffiths, P. E. (2003). Basic Emotions, Complex Emotions, Machiavellian Emotions. In *Philosophy and the Emotions* (ed. A. Hatzimoysis), pp. 39–67. Cambridge University Press, Cambridge.

Kenny, A. (1963). *Action, emotion & will.* Routledge & Kegan Paul, London.

Lazarus, R. S. (1991). *Emotion and adaptation.* Oxford University Press, New York.

Lazarus, R. S., Coyne, J. C., and Folkman, S (1984). Cognition, emotion & motivation: doctoring Humpty Dumpty. In *Approaches to Emotions* (ed. K. Scherer and P Ekman), pp. 221–37. Erlbaum, Hillsdale, New Jersey.

LeDoux, J. (1996). *The emotional brain: the mysterious underpinnings of emotional life.* Simon and Schuster, New York.

LeDoux, J. E. (1993). Emotional networks in the brain. In *Handbook of Emotions,* (ed. M. Lewis and J. M. Haviland), pp. 109–18. Guildford Press, New York.

Lettvin, J. Y., Maturana, H. R., and McCulloch, W. S. P. (1959). What the frog's eye tells the frog's brain. *Proceedings of Institute of Radio Engineers,* 11, 230–55.

Lyons, W. (1980). *Emotion.* Cambridge University Press, Cambridge.

Mason, W. A. (1985). Experiential influences on the development of expressive behaviors in Rhesus monkeys. In *The Development of Expressive Behavior* (ed. G. Zivin), pp. 117–52. Academic Press, New York.

Millikan, R. G. (1984). *Language, thought & other biological categories.* MIT Press, Cambridge, MA.

Nussbaum, M. C. (2001). *Upheavals of thought: the intelligence of emotions.* Cambridge University Press, Cambridge, New York.

Öhman, A. (1986). Face the beast and fear the face: animal and social fears as prototypes for evolutionary analyses of emotion. *Psychophysiology,* 23, 123–45.

Öhman, A. (2002). Automaticity and the amygdala: nonconscious responses to emotional faces. *Current Directions in Psychological Science,* 11(2), 62–6.

Öhman, A. and Soares, J. J.F. (1994). Unconscious anxiety: phobic responses to masked stimuli. *Journal of Abnormal Psychology,* 102, 121–32.

Papineau, D. (1987). *Reality and Representation.* Blackwells, NY.

Prinz, J. (Forthcoming) *Emotional perception.* Oxford University Press, Oxford.

Russell, J. A. and Fernández-Dols, J. M. (1997). *The psychology of facial expression.* Cambridge University Press, Cambridge.

Salovey, P., Bedell, B. T., Detweiler, J. B., and Mayer, J. D. (2000). Current directions in emotional intelligence research. In *Handbook of emotions*, 2nd edition (ed. M. Lewis and J. M. Haviland-Jones), pp. 5–4–520. Guildford, New York.

Sartre, J. P. (1962). *Sketch for a theory of the emotions* (P. Mairet, Trans.). Methuen, London.

Scarantino, A. (In Press 2004) Affordances explained. *Philosophy of Science*, 71 (Supplement: Proceedings of the 2002 Biennial Meeting of the Philosophy of Science Association. Part II: Symposia Papers).

Scherer, K. R. (1999). Appraisal theory. In *Handbook of emotion and cognition* (ed. T. Dalgleish and M. J. Power), pp. 637–63. Chichester, New York.

Solomon, R. (1976). *The passions.* Doubleday, New York.

Solomon, R. C. (1993). The philosophy of emotions. In *Handbook of emotions* (ed. M. Lewis and J. M. Haviland), pp. 3–15. Guildford, New York.

Stein, N. L., Trabasso, T., and Liwag, M. (1993). The representation and organization of emotional exierence: unfolding the emotion episode. In *Handbook of emotions* (ed. M. Lewis and J. M. Haviland), pp. 279–300. Guildford, New York.

Stich, S. (1983). *From folk psychology to cognitive science.* MIT Press, Cambridge, U.K.

Teasdale, J. D. (1999). Multi-level theories of cognition-emotion relations. In *Handbook of cognition and emotion*, (ed. T. Dalgleish and M. J. Power), pp. 665–81. John Wiley and sons, Chichester.

Tooby, J. and Cosmides, L. (1992). The psychological foundations of culture. In *The adapted mind: evolutionary psychology and the generation of culture* (ed. J. H. Barkow, L. Cosmides, and J. Tooby), pp. 19–136. Oxford University Press, Oxford and New York.

Whiten, A. and Byrne, R. W. (ed.) (1997). *Machiavellian intelligence II: extensions and evaluations.* Cambridge University Press, Cambridge.

Zajonc, R. B. (1980). Feeling & thinking: preferences need no inference. *American Psychologist*, 35, 151–75.

Zajonc, R. B. (1984a). On the primacy of affect. In *Approaches to emotion* (ed. K. Scherer and P. Ekman), pp. 259–70. Lawrence Erlbaum, Hillsdale, NJ.

Zajonc, R. B. (1984b). The interaction of affect and cognition. In *Approaches to emotions* (ed. K. Scherer and P. Ekman), pp. 239–46. Lawrence Erlbaum, Hillsdale, NJ.

CHAPTER 6

UNPICKING REASONABLE EMOTIONS

BRIAN PARKINSON

One of the simplest ways to make sense of emotions is by reference to their apparent functions. Anger, so the story goes, is a way of warding off potential antagonists, and fear facilitates escape from a variety of threats. Invoking natural selection to explain how these functions operate further enhances the apparent rationality and coherence of this account: emotions are solutions to adaptive problems faced by our evolutionary ancestors. But how well does this neat package hang together? Does it actually give a complete picture of how emotions unfold in real-time transactions?

This chapter focuses on the particular formulation of the adaptive functionality of emotions provided by recent versions of appraisal theory (e.g., Lazarus 1991, Smith and Lazarus 1993, Roseman 2001). Their basic idea is that emotions are prepackaged bundles of response designed to address broad classes of functional demands. Selective forces have stitched together the various components of emotional reaction, picking the ones that provide survival and reproductive advantages. I shall tug at the seams of this tidy narrative by arguing first that the prestructuring of emotional response syndromes has often been overestimated or oversold. Indeed, coherence emerges piece by piece from real-time affordances and resistances inherent in unfolding situations, rather than running off in a preprogrammed way because of decisions made in evolutionary prehistory. Second, any inherent integrity of response packages derives as much from culturally variant socialization practices as adaptive pressures. For functional reasons, there is merit in a system whose parameters stay unspecified until the particularities of the cultural problem-frame become apparent. This is not to claim that our minds enter the world as blank slates, only that too rigid a structure unduly restricts flexibility in rapidly changing circumstances.

My claim then is that evolution is not the glue or thread holding emotions together, but instead that they are loosely assembled over phylogenetic and ontogenetic history, then channelled into niches situated in contemporary unfolding ecologies. Although few would want to deny the importance of socialization and on-line responsivity in emotion, current emphases often detract from their thorough investigation.

This chapter begins with a brief description of appraisal theory and its evidential base, before providing evidence that the coherence and consistency of relational meanings underlying one particular emotion are not easily subsumed into a unitary theme. Correspondingly, I argue that the various functional demands associated with the variety of occasions for any given emotion cannot readily be solved by any single action or strategy.

In summary, two basic issues are addressed:

1. Viability: How well would a system of prepackaged emotions meet its functional requirements in principle?

2. Accuracy: Are emotions really structured in the way that this account implies in practice?

Functional appraisals and emotions

Appraisal theory works from a decision-making metaphor (see Lazarus 1991). Events present problems for the organism to solve. Evolution has equipped humans with mechanisms that facilitate this problem-solving (the relevant decision rules having been preset at some point in evolutionary history). First, an appraisal mechanism allows rapid and economical detection and identification of adaptively relevant concerns, setting the agenda for functional response by characterizing the nature of the problem and available resources for dealing with it. Correspondingly, an emotion mechanism provides (partly) preformulated solutions to these problems matching the identified character of the eliciting situations. For example, the presence of a potential antagonist is detected by appraisals relating to other-blame which directly induce the emotion of anger that invokes appropriately antagonistic action tendencies. Appraisal determines the nature of the problem, emotion provides a strategy for its solution.

The particular advantage of emotional response is that it is quicker and more efficient than deliberative reasoning but not as rigid as a reflex. According to the appraisal account, we do not have the time or resources to consider the full range of alternatives in many situations, yet still need to be responsive to the particularities of the current circumstances. Emotion can then steer us through. As Smith and Ellsworth (1987) argue: 'Emotions represent an evolutionary step beyond innate releasing mechanisms and fixed-action patterns in that they provide a way of motivating behaviour that allows a measure of flexibility both in the eliciting conditions and in the form of the behavioural response' (475).

Relatedly, Scherer (e.g., 2001) considers emotions to be 'decoupled reflexes' setting up a readiness to respond with a default action but not compelling such a response. In both these views, emotional reactions are constrained but not wholly; they are flexible but not entirely. Further, the idea is that constraints come from internal mental structures (which provide incomplete specification of action): On the input side, cues are represented in terms of appraisals. On the output side, action is shaped by action tendencies.

To summarize, the reasoning behind appraisal theory runs roughly as follows: If preprogrammed emotions are to serve adaptive functions, the system needs to know *what to get emotional about* (when to output an emotion) and *how to cope* (what kind of responses to output). Appraisal allows detection of adaptively relevant transactions. Emotion involves a state of action readiness designed to deal with whatever needs attention in these transactions.

Although the theory I am addressing specifically in this chapter is appraisal theory, its account of emotions is not too dissimilar to that offered by other influential evolutionary psychologists. For example, Cosmides and Tooby (2001) argue as follows: 'Evolved psychological adaptations are selected to use cues that (1) can be reliably and easily detected by the individual, and (2) reliably predicted the hidden structure of conditions relevant to determining what course of action one should take' (100).

This view of emotions as adaptive plans or preset decision rules also fits well with a common sense rationalistic view of emotions: the way we like to justify them in everyday conversation. We discover that someone is to blame for something bad that has happened and consequently get angry, and this prepares us for retaliation. The basic assumption of all these interrelated explanations is that contexts do not reveal their structure directly to perception but need decoding (by an appraisal mechanism) in order to determine appropriate response.

Appraisals underlying different emotions

The decision points that the appraisal system needs to pass through, before outputting a functionally appropriate emotion, have been formalized in a range of classificatory schemes. There are differences of detail (see Scherer 1999) but the main themes are similar, so I shall focus on just one of the more influential and cogent models as developed by Smith and Lazarus (1993). The components of appraised meaning are specified in Table 6.1. Working downwards from the top of this table, an appraisal of motivational relevance is

Table 6.1 Appraisals associated with some common emotions (adapted from Smith, Haynes, Lazarus, and Pope, 1993)

EMOTIONS	Happiness	Hope	Sadness	Fear	Anger	Guilt
PRIMARY APPRAISALS	Motivational Relevance					
	Motivational Congruence		Motivational Incongruence			
SECONDARY APPRAISALS **Coping Potential**		High problem-focused coping potential	Low problem-focused coping potential	Low or uncertain coping potential		
Accountability					Other-accountability	Self-accountability
Expectations		Positive future expectations	Negative future expectations			
CORE RELATIONAL THEME	Success	Potential for success	Irrevocable loss	Danger	Other-blame	Self-blame

considered a precondition for the occurrence of any kind of emotion: Unless what is happening bears in some way on current projects, plans or goals ('concerns' in Frijda's (1986) useful terminology), there is nothing to get emotional about. A second primary appraisal concerns motivational congruence: If what is happening impedes progress towards goals or otherwise interferes with our projects, the consequent emotion will be unpleasant (negative), whereas if our plans are faciliated, we will feel good about things (positive emotion).

The particular nature of the positive or negative emotion that is experienced is thought to depend on secondary appraisals (appraisals not of the event itself but of how well we can deal with it, practically or emotionally, and relatedly on who or what is accountable for what has happened). For example, if someone else is perceived as responsible for a motivationally relevant and incongruent event (other-accountability), there will be anger, but if the person perceives himself or herself as responsible for a comparable event, then guilt will ensue.

It is important to note that Smith and Lazarus (1993) do not intend to imply a strict temporal sequence to primary and secondary appraisals. Indeed the appraised meaning may well be apprehended holistically and all in one go, by reference to a core relational theme that encapsulates the meaning of the emotional transaction (other-blame for anger, and self-blame for guilt). In any case, the theory argues that arriving at this appraised meaning *always* automatically and directly produces the associated emotion. Each appraisal pattern represents both a necessary and sufficient condition for its occurrence (see Lazarus 1991).

The first thing to note about this formulation is that it succeeds in making emotions sound eminently reasonable. It certainly makes sense that emotions should be accompanied by the judgements implied here (with maybe one or two quibbles about the precise details). The second is that the scheme seems to work best when the trigger for the emotion is a temporally isolated event: Something happens, we appraise it, and then emotion occurs. Although Lazarus (1991) is quite explicit that it is 'transactions' (involving a higher-level fusion of person embedded in unfolding environment) that are appraised, this does not sit so easily with his distinctions between primary and secondary appraisal, or problem-focused and emotion-focused coping potential (ability to deal with the event and with how the event makes you feel, respectively). The applicability of the appraisal analysis to emotions that emerge over the course of unfolding lines of action is explicitly addressed by Parkinson (2001) but this issue is also touched upon on later in the present chapter. However, let us start by considering the evidence marshalled in support of the appraisal model just outlined.

Evidence for appraisal–emotion connections

The usual methodology deployed in tests of appraisal theory is self-report. Smith and Ellsworth (1985) pioneered this approach (see also Roseman 1979). In their study, 16 participants rated 15 recent emotional experiences along 6 appraisal dimensions, many of which were conceptually related to those specified in Smith and Lazarus's (1993) scheme as outlined above (including pleasantness [motivational congruence], anticipated effort [future expectancy], self/other responsibility [self- and other-accountability] etc.)

The basic finding in this and similar studies is an unsurprising one: Different emotions are associated with distinctive appraisal profiles. This is also true when participants report on concurrent rather than recalled emotional experiences (Smith and Ellsworth 1987). For instance, the appraisals associated with three contrasting emotions are presented in Fig. 6.1. Anger and guilt differ mainly on the appraisal dimension of 'self/other responsibility' with anger associated with the judgement that someone else is responsible for what is happening and guilt associated with the judgement that the self is responsible. Pride is similar to guilt except that it is associated with situations appraised as pleasant (motivationally congruent) rather than unpleasant (motivationally

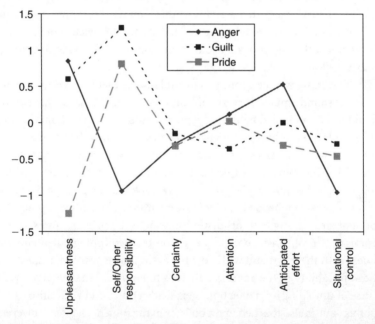

Figure 6.1   Appraisal profiles for anger, guilt, and pride (based on data from Smith and Ellsworth 1985).

incongruent). Each emotion is thus characterized by a distinctive profile along the specified appraisal dimensions.

What do these results tell us? On the surface, they seem to imply that self-reported emotions are connected with, if not actually caused by, specific appraisal patterns. Leaving aside the question of whether this fact confirms an empirical link between real emotions and occurrent appraisals or simply a representational connection between our ideas of appraisal and emotion (see Parkinson 1997), there is still an issue about the representativeness of sampling of emotions in these studies. The appraisal model is consistent with attempts to account for and justify our emotions in everyday language: Perhaps the emotion examples generated by participants in these studies are exactly those that they find easiest to justify.

Looking at the specific instructions given to participants by Smith and Ellsworth in order to elicit emotion examples, there is some support for this reasoning. They told people to imagine they were explaining their emotions to a Vulcan such as Mr Spock from the first Star Trek TV series (someone who the experimenters said had never experienced an emotion). Under these circumstances, it would not be surprising if participants selected instances of emotion that were most amenable to a logical analysis.

More generally, it seems plausible that the fact of taking part in an obviously scientific study of emotions brings demand characteristics relating to the generation of reasonable emotions, ones that can be easily analyzed in rational terms. Further, it may be that when we think about emotions, the ones that come most readily to mind are those that conform readily to a rational prototype that allows their easy explanation. In many everyday contexts, maybe it is difficult to think of emotions that don't fit the common-sense pattern.

Reasonable and unreasonable anger

In a recent study (Parkinson 1999), I tried to circumvent the problems of obtaining a representative sample of self-reported emotions by giving explicit instructions about what kind of examples should be generated by participants. The focus of the study was on anger and guilt, but here I shall focus mainly on the results relating to anger. In the reasonable anger condition, each participant was asked to: 'think back to the most recent occasion when you felt angry for a good reason. ... try to remember the last time that something happened which made you feel angry and which you feel you were right to feel angry about.' The instructions were the same for the unreasonable anger condition, except that in this case participants had to recall the most recent occasion on which they had felt angry without good reason ('when something happened which made you feel angry but which you feel it was inappropriate to feel angry about'). A third condition was included to assess whether it was possible to appraise situations in ways supposedly directly associated with anger, but without experiencing the emotion itself. Participants in this non-emotional blame condition were asked to remember an occasion when they had: '... blamed someone for something bad that had happened but didn't get angry about it.'

Table 6.2 presents examples of the incidents reported in response to these three kinds of instruction. The reasonable anger incidents mostly referred to episodes in which someone else was to blame for something bad that had happened in accordance with the appraisal account. The unreasonable incidents included some in which others were seen as to blame, but this blame was considered unreasonable, and other incidents involving events that are not easily seen in terms of other blame. The incidents reported in the non-emotional blame condition seem broadly comparable to those reported in the reasonable anger condition.

Ratings of the three kinds of incidents along Smith and Lazarus's (1993) self-report appraisal items confirmed these differences. As Fig. 6.2, shows, appraisals accompanying reasonable anger and nonemotional blame were highly similar, both characterized by high motivational relevance, incongruence, and other-accountability. However, the appraisal profile for unreasonable anger differs from both, especially with regard to the appraisal dimensions of other- and self-accountability. Unreasonable anger occurred in situations that participants rated as lower in other-accountability and higher in

Table 6.2 Examples of reported incidents from Parkinson (1999)

Reasonable anger

• A friend lied about something she did, saying she had done something when she hadn't, thus endangering the welfare of someone else's horse.

• Found out my ex-boyfriend had cheated on me while we were together.

Unreasonable anger

• Losing at pool three times in a row.

• I had gone out but had not had a good time and on the way home it started to pour down with rain and I got very wet.

Non-emotional blame

• A girl in my block was reading some of my personal letters in my room when I was not there.

• My boyfriend went off with another woman.

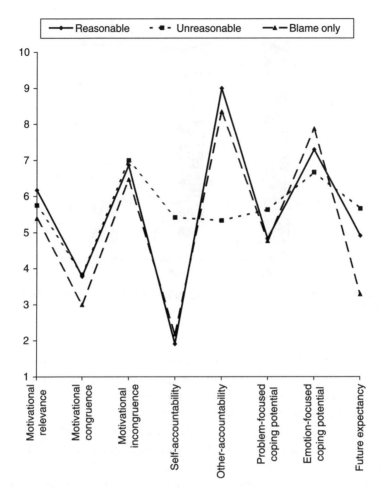

Figure 6.2   Appraisal profiles for reasonable and unreasonable anger and non-emotional other-blame (adapted from Parkinson 1999).

self-accountability. Further, in a second study, participants' scores on Smith and Lazarus's (1993) questionnaire measure of the core relational theme associated with anger ('other-blame') were significantly lower in the unreasonable anger condition than in either the non-emotional blame condition or the reasonable anger condition. Correspondingly, self-reported anger intensity was significantly lower for non-emotional blame than either anger condition (see Fig. 6.3). Thus, participants rating themselves relatively low on other-blame still reported experiencing anger in the unreasonable anger condition, and participants reporting relatively less anger reported relatively strong

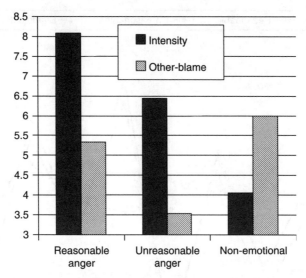

Figure 6.3 Is other-blame a necessary and sufficient condition for anger? (adapted from Parkinson 1999).

other-blame in the non-emotional blame conditions. If we assume that the self-report indices are valid measures of appraisal and emotion, these results are problematic for any model that sees these appraisals as necessary and sufficient conditions for this emotion.

Of course, there are many reasons for doubting that people's reports of appraisal correspond precisely to underlying appraisal processes, not least the point that appraisal is thought to be often unconscious (Arnold 1960, Lazarus 1991). For example, we often get angry without being aware of any prior appraisal of other-blame. However, questioning the validity of self-report appraisal measures also casts doubt on the main positive evidence for the appraisal view in the first place. Further, inspection of the incidents reported in the unreasonable anger condition do not seem to provide the basis for any appraisal of other-accountability whether conscious or unconscious, but more of this in a moment ...

One possible criticism of this study is that participants may have confabulated unreasonable anger incidents in response to the demand characteristics of the instructions. However, a more recent study (Parkinson and Roper, 2002) simply asked participants to report all anger incidents, however apparently trivial or unreasonable, over the period of a week as soon as possible after they occurred. Here too, anger experiences reported as more unreasonable were rated as significantly lower in other-accountability. Further, ratings of the other two appraisals supposedly characterizing anger (motivational relevance and incongruence) were also lower. If anger is fully explained by these appraisals, it is hard to explain why it still occurs at comparable strength even when they are all at lower levels.

From the present perspective, the fact that the everyday reports of emotion generated in previous questionnaire studies tend to accord with an appraisal account is no accident. When people usually think about their emotions, the default option is to think of justifiable, reasonable examples as specified in everyday common sense. Appraisal theory has similar origins. It extends the everyday account of emotion as caricatured and contested by William James (1898): 'Our natural way of thinking ... is that the mental perception of some fact excites the mental affection called the emotion ... Common sense says, we lose our fortune, are sorry and weep; we meet a bear, are frightened and run; we are insulted by a rival, are angry and strike.' (449).

Appraisal theory simply specifies more precisely how events in the world attain their power to excite us, and what determines the nature of the ensuing emotion. According to appraisal theory, then, we are insulted by a rival, perceive the insult as motivationally incongruent and the other person as to blame for it, and consequently become angry (or ourselves as to blame for it and consequently feel guilty). But emotions do not always unfold in such a reasonable way in practise despite what our superficial intuitions might seem to suggest.

Range of anger incidents

If we consider the full range of possible occasions for anger, rather than only those that are commonly represented in appraisal studies, it becomes difficult to sustain the view that they can all be encoded in terms of other-blame appraisals. Let me illustrate this point by reference to descriptions of situations in which people report becoming angry, collected from a series of my recent studies including those described above.

Of course, many of these reported instances of everyday anger fit quite neatly with the reasonable analysis offered by appraisal theory. Something specific happens that can be interpreted in terms of other-blame and people get angry about it. Consider the following two incidents, for example:

- Someone crashed into my car and wrote it off.
- Found out my ex-boyfriend had cheated on me while we were together.

However, even here, the isolation of a particular emotional event is not so clear as it might immediately seem. For example, was the respondent's immediate initial reaction to the impact in the first example, one of anger? Didn't this form of response evolve over time as the person worked her way through the unfolding situation? How was the news of the ex-boyfriend's cheating imparted in the second example? Was it out of the blue? Was it immediately accepted as true if there were no prior suspicion and so on? What initially seem to be simple localized events usually need some degree of temporal articulation for their emotional relevance to be established. Appraisal of other-blame may therefore not be a temporally delimited process, but may emerge over time as part of the actor's ongoing transaction (cf. Lazarus 1991, Parkinson 2001).

Although many reported anger events superficially followed this pattern of some specific misdemeanour or frustration, others have more explicit temporal articulation:

- My sister and I were shopping for clothes and she kept complaining that the clothes were wrong for her, too expensive etc.

- I was really busy; I had a lot of reading and notes to make before I went out, and my Mum was asking me to do something for her, then someone came round and delayed me from getting on with what I wanted to do, which made me late.

- I was in a bad mood anyway and loads of people were in my room watching telly and I was trying to concentrate and one of my flatmates would not stop talking really, really loudly.

In these latter situations, it is difficult to say exactly what event triggered the emotion, and to pinpoint exactly where the emotion is supposed to start. There is presumably a longstanding pattern of relationship in the first of these examples that sets the context for this specific incident. What is already in place is not only an appraisal but also a habitual mode of affective response. Similarly, in the third example, a previous mood state explicitly feeds into the blame appraisal and (perhaps directly) the emotion of anger too. Relatedly, whatever the emotion is about in these examples is not just some external event that happens to the individual (as in most psychological experiments into emotion) but rather an unfolding transaction with the physical and social world (cf. Lazarus 1991). The emotion does not arise in response to a specific event or its interpretation, but emerges from ongoing situated action. Since these situated actions already carry their own (developing) agenda, it is not necessary for a separate appraisal-emotion process to reset goal priorities.

All of the anger incidents mentioned so far are amenable to analysis in terms of other-blame even if this other-blame is not a simple cognitive mediator of the emotion. But people also report anger in situations when there is no-one else who could reasonably be held accountable for events. Consider the following incidents:

- Having to wake up early when really, really tired.

- I found out that one of my friends had been killed in a car crash, and I started to feel angry with him, and other people and I don't really know why.

- Whilst washing the dishes I began to feel angry. There was no specific event causing me to feel angry but thinking about my brother made me angrier.

One response to the apparent diversity of reported anger examples is to deny that there are any necessary common factors and that the episodes cluster loosely around a prototypical script (Russell and Fehr 1994). It certainly seems that any account treating other-accountability as intrinsic to anger appraisal (e.g., Ortony, Clore, and Collins 1988, Smith and Lazarus 1993) would need to reclassify some of these instances as pseudo-anger. Alternatively, it might be claimed that the appraiser often goes well beyond the information given, and attributes agency to impersonal forces (perhaps by invoking god or fate or whatever). This claim has a certain intuitive plausibility, since we do sometimes hit out at inanimate objects (e.g., think of Basil Fawlty berating then beating his broken down car, or recall the last time you swore at your computer). However, there is an issue here about whether any object-directed blame precedes the initiation of anger itself. Do we always anthropomorphise entities prior to our frustration with them? Or does our existing irritation make us want to hit out at something we can treat as if it were suffering as a consequence?

Contrary to prototype theory, my own view *is* that there is a common core to anger occasions, but at a more basic level than specified by appraisal theories. Two further examples help to clarify what this common core might be. The first is the procedure developed by Stemmler (1989) to induce 'real-life' anger so that its physiological correlates could be assessed:

> Anagrams were displayed for 5 s, and the first 15 items were solvable. Then unexpectedly, the task was interrupted, 'Listen, we can hardly understand you, although the amplifier's volume is already turned up to maximum. It would be best if you could speak louder!' The following anagram was solvable. Then in a brusque voice, a second interruption, 'Louder, please!' The next anagram was unsolvable. After the subject's answer, it was aggressively insisted, 'Can't you speak up?' (622)

Clearly, in this situation, there is someone who can be held accountable for the motivationally incongruent events that are happening. However, what seems to fuel the emotion is something to do with the implacable resistance of this person to any attempt to get through to them.

The second related example stems from findings that sustained arm restraint consistently produces anger-like reactions in very young infants (e.g., Camras et al. 1992, Watson 1929). Frijda's (1993) notion that the minimal condition for anger is 'acute goal interference' seems compatible with this and all other examples offered so far. To say that the infant has an articulated goal, however, buys into an account that assumes central executive control of action, and a more ecological formulation in terms of struggling against resistance is preferable. For anger to occur then, we need to be pursuing some action that is impeded by counterforce, so that effort is escalated in order to get through.

But isn't that simply frustration rather than anger per se? It does seem that social resistance (or at least resistance that can be reduced by social means) provides more prototypical cases of anger (as in the Stemmler example, above). In this regard, it is interesting to note that when subjected to arm restraint, 4-month-old infants mostly direct their communicative movements at the direct source of physical obstruction, the adult's hands. However, by the age of 7 months, their 'angry' faces are redirected to the face of the person doing the restraining (Campos, Campos, and Barrett 1989). What makes these infants genuinely angry in the latter situation may be the fact that the restriction can be released by the actions of another person. Indeed, Stenberg, Campos, and Emde (1983) report that 7-month-olds show more intense facial signals towards their mothers than towards strangers when restrained, probably because mothers are perceived as more likely to respond by releasing them. Anger, in short, may be a strategy for getting someone else to help with a restraining force, even though its more primitive developmental origins lie in acts of struggle themselves, rather than their communicative content.

This analysis bears comparison with Vygotsky's (1934/1986) argument that the meaning of instinctual impulses is transformed as a consequence of them entering the realm of human social interaction. For example, he argues that pointing as an intended act with an internalized meaning derives from a more basic behavior of reaching for something. This reaching is perceived by the caregiver as an indication of the child's inner desires, and the caregiver then co-operates with the child by giving it the object that was being reached for. The child thus learns that the initial act of stretching in the direction of an object often elicits its provision by the caregiver, and ultimately comes to use the movement intentionally in order to achieve this social rather than directly practical effect. Similarly, I would argue that the child's primitive struggle to get free changes its meaning as soon as the restrainer or someone else responds to it as an indication of desire or action tendency. At this stage, anger stops being simply a struggle against resistance, and becomes a request for release or assistance: 'Let me go!' or 'Help me with this!'

Crucially, the specific pragmatic meaning of anger depends on exactly how the initial primitive act of struggling against resistance is interpreted and evaluated (appraised) by caregivers. For example, there are cross-cultural differences in whether anger is considered a legitimate or illegitimate response (Briggs 1970, Stearns and Stearns 1986). There are also variations in how much individual desires are valued and respected (Markus and Kitayama 1991). Caregivers in different societies therefore react differently to an infant's perceived desires and struggles, some co-operating, some punishing, some simply continuing to resist. The specific form of emotion that emerges in these contexts would not always conform to a Western prototype of reasonable or justifiable anger.

My conclusion then is that the minimal precondition for anger is simply resistance stopping us from getting through (cf. Berkowitz 1993, Frijda 1993). This might be physical resistance (as when the door stays resolutely jammed however hard we push against it, refusing to co-operate with our need to get indoors), or it may be social resistance (when someone just will not listen or acknowledge our point, when we cannot get through to them, to coin an appropriate metaphor). However, because of our early experiences of struggling in specific interpersonal contexts, it is unusual to get angry without, at some stage, also appealing for help or release, even if the only possible audience for this appeal is god or fate. Further, this intrinsic pragmatic aspect means that anger may also occur when the physical or social environment does not offer resistance that would normally trigger intensification of struggle, but when another person can anyway help with whatever project is being pursued, or when someone else is getting in the way but anger is easier than otherwise pushing through.

Although some element of resistance seems close to a necessary condition for the emotion, this is not something that needs detection by some separate evolutionarily determined appraisal mechanism. Further, the emergence of interpersonal functions of anger in the context of specific cultural patterns of socialization means that the range of situations in which it occurs will differ, not because 'other-blame' is differentially decoded, but simple because different social effects occur as the emotion develops and when it is currently presented. Anger means different things and has different effects in different circumstances.

Let me be clear about what I have been saying so far. I do not mean to imply that specifically *unreasonable* emotions (of the sort described in the experiments referred to above) cannot, in principle, serve (or ever have served) adaptive functions. Naturally, reactions that seem to make no sense at the time may have a deeper function. However, as soon as emotions are sampled outside the confines of commonsense stereotypes, the wide variety of occasions for their occurrence makes it difficult to see any unitary set of cues or themes that might be extracted in order to elicit them. Often no coherent relational meaning seems to be specified in advance of starting to get emotional. This seems inconsistent with at least some views of the evolutionary functions of distinct emotions.

Another way of looking at this is with respect to optimizing the functionality of any specific emotional response. Is there really a specifiable set of relational themes that could be extracted to cover all the situations in which an emotion would be an adaptive response? Taking anger as an example, is preparation for attack or signaling a readiness to attack something that only or best improves chances of survival or reproduction when someone else is perceived as to blame? Clearly, there might some archetypal anger situations from which metaphorical generalizations are made, but even this does not allow for a simple detection strategy in terms of abstract thematic content.

Emotions as adaptive plans of action

Having considered the coherence of the appraisal structure that supposedly elicits emotions, I now turn to the specification of emotions themselves. From the point of view of most versions of appraisal theory, emotions are patterns of response that are structured to meet specific sets of functional demands. Having weighed up the evidence contained in the event, a plan is formulated for dealing with the challenge or problem identified. For example, according to Lazarus (1991) 'each kind of emotion comprises a distinctive cognitive, motor, and physiological response configuration that is defined by the common adaptational (psychological and physiological) requirement of the person–environment relationship, as these are appraised' (202). Thus, rather than seeing emotions as some specific feeling state (quale), theorists have concluded that emotions are response syndromes with some level of internal organization. In Lazarus's view, emotions are prepackaged and co-ordinated reactions whose structure is specified in advance by the relevant core relational theme. Similarly, Roseman (1996) argues: 'Appraisals guide the emotion system in selecting the particular emotion whose strategy is most likely to be adaptive in the type of situation that the person is facing' (108).

As mentioned earlier, however, whatever influence emotions might have on behavior, the connection cannot be entirely fixed and determinate. If it were, emotions would simply be reflexes without the flexibility that supposedly gives them their specific evolutionary advantage. So emotions prepare the organism for action but do not compel it to act. What exactly does this loose, contextually sensitive specification involve in practice?

A range of interrelated possibilities have been considered in this regard. First, there may be some aspects of emotional responding that do follow appraisal in a reflex-like manner, and somehow constrain other reactions. Ekman (1972), for example, argues that distinctive facial action programs are initiated by the occurrence of any of the so-called basic emotions. The main problem for this view is that we can apparently experience intense emotions without corresponding expressions showing on our faces even when there are no obvious countervailing forces like display rules in play. For example, Fernandez-Dols and Ruiz-Belda (1995, 1997) found that Olympic gold medallists did not smile immediately after winning their events unless there was someone else there to read their facial signals. However, it is still plausible that some of the processes contributing to emotional responses are reflex-like. The struggle against restrictive embrace in early anger, for example, may be a good candidate, as might components of responses to 'threat' stimuli (e.g., LeDoux, 1996; Robinson, 1998).

Most appraisal theorists, however, believe that the parameters shaping emotional action are specified at a more abstract level than simple reflexes. The central notion here is that of 'action readiness.' Emotions set the cognitive and/or physiological system in a mode that prepares it to engage in certain kinds of behavior (Frijda 1986). For anger, the action readiness mode presumably involves something like retaliation, acting in some way against the person who has been appraised as to blame for the motivationally congruent event that has happened. In common-sense terms, this seems superficially consistent with the urge to strike we sometimes experience when in a rage. Indeed, Frijda argues that one of the characteristics of emotional action tendencies is their control precedence. Emotions reprioritize our goals and impulses to fit with their own agenda (Oatley and Johnson-Laird 1987).

Like the idea of appraisals as core relational themes, the action readiness story only really hangs together up to the point where it attempts to specify behavior modes that apply across the range of occasions for any given emotion. There are many anger-inducing situations, for example, in which we do not strike out physically, and where striking out physically would clearly be dysfunctional. Of course, this point is not fatal for an evolutionary account of adaptive action readiness modes, because we can assume that one kind of action strategy originally brought a probabilistic rather than absolute advantage. Maybe it made sense to be prepared to fight when faced with an antagonist because this aided survival or reproductive success more often than not. The fact that a strategy that worked on average in the environment of evolutionary adaptiveness does not mean that it will work as commonly in contemporary settings.

But even if we simplify the ecological parameters within which our hunter-gatherer ancestors operated in a just-so fashion, it is hard to see a consistent mode of action readiness serving its function adequately. The reason is that it apparently lacks the necessary context sensitivity. Someone else blocking one's goals should only elicit anger if they are potentially weaker, or less prepared than oneself, if future co-operation is not important, and so on. No simplifying heuristic seems capable of taking into account enough of the moderating factors.

The other issue concerns how action readiness modes are actually specified and instantiated. Some theorists have argued that they represent specific preparation of the metabolism for certain kinds of physical or psychological demands. This resembles Cannon's (1927) notion that emotions are emergency situations in which vigorous activity is likely to be required. Energy is therefore released to necessary muscles by a sympathetic activation response. Appraisal theorists do not believe that generalized energy mobilization accompanies all emotions, but rather that specific metabolic responses are associated with particular emotions to support particular kinds of action (e.g., Smith 1989).

Evidence for this kind of autonomic specificity is inconsistent, despite more than half a century's worth of empirical investigations into this issue (see, e.g., Cacioppo *et al.* 1993, Stemmler 1989). At any rate, there are sound conceptual reasons for doubting whether such specificity is likely, related to some of the points made above. In the example of fear, when faced with a predator, does it always maximize survival to run, or even to do anything active at all? Sometimes it might work better to hide or stay absolutely still (each of these responses is commonly associated with fear). Given this range of responses, what kind of underlying structure for action could an autonomic response pattern actually provide? As Davidson (1994) argues: 'Fear can be associated with both fleeing and freezing, while anger is sometimes associated with approach movements (i.e., attack) and other times with withdrawal tendencies. The autonomic supports for these different forms of each emotion should differ considerably. For example, cardiovascular mobilization should be greater during fleeing than during freezing' (239).

Similar arguments apply to the claim that emotions reset goals or motivational agendas at a more abstract, cognitive level. For example, Roseman (1996) attempted to specify 'emotivations' characteristic of each particular emotions. Fear, in his view involves a goal described as 'Get to safety, prevent' and an integrating strategy: 'prepare to move away from or stop moving toward it.' The conjunction contained in this description already seems to imply that there is no unitary agenda underlying this emotion. Other emotivations are phrased in such abstract terms that it is hard to see them providing anything but the loosest guidance for action. Anger, for example, sets a command of moving against another person, but precisely how this is to be achieved is not specified. In order to shape the specific response, the would-be actor presumably needs to take into account all kinds of contextual factors. Once this has been done, one wonders why the agenda needed setting in advance anyway. Furthermore, as we have seen above, many of the common occasions of anger involve no specific other we could conceivably move against in the first place.

The central lesson here is that in order to serve their obvious variety of functions across the broad range of possible circumstances, emotions cannot be tightly specified in advance. As Cosmides and Tooby (2001) acknowledge: '... some recurrent situations have less structure (i.e., they share fewer properties in common), and so the emotion mode makes fewer highly specialized adjustments, imposes fewer specialized and compelling interpretations and behavioral inclinations and so on' (101).

Of course, I don't want to argue that the behavior associated with any given emotion is infinitely flexible. Some things may be clearly inappropriate or non-viable when angry, for example. However, what determines appropriateness does not seem to be a preset agenda or physiologically implemented action readiness mode, but rather an attentiveness to whatever circumstance provoked the emotion and a sensitivity to its particular demands and characteristics. Further, many of the relevant goals are often already in place before the emotion itself occurs. When someone obstructs my progress, I am already heading in a specific direction, and my anger simply reflects an intensification of my attempt to get there.

If emotions are not wholly specified in advance, at least some of their structure must derive from the contingencies of the unfolding interaction. In my view, emotional modes of action are often pieced together over time bottom-up in continual responsiveness to the pressures and affordances of their developing ecology. What tracks the course of ongoing involvements is not any appraisal registering and recording conclusions which are integrated prior to generation of emotion, but rather the immediate effects of each aspect of the ongoing involvement with the transaction. For example, struggle against counterforce leads to changing patterns of muscle tension, ongoing communicative displays are negotiated dynamically over time and these components coalesce into a pattern of emotion without the need for central integration. (Of course, there are also constraints on subprocesses arising from their mutual interactions). So we don't need a separate appraisal process to record conclusions and piece them together into emotional themes because the emotional meaning is directly represented by the embodied collection and concatenation of interconnective subprocesses. Structure derives from dynamic situated action and internal interdependences rather than from any central executive process.

However, there are times when there may be strategic, top-down control of emotional components. Even here, though, it is not necessary to register any emotion-specific core relational theme in advance. Emotion plans are selected and implemented not to fit an abstractly defined emotion meaning but to fulfil specific practical requirements in their given setting. We have to learn when and where emotional responses of the various kinds are appropriate.

I have argued that any prestructuring of emotional response syndromes derives as much from socialization as from genetic determination. There are good adaptive reasons for this. Any prespecified response strategy has a limited range of functional application. Fleeing, for example, works with certain classes of predators, but when new threats arrive on the scene its appropriateness may rapidly disappear. When survival-relevant situations change quickly or are location-specific, what is required is a system with inbuilt context-sensitivity. Rather than having loosely specified response modes that are unalterable in their constitution, why not instead equip the animal with the potential to assemble strategies on the basis of actual and vicarious experience. Many of human beings' survival advantages apparently derive from their neoteny. Humans spend more of their lives relatively helpless, being cared for by others than almost any other terrestrial organism. This enables cultural transmission of tools, symbols, practices that are specifically appropriate to (historically and geographically) local circumstances. Humans do not usually face situations that are directly survival- or reproduction-relevant until they have been well-socialized so they do not need to be hard-wired to deal (relatively inflexibly) with them.

Which aspects of emotions are preadapted?

Humans do not enter the world as blank slates. They are also not automata preset to react in a machine-like manner to all specific inputs. Everybody accepts that both these extreme formulations are false. Between them however lie a range of alternatives about what is inherited and what is not (cf. Parkinson 1998). I am certainly prepared to acknowledge that many aspects of emotional function are genetically programmed, but I do not think that emotions themselves spring forth fully formed even as loose specifications for action. Certain events are inherently rewarding and others bring unavoidable pain (e.g., Rolls 1999). We start out with an urge to move, to be active, and impedance of this leads to struggle (perhaps because persistent physical restriction is intrinsically punishing). More importantly, however, we are specifically attuned to pick up information and copy movements of the most vivid and dynamic objects in our earliest environment, namely other people. Their reactions to our reflex responses initiate us into emotional society and train us from our earliest moments in the art of emotional conduct. In such a view, it is not emotional syndromes that are inherited but the conditions for their socialization.

The appraisal account sees emotions as serving practical action, facilitating adaptive response to events that hinder or facilitate progress towards goals. However, emotions are also about negotiating a complex and changing interpersonal reality. We present emotions to one another to warn or cajole, persuade, punish, congratulate. We use them to endorse shared values or to contest others' opinions. These functions are not secondary to some original practical function, even if the action components have practical origins. I turn my nose up to indicate a metaphorical bad smell, but as Darwin (1872/1998) acknowledged, the movement itself long ceased to have this direct purpose.

Summary

Appraisal theory's story, in essence, is that the various components of emotional response syndromes are stitched together over the course of evolutionary history, and picked out by natural selection because of the survival or reproductive advantage they provide. I have argued that some of the structure of emotional response derives from non-universal socialization, and that other aspects derive from the on-line constraints and affordances of unfolding emotional situations themselves. By prepackaging the emotional response, appraisal theory draws attention away from the processes whereby real emotions are structured over recent and current history.

One of the attractions of evolutionary accounts is that complex and multifarious outcomes are explained not in terms of pre-given design but by pressures that shaped events over time. It might therefore seem paradoxical that recent theories in evolutionary psychology assume that the psychological system has built-in plans and strategies. The mind does not need to know fully in advance when and how to get emotional because the body's movements are pushed and pulled by the forces directly bearing on it.

References

Arnold, M. B. (1960). *Emotion and personality: psychological aspects*, Vol. 1. Columbia University Press, New York.

Berkowitz, L. (1993). *Aggression: its causes, consequences, and control*. McGraw-Hill, New York.

Briggs, J. (1970). *Never in anger: portrait of an Eskimo family*. Harvard University Press, Cambridge, MA.

Campos, J. J., Campos, R. G., and Barrett, K. C. (1989). Emergent themes in the study of emotional development and emotion regulation. *Developmental Psychology*, **25**, 394–402.

Cacioppo, J. T., Klein, D. J., Berntson, G. G., and Hatfield, E. (1993). The psychophysiology of emotion. In *Handbook of emotions* (ed. M. Lewis and J. M. Haviland), pp. 119–42. Guilford, New York.

Camras, L. A., Oster, H., Campos, J. J., Miyake, K., and Bradshaw, D. (1992). Japanese and American children's responses to arm restraint. *Developmental Psychology*, **28**, 578–83.

Cannon, W. B. (1927). The James-Lange theory of emotions: A critical examination and an alternative theory. *American Journal of Psychology*, **39**, 106–24.

Cosmides, L. and Tooby, J. (2001). Evolutionary psychology and the emotions. In *Handbook of emotions*, 2nd edition (ed. M. Lewis and J. M. Haviland-Jones), pp. 91–115. Guilford, New York.

Darwin, C. (1872/1998). *The expression of the emotions in man and animals*, (3rd edn). HarperCollins, London.

Davidson, R. J. (1994). Complexities in the search for emotion-specific physiology. In *The nature of emotion* (ed. P. Ekman and R. J. Davidson), pp. 237–42. Oxford University Press, Oxford.

Ekman, P. (1972). Universals and cultural differences in facial expressions of emotion. In *Nebraska symposium on motivation*, Vol. 19 (ed. J. K. Cole), pp. 207–83. University of Nebraska Press, Lincoln, NE.

Fernandez-Dols, J.-M. and Ruiz-Belda, M.-A. (1995). Are smiles a sign of happiness? Gold medal winners at the Olympic games. *Journal of Personality and Social Psychology*, **69**, 1113–9.

Fernandez-Dols, J. M. and Ruiz-Belda, M. A. (1997). Spontaneous facial behavior during intense emotional episodes: artistic truth and optical truth. In *The psychology of facial expression* (ed. J. A. Russell and J. M. Fernandez-Dols), pp. 255–94. Cambridge University Press, Cambridge.

Frijda, N. H. (1986). *The emotions*. Cambridge University Press, Cambridge.

Frijda, N. H. (1993). The place of appraisal in emotion. *Cognition and Emotion*, **7**, 357–87.

James, W. (1898). *The principles of psychology*, Vol. 2. Macmillan, London.

Lazarus, R. S. (1991). *Emotion and adaptation*. Oxford University Press, New York.

LeDoux, J. E. (1996). *The emotional brain*. Simon & Schuster, New York.

Markus, H. R. and Kitayama, S. (1991). Culture and the self: Implications for cognition, emotion, and motivation. *Psychological Review*, **98**, 224–53.

Oatley, K., and Johnson-Laird, P. N. (1987). Towards a cognitive theory of emotions. *Cognition and Emotion*, **1**, 29–50.

Parkinson, B. (1997). Untangling the appraisal-emotion connection. *Personality and Social Psychology Review*, **1**, 62–79.

Parkinson, B. (1998). What we think about when we think about emotions. *Cognition and Emotion*, **12**, 615–24.

Parkinson, B. (1999). Relations and dissociations between appraisal and emotion reports in reasonable and unreasonable anger and guilt. *Cognition and Emotion*, **13**, 347–85.

Parkinson, B. and Roper, A. (2002). *Comparing reasonable and unreasonable anger: A prospective study.* Poster presented at the XIIth conference of the International Society for Research on Emotion, Cuenca, July 2002.

Robinson, M. D. (1998). Running from William James' bear: a review of preattentive mechanisms and their contributions to emotional experience. *Cognition and Emotion,* **12,** 667–96.

Rolls, E. (1999). *The brain and emotion.* Oxford University Press, Oxford.

Roseman, I. J. (1979, September). *Cognitive aspects of emotion and emotional behaviour.* Paper presented at the 87th Annual Convention of the American Psychological Association, New York.

Roseman, I. J. (1996). Why these appraisals? Anchoring appraisal models to research on emotional behavior and related response systems. In *ISRE '96: Proceedings of the IXth Conference of the International Society for Research on Emotions* (ed. N. H. Frijda), pp. 106–10. ISRE Publications, Toronto.

Roseman (2001). A model of appraisal in the emotion system. In *Appraisal processes in emotion: Theory, research, application* (K. R. Scherer, A. Schorr, and T. Johnstone), pp. 68–91. Oxford University Press, Oxford.

Russell, J. A. and Fehr, B. (1994). Fuzzy concepts in a fuzzy hierarchy: varieties of anger. *Journal of Personality and Social Psychology,* **67,** 186–205.

Scherer, K. R. (1999). Appraisal theory. In *Handbook of cognition and emotion* (ed. T. Dalgleish and M. Power), pp. 637–63. Wiley, London.

Scherer, K.R. (2001). Appraisal considered as a process of multilevel stimulus checking. In *Appraisal processes in emotion: theory, research, application* (ed. K. R. Scherer, A. Schorr, and T. Johnstone), pp. 92–120. Oxford University Press, Oxford.

Smith, C. A. (1989). Dimensions of appraisal and physiological response in emotion. *Journal of Personality and Social Psychology,* **56,** 339–53.

Smith, C. A. and Ellsworth, P. C. (1985). Patterns of cognitive appraisal in emotion. *Journal of Personality and Social Psychology,* **48,** 813–38.

Smith, C. A. and Ellsworth, P. C. (1987). Patterns of appraisal and emotion related to taking an exam. *Journal of Personality and Social Psychology,* **52,** 475–488.

Smith, C. A., Haynes, K. N., Lazarus, R. S. and Pope, L. K. (1993). In search of the "hot" cognitions: attributions, appraisals, and their relation to emotion. *Journal of Personality and Social Psychology,* **65,** 916–29.

Smith, C. A. and Lazarus, R. S. (1993). Appraisal components, core relational themes, and the emotions. *Cognition and Emotion,* **7,** 233–69.

Stearns, C. Z. and Stearns, P. N. (1986). *Anger: the struggle for emotional control in America's history.* University of Chicago Press, Chicago.

Stemmler, G. (1989). The autonomic differentiation of emotions revisited: convergent and discriminant validation. *Psychophysiology,* **26,** 617–32.

Stenberg, C.R., Campos, J.J. and Emde, R.N. (1983). The facial expression of anger in seven-month-old infants. *Child Development,* **54,** 178–84.

Vygotsky, L. S. (1934/1986). *Thought and language.* MIT Press, Cambridge, MA.

PART III

EVOLUTION AND THE RATIONALITY OF EMOTION

EVOLUTION, CULTURE AND THE IRRATIONALITY OF THE EMOTIONS

CHANDRA SEKHAR SRIPADA AND STEPHEN STICH

Introduction

For about 2500 years, from Plato's time until the closing decades of the 20th century, the dominant view was that emotions are quite distinct from the processes of rational thinking and decision-making, and are often a major impediment to those processes. But in recent years this orthodoxy has been challenged in a number of ways. Damasio (1994) has made a forceful case that the traditional view, which he has dubbed *Descartes' Error*, is quite wrong, because emotions play a fundamental role in rational decision-making. When the systems underlying the emotions do not function properly, Damasio maintains, rational decision-making breaks down. Other theorists, most notably Robert Frank (1988), have argued that if we view the emotions through the longer lens of evolutionary theory, we can see that much of what looked to be irrational in the emotions is actually part of an effective strategy for achieving agents' goals and maximizing their reproductive success. In the wake of this and other recent work, the pendulum of received opinion has swung in the other direction. The emotions are now increasingly regarded as inherently rational, as Frank maintains, and as important components of other rational processes.

One of our goals in this paper is to argue that the pendulum has swung too far, and to push it back a bit in the other direction. Though we will not disagree with either Damasio or Frank, we argue that their work tells only part of the story about the rationality of the emotions. Emotions, we will maintain, are intrinsically linked to a mentally represented set of norms, goals and values which we call a *value structure*. Moreover, there are good reasons—indeed good *evolutionary* reasons—to think that the contents of value structures will often be *mal*adaptive. When they are, the emotions and the behavior they lead to will typically be *ir*rational.

The paper is divided into four sections. In Section 1, we sketch several quite different accounts of rationality, and focus on the account that we propose to use in assessing the rationality of the emotions. In Section 2 we will introduce the notion of a value structure and explain the central role that value structures play in many recent theories about the mental mechanisms subserving the emotions. In Section 3, we ask how value structures arise. There are, we maintain, three sources from which value structures arise: genes, the environment, and culture. In Section 4 we argue that each of the three sources which influence the formation of value structures can give rise to value structures with importantly irrational components. These are illustrated with some quite varied examples, drawn from the literature on attitudes toward violence, food taboos and psychopathology. Some of the most interesting reasons for thinking that value structures and emotions will often be irrational are suggested by recent work on gene-culture co-evolution by Robert Boyd, Peter Richerson and others. To date, this work has made relatively little impact on research on the emotions. A second major goal of the paper is to argue for the importance of Boyd and Richerson's work in this area.

Some approaches to rationality

As Samuels *et al.* (2003) have argued, accounts of rationality can be usefully divided into two major categories. *Deontological accounts* assess the rationality of instances or patterns of reasoning and decision-making by appeal to normative rules or principles like those of logic and decision theory. In *consequentialist accounts*, by contrast, instances or patterns of reasoning and decision-making are evaluated by attending to their consequences—the states of affairs they lead to—in one or another environment, with different consequentialist accounts focusing on different sorts of consequences and environments. In reliabilist epistemology, true belief is the consequence that looms large in the assessment of rationality, while in both pragmatist epistemology and decision theory the focus is on desire satisfaction or the maximization of subjective utility.[1] Individual (or occasionally group) well-being is another sort of outcome that a consequentialist account of rationality might seek to maximize. The notion of well-being is, notoriously, much more philosophically controversial and much harder to pin down than the notion of subjective utility. But it is clearly a distinct notion since, sometimes at least, what people

---

1 For a defense of reliabilist epistemology, see Goldman (1986); for a defense of pragmatist epistemology, see Stich (1990).

want does not contribute to their well-being (Kahneman *et al.* 1999). Inclusive fitness is yet another property that consequentialist theorists have thought to be important. When evolutionary psychologists like Cosmides and Tooby assess the rationality of belief-forming and decision-making processes, it is clear that what they often have in mind is an evaluation of the contribution that the processes make to the inclusive fitness of those who employ them (Cosmides and Tooby 1994). Similarly, the notion of 'ecological rationality' that is used in the work of Gerd Gigerenzer and his collaborators (Gigerenzer *et al.* 1999, Gigerenzer 2000) is sometimes best understood as a consequentialist notion where what is being maximized is inclusive fitness in some environment. Consequentialist assessments of the rationality of a psychological mechanism or process will, of course, often be quite sensitive to the environment in which the mechanism is assumed to operate. One obvious choice of environment is the one in which the mechanism is actually embedded. For other purposes, however, a theorist might focus on what Sperber (1996) has called the 'proper' environment—the environment in which the mechanism in question evolved. For still other purposes, accounts of rationality might focus on one or another sort of idealized environment in which certain theoretically important assumptions are assumed to obtain (Goldman 1986). The taxonomy of accounts of rationality that we have sketched is summarized in Fig. 7.1.

In exploring the rationality of the emotions in this paper, we will be primarily concerned with the consequentialist notion of rationality that links it to inclusive fitness in the actual environment—the square labelled 'A' in Fig. 7.1.

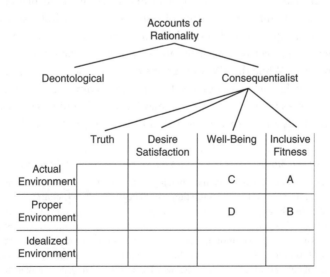

Figure 7.1 A taxonomy of accounts of rationality.

We adopt this notion of rationality for several reasons. First, as argued in Samuels *et al.* (2003), deontological accounts of rationality are problematic in a variety of ways. Second, much discussion of the rationality of the emotions, in recent years, has explicitly or implicitly relied on some version of a consequentialist/inclusive fitness account of rationality (Tooby and Cosmides 1990, Frank 1988, Fessler 2001). Third, assessments of rationality in accordance with the account we will be focusing on often (though not always!) roughly coincide with assessments that would result if we instead used inclusive fitness in the proper environment (square B) or well-being in the actual or proper environment (squares C and D), and when these assessments diverge significantly, there is often something important to be learned. Finally, and perhaps most importantly, sociobiologists, human behavioral ecologists and other advocates of robust versions of adaptationism maintain that the existence of maladaptive mental dispositions or processes is unlikely on evolutionary grounds.[2] This paper can be viewed, inter alia, as an extended argument against this view.

Emotions and value structures

In this section we will explain our notion of a *value structure* and indicate why we think that value structures, or something quite like them, play a role in the account of the emotions offered by a number of leading researchers. We will start with Paul Ekman's highly influential affect program theory. Affect programs, according to Ekman, are universal, largely automated (or involuntary) suites of coordinated emotional responses subserved by innate psychological and physiological mechanisms present in all normal members of the species. In humans, the suite of responses often includes an emotion specific facial expression, characteristic autonomic nervous system activity, characteristic subjective experience and emotion-specific action tendencies (Ekman 1992). While the affect programs themselves are taken to be innate and universal, Ekman's work on display rules soon convinced him that emotional responses further 'downstream' may be strongly influenced by culturally local beliefs and norms (Ekman 1972).[3] For our purposes, what is most

------

2 See Laland and Brown (2002), chs. 3 and 4 for a useful overview of the relevant literature.

3 In one experiment Ekman found that when Japanese subjects were shown unpleasant films in the presence of an authority figure they would begin the muscle contractions required to produce the facial expressions of negative emotions, but then immediately mask these expressions with a polite smile. American subjects, by contrast, made no attempt to mask the expression of negative emotions, nor did Japanese subjects when they viewed the distressing films alone. Ekman and his colleagues explained these findings by positing the existence of culturally local 'display rules' which can override or radically alter the pattern of emotional expression after an affect program has begun to unfold (Ekman 1972).

important is the question of what happens 'upstream,' that is, what determines the elicitation of an emotion episode. On Ekman's account, affect programs are typically triggered by an innate 'appraisal mechanism' that selectively attends to external and internal stimuli indicating that the emotion is appropriate. It is uncertain whether Ekman ever thought that there are some stimuli which the appraisal mechanism is built to respond to directly, without the mediation of other cognitive states and processes. By the mid-1990s, however, Ekman had clearly adopted the view that much of the activity of the appraisal mechanism is affected both by culturally local beliefs and by culturally local norms, values and goals (Ekman 1994). The mental representation of these norms, values and goals are what we call a value structure.[4]

Other researchers, influenced by Ekman, have elaborated his notion of an appraisal mechanism in useful ways. Lazarus (1994) suggests that each emotion is linked to its own innate principle, which he calls a 'core relational theme,' specifying the conditions under which it is appropriate to have the emotion. The innate specifications of these conditions are quite abstract, however, and thus lots of culturally local information is required to determine when the conditions are satisfied. The core relational theme that Lazarus proposes for anger, for example, is 'a demeaning offense against me and mine'. Obviously, there is no way of knowing when such an offense has occurred without knowing a fair amount about locally prevailing norms and values. Synthesizing the ideas of a number of theorists, Robert Levenson has proposed a 'biocultural model' of the emotions, depicted in Fig. 7.2, which 'reflects a confluence between innate and learned influences' (Levenson 1994, 125). The 'innate hardwired' parts of the model—corresponding roughly to Ekman's affect program mechanisms—are in the center of the diagram, between the black boxes. Emotion prototypes are the equivalent of Lazarus's core relational themes. The black boxes, indicating the appraisal system and the display and feeling rules are the 'primary loci of cultural influences' and can access the agent's beliefs and values, many of which will be culturally local. In Fig. 7.3, we have elaborated on Levenson's model to make the role of beliefs and value structures in this account more explicit.

The idea that emotions are typically elicited by appraisal processes that are sensitive to the contents of a person's value structure is endorsed by theorists who approach the emotions from a variety of theoretical perspectives.

---

4 There is much more to be said about the distinctions between norms, values and goals. But the details are a long story which we don't have time for here.

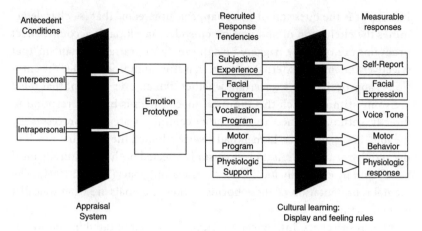

Figure 7.2 Levenson's Bio-Cultural Model of the Emotions. Permission sought.

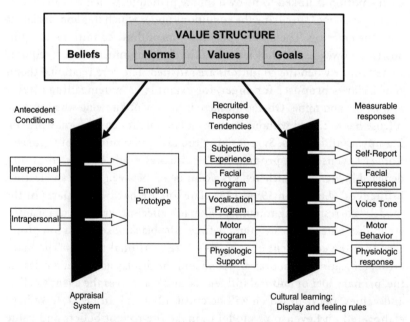

Figure 7.3 An elaboration of Levenson's model in which the role of beliefs and value structures are made explicit.

Nico Frijda, Klaus Scherer, Keith Oatley, and Andrew Ortony and his colleagues and many other leading theorists have all emphasized that the goals, norms and values that constitute a person's value structure are crucial in the antecedents of emotion (for a review see Scherer 1988). Of course, there are many important differences among these theorists.[5] What is important for our purposes is that these theorists *agree* that value structures—norms, values and goals—do, in fact, play a crucial role in the psychological processes that elicit emotions.

It might be thought that the widely discussed work of Joseph LeDoux is an important exception to the claim that leading researchers recognize the role of value structures in triggering emotions, since his work shows that there are emotion-triggering pathways which are not mediated by higher cognitive processes at all. LeDoux maintains that some emotions are elicited by a 'low-road' pathway which bypasses appraisal mechanisms and value structures altogether (LeDoux 1996). In claiming that value structures play an important role in the antecedents of emotions, we do not deny that there are alternate routes to the elicitation of emotions such as the route that LeDoux has characterized. Moreover LeDoux himself views appraisal mechanisms as part of the explanation of what establishes some instances of low-road circuits. So even LeDoux would endorse our contention that value structures play a crucial role in the antecedents of many (though not necessarily all) emotions.

What we have argued so far is that there is a broad consensus in support of the claim that the antecedents of many emotion episodes (though perhaps not all) are tightly linked to aspects of people's value structures. In the following two sections, we will argue that some of the sources which causally influence the contents of value structures can (and do) lead to the production of *maladaptive* value structure components. We will also argue that these maladaptive value structure components can generate maladaptive (and thus irrational) emotions.

Three sources of the contents of value structures

There has been little systematic work aimed at explaining how the contents of value structures arise. Following Boyd and Richerson (1985), we propose that it is useful to distinguish three importantly different sources which contribute to the contents of value structures: genes, the environment and culture.

---

5 For example, they disagree about the exact sequences of cognitive evaluations which occur during the appraisal process (Scherer 1993, Ortony et al 1988), about how appraisals might be neurally implemented (Chewlos and Oatley 1994) and even about the methods by which such questions could be answered (Ekman 1994). There is also considerable disagreement about how emotions should be typed, with Scherer and Ortony et al. claiming that appraisal principles are constitutive of emotion types, Frijda (1986) favoring an approach which also relies on emotion-specific action tendencies and Ekman favoring the individuation of emotions in terms of structural mechanisms. We will not take any sides in these important disputes.

In both this section and the one that follows, we will elaborate on these sources and offer examples of value structure elements that could well have originated from them. We propose this taxonomy only as a rough first pass at addressing the largely unasked question of why value structures end up having the contents they do. It is important to keep in mind that in distinguishing these three sources, we are not claiming they are independent, and we stress that they can and often do *jointly* contribute to the formation of elements of value structures. With this caveat in place, we now turn to the task of clarifying and explicating the sources from which the contents of value structures arise.

It is clear that *genes* causally contribute to the formation of some elements of value structures since genes play an important and wide-ranging role in phenogenesis more generally. In some cases, genes play the predominant role in causally contributing to some phenotypic outcome, and we will follow a standard practice in referring to such outcomes as *innate*. There is much dispute about how best to understand innateness (Samuels 2002, Griffiths 2002). However, on any reasonable account, core cases of innateness include phenotypic characteristics such as color vision and blood type, and disorders such as phenylketonuria. We will be discussing some innate psychological traits which contribute to the contents of value structures in the next section.

A second source of causal influences which shape the contents of value structures is the *environment*. Boyd and Richerson use the term *individual learning* as a label for a cluster of processes by which people acquire and modify beliefs, skills and elements of their value structures by interacting with, and getting feedback from, the (non-social) environment. Examples of individual learning processes include classical conditioning, trial and error instrumental learning and various forms of inductive learning. In individual learning, interaction with the environment can lead to changes in a number of different kinds of mental states, including both beliefs and preferences. For example, a person may try many different routes to work and discover which is shortest (change in belief) or may try all the different flavors of Baskin Robbins ice cream and find out which one she likes best (change in preferences).

The last and probably most important source of causal influences which shape the contents of value structures is *culture*. We define culture in terms of its relation to a transmission process often called *social learning*. In social learning, a mental state in one person causally contributes to the formation of a mental state in another person, where the latter mental state *resembles* the former.[6] Two paradigmatic examples of social learning processes are *teaching* and

---

6 There are a number of ways in which the notion of resemblance can be formalized and made more precise. For the purposes of this paper, an intuitive notion of resemblance will suffice.

imitation. Social learning is important because it can lead to the transmission of information such as beliefs, values and skills between individuals and across generations. In this respect, social learning differs profoundly from individual learning, since the products of individual learning will die with the learner unless some social learning process is introduced. Following Boyd and Richerson, we view *culture* as the body of information residing in the minds of people that was acquired by social learning. We think it is plausible to suppose that social learning contributes significantly to the formation of peoples' value structures, so value structures are intimately connected with culture.

Culture understood in this way can be usefully viewed as an *inheritance system.* The cultural inheritance system can best be explained by analogy with the more familiar genetic inheritance system. In the genetic inheritance system, there is a statistically defined pattern of resemblance between biological parents and children—for example, on average, taller parents have taller children and shorter parents have shorter children—and parents causally contribute to this resemblance by means of well-known genetic mechanisms. The existence of mechanisms which produce patterns of resemblance between individuals, whether based on genes or any other process, is the crucial feature which defines the highly general and useful notion of an inheritance system.

In any inheritance system, a range of forces can potentially act to produce evolutionary change in the distribution of the characteristics of individuals in a population over time. A full specification of these forces depends on the particular structure and properties of the system. For example, one important force which can operate in the genetic inheritance system is *natural selection.* Other forces which might be potentially operative include genetic drift, recombination and migration.

The case of culture is formally analogous to the genetic case. In the social learning process, a mental state of a *cultural parent* causally facilitates the formation of a type-similar mental state in a *cultural child.* As a result, there is a statistically defined pattern of resemblance between cultural parents and children. For example, on average, the religious beliefs and practices of Muslim children resemble those of their Muslim parents, while the beliefs and practices of Mormon children resemble those of their Mormon parents. Thus, culture can be viewed as an inheritance system, with social learning providing the mechanism of inheritance.[7]

As in the case of the genetic inheritance system, a range of forces can potentially act on the cultural inheritance system. The list of forces which can

---

7 It is important to keep in mind that 'cultural parents' need not be biologically related to (nor older than) their 'cultural children.' Moreover, with respect to a given trait, a cultural child may have one, several or many cultural parents.

operate on the cultural system is different than the analogous list for the genetic system because while the cultural system exhibits many properties which are similar to the genetic system, it also exhibits many which are unique and have no parallel in the genetic system. Like the genetic system, change in the cultural system is *cumulative*. Many cultural variants, for example, the technologies of kayak building or watch-making,[8] arose by something like the familiar Darwinian process of descent with modification over extended stretches of time. Unlike the genetic system, however, in the cultural system novel cultural variants can emerge by a *directed process*. A person can create a novel cultural variant whose cultural fitness is better than one would expect were that variant generated by chance.[9] Furthermore, these novel variants are heritable in that they can be transmitted by social learning. The cumulative and directed nature of the cultural inheritance system makes it an enormously powerful tool for generating innovations that have enabled humans to adapt to environmental change and to survive in a wider variety of environments than any other animal species. Indeed, cumulative social learning is *uniquely human*. There are only a few good examples of social learning in other species, and no other species exhibits the sort of cumulative social learning that humans do (Henrich and Boyd 1998).

Sometimes the social learning process is *unbiased*—an existing cultural variant is picked at random. However, a unique feature of the cultural system is that often social learning is mediated by important and powerful biases. A bias is a process that determines which cultural variant a person will adopt, and there are several possible kinds of biases that a person may utilize. In *direct bias*, a person tries out the different variants that are available and sees which one she prefers. In *indirect bias*, a person selects a cultural variant based on some feature or marker that characterizes the variant. There are two important kinds of indirect biases which we will be focusing on. In *conformist bias*, a person adopts a variant that is common in his or her environment. In *prestige bias*, a person adopts a variant exhibited by a high prestige person.[10]

We have now completed our taxonomy of the sources from which the contents of value structures arise and distinguished three principal sources: genes,

8   Two of Boyd and Richerson's favorite examples!

9   Analogous to genetic fitness, the cultural fitness of a cultural variant is the variant's chances of surviving and being socially transmitted.

10   Our terminology here differs slightly from Boyd and Richerson's; as they use the term, prestige bias counts as an 'indirect bias' but conformist bias does not.

the environment and culture. As we have noted, these three sources need not be independent; rather, they will often interact in jointly contributing to some aspect of phenotype. Indeed, such interaction occurs in many familiar cases such as language learning and moral development. But despite the fact that they interact in many domains, there are a number of reasons why it is important to keep these three sources of causal influence separate, at least conceptually. One reason emerges when constructing models of genetic and cultural evolution in which all three sources play a role. As we have noted, genes, the environment and culture have different properties (for example, genes and culture can exhibit different inheritance structures). Because of these differences, causal influences arising from each source contribute in very different ways to the overall population-level dynamics which such models attempt to capture (Boyd and Richerson 1985). For our purposes, another reason for distinguishing these three sources is that contributions from each source can (and often do) '*fail*' independently of the others. By 'fail,' we mean that causal influences originating from these sources end up contributing to the production of *maladaptive* phenotypic outcomes. By distinguishing these three sources from which the contents of value structures arise and studying how contributions from each might independently fail, we can gain a deeper understanding of how value structures for a single individual, or for a population of individuals in a community, can come to have maladaptive elements, leading to emotions which are (in our sense) irrational.

Maladaptive value structures and irrational emotions

We suggest that there are two basic ways in which the contributions from genes, the environment or culture might end up producing maladaptive elements of value structures. For want of better names, we will refer to these two kinds of failure as *failure due to inertia* and *failure due to inevitable misfiring*. We will clarify what these two kinds of failure amount to as we proceed. Since we propose that there are three basic sources from which elements of value structures arise, and two ways in which the contribution from these sources might fail, the result is a two by three matrix as shown in Fig. 4. Our main task in this section is to fill in this matrix with examples that plausibly illustrate cases in which the contributions from these three sources end up producing maladaptive elements of value structures and irrational emotions. Because space is limited, we will not try to fill in every box; we will leave 2 and 4 empty. We are inclined to think that the remaining four boxes in our matrix are in many ways the most interesting. The examples to be used are indicated in Fig. 7.4.

Sources of the Contents of Value Structures

		Genes	Environment	Culture
Phenomena Generating Maladaptive Value Structures	Inertia	1 Specific Phobias	2	3 Cultures of Honor
	Inevitable Misfires	4	5 Garcia Aversions	6 Food Taboos

Figure 7.4 Contribution from genes, the environment or culture might end up producing maladaptive elements of value structures via inertia or via inevitable misfires.

4.1

We begin with box 1—inertial failure in the genetic system. The idea behind genetic inertia is quite simple: Natural selection operating on genetic variation can be quite slow and phenotypic change often requires extended periods of time. Thus, even though natural selection may have produced phenotypic variants adaptive in an ancestral environment, as environments change there is substantial scope for mismatches between an organism's phenotype and the phenotype that would be most adaptive in the current environment. When such a mismatch occurs, we say it is due to *genetic inertia*. This theme is often emphasized in the evolutionary psychology literature. Indeed, the importance of genetic inertia is a point on which evolutionary psychologists and socio-biologists (or human behavioral ecologists) differ sharply (Tooby and Cosmides 1990, Laland and Brown 2002). We have suggested that genes causally contribute to the formation of some elements of value structures, and it is plausible that one way in which these elements might fail to be adaptive is due to the operation of genetic inertia. We believe that certain kinds of specific phobias illustrate genetic inertia leading to maladaptive elements of people's value structures and irrational emotions.

Specific phobias are psychiatric disorders characterized by pathological experience of the emotion of fear. We propose that at least some phobias arise from *innate* fears. Plausible candidates for innate fears are those directed at recurrent threats faced by human ancestors. The underlying adaptive logic is that an innate and rapid fear response to a recurrent threat would have conferred a selective advantage on human ancestors who possessed such a trait.

Some specific situations that are plausible candidates for being recurrent threats to human ancestors, and thus triggers for innate fears, include the following: being constrained in a small space without clear means of leaving, being near snakes, being at a great height from the ground, being alone in open spaces far from home, being near blood or injuries and being near large numbers of unfamiliar individuals. Indeed, there is significant evidence that fears triggered by these situations are, in fact, substantially innate (see Marks 1987).

Innate fears can have a wide-ranging impact on behavior by contributing to the acquisition of elements of value structures. In some cases, these value structure elements can be quite maladaptive. For example, a person with a particularly strong innate fear of closed spaces will typically, over time, come to acquire a host of *avoidances*, that is goals and preferences for avoiding situations or activities which involve closed spaces, as elements of their value structures. In ancestral environments, these value structure elements might have been directed at such things as deep caves or dense underbrush, and were presumably adaptive. However, in modern environments, strong fear of closed spaces can lead to avoidances towards elevators, subways, phone booths and a host of other places and activities. Such avoidances, when they are sufficiently debilitating, are the hallmark claustrophobia. Similar kinds of maladaptive avoidances can also occur with the other innate fears listed above, each of which is implicated in a sub-type of phobic anxiety disorder commonly seen in modern clinical practice, namely: ophidophobia, acrophobia, agoraphobia, hemophobia and social phobia (DSM-IV 1994).

We believe that certain strong innate fears, which presumably led to adaptive avoidances in ancestral environments, now contribute to producing the burdensome and maladaptive constellation of avoidances characteristic of phobias.[11] Some kinds of phobic disorders appear to be heritable, and like many complex psychological disorders which are presumed to involve polygenetic inheritance, one could reasonably expect that the strengths of peoples' innate fear dispositions are distributed over some range. We suspect that the

---

11 While we believe that certain strong innate fears dispose one to phobias, we do not mean to imply that all phobias arise from innate fears. The phobic fear of guns, hoplophobia, for example, presumably does not arise from an innate fear, but rather reflects the highly salient danger of these weapons in contemporary environments. Interestingly, at least one worker has argued that pathological fear of spiders—arachnophobia—may not arise from an innate fear, but rather from a culturally transmitted fear. Spiders appear to have become (falsely) associated with disease in Western societies during the Middle Ages during the course of several epidemics, and arachnophobia appears less prominent in non-Western cultures (Davey 1994). We thank Luc Faucher for bringing this case to our attention.

optimal distribution of strengths of innate fear dispositions for ancestral environments is significantly *mismatched* with respect to what would be most
adaptive in modern environments (see also Marks and Nesse 1994, Murphy
and Stich 2000). A high level of sensitivity to an innate fear trigger which
would be unproblematic, or even adaptive, in ancestral environments leads to
morbidity in modern environments.[12]

4.2

We turn now to box 3—cases of inertia in the cultural domain. Earlier we
noted that culture is an inheritance system with social learning providing the
mechanism of inheritance. Like the genetic system, the cultural system
exhibits cumulative change. But culture is unique in that it is also *directed*, that
is, cultural change can be more rapid because novel variants can be introduced
by processes that reliably produce variants whose cultural fitness is higher
than one would expect by chance. Because culture is both cumulative and
directed, culture has a *unique* ability to produce highly complex adaptations to
local conditions in relatively short periods of time. For this reason, culture-
wielding creatures are typically highly *specialized* to their local surroundings.
Consider for example Copper Eskimos (another favorite Boyd and Richerson
example) who exhibit a spectacular array of socially acquired traits related to
matters such clothing, housing, hunting, alliance formation, and on and on.
Two features of these cultural traits are noteworthy. First, they were not
acquired by the slow process of genetic evolution (there is no reason to suppose these cold-climate adaptations have a genetic basis) or by individual
learning. Second, many of these cultural traits represent ecological specializa-
tions; they would be inappropriate in any environmental or social context significantly different from the one which the Copper Eskimos do in fact inhabit.
Thus while *Homo sapiens* is perhaps the world's most preeminent ecological
and geographic generalist, individual cultural groups are largely specialists,
achieving high degrees of adaptation to their local environment by means of
the cultural inheritance system. By facilitating specialization, the cultural system certainly does promote adaptiveness. But specialization has the trade-off
that a specialized individual is more susceptible to mismatch due to *cultural
inertia* when environments change. An example which plausibly illustrates

12   While phobias clearly lead to significant dysfunction, it is less clear that they lead to a
     reduction in biological fitness, since claims about reproductive success are notoriously
     hard to test. Nevertheless, we believe that it is at least plausible that dysfunction due to
     phobias does indeed impact fitness. Additionally, it is worth noting that the dysfunc-
     tion associated with phobias clearly does impact well-being in the actual environment,
     which is another notion of rationality that we distinguished earlier.

cultural inertia in the domain of emotions is Nisbett and Cohen's well-known study, *Culture of Honor* (Nisbett and Cohen 1996).

Cultures of honor have been documented by anthropologists in many groups around the world. While these groups differ in many respects, they are classified as cultures of honor because they share important commonalities. A central feature of cultures of honor is that males in these cultures are prepared to protect their reputation for strength and probity by resorting to violence. The importance placed on a reputation for strength leads to a corresponding importance placed on insult and the necessity to respond to it. An individual who insults someone must be forced to retract. If the instigator refuses, he must be punished with violence or even death. Cultures of honor have arisen in many parts of the world in situations where resources are liable to theft and where the state's coercive apparatus cannot be relied upon to prevent or punish theft. These conditions often occur in relatively remote areas where herding is the main viable form of agriculture; the 'portability' of herd animals makes them prone to theft. Since cultures of honor have repeatedly and independently emerged in circumstances where placing high degrees of importance on a reputation for strength would be a highly effective social strategy with clear adaptive benefits, we believe that they are cultural adaptations which have been independently invented in different places in response to similar environmental pressures. Thus cultures of honor are an example of *convergent evolution* of traits within the cultural system.[13]

What makes cultures of honor particularly interesting for our purposes is that they exhibit considerable cultural inertia and they have a profound effect on the emotions and on the physiological mechanisms subserving them. Both points are vividly illustrated in pair of experiments by Nisbett and Cohen. In the first experiment, unsuspecting white male subjects walked down a long hall, and as they did so they were bumped by a (large!) male confederate who also called the subject an 'asshole'. Two observers who were pretending to work in the hall observed the subject's face when he was bumped, noted his body language and rated his emotional reactions. The results of the experiment are shown in Fig. 7.5; they indicate (dramatically) that culture of honor subjects were much more likely to be rated as having higher levels of anger versus amusement, while for non-culture of honor subjects, the reverse is true.

13 An alternative suggestion is that cultures of honor are part of evoked, as opposed to transmitted, culture. That is, one might claim that innate human nature provides both culture of honor and non-culture of honor options, and that one or the other of these options is toggled by local environmental cues. We regard this suggestion as unlikely because agriculture and herding are too recent for it to be plausible that cultures of honor are evoked biological adaptations.

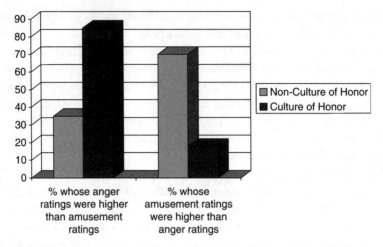

Figure 7.5 The results of an experiment by Nisbett and Cohen in which male subjects were bumped and insulted by a confederate. Most culture of honor subjects were more angry than amused. Permission sought.

The second experiment was similar to the first in that male subjects again walked down a long hallway where they were bumped by a large male confederate who called the subject an 'asshole'. This experiment differed from the first one in that both before and after walking down the hallway and getting bumped, subjects were asked to provide a saliva sample (a cover story involving measurement of blood sugar during tasks was given). The saliva samples were tested for cortisol (associated with stress, anxiety, and arousal) and testosterone (associated with aggression and dominance behavior). Again the results, depicted in Fig. 7.6, are dramatic. For culture of honor subjects, both cortisol and testosterone were much higher after the bumping and the insult, while this was not the case for non-culture of honor subjects.

Thus far, we have not said anything about who these 'culture of honor' and 'non-culture of honor subjects' actually are. The crucial point of the experiments, for our purposes, is that all the subjects were students at the University of Michigan. The non-culture of honor subjects were white northerners, while the culture of honor subjects were whites who had spent most of their lives in the American South. Nisbett and Cohen's thesis is that the South is a region whose cultural environment was shaped by members of earlier generations, for example Scotch–Irish immigrants, who had been herders for centuries, and who brought with them and helped entrench a culture of honor within this region. However, the American South has long

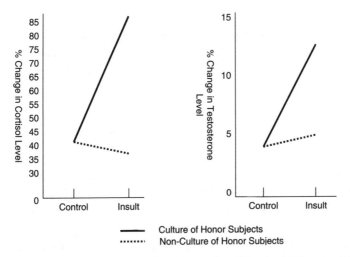

Figure 7.6 The results of a second experiment by Nisbett and Cohen in which levels of cortisol and testosterone increased much more substantially in culture of honor subjects who were insulted by a confederate. Permission sought.

ceased to be a sparsely populated frontier region, herding has all but disappeared in the South, and reliable policing by the state is available virtually throughout this region. Furthermore, these culture of honor subjects, though raised in the South, were attending the University of Michigan and had relatively high socio-economic status. For several generations, at least, these students' families and their neighbors' families had made their living in non-herding livelihoods like business, the professions and the civil service. Thus the conditions which would have made a culture of honor adaptive in the American South have long since disappeared. Nevertheless, Nisbett and Cohen's experiments show that among subjects raised in the South, a culture of honor persists and these subjects' emotional reactions to insult are profoundly affected by a culturally conveyed value structure that exhibits remarkable *inertia*.[14]

14 Cohen and his colleagues have also conducted a series of experiments that suggest that honor norms are no longer as deeply internalized among contemporary Southerners as they once were. In particular, Southerners no longer view another person's failing to respond to insult as a reason to view him as less manly, though they continue to expect that others would view the person as less manly. The result is that people continue to heed honor norms because they mistakenly believe that others would think less of them if they did not. Cohen and Vandello (2001) call this state 'a plurality of ignorance,' which again underscores the maladaptive nature of honor norms in the contemporary South (see Cohen and Vandello 2001 for a review).

4.3

We turn now to cases of irrational emotions that arise from failure due to inevitable misfires, considering first an example of inevitable misfire in the domain of individual learning from the environment. In a series of important experiments, John Garcia and his colleagues demonstrated that rats acquire a strong aversion to distinctively flavored food if they experience gastro-intestinal distress within 12 hours after eating the food (Garcia 1974). Other animals, including humans, also develop 'Garcia aversions'—indeed about 30% of Americans report such aversions. Based on these findings, Garcia and his colleagues proposed that that individual learning of food aversions is sub-served by a phylogenetically conserved system specifically dedicated to the defense of the gut. The mechanism subserving Garcia aversions differs in many respects from standard classical conditioning. For example, Garcia aver-sions are elicited by the taste and smell of food (and not by the food's visual, auditory, or tactile properties). Also, Garcia aversions develop despite the fact that the unconditioned stimulus (gastro-intestinal distress) is temporally remote (by up to 12 hours) from the conditioned stimulus (the food). For our purposes, the most important difference is the sensitivity of the mechanism. Unlike standard classical conditioning, the mechanism subserving the acquisi-tion of Garcia aversions is extremely sensitive and only a single trial is required for the acquisition of the conditioned response. The high sensitivity of the learning mechanism subserving Garcia aversions was presumably adaptive in an ancestral environment (and may *still* be adaptive in the modern environ-ments)—in a sense the mechanism is following the old adage 'better safe than sorry'. Nevertheless, because of the high sensitivity of the mechanism, many of the aversions generated by the mechanism are to harmless foods.

The case of Garcia aversions illustrates the important distinction between the adaptiveness of individual learning mechanisms which modify value structure elements in response to environmental contingencies, and the adap-tiveness of the value structure elements generated by those mechanisms. Many of the aversions generated by the Garcia mechanism are to perfectly harmless food, and therefore these aversions, and the emotions they trigger, are mal-adaptive (and, in our sense, irrational). Thus the inevitable misfire of *adaptive* individual learning mechanisms like the Garcia mechanism can lead to *mal-adaptive* value structure components.

4.4

We believe that some of the most interesting and important examples of mal-adaptive value structure elements are due to inevitable misfires in the cultural domain. That will be our theme for the remainder of the paper.

Earlier we discussed the distinction between directly and indirectly biased social learning. In directly biased social learning, a person tries out different cultural variants in order to see which one works best. In indirectly biased social learning, a person uses some marker, such as the commonness of a cultural variant or the prestige of the person from whom a cultural variant will be copied, to bias the selection of cultural variants. Our focus in this section will be on inevitable misfires that occur as a result of indirect biases. We believe the importance of indirect biases in cultural transmission has not been widely recognized. One of the most original aspects of the work of Boyd and Richerson and their colleagues, and the feature which differentiates them most from other workers who have adopted Darwinian approaches to culture, is their extensive analysis of the conditions of use and consequences of using indirect biases. For our purposes, indirectly biased social learning is particularly interesting because it produces a number of surprising and counterintuitive effects, one of which is the propagation of maladaptive cultural variants, which Boyd and Richerson sometimes call *rogue memes*. Boyd and Richerson and their colleagues have constructed a family of models demonstrating that natural selection will favor the use of social transmission and indirect biases in a wide variety of circumstances when the environment is variable (but not too variable), and information is costly and thus direct biases are not feasible (Boyd and Richerson 1985). When these circumstances obtain, the optimal cultural system, from the point of view of maximizing genetic fitness, is one that leaves abundant scope for *rogue memes*. Though this is not the place to present these sophisticated mathematical models in detail, it is easy enough to see the intuitive ideas underlying them by examining the conditions under which these models show that indirect biases will tend to be effective, leading to the spread of adaptive cultural variants, and contrasting them with the conditions under which indirect biases tend to lead to the spread of rogue memes.

We begin with prestige bias. Though a person's prestige can be based on a number of factors, there is typically a significant correlation between a person's prestige in a culture and his or her *success* in aspects of life that are of importance in that culture. Mathematical modeling shows that when reliable information about the adaptiveness of cultural variants is hard to come by, prestige bias—adopting the cultural variants that high prestige people have adopted—can be a very successful strategy (Henrich and Gil-White 2001, Boyd and Richerson 1985). But it is often difficult to determine which values, practices and beliefs contribute to prestigious people's success and which do not. People will thus often adopt a sizeable chunk of a prestigious person's repertoire of knowledge, skills, values and practices, some of which might be useless or even seriously maladaptive. Thus, prestige bias, though an adaptive strategy overall, will nevertheless also lead to the propagation of neutral and maladaptive cultural variants.

Now we turn to conformist bias. In a spatially variable environment, it is reasonable to suppose that different practices, beliefs and values may be adaptive in different places. Mathematical modeling shows that under these conditions, prior episodes of individual learning on the part of others will often make it the case that the most common cultural variant in a given location will also be the most adaptive cultural variant for that location (Henrich and Boyd 1998). Because commonness can serve as a reliable marker for adaptiveness, conformist bias is often effective, which is why its use is so widespread. However, these models also show that there is a range of conditions, including fast environmental change and circumstances in which individual learning is highly inaccurate, under which conformist bias will favor the spread of *maladaptive* cultural variants. Conformist bias will also tend to preserve maladaptive cultural variants that become widespread as the result of other processes, e.g. prestige bias.

In addition to the mathematical models of Boyd and Richerson and their colleagues, the importance, and sometimes untoward effects, of indirect biases are also supported by (the admittedly limited) empirical data. The literature on the diffusion of innovations plays a unique role as an empirical database because it offers perhaps the only systematic cross-cultural analysis of the relative role of direct versus indirect biases in adoption of novel cultural variants. Everett Rogers, who is by far the best known investigator in the study of the diffusion of innovations, surveys some 3000 articles in the literature and proposes a model of innovation adoption which is consistent with an important role for prestige and conformist biases in innovation adoption (Rogers 1995, Henrich 2000). If indirect bases are widespread, then we should be able to document cases in which their use leads to acquisition of maladaptive innovations. The diffusion of innovations literature does indeed offer many examples of maladaptive innovations and practices acquired by means of indirect biases. In all these cases, a recurring theme is that people are simply not able to properly assess the goodness or badness of the innovation and must thus make use of indirect biases.[15]

We believe the diffusion of innovations literature suggests two things: the use of indirect biases is widespread and indirect bases do in fact lead to the

---

15 An illustrative example is the case of third-world mothers who rapidly adopted the highly maladaptive practice of formula feeding, at least partly due to advertising deliberately designed to suggest that high-status people formula feed their own children (Rogers 1995).

propagation of rogue memes. It should be kept in mind that innovations are an ideal case for direct biases since often they are the kinds of things one can try out and 'see how good they are'. In the case of the social transmission of norms and values, we believe the use of indirect biases will, if anything, be more widespread. In contrast to innovations, it is typically very hard to see how one can use direct biases to guide the acquisition of norms and values since there is little scope to assess how good they are. Thus, even though the empirical evidence is less abundant, we expect that in the social transmission of elements of people's value structures, indirect biases play an even stronger role. And since indirect biases often leave ample scope for the propagation of rogue memes, we suspect that indirectly biased social transmission might account in a significant way for maladaptive elements of people's value structures, and thus for irrational emotions. What we aim to do in the rest of this section is briefly establish at least a circumstantial case for the thesis that irrational emotions do indeed arise as a consequence of rogue meme norms and values propagated by indirect biases. The example we will focus on is the case of irrational reactions of *disgust*, which occur in the context of *food taboos*.

All societies have rules which prohibit consumption of certain types of foods. While the category of food prohibitions is markedly heterogeneous—prohibitions may be applied to an almost boundless variety of food types, be binding on different classes of people, and may be invoked in a number of different social contexts—we shall refer to all such prohibitions on food as 'food taboos'. The emotion of disgust plays an important role in mediating food taboos. There is abundant anecdotal evidence in the ethnographic literature indicating that the prospect of eating tabooed food items elicits powerful feelings of revulsion, nausea, and the gape expression characteristic of disgust (Whitehead 2000, Simoons 1994). Moreover, consistent with the prominent role of disgust in mediating food taboos, Rozin and his colleagues have proposed that the psychological mechanisms of disgust originated as an elaboration of an ancestral system specialized for the rejection of food (Rozin *et al.* 2001). The question we will be focusing on is: by what mechanisms do particular food items come to be the object of taboos within a society? To the extent that these mechanisms systematically allow for taboos to attach to beneficial foods items rather than harmful ones, the taboos will often be maladaptive, and the result will be irrational emotions, in particular irrational reactions of disgust.

In addressing the question of how taboos become attached to particular food items, we begin by reiterating that across human societies, a startlingly heterogeneous variety of food items are tabooed. This *diversity* alone leads one to suspect that the objects of taboos are quite arbitrary, and that historical accident plays an important role in the explanation of why one food item is tabooed and another is not.[16] We believe that in order to gain a deeper understanding of the mechanisms by which taboos attach to particular food items, we must first recognize the unique role that social learning plays in the domain of food. Humans are exceptional in the extent to which they rely on social learning as a source of information. Furthermore, the food domain is particularly apt for utilizing social learning, since copying the food practices of others is relatively easy, while the costs of making errors in food selection can be disastrous (Galef 1998). Thus we believe that a social learning-based approach to understanding food taboos is promising. There are two distinct questions that such an explanation needs to address: how do food taboos *originate*, and how are they *sustained* over generations within cultural groups.

We begin with the first question: How does a particular kind of food originally come to be the object of a taboo within a particular culture? Here we follow evolutionary anthropologists Daniel Fessler and Carlos Navarrete, who suggest an account that invokes a number of interacting psychological and social processes, with indirectly biased cultural transmission playing a crucial role (Fessler and Navarrete unpublished). According to Fessler, food aversions plausibly originate as a consequence of post-ingestion sickness, in the manner of the Garcia phenomenon discussed earlier.[17] Once aversions have been developed, they may spread through direct observation of others—one's sight of a conspecific's aversive response to a food is a potent stimulus for developing

---

16 One well-known approach to explaining taboos draws on the functionalist perspective in anthropology which assumes that many seemingly arbitrary cultural practices are actually functional, and their adaptive benefits, which are often hidden, play an important role in explaining how the practices originated or are sustained. (For a contemporary approach to functionalism, see the defense of cultural materialism in Harris 1979). While there are few decisive arguments in the social sciences, the weight of evidence strongly suggests that, at least in the domain of food taboos, functionalist justification is often absent, and indeed many food taboos appear to be clearly maladaptive (Fessler unpublished manuscript). Particularly difficult for a functionalist hypothesis to explain are cases in which closely related groups living in the same environment, and otherwise sharing similar social structures, exhibit widely different food taboos. Henrich (2000) reports a series of cases of this type from the ethnographic literature. For example, among the Machigueanga of the Peruvian Amazon, snake, a widely available source of protein, is rejected even when it is known to be non-poisonous. Among the Warao of the Peruvian Orinoco river delta, large mammals are not hunted because they have 'blood like people'. Nevertheless, closely related groups living in the same region have no such prohibitions (Henrich personal communication).

17 Fessler and Navarrete add that meat, for various reasons which we will not elaborate on here, may be disproportionately salient as a source of aversions.

aversive reactions oneself.[18] Crucially, prestige bias and conformist bias are likely to play a pivotal role in propagating aversions from a small sub-set of the population to a much wider section of the population; prestige bias when the aversion is still rare, and conformist bias when the aversion has reached a critical mass. Additionally Fessler and Navarrete propose that prestige bias, by itself, might account for the origination of some food taboos—the idiosyncratic dislikes of a prestigious person, even if not related to post-ingestion sickness, might spread by prestige-biased transmission. Finally, they propose that when an aversion is widespread, it eventually comes to be normatively moralized in the form of a taboo. Consumption of a food item which was previously regarded as merely aversive now comes to be regarded as morally wrong and deserving of sanctions (Fessler and Navarrete unpublished manuscript).[19]

While Fessler and Navarrete's account explains how taboos originate, a second puzzle concerns how taboos are sustained over time within cultural traditions. In order to see that there is a puzzle here, one needs to keep in mind that the objects of taboos are enormously diverse across cultural groups, but quite uniform within cultural groups. This stable pattern of uniformity and diversity requires explanation because it is inconsistent with many kinds of cultural transmission. Boyd and Richerson and their colleagues have constructed an elegant series of mathematical models which demonstrate an interesting and unanticipated result: Given plausible assumptions about base rates for mutation and migration, processes like directly biased social transmission or individual learning cannot maintain stable differences between groups and instead lead to the dissipation of diversity between groups, contrary to what is in many cases in fact observed. However, indirect biases, in particular conformist biases, are capable of maintaining sharp within-group homogeneity and between-group differences with respect to practices such as taboos, thus providing a plausible mechanism for the pattern of diversity we actually see (Boyd and Richerson 1985, Henrich and Boyd 1998).[20] In the absence of empirical evidence which addresses questions about proximal mechanisms directly, these models serve as part of a reasonable circumstantial case that indirect biases are in fact operative in sustaining cross cultural diversity with

18   Fessler and Navarrete call this process 'socially mediated ingestive conditioning'—it is a member of a family of social learning processes which humans and other animals use in the acquisition of food preferences (see Zental and Galef 1998 for discussion of a number of other social learning processes used in the domain of food).

19   The process of normative moralization is poorly understood. For one account of this process, see Sripada and Stich (in preparation).

20   In addition to conformist bias, there are other processes which maintain stable within-group homogeneity and between-group differences. See Sripada and Stich (in preparation).

respect to cultural practices such as taboos. Thus, to sum up, we believe the inevitable misfiring of indirectly biased social transmission can and does lead to the genesis, propagation and maintenance of maladaptive food taboos, and the norms and values which mediate these maladaptive practices. When indirectly biased social transmission misfires and leads people to acquire maladaptive norms and values as elements of their value structures, the result is irrational emotions.

Conclusion

In recent years, the question of the rationality of the emotions has often been addressed by theorists interested in showing how emotions can perform rational mental functions or at least can be important components in other rational processes. A central theme of this paper has been that such approaches are not complete because they fail to deal with the antecedents of emotions, that is the cognitive structures which underwrite the link between emotion episodes and particular contexts of elicitation. In constructing a general framework for analyzing the antecedents of emotions, we introduced the crucial idea of a value structure, which consists of the mental representation of the full range of a person's evaluative attitudes, such as goals, values and norms. Using Boyd and Richerson's dual-inheritance analytic framework, we suggested three sources from which elements of value structures arise and two ways in which these three sources might contribute to maladaptive elements of value structures. We illustrated these proposed kinds of failure with specific examples drawn from the empirical literature. The kinds of cases of irrational emotions we described have largely been neglected by theorists interested in the question of the rationality of the emotions. By suggesting new and more precise ways of thinking about the antecedents of emotions, we hope to have provided a novel perspective on the venerable and contentious question of the rationality of the emotions.

References

Boyd, R. and Richerson, P. (1985). *Culture and the evolutionary Process*. The University of Chicago Press, Chicago.

Chewlos, G. and Oatley, K. (1994). Appraisal, computational models, and Scherer's expert system. *Cognition and Emotion*, 8(3), 245–57.

Chomsky, N. (1981). Principles and parameters in syntactic theory. In *Explanation in linguistics: the logical problem of language acquisition* (ed. N. Hornstein and D. Lightfoot), pp. 32–75, Longman, London.

Cosmides, L. and Tooby, J. (1994). Better than rational: evolutionary psychology and the invisible hand. *American Economic Review*, 84(2), 327–32.

Damasio, A. (1994). *Descartes error.* Avon Books, New York.

Davey, G. (1994). The 'disgusting' spider. *Society and Animals,* **2**(1).

Diagnostic and Statistical Manual of Mental Disorders, Fourth Edition (1994) American Psychiatric Association, Washington D.C.

Ekman, P. (1972). Universals and cultural differences in facial expressions of emotions. In *Nebraska Symposium on Motivation 1971,* Vol. 4 (ed. J. K. Cole), pp. 207–83. University of Nebraska Press, Lincoln.

Ekman, P. (1992). Are there basic emotions? *Psychological Review,* **99**(3), 550–53.

Ekman, P. (1994). All emotions are basic. In *The nature of emotions: fundamental questions* (ed. P. Ekman and R. J. Davidson), pp. 15–19. Oxford University Press, New York.

Fessler, D. M. T. (2001). Emotions and cost/benefit assessment: the role of shame and self-esteem in risk taking. In *Bounded rationality: the adaptive toolbox* (ed. R. Selten and G. Gigerenzer), pp. 191–214. MIT University Press, Cambridge, MA.

Fessler, D. M. T. and Navarrete, C. D. (unpublished manuscript). Meat is good to taboo: dietary proscriptions as a product of the interaction of psychological mechanisms and social processes.

Frank, R. (1988). *Passions within reason.* W. W. Norton and Company, New York.

Frijda, N. (1986). *The emotions.* Cambridge University Press, New York.

Galef, B. G. (1998). Communication of information concerning distant diets in a social, central-place foraging species: *Rattus norvegicus.* In *Social learning: psychological and biological perspectives* (ed. T. R. Zentall and B. G. Galef), pp. 119–40. Lawrence Erlbaum Associates, Hillsdale, NJ.

Garcia, J., Hankins, W. G., and Rusiniak, K. (1974). Behavioral regulation of the milieu interne in man and rat. *Science,* **185**, 824–31.

Gigerenzer, G. (2000). *Adaptive thinking: rationality in the real world.* Oxford University Press, Oxford.

Gigerenzer, G., Todd, P., and the ABC Research Group. (1999). *Simple heuristics that make Us smart.* Oxford University Press, Oxford.

Goldman, A. (1986). *Epistemology and cognition.* Harvard University Press, Cambridge, MA.

Griffiths, P. E. (2002). What is Innateness? *The Monist,* **85**(1), 70–85.

Harris, M. (1979). *Cultural materialism: the struggle for a science of culture.* Random House, New York.

Henrich, J. (2000). Cultural Transmission and the Diffusion of Innovations. Unpublished Manuscript.

Henrich, J. and Boyd, R. (1998). The evolution of conformist transmission and the emergence of between group differences. *Evolution and Human Behavior,* **19**, 215–41.

Henrich, J. and Gil-White, F. (2001). The evolution of prestige: freely conferred deference as a mechanism for enhancing the benefits of cultural transmission. *Evolution and Human Behavior,* **22**, 165–96.

Laland, K. and Brown, G. (2002). *Sense and nonsense: evolutionary perspectives on human behavior.* Oxford University Press, Oxford.

Lazarus, R. (1994). Universal antecedents of the emotions. In *The nature of emotions: fundamental questions* (ed. P. Ekman and R. J. Davidson), pp. 163–71. Oxford University Press, New York.

LeDoux, J. (1996). *The emotional brain.* Touchstone, New York.

Levenson, R. (1994). Human emotion: a functional view. In *The nature of emotion: fundamental questions* (ed. P. Ekman and R. J. Davidson), pp. 123–30. Oxford University Press, New York.

Marks, I. M. (1987). *Fear, phobias, and rituals.* Oxford University Press, New York.

Marks I. M. and Nesse, R. (1994). Fear and fitness: and evolutionary analysis of anxiety disorders. *Ethology and Sociobiology,* 15, 247–61.

Murphy, D. and Stich, S. (2000). Darwin in the madhouse: evolutionary psychology and the classification of mental disorders. In *Evolution and the human mind: modularity, language and meta-cognition* (ed. P. Carruthers and A. Chamberlain), pp. 62–92. Cambridge University Press, Cambridge, MA.

Nisbett, R. and Cohen, D. (1996). *Culture of honor.* Westview Press, Boulder, CO.

Ortony, A., Clore, G., and Collins, A. (1988). *The cognitive structure of emotions.* Cambridge University Press, New York.

Rogers, E. (1995). *The diffusion of innovations,* 4th edition. The Free Press, New York.

Rozin, P., Haidt, J., and McCauley, C. (2000). Disgust. In *Handbook of emotions* (ed. M. Lewis and J. Haviland), pp. 637–53. The Guilford Press, New York.

Samuels, R. (2002). Nativism in cognitive science. *Mind and Language,* 17(3), 233–65.

Samuels, R., Stich, S., and Faucher, L. (2003). Reason and rationality. In *Handbook of epistemology* (ed. M. Sintonen, I. Niiniluoto, M. Sintonen, and J. Wolenski), pp. 1–50. Kluwer, Dordrecht.

Scherer, K. (1988). Criteria for emotion antecedent appraisal: a review. In *Cognitive perspectives on emotion and motivation,* Vol. 10 (ed. V. Hamilton and G. H. Bower), pp. 89–126. Nijhoff, Dodrecht.

Scherer, K. (1993). Studying the emotion-antecedent appraisal process. *Cognition and Emotion,* 7(3/4), 325–55.

Simoons, F. (1994). *Eat not this flesh.* The University of Wisconsin Press, Madison.

Sperber, D. (1996). *Explaining culture: a naturalistic approach.* Cambridge University Press, Cambridge, MA.

Sripada, C. and Stich, S. (in preparation) The psychology and evolution of moral diversity.

Stich, S. (1990). *The fragmentation of reason.* MIT Press, Cambridge, MA.

Tooby, J. and Cosmides, L. (1990). The past explains the present: emotional adaptations and the structure of ancestral environments. *Ethology and Sociobiology,* 11, 375–424.

Whitehead, H. (2000). *Food rules.* The University of Michigan Press, Ann Arbor.

Zental T. R. and Galef B. G. (1998). *Social learning: psychological and biological perspectives.* Lawrence Erlbaum Associates, Hillsdale, NJ.

CHAPTER 8

THE ROLE OF EMOTIONS IN ECOLOGICAL AND PRACTICAL RATIONALITY

MATTEO MAMELI

Ecological rationality is that property we refer to when we say that an organism is rational if it copes successfully with its environment. Practical rationality is that property we refer to when we say that an organism is rational if it 'makes the right choices.' More precise accounts of these notions are given below. A lot has been written about emotions and ecological rationality. A lot has been written about the role that emotions play in making humans and other mammals capable to cope successfully with their environment (e.g. Darwin 1872, Trivers 1971, Frank 1988, Ekman 1992, Nesse 1990, Tooby and Cosmides 1990, Cosmides and Tooby 2000, Fridlund 1994, Griffiths 1997, LeDoux 1998, Panksepp 1998, Buss 2000, Gibbard 1991, Haidt 2002, Ohman 2000, Rozin *et al.* 2000, Hatfield and Rapson 2000, Hrdy 1999). Some of these theories—especially those about the higher-cognitive and the moral emotions—are controversial. But the claim that mammals need emotions in order to cope successfully with their environment isn't. No one doubts that fear plays an important role in mammals' being able to avoid predators, or that disgust plays an important role in mammals' being able to avoid contaminating foods and contaminating acts, or that emotional facial expressions have important communicative functions in primates, etc. The claim that emotions are important for mammals' ecological rationality isn't under dispute.

The same cannot be said about the relation between emotions and practical rationality. It is part of the folk-psychological conception that emotions interfere with our ability to 'make the right choices.' And this view has been the received view in psychology and philosophy since Plato. Only a few have opposed the received view. In particular, this view has been attacked by neurobiologist Antonio Damasio (1994, 1996), who argues that emotions play an important positive role in decision-making. (For other critiques of the received view see Haidt 2001, Zhu and Thagard 2002.) In this paper, I attempt to identify what is right and what is wrong with Damasio's theory. The upshot of my discussion is going to be that emotions may be even more important for practical rationality than Damasio suggests.

Ecological and Practical Rationality

Here is a possible definition of ecological rationality:

> **EcoR***: An organism O is **ecologically rational** to the extent that O copes successfully with its environment E.

This definition is not satisfactory because it does not distinguish organisms that cope successfully with their environment because they are lucky from organisms that cope successfully with their environment because of the way they 'work.' If we want to take this distinction into account, we should define ecological rationality as follows:

> **EcoR**: An organism O is **ecologically rational** to the extent that O copes successfully with its environment E because, thanks to its internal constitution, O has a tendency to cope successfully with E.[1]

First, any concept of rationality must involve a standard to be achieved. Ecological rationality is that kind of rationality for which the to-be-achieved standard is coping successfully with one's environment. Second, any theoretically useful concept of rationality must require that the relevant standard isn't achieved accidentally. If we know that an organism has met a standard accidentally, then we cannot infer anything about how the organism works or about whether the organism will be able to meet the same standard in the future. *Luck isn't projectible.* In contrast, if we know that an organism has met a standard because, in virtue of its internal constitution, it has a tendency to meet that standard, we may be able to infer something about the way the organism works and we may be able to infer that the organism will meet the same standard again in the future. It is for this reason that EcoR is a better definition of ecological rationality than EcoR*.

---

1 An ascription of a tendency is an ascription of causal powers, or capacities. For a discussion see Cartwright (1989, 1999).

In spite of this, EcoR is incomplete. Completeness requires that we know what 'coping successfully with one's environment' means. (1) It could be read as equivalent to 'managing to maximize one's inclusive fitness.' (2) Or it could read as equivalent to 'managing to maximize one's utility.' (3) Or it could be read as equivalent to 'being capable of solving those adaptive problems that were faced by one's ancestors and that are responsible for the evolution of one's cognitive abilities.' And there are many other possibilities. To each different interpretation of 'copying successfully with one's environment' there corresponds a different notion of ecological rationality. The expression *ecological rationality* was introduced by Gigerenzer and Todd (1999). Even though they do not give an explicit definition of what it takes for an organism to be ecologically rational—they only talk about the ecological rationality of heuristics—from what they say it can be inferred that, according to them, an organism is ecologically rational to the extent that it can solve those adaptive problems that were responsible for the evolution of its cognitive abilities. That is, they adopt the third reading of 'coping successfully with one's environment' (Gigerenzer and Todd 1999, Gigerenzer 2000, Todd and Gigerenzer 2000, Gigerenzer and Selten 2001). How can we choose between the different notions of ecological rationality? This is a hard question and cannot be discussed here. Luckily, for the purposes of this paper, no answer is needed. I shall be neutral. Everything I say will be compatible with the three possible interpretations of 'coping successfully with one's environment' as well as with other plausible interpretations of this expression.[2]

---

2 My view is that different interpretations of 'coping successfully with one's environment'—and, thereby, different versions of EcoR—are useful in different theoretical contexts. Note that the three kinds of ecological rationality that correspond to the three suggested readings of 'coping successfully with one's environment' often go together. Here are some of the reasons why: (a) Often organisms have desires designed by natural selection to bring about fitness-increasing outcomes; if the selective environment has not changed in dramatic ways, the satisfaction of these desires leads to higher inclusive fitness. (b) Often organisms have desire-acquisition devices designed by natural selection to bring about the development of fitness-increasing desires; if the selective and the developmental environment have not changed in dramatic ways, these devices bring about the development of desires whose satisfaction leads to higher inclusive fitness. (c) If the selective environment has not changed in dramatic ways, organisms capable of solving ancestral adaptive problems have high inclusive fitness. (d) Organisms with high inclusive fitness are usually organisms that have inherited devices that can solve ancestral adaptive problems and they are organisms whose selective environment has not changed in dramatic ways. (e) Organisms capable of satisfying their desires usually can do so because they have inherited devices which helped their ancestors to solve adaptive problems by helping them to satisfy their own desires.

But ecological rationality isn't the only interesting kind of rationality. There are many interesting kinds of rationality. One kind is what philosophers call *practical rationality*. This is the kind of rationality Tom Pink is talking about in the following passage:

> Not all agents need be rational. To be a rational agent, one needs, first, a practical intellect or deliberative capacity to form practical judgements about what actions are rationally justified; and second, one needs an executive capacity to apply these judgements in one's actions. Animals, in particular, have often been seen [...] to lack practical intellect. [...] Notice that rational agents, on our definition, can act irrationally, through a defective use of their deliberative and executive capacities. They might make a deliberative mistake as to what actions are justified or [...] the defect might be purely executive, in their deliberate performance of an action despite their judgement of this action as unjustified. Someone who does count as a rational agent can be said to possess a rational appetite—a capacity to become motivated to act through rational decision-making, thereby forming intentions to act, decisions and intentions based in turn on their deliberations about what actions would be justified. (Pink 2000)

Here is a standard definition of practical rationality:

> **PraR***: An organism O is **practically rational** to the extent that (1) O deliberates correctly (i.e. O 'makes the right decisions') and (2) O carries out its deliberations.

This standard definition is incomplete. We need to know what it takes to deliberate, and to deliberate correctly, in order to have a complete definition. These issues have been debated at length by philosophers, psychologists, and economists. I shall present my own (partial) account and put it to use in the rest of the paper.

What is deliberation? It is that process by means of which we choose what to do and not to do.[3] Not all the things we do are the result of choice. Sometimes we deliberate, but often we don't. Sometimes our environment, perceptions, beliefs, desires, habits, emotions, moods, and cravings cause us to behave by first causing us to choose a particular action; those are the cases in which we deliberate. But often our surroundings, perceptions, beliefs, desires, habits, emotions, moods, and cravings cause us to behave without first causing us to choose an action; those are the cases in which we don't deliberate. A simple way to distinguish between behaviors that are caused (among other things) by our choosing to do something and behaviors that

---

3 Despite claims to the contrary (Williams 1973), in some circumstances, we can decide not only what to do (and not to do), but also what to want (and not want) and what to believe (and not believe). For simplicity, I shall talk only about deliberation concerning action. But the definitions I offer can be easily modified so as to account for deliberation about one's own mental states as well.

are not can be formulated by using the notion of intention to act.[4] Deliberation (choosing to do A) is that causal process that results in the tokening of an intention to do A, and carrying out one's deliberations is that causal process that goes from the tokening of the intention to do A to the performance of A. Deliberation (or decision-making) is nothing but intention-tokening.

What is correct deliberation then? There are two interesting strategies for distinguishing correct from incorrect intention-tokening. On the first strategy, what makes intention-tokening correct or incorrect is the kind of process that causes it. One view is that an instance of intention-tokening is correct if and only if it is caused by an inferential process that does not violate the rules of logic and probability. This is the received view of correct deliberation. The problem with this view is that it does not tells us what is good about deliberating in accordance with the rules of logic and probability. In many cases, trying to reason in accordance with the rules of logic and probability seems to be the wrong thing to do. Similar problems are faced by other accounts of correct deliberation in terms of the process that causes intention-tokening. On the second strategy, what makes a particular instance of intention-tokening correct or incorrect is the kind of effects that it can bring about. I follow this strategy. My account is that an organism deliberates correctly to the extent that it tokens intentions to act that, if carried out, would increase the organism's ecological rationality. What is good about correct deliberation is its positive contribution to the organism's being able to cope successfully with its environment. Given this way of thinking about correct deliberation, we can define practical rationality as follows:

> **PraR:** An organism O is **practically rational** to the extent that (1) O tokens intentions to act that, if carried out, would make a positive contribution to O's ecological rationality and (2) these intentions bring about their corresponding actions.

Practical rationality is an aspect of ecological rationality which can be present only in organisms capable of deliberation. If, as many believe, non-human animals are not capable of deliberation, practical rationality is an aspect of ecological rationality which is present only in humans. Humans are not *perfectly* practically rational. Many—starting with Plato and Aristotle—have

---

4 Intentions are a special kind of mental states, not reducible to perceptions, beliefs, desires, emotions, or cravings. They are mental states with a distinctive kind of effect on behaviour. It is not easy to give an account of the distinctive way in which intentions control behavior. For some attempts see Bratman 1987, Velleman 1989, Mele 1992 and the papers in Malle *et al.* 2001.

written about the failures of human practical rationality. And many have written about the role emotions play in such failures. But even though we are not *perfectly* practically rational, we are practically rational *to a degree*. We can and sometimes we do make decisions that contribute positively to our coping successfully with our social and non-social environment—and this is true on any plausible reading of 'copying successfully with the environment.' Do emotions play a positive role in our being able to be practically rational? According to folk-psychology (and many philosophers, psychologists, and economists) they don't. According to Antonio Damasio, they do. In the next section, I shall examine Damasio's views.

Damasio's somatic marker hypothesis

One hypothesis about the role of emotions in human practical rationality is Damasio's somatic marker hypothesis. One of the reasons why Damasio's theory is interesting is that he does not define emotions in terms of their functional role in deliberation, but rather in neurobiological terms (Damasio 1994, 1996, 1998, 1999, 2001). Damasio distinguishes between *emotional states* and *emotional feelings*. Emotional states are collections of bodily responses, changes in visceral and musculoskeletal state and changes in internal milieu. These states are triggered by perceptions and thoughts—beliefs included. The triggering mechanism can be innate or learned; if it is innate, the triggered emotional state is said to be *primary*; if it is learned, the triggered emotional state is said to be *secondary*. For example, a state of fear is a collection of bodily changes—changes in heartbeat, in blood pressure, in skin temperature, in the amount of blood in different parts of the body, in muscular tension, etc.—which can be triggered by an innate unconditioned stimulus or by a perception or thought of a situation of a kind that has been previously associated with fear. Emotional states, according to Damasio, need not be felt. They can exist without being perceived. Emotional *feelings* are brain states that represent the bodily and cerebral changes that constitute emotional states. They are perceptions of emotional states. *Being* in fear and *feeling* fear are two different things on this theory—the latter is a perception of the former. A feeling of fear is the perception of the changes in heartbeat, blood pressure, skin temperature, etc., that constitute the state of fear—this is the Jamesian part of Damasio's theory (James 1884). But there is a non-Jamesian part to the theory too. Not only emotional states need not be felt, but emotional feelings need not be conscious. Emotional feelings, just like other kinds of perceptions, can be unconscious—this is the non-Jamesian part of Damasio's theory (Prinz forthcoming).

According to Damasio, emotional feelings work as *somatic markers*. An emotional feeling *marks* the content of the mental state, M, that triggered the emotional state of which the emotional feeling is a perception. The emotional feeling marks the content of M in terms of the effects that M produced on the body. Consider a child who has done something about which his mother is angry. Suppose the perception of his mother reproaching him causes the child to *be* sad. This state of sadness is then immediately perceived—i.e. the child *feels* sad. The state of sadness is perceived in conjunction with (or just after) the perception of being reproached. Because of this, the feeling of sadness marks the content of the perception—being reproached by mother—in terms of the bodily changes produced by the perception. That is, the feeling of sadness marks the content of the perception in terms of the state of sadness. It marks the reproach as *sadness-producing*. Since the state of sadness is unpleasant (it has a negative valence, see Prinz forthcoming), the feeling of sadness marks the reproach as *to-be-avoided*.

Somatic markers can guide behavior. The day after being reproached the child may consider whether or not to play with his friends after school. He knows that his mother wants him to be home early today. And he knows that if he stays with his friends, his mother will reproach him. The thought of being reproached causes him to *feel* sad. And feeling sad influences the decision process and causes the child to decide to go home. In Damasio's terminology, the thought of the mother's reproaching him causes the somatic marker to be *reconstituted* and helps the child avoid being reproached again. The somatic marker can be reconstituted in two ways. It can be reconstituted via what Damasio calls the *body-loop*. In this case the child *feels* sad because the thought of being reproached causes him to *be* sad and this state of sadness is perceived by the somatosensory cortices. But the somatic marker can also be reconstituted via what Damasio calls the *as-if-body-loop*. In this case, the thought of possibly being reproached activates the somatosensory cortices in such a way that the child *feels* sad without actually *being* in a state of sadness. Moreover, the reconstituted somatic marker—a feeling of sadness—may be conscious or unconscious, i.e. there child does not need to know that he feels sad in order for the feeling to play its role in disposing the child to choose to go home.

If the reconstitution of the somatic marker is subject to stimulus generalization, the child may start feeling sad at the thought of being reproached not only by his mother but also by his relatives, by his teachers, by an impersonal authority, etc. If this happens, the somatic marker can help the child avoid being reproached by any authority he may care about.

We now have the tools to understand Damasio's *somatic-marker hypothesis*:

Before you apply any kind of cost-benefit analysis to the premises, and before you reason toward the solution to the problem [deciding what to do], something quite important happens: When the bad outcome connected with a given response option comes into mind, however fleetingly, you experience an unpleasant gut feeling. Because the feeling is about the body, I gave the phenomenon the technical term *somatic state* [...] and because it 'marks' an image, I called it a *marker*. [...] What does the somatic marker achieve? It forces attention on the negative outcome to which a given action may lead, and functions as an automated alarm signal which says: Beware of danger ahead if you choose the option which leads to this outcome. The signal may lead you to reject, *immediately*, the negative course of action and thus make you choose among other alternatives. The automated signal protects you against future losses, without further ado, and then allows you to *choose among fewer alternatives*. There is still room for using a cost-benefit analysis and proper deductive competence, but only *after* the automatic step drastically reduces the number of options. Somatic markers may not be sufficient for normal human decision-making since a subsequent process of reasoning and final selection will still take place in many though not all instances. Somatic markers probably increase the accuracy and efficiency of the decision process. Their absence reduces them. This distinction is important and can easily be missed. The hypothesis doesn't concern the reasoning steps which follow the action of the somatic marker. In short, *somatic markers are a special instance of feelings generated by secondary emotions*. Those emotions and feelings *have been connected, by learning, to predicted future outcomes of certain scenarios*. When a negative somatic marker is juxtaposed to a particular future outcome the combination functions as an alarm bell. When a positive somatic marker is juxtaposed instead, it becomes a beacon of incentive. (Damasio 1994, 173–174)

The hypothesis thus suggests that somatic markers normally help constrain the decision-making space by making that space manageable for logic-based, cost-benefit analyses. In situations in which there is remarkable uncertainty about the future and in which the decision should be influenced by previous individual experience, such constraints permit the organism to decide efficiently within short time intervals. In the absence of a somatic marker, options and outcomes become virtually equalized and the process of choosing will depend entirely on logic operations on many option-outcome pairs. The strategy is necessarily slower and may fail to take into account previous experience. [...] Random and impulsive decision-making is a related pattern. (Damasio 1996, 1415)

According to Damasio, reconstituted somatic markers generated by the thought of possible outcomes are important in humans in order 'to decide efficiently and within short time intervals' in those 'situations in which there is remarkable uncertainty about the future and in which the decision should be influenced by previous experience.' They are important because in these circumstances it is too difficult for us to calculate all the costs and benefits of all the possible outcomes of all the available options. By means of somatic markers, we can avoid calculating the costs and benefits of a large class of these options. Whenever we consider an option and we predict that it will lead to a certain outcome and the thought of the outcome triggers a (conscious or unconscious) strong negative emotional feeling, the option is automatically taken off the list of actions worth considering. In this way, we reduce the list of options to a size that can be dealt with entirely by means of unemotional cost-benefit analysis. Thus, if one has to decide how to use one's money, some possible options (e.g. spending it all on entertainment) will be automatically eliminated because of the emotional feelings (e.g. sadness and fear) caused by the thought of the outcomes of such options (e.g. no money for buying food next week). After many such options have been discarded in this way, one can start making an unemotional cost-benefit analysis of the remaining possibilities (e.g. whether to rent a big expensive flat or a small cheap one) and finally decide what to do. Damasio's view of the role of emotions in decision-making can be summarized as follows:

> **EmoP (Emotional Preselection Theory of Action Choice)**: In humans, emotional feelings triggered by the thought of possible outcomes of possible actions—i.e. reconstituted somatic markers—reduce the number of options that need to be evaluated by unemotional cost-benefit analysis in order to decide what to do.

Damasio adds to EmoP the thesis that, in organisms with computational limitations like the ones humans have, unemotional cost-benefit analysis cannot work properly if the options to be evaluated are too many or if it is too computationally difficult to evaluate the costs and the benefits. He concludes that, in humans, emotional feelings are important for efficient decision-making:

> **Damasio's Somatic-Marker Hypothesis**: In humans, emotional feelings triggered by the thought of possible outcomes of possible actions—i.e. reconstituted somatic markers—contribute to correct deliberation (and thereby to practical rationality) because they reduce to a computationally manageable size the number of options that need to be evaluated by unemotional cost-benefit analysis in order to decide what to do.

What's the evidence for this hypothesis? Damasio thinks his hypothesis is a plausible explanation for the behavior of patients with damaged ventromedial prefrontal cortex. These patients present severe impairments in their decision-making abilities in spite of normal intellectual abilities. Here is what happened to Elliot—a man who had been successful in all respects (family, work, friends, etc.)—after the removal of a brain tumor caused damage to his ventromedial prefrontal cortex:

> [Elliot] was unable to manage his time properly; he could not be trusted with a schedule. When [his] job called for interrupting an activity and turning to another, he might persist nonetheless, seemingly losing sight of his main goal. Or he

might interrupt the activity he had engaged, to turn to something he found more captivating at that particular moment. Imagine a task involving reading and classifying documents of a given client. Elliot would read and fully understand the significance of the material, and he certainly knew how to sort out the documents. [...] The problem was that he was likely, all of a sudden, to turn from the sorting task he had initiated to read one of those papers, carefully and intelligently, and to spend an entire day doing so. [...] His knowledge base seemed to survive, and he could perform many separate actions as well as before. But he could not be counted on to perform an appropriate action when it was expected. [...] His ability to reach decision was impaired, as was his ability to make an effective plan for the hours ahead of him, let alone to plan for the months and years of his future. (Damasio 1994, 35–37)

Elliot and people with the same kind of brain damage are mentally normal in very many respects (Damasio 1994, 1996, Saver and Damasio 1991), at least according to the results of standard psychological tests. The perceptual, motor, and linguistic abilities of these patients are normal. Their reasoning abilities and their IQ are normal. Their memory and attention skills are normal. Their beliefs about social and non-social reality are normal. Their desires (as reported by the patients) are normal. Their ability to imagine possible situations and to predict and imagine the outcome of possible actions is normal. The patients are as good as anyone else at figuring out what are the best means to achieve a certain outcome. And they are as good as anyone else at carrying out their decisions. Despite all this, these patients deliberate in 'the wrong way'. Their choices of friends and activities often lead to losses in financial and social standing and, as a consequence, the patients are often abandoned by their friends and relatives. They make decisions and they carry them out. But many of their decisions (many of the intentions they token) are no longer personally advantageous. By using the definitions provided in the previous section of this paper, we can say that in many cases the decisions (the intentions) of these patients, when carried out, do not contribute in a positive way to the patients' ecological rationality. That is, the patients are practically irrational— or, at least, they are less practically rational than are normal subjects.

What explains the patients' irrationality? According to Damasio, the explanation is that the patients are unable to reconstitute their somatic markers. No emotional feeling is triggered when they think about the possible outcomes of their actions. So, their deliberation process can only proceed through an unemotional cost-benefit analysis. Hence, in all those cases in which it is not possible (for organisms with computational limitations like the ones humans have) to establish which option is good and which option is bad by means of an unemotional cost-benefit analysis, the patients generate 'random and impulsive decision-making'.

What is the evidence for the claim that the patients are unable to reconstitute their somatic markers? Important evidence comes from *the gambling experiments*. In these experiments, the subjects sit in front of four decks of cards identical in appearance and size. They are given $2,000 of play money and they are told that the game requires to select a card at the time from any of the decks until they are told to stop; that they must make as much profit as they can; and that they are free to switch from a deck to another whenever they want and how many times they want. The subjects aren't told in advance how many card selections they will be allowed to make. After each card selection, they receive some money. After turning a card from decks A and B, they are given $100. After turning a card from decks C and D, they are given $50. After turning some cards, the subjects are also asked to pay a penalty. The amount varies with the deck and the position in the deck according to a schedule unknown to the subjects. The schedule of penalty is organized so that the high-paying decks lead quickly to a net loss, while the low-paying decks lead to a net gain. After encountering a few losses, normal participants begin to generate skin-conductance responses (SCRs) before selecting from the high-paying decks and they also begin to avoid these decks. Patients with ventromedial-prefrontal-cortex damage do neither. Normal subjects show SCRs before selecting from the bad decks even before they realize consciously that A and B are indeed the bad decks. Brain-damaged patients show no SCRs before selecting from the bad decks and they keep selecting from the bad decks even after realizing and reporting that A and B are the bad decks (Bechara *et al.* 1994, 1996, 1997).[5]

According to Damasio, the results of these experiments should be interpreted as follows. In all subjects, selecting a card from A and B causes big losses and thereby frustration at having lost so much money. In normal subjects, the emotional feeling caused by such frustration negatively marks the selection of a card from A and B. When normal subjects consider the possibility of selecting a card from A or B, the negative somatic marker associated with this action is reconstituted (as shown by the SCRs) and (unconsciously at first) the reconstituted somatic marker causes the subjects to decide not to select from those decks. In the patients with damage to the ventromedial prefrontal cortex, the big losses caused by selecting from A and B cause frustration. But the feeling of frustration is not reconstituted when the patients consider the possibility of selection from such decks afterwards. This explains both why the patients do not generate SCRs before selecting from the bad decks and why they keep

5 For a different experiment see Damasio *et al.* 1990, 1991, Tranel 1994.

selecting from them even when they realize that they are indeed the bad decks.[6]

The experiments seem to show that patients with vetromedial-prefrontal-cortex damage are unable to reconstitute (*some of*) their somatic markers. Given this, can we explain the behavior of the patients by appealing to Damasio's Somatic Marker Hypothesis? Consider Elliot's behavior. While at the office, Elliot must decide whether to keep filing the documents, as he has been told to do by his boss, or to start reading an interesting document. The data about Elliot's intellectual abilities show that he is able to figure out that if he starts reading the document, he will be reproached by his boss and eventually he will lose his job. And the data show that Elliot knows that losing one's job is something that he should avoid. And yet Elliot decides to start reading the interesting document. He makes the wrong decision. Why? This is Damasio's explanation: since Elliot is unable to reconstitute somatic markers, there can be no emotional preselection of the possible options in his mind; so, Elliot must rely entirely on unemotional cost-benefit analysis in order to make his decision; but since this is a situation in which it is too difficult for organisms with our computational limitations to perform an unemotional cost-benefit analysis, Elliot has no other choice than to choose randomly and impulsively. In the following section, I say what I think is wrong with this explanation and I propose a new one.

A New Somatic Marker Hypothesis

Damasio's explanation of Elliot's behaviour cannot be right. The situation described isn't one in which it is too difficult to carry out an unemotional cost-benefit analysis. Elliot knows what is likely to happen if he does not do what he has been told to do. And he knows that what is likely to happen is not good. Calculating costs and benefits is easy in this case. Thus, if Elliot could choose what to do by means of an unemotional cost-benefit analysis, he could easily deliberate correctly in this case.

Damasio's Somatic Marker Hypothesis entails that Elliot can choose what to do by means of an unemotional cost-benefit analysis in simple cases. So, it

---

6 Alternative explanations, like hypersensitivity to reward and insensitivity to punishment, are ruled out by a change in the task's design (Anderson *et al.* 1996). When the schedules of punishment and reward are reversed—i.e. punishment is placed after every selection and reward is made unpredictable—the brain-damaged subjects still choose the less advantageous strategy. They prefer the decks which generate fewer losses on a card by card basis (even if these decks do not generate net gains in the longer run) to the decks which generate bigger losses on a card by card basis (even if these decks generate net gains in the longer run).

entails that Elliot can deliberate correctly in this case. This is why Damasio's theory cannot fully explain Elliot's behavior. The same is true of other theories that allow for the possibility that action-choice can be determined by unemotional cost-benefit analysis.

An alternative to EmoP is this:

> **EmoS (Emotional Selection Theory of Action Choice)**: In humans, the choice between different actions (included the choice between doing and not doing something) is always determined by the emotional feelings caused by the thought of possible outcomes of possible actions—i.e. by somatic markers—and not by an unemotional cost-benefit analysis.

EmoP and EmoS are very different. According to EmoP, in normal people, after the emotional preselection has been made, 'cost-benefit analysis and proper deductive competence' take charge and choose among the options that have survived. EmoS denies this possibility. According to this theory, *in no case* does unemotional cost-benefit analysis determine action-choice (intention-tokening) in humans; emotional feelings are involved not only in the preselection phase of decision-making but in all the rounds, including the final one.

EmoS does not imply that no cost-benefit analysis is ever involved in choosing an action. A cost-benefit analysis takes place all the time when we decide what to do, but the costs and the benefits are evaluated and compared by means of emotional feelings. We try to predict what outcomes an action may cause. If the predicted outcomes trigger good feelings, then we implicitly classify those outcomes as possible benefits and we are more disposed to choose to perform the action. If the predicted outcomes trigger bad feelings, then we implicitly classify those outcomes as possible costs and we are more disposed to choose to avoid the action. The cost-benefit analysis of possible actions is implemented by the triggering of emotional feelings.

Moreover, EmoS does not imply that beliefs about what is rational to do or beliefs about what one ought to do cannot influence decision-making. According to EmoS, they can, but only if they are associated with the right emotional feelings. Beliefs about what is morally or socially or rationally appropriate in certain circumstances do not exert any motivational force on decision-making unless they can trigger emotional feelings that motivate one to choose according to the contents of these beliefs. On this view, in normal people the acquisition of knowledge about what is morally, socially or rationally appropriate goes together with the acquisition of the dispositions to trigger certain kinds of emotional feelings. When the acquisition of this knowledge occurs in the absence of the acquisition of the right emotional dispositions, the result is people who—like psychopaths—know what is morally, socially and rationally appropriate but are not motivated to choose in accordance to what they know.

Finally, EmoS does not imply that we cannot choose to do things we do not like to do. Many of the possible actions we consider while trying to decide what to do have both predicted outcomes that trigger good feelings and predicted outcomes that trigger bad feelings. According to EmoS, one *can* decide to perform an action with predicted outcomes that trigger very bad feelings, but only if other predicted outcomes of the action cause good feelings *and* the good feelings outweigh the bad ones. A complete formulation of EmoS would need to tell us about the details of how good and bad feelings are pitted against each other. One possibility for example is that the feelings caused by attended predicted outcomes have more power in determining the final decision than the feelings caused by unattended predicted outcomes. This would explain why sometimes we can change our mind as a result of attending or not attending to some of the predicted outcomes of our possible actions. The complete theory would also have to tell us what happens in those cases in which the bad feelings and the good feelings triggered by the thought of the outcomes of an action are equally strong. Does the intention-tokening mechanism 'flip a coin' in those cases?

These details are not of much concern right now. I am concerned with making EmoS intelligible and plausible. According to EmoS, decision-making is a process constituted by an emotional and an unemotional part. The unemotional part of the process is the inferential process that allows us to predict which effects our actions are likely to produce. This part of the process cannot by itself cause us to choose any action. The emotional part is that process by which the emotional feelings caused by the predicted effects of action get pitted one against each other and determine the final choice of action.

If EmoS is true, emotional feelings play an even more fundamental role in human practical rationality than Damasio says. According to Damasio's theory, emotional feelings aren't necessary for deliberation; they are only important for correct deliberation in computationally difficult circumstances. In contrast, according to EmoS, emotional feelings are necessary for deliberation. Here is the new somatic-marker hypothesis:

> New Somatic-Marker Hypothesis (part 1): In humans, emotional feelings triggered by the thought of the possible outcomes of possible actions—i.e. reconstituted somatic markers—are necessary for deliberation (and thereby for correct deliberation, and thereby for practical rationality) because no choice between actions can be produced by unemotional cost-benefit analysis.

How can EmoS and the new somatic-marker hypothesis explain the behaviour of Elliot-like patients? The patients seem capable of deliberating. So, according to EmoS, they must have emotional feelings triggered by the thoughts of the possible outcomes of their actions—they must be able to reconstitute at least *some* somatic markers. And indeed they are. When Elliot thinks about the prospect of starting to read an interesting document, he has a positive emotional feeling. It is for this reason that he chooses to read the document. And when he thinks about the prospect of taking a card from the high-paying decks, he has a positive emotional feeling. It is for this reason that he chooses to select a card from those decks. What Elliot-like people lack is a *particular kind* of emotional feelings. They lack emotional feelings caused by the thought of *non-immediate* outcomes. The thought of the *immediate prospects* of actions cause feelings in the patients, but the thought of the *non-immediate* prospects of actions don't. When he thinks about the future prospect of losing his job as a result of not doing what he has been told to do, Elliot does not have the negative emotional feelings that a normal person has in such circumstances. It is for this reason that he is not motivated to avoid the action that will cause him to lose his job. And when he thinks about the future prospect of losing the game as a result of continuing to select from the high-paying decks, Elliot does not have the negative emotional feelings that a normal person has in such circumstances. It is for this reason that he is not motivated to avoid the high-paying decks.

Elliot-like people are *time-slice* agents. These patients can decide what to do, but their choice of action is not influenced by the predicted non-immediate outcomes of the possible actions they consider when they are trying to decide what to do. Their choice of action is determined entirely by the predicted immediate prospects of the actions. The predicted non-immediate future does not enter into the implicit cost-benefit analysis. It does not enter into it because the predicted future outcomes do not cause emotional feelings and because the implicit cost-benefit analysis is implemented by the triggering of emotional feelings. The thought of the non-immediate future cannot motivate the patients to choose one action rather than another. But our being able to cope successfully with our environment often depends on the non-immediate consequences of our actions. It is for this reason that the patients cope less successfully with their environment than normal people do. It is for this reason that they are less practically rational than are normal people.

This explanation is consistent with *some* of the things Damasio says about why the patients fail to decide advantageously. Damasio claims that the patients are 'insensitive to future consequences', that they have a sort of 'myopia for the future' (Bechara *et al.* 1994, Damasio 1994, 1996). And he has identified where the malfunctioning is: the inability to reconstitute somatic markers. But Damasio thinks that the patients cannot reconstitute *any* somatic markers. While the evidence (the gambling experiments, Elliot's behavior, etc.) only suggests that they cannot reconstitute *some* somatic markers, those that should be triggered by the thought of non-immediate future out-comes. Moreover, the patients' insensitivity to future consequences is not con-sistent with Damasio's somatic-marker hypothesis. According to his hypothesis, the decisions of Elliot-like people in computationally simple circumstances can be sensitive to predicted future outcomes because the thought of the future can influence decision-making by influencing an unemotional cost-benefit analysis. Elliot's behavior seems to show that, even in computationally simple circumstances, Elliot's decisions are insensitive to predicted non-immediate outcomes.

Some have pointed out that humans sometimes fail to be practically rational because they discount the future too much (Ainslie 2001). EmoS suggests a mechanism for such a phenomenon. Normal subjects discount the future because the emotional feelings caused by the thoughts of non-immediate future outcomes are weaker than the emotional feelings caused by immediate outcomes. Sometimes they are *too* weak, from the point of view of the standard of practical and ecological rationality. When that happens, normal subjects behave a bit like Elliot.

According to this theory, emotional feelings caused by the thought of non-immediate outcomes of action are necessary for correct deliberation and, thereby, for practical rationality. Obviously, it does not follow that they are sufficient. The ability to infer the likely consequences of different actions is also needed. And emotional feelings caused by the thought of immediate prospects are needed too. And this isn't all. Psychopaths have all these things and yet they are not able to deliberate correctly. They are practically irrational. The problem with them is that they have the *wrong* emotional feelings. For example, when thinking about the possibility of murdering someone and its possible outcomes (e.g. being jailed), they feel excitement rather than fear, guilt, sadness, etc. One can be practically rational only if one has the right emotional feelings, or to be more accurate:

> **New Somatic-Marker Hypothesis (part 2)**: In order to be practically rational, a human being must be such that bad (negatively valenced) emotional feelings are trig-gered by the thought of possible outcomes that would reduce ecological rationality and such that good (positively valenced) emotional feelings are triggered by the thought of possible outcomes that would increase ecological rationality. Moreover, the intensity of the emotional feelings must be proportional to the effects that the predicted outcomes would have on ecological rationality.

Conclusions

After having defined ecological and practical rationality, and having discussed and criticized Damasio's somatic-marker hypothesis, I have argued for these theses:

> **EmoS (Emotional Selection Theory of Action Choice)**: In humans, the choice between different actions (included the choice between doing and not doing something) is always determined by the emotional feelings caused by the thought of possible outcomes of possible actions—i.e. by somatic markers—and not by an unemotional cost-benefit analysis.

> **New Somatic-Marker Hypothesis (part 1)**: In humans, emotional feelings triggered by the thought of the possible consequences of possible actions—i.e. reconstituted somatic markers—are necessary for deliberation (and thereby for correct deliberation, and thereby for practical rationality) because no choice between actions can be produced by unemotional cost-benefit analysis.

> **New Somatic-Marker Hypothesis (part 2)**: In order to be practically rational, a human being must be such that bad (negatively valenced) emotional feelings are triggered by the thought of possible outcomes that would reduce ecological rationality and such that good (positively valenced) emotional feelings are triggered by the thought of possible outcomes that would increase ecological rationality. Moreover, the intensity of the emotional feelings must be proportional to the effects that the predicted outcomes would have on ecological rationality.

If these theses are true, the common-sense picture of the role of emotions in deliberation and practical rationality is extremely incomplete. One possible explanation of this oversight of folk-psychology is that many of the emotional feelings that determine action choice are unconscious and unattended. That is, often deliberation is determined by *covert* emotional feelings (Bechara *et al.* 1997).

Folk-psychology to one side, why should we be built the way EmoS says we are? After all, it is very easy to conceive of different cognitive architectures. We can imagine a computer that deliberates (tokens intentions) entirely by unemotional cost-benefit analysis. Why can we not do that? One possible answer is that our deliberative capacities are built on top of (and out of) our emotional capacities—both evolutionarily and developmentally. It is plausible to think that it is because of the kind of organisms we were before we evolved the ability to deliberate (the ability to token intentions) that we ended up being able to deliberate only if helped by our emotions.

Acknowledgements

Many thanks to Lisa Bortolotti, Paul Griffiths, David Papineau, Jesse Prinz, Mark Sainsbury, Nick Shea, Dan Sperber, and Finn Spicer for many useful comments.

References

Ainslie, G. (2001). *Breakdown of will.* Cambridge University Press, Cambridge.

Anderson, S. W., Bechara, A., Tranel, D., Damasio, H., and Damasio, A. R. (1996). Characterization of the decision-making defect of subjects with ventromedial frontal lobe damage. *Society for Neuroscience Abstracts* 22.

Bechara, A., Damasio, A. R., Damasio, H., Anderson, S. W. (1994). Insensitivity to future consequences following damage to human prefrontal cortex. *Cognition,* **90,** 7–15.

Bechara, A., Tranel, D., Damasio, H and Damasio, A. R. (1996). Failure to respond autonomically to anticipated future outcomes following damage to prefrontal cortex. *Cerebral Cortex,* **6,** 215–25.

Bechara, A., Damasio, H., Tranel, D., and Damasio, A. R. (1997). Deciding advantageously before knowing the advantageous strategy. *Science,* **275,** 1293–5.

Cartwright, N. (1989). *Nature's capacities and their measurement.* Oxford University Press, Oxford.

Cartwright, N. (1999). *The dappled world.* Cambridge University Press, Cambridge.

Cosmides, L. and Tooby, J. (2001). *Evolutionary psychology and the emotions.* In *Handbook of emotions,* 2nd edition, (ed. M. Lewis and J. M. Haviland-Jones). Guilford, New York.

Damasio, A. R. (1994). *Descartes' error: emotion, reason and the human brain.* Grosset/ Putnam, New York.

Damasio, A. R. (1996). The somatic-marker hypothesis and the possible functions of the prefrontal cortex. *Philosophical Transactions of the Royal Society of London,* B **351,** 1413–20.

Damasio, A. R. (1998). Emotion in the perspective of an integrated nervous system. *Brain Research Reviews,* **26,** 84–6.

Damasio, A. R. (1999). *The feeling of what happens: body, emotion and the making of consciousness.* Random House, London.

Damasio, A. R. (2001). Reflections on the neurobiology of emotion and feeling. In *The foundations of cognitive science* (ed. J. Branquinho). Oxford University Press, Oxford.

Damasio, A. R., Tranel, D., and Damasio, H. (1990). Individuals with sociopathic behavior caused by frontal damage fail to respond autonomically to social stimuli. *Behavioral and Brain Research,* **41,** 81.

Damasio, A. R., Tranel, D., and Damasio, H. (1991). Somatic markers and the guidance of behavior: theory and preliminary testing. In *Frontal lobe function and dysfunction* (ed. H. S. Levin, H. M. Eisenberg, and A. L. Benton). Oxford University Press, Oxford.

Darwin, C. (1872). *The expression of the emotions in man and animals.* D. Appleton and Company, New York.

Ekman, P. (1992). An argument for basic emotions. *Cognition and Emotion,* **6,** 169–200.

Fodor, J. (2000). *The mind doesn't work that way.* MIT Press, Cambridge MA.

Frank, R. H. (1988). *Passions within reason: the strategic role of the emotions.* Norton, New York.

Fridlund, A. J. (1994). *Human facial expression: an evolutionary view.* Academic Press, San Diego.

Gibbard, A. (1991). *Wise choices, apt feelings.* Harvard University Press, Cambridge MA.

Gigerenzer, G. (2000). *Adaptive thinking.* Oxford University Press, Oxford.

Gigerenzer, G. and Selten, R. (ed.) (2001). *Bounded rationality.* MIT Press, Cambridge MA.

Gigerenzer, G. and Todd, P. M. (1999). *Simple heuristics that make us smart.* Oxford University Press, Oxford.

Godfrey-Smith, P. (1996). *Complexity and the function of mind in nature.* Cambridge University Press, Cambridge.

Griffiths, P. E. (1997). *What emotions really are: the problem of psychological categories.* Chicago University Press, Chicago.

Haidt, J. (2001). The emotional dog and its rational tail. *Psychological Review,* **108**, 814–34.

Haidt, J. (2002). The moral emotions. In *Handbook of affective sciences* (ed. R. J. Davidson). Oxford University Press, Oxford.

Hrdy, S. (1999). *Mother nature: natural selection and the female of the species.* Pantheon Books, New York.

Hatfield, E. and Rapson, R. L. (2000). Love and attachment processes. In *Handbook of emotions* (ed. M. Lewis and J. M. Havilan-Jones), 2nd edition. Guilford, New York.

James, W. (1884). What is an emotion? *Mind,* **9**, 188–205.

LeDoux, J. E. (1998). *The emotional brain.* Weidenfeld & Nicolson, London.

Malle, B. F., Moses, L. J., and Baldwin, D. A. (2001). *Intentions and intentionality: foundations of social cognition.* MIT Press, Cambridge MA.

Mele, A. R. (1992). *Springs of action.* Oxford University Press, Oxford.

Nesse, R. M. (1990). Evolutionary explanations of emotions. *Human Nature,* **1**, 261–89.

Ohman, A. (2000). Fear and anxiety: evolutionary, cognitive, and clinical perspectives. In *Handbook of emotions,* 2nd edition (ed. M. Lewis and J. M. Havilan-Jones). Guilford, New York.

Panksepp, J. (1998). *Affective neuroscience: the foundations of human and animal emotions.* Oxford University Press, New York.

Pink, T. (2000). The will. In *Routledge encyclopedia of philosophy.* Routledge, London.

Prinz, J (forthcoming) *Emotional perception.* Oxford University Press, Oxford.

Rozin, P., Haidt, J., and McCauley, C. R. (2000). Disgust. In *Handbook of emotions,* 2nd edition, (ed. M. Lewis and J. M. Havilan-Jones). Guilford, New York.

Saver, J. L. and Damasio, A. R. (1991). Preserved access and processing of social knowledge in a patient with acquired sociopathy due to ventrometial frontal damage. *Neuropsychologia,* **29**, 1241–9.

Tooby, J. and Cosmides, L. (1992). The psychological foundations of culture. In *The adapted mind* (ed. J. Barkow, L. Cosmides, and J. Tooby). Oxford University Press, Oxford.

Todd, P. M. and Gigerenzer, G. (2000). Simple heuristics that make us smart. *Behavioural and Brain Sciences,* **23**, 727–41.

Tooby, J. and Cosmides, L. (1990). The past explains the present: emotional adaptations and the structure of ancestral environments. *Ethology and Sociobiology,* **11**, 375–424.

Tranel, D. (1994). 'Acquired sociopathy': the development of sociopathic behavior following focal brain damage. In *Progress in experimental personality and psychopathology research* 17 (ed. D. C. Fowles, P. Sutker, and S. H. Goodman). Springer, New York.

Trivers, R. L. (1971). The evolution of reciprocal altruism. *Quarterly Review of Biology*, **46**, 35–57.

Velleman, J. D. (1989). *Practical reflection*. Princeton University Press, Princeton.

Williams, B. (1973). Deciding to believe. In *Problems of the self* (ed. B. Williams). Cambridge University Press, Cambridge.

Zhu, J. and Thagard, P. (2002). Emotion and action. *Philosophical Psychology*, **15**, 19–36.

CHAPTER 9

THE SEARCH HYPOTHESIS OF EMOTION

DYLAN EVANS

Introduction

How do the emotions affect reason? This question has been debated since Plato, who proposed what may be called 'the negative view of emotion' (Evans 2001). According to the negative view, emotions usually affect reasoning for the worse. To the extent that humans can free themselves of emotion, therefore, they can become more rational. Until recently, most philosophers and psychologists have tended to agree with Plato on this matter.

In the past couple of decades, however, a growing number of thinkers have challenged the traditional consensus (see, for example, de Sousa 1987, Frank 1988, Damasio 1994, Elster 1999, Evans 2001). They argue for what may be called 'the positive view of emotion'. According to the positive view, emotions usually affect reasoning for the better. The positive view suggests that, other things being equal, humans will be *less* rational to the extent that they lack emotion.

The positive view of emotion is mere hand-waving, of course, unless we can spell out exactly *how* emotions are supposed to aid rationality. The various proponents of the positive view have risen to this challenge in a number of different ways. In this paper, I will examine one particular way of elucidating how emotions help reason which, for want of a better name, I will call 'the search hypothesis of emotion'.

In the next section, I provide a brief sketch of the search hypothesis of emotion. In the following section, I dispense with a red-herring that has marred previous statements of the search hypothesis. I then set out the model of rational decision-making that is implicit in the search hypothesis. I go on to distinguish two possible ways of reading the search hypothesis, and conclude that the hypothesis can only be evaluated in the context of a specific theory on what emotions are.

The search hypothesis of emotion

Ever since Thomas Hobbes denied that reason can fix our ends or desires, an instrumental conception of rationality has dominated Western thought. According to this view, reason is, in Hume's famous phrase, a mere 'slave of the passions'. It has no motivating force, and is limited to finding the right means to attain the ends which are 'given' by the emotions.

This view has the merit of providing a neat explication of the reason–emotion distinction. Perhaps, however, it is rather *too* neat. Not only does it rule out the possibility of asking people to justify their ends—*de gustibus non disputandum est*—but it also, conversely, rules out the possibility of any emotional influence in rational choice. First, one supposes, emotions assign a subjective utility to each end, without any help from reason; then, whenever we have to make a decision or choose between a number of actions, reason calculates the expected utility for each action and automatically selects that action with the highest expected utility. Reason is thus reduced to computation, in true Hobbesian fashion.

One problem with this view of reason is that it tells us nothing about how we predict the possible outcomes of each action. In rational choice theory, the range of possible outcomes (and the conditional probabilities relating outcomes to actions) are assumed to be given, just like the subjective utilities of the outcomes. The latter are supposed to be given by the emotions; but what about the former? We cannot simply appeal to the agent's beliefs, since belief-fixation is supposed to be a rational process itself, so that simply leads to an infinite regress.

An example may serve to make this problem a bit clearer. Suppose that I wish to arrange an appointment with my doctor, and he suggests two alternative days—say, next Monday or next Tuesday. If I am a rational agent (according to the instrumental view of rationality), I will calculate the expected utility of going to the doctor's on each of these days and choose that which has the higher. Before I can do this, I need to assign a conditional probability $Pr(\omega|x)$ to each outcome, where ω is the outcome and x is the action. Before I can do *that*, however, I must first of all list all the possible outcomes. And, to borrow a phrase, there's the rub; for who knows 'what dreams may come, when we have shuffled off this mortal coil'—or even what might ensue from arranging to see the doctor on Monday? If I have already agreed to take my kids out to the zoo on Monday, then arranging the appointment for Monday would mean having to reschedule the trip to the zoo. Rescheduling the trip to the zoo would be one outcome of arranging the appointment for Monday, but why stop there? Why not also consider the possible consequences of *that*? My kids might get annoyed with me; I might tell them off for being intransigent, this might lead them to be more flexible, which might help them to be happier later in life ... and so on, *ad infinitum*. Since the relation *being an outcome of* is transitive, it follows that all these are also outcomes of arranging the appointment for Monday. So even for a simple decision like arranging an appointment with the doctor, the set of possible outcomes for each action is in principle unbounded. Therefore, listing the possible outcomes of any given action is a potentially endless task. Yet, if I am to make a decision, I must stop listing outcomes at some point. Looking before you leap is all very well, but the point is to leap. At some point, you must stop thinking, and start acting. Let us call this 'Hamlet's problem'.[1]

Note that we cannot solve Hamlet's problem by recourse to rational decision theory by, say, assigning a utility function to thinking-time. That would simply lead to an infinite regress, for it would mean that, before making any decision, we would have to decide how much time to spend on making it. But before we could decide *that*, we would first have to decide how much time to spend on *that* decision, and so on, *ad infinitum*. So, it seems that reason cannot even get off the ground unless some prior, non-rational procedure is used to delimit the time for decision-making, or the range of consequences to be considered, or both (or perhaps they just amount to the same thing).

According to the search hypothesis of emotion, this non-rational procedure for delimiting the range of consequences to be considered in a rational decision-process is governed by the emotions. The emotions, on this account, play more than one role in rational choice. Not only do they assign a subjective utility to each outcome; they also delimit the range of outcomes to be considered.

The search hypothesis of emotion is a relatively recent idea. The first person to have put it forward explicitly is, as far as I can tell, the philosopher Ronald de Sousa. In his book, *The Rationality of Emotion* (1987, 195), he argued that emotions limit 'the range of information that the organism will take into account, the inferences actually drawn from a potential infinity, and the set of live options among which it will choose'. In his article on emotion for the

---

1   Jerry Fodor (1987, 140) used this term to describe a similar, though more general kind of problem.

Blackwell Companion to the Philosophy of Mind, de Sousa (1994, 276) re-iterates the idea, stating that 'in the process of rational deliberation itself, emotions render salient only a tiny proportion of the available alternatives and of the conceivably relevant facts'.

More recently, similar views have been expressed by a number of evolutionary psychologists. Timothy Ketelaar and Peter Todd, for example, have suggested that 'specific emotions might help to solve the problem of what information to attend to in specific environmental circumstances' (Ketelaar and Todd 2000, 21–2). Spelling out the idea in more detail, they go on to state:

> Thus, when the future outcome of various courses of action cannot be objectively 'calculated', often because there are simply too many plausible consequences to consider (i.e., the frame problem), it may pay to 'let your emotions be your guide' in selecting which course of action to pursue. (2000, 21–2)

So far so good, or so it seems. The search hypothesis of emotion seems, on the face of it, to be a neat way of fleshing out the claim that emotions play a positive role in aiding rational choice. However, when one probes it a little, it turns out to have some serious problems. In a short while, I will look at these problems, but first I want to dispense with a red-herring.

A red-herring: the frame problem

In the passage just cited, Ketelaar and Todd refer to 'the frame problem'. De Sousa does too. In the article on emotion in the Blackwell *Companion* (1994, 276) he makes the following claim:

> ...the number of goals that it is logically possible to posit at any particular time is virtually infinite, and the number of possible strategies that might be employed in pursuit of them is orders of magnitude larger. Moreover, in considering possible strategies, the number of consequences of any one strategy is again infinite, so that unless some drastic preselection can be effected among the alternatives their evaluation could never be completed. This gives rise to what is known among cognitive scientists as the 'Frame Problem': in deciding among any range of possible actions, most of the consequences of each must be eliminated from consideration a priori, i.e. without any time being wasted on their consideration. That this is not as much of a problem for people as it is for machines may well be due to our capacity for emotions.

So it seems that what I have called 'the search hypothesis of emotion' could be re-phrased in something like the following terms: *emotions help humans to solve the frame problem.* This is, in fact, more or less how Ketelaar and Todd describe their view of emotion: 'a simple emotion mechanism might help us surmount the frame problem' (Ketelaar and Todd 2000, 11). So, might we not refer to the search hypothesis of emotion instead as, say, 'the *frame* hypothesis of emotion'?

The reason why I have chosen *not* to coin such a phrase, and to talk instead about 'the *search* hypothesis of emotion', is that there is no consensus about what exactly the frame problem *is*. The phrase was coined by John McCarthy in 1969 to denote a difficulty with a particular formalism that he and Patrick Hayes had developed for temporal reasoning in computer programs (McCarthy and Hayes 1969). As time went on, however, the term was increasingly used by philosophers in more general ways. By the early 1980s, for example, Jerry Fodor was using the term to designate the problem of how to program digital computers to make good abductive inferences (Fodor 1983). Patrick Hayes, who co-authored the original paper with John McCarthy in which the term first appeared, has accused these broader definitions of the frame problem of muddying the waters. For Hayes, these broader definitions are unconnected with the original frame problem, which is simply a technical problem with a particular kind of formalism (Hayes 1987). Philosophers such as Fodor and Dennett disagree, and the debate has raged through several edited collections of essays (Pylyshyn 1987, Ford and Pylyshyn 1996). My reason for not wishing to speak of 'the frame hypothesis of emotion' is pragmatic; I do not wish to get bogged down in endless disputes about what the frame problem 'really is'. It is not necessary to resolve these disputes before addressing the search hypothesis of emotion.

When de Sousa, Ketelaar and Todd refer to the frame problem, they all have in mind a much broader definition of the frame problem than that which is common in artificial intelligence. The problem that they think emotions solve is that of when to stop listing what the possible consequences of an action will be. This is a long way from what most researchers in artificial intelligence understand by the frame problem. If we wish to label the problem identified by de Sousa, Ketelaar and Todd with some technical term drawn from the jargon of artificial intelligence, we should probably call it 'the search problem'. In the following section, I explain what the search problem is.

The search problem

One of the conceptual mainstays of artificial intelligence is the insightful idea, first proposed by Allen Newell, Cliff Shaw and Herbert Simon, of conceiving problem-solving as a kind of *search*. Imagine a state space consisting of many potential solutions to a problem; finding the right solution then involves searching through the state space. Now, if we had to generate the state space of potential solutions in entirety in advance of the search, we would often be stuck with Hamlet's problem, since the state space of many problems is infinite. To get round this, Newell, Shaw and Simon proposed that the state space can be expanded step by step, with the current state being tested to see whether or not it qualifies as an acceptable solution before the next expansion. If the current state space *does* qualify as an acceptable solution, the search is terminated and the problem is solved; otherwise, the state space is expanded by generating another state. The new state is then tested, and so on.

It is this step-by-step process of generating and testing that makes all the difference between the idealized models of rational choice theory and the bounded rationality of artificial intelligence systems. Instead of trying to figure out all the consequences of an action before evaluating them, the search procedure generates one consequence at a time and then evaluates it before going on to generate another one. The test it uses to evaluate the consequence must be a simple algorithm that returns a quick 'yes' or 'no'. If the answer is positive, a solution has been found and the search stops. If the answer is negative, the search continues.

This simple process can solve Hamlet's problem—or the problem of arranging an appointment to see the doctor. Instead of imagining all the consequences of each action, and then assigning utilities and conditional probabilities to each of the consequences before finally calculating the overall expected utility of each action—a potentially infinite task, as we have seen—I simply imagine the consequences of each action one at a time, and apply some test. The test might be something simple such as meeting some aspiration level. I might, for example, think of the first consequence of arranging to see the doctor on Monday—re-arranging the trip to the zoo—and ask whether that would be too much bother for me. If it is not, I arrange my appointment for Monday. Otherwise, I go on to consider other consequences of this action and/or the consequences of other actions.

Now, what makes this way of deciding rational is that—providing the right kind of test is used, and the right search strategy[2]—decisions made on the basis of a search process like this can regularly lead to decisions that closely approximate those made by an ideally rational agent operating according to classical decision theory. This, at least, is what proponents of bounded rationality maintain, following the work of Herbert Simon (Simon 1955).

---

2 A 'search strategy' is defined by the criterion used to decide which state to expand first. If we represent the search process as building up a search tree, then the search strategy tells us which node of the tree to expand first. A 'breadth-first' search, for example, expands all the nodes at one level before expanding any of the nodes at the next level. A 'depth-first' search, on the other hand, always expands one of the nodes at the deepest level of the tree; only when the search hits a dead end (a non-goal node with no expansion) does the search go back and expand nodes at shallower levels. More informed kinds of search strategy— ones that use problem-specific knowledge—are also possible (Russell and Norvig 1995).

Picking the right test to use for the given problem at hand, and the right search strategy, is thus crucial. This is the search problem.

The search hypothesis of emotion can now be re-stated; it is the claim that emotions enable humans to solve the search problem. Emotions prevent us from getting lost in endless explorations of potentially infinite search spaces by providing us with both the right kind of test and the right kind of search strategy for each kind of problem we must solve. Only when emotions fail us do we end up in Hamlet's situation, suffering from a severe case of analysis paralysis.

Two readings of the search hypothesis

There are two ways in which the search hypothesis can be construed. The first is that the hypothesis is a metaphysical claim about what emotions really *are*; the second is an empirical claim about what emotions typically *do*. There is at least one good reason, however, why the first reading is not tenable. This is that the search hypothesis, when construed as a definition of emotion, becomes vacuous. If it were intended as a definition, of course, it would imply a functionalist account of mental states, since it would define emotions by what they typically do. And what emotions typically do, according to the search hypothesis, is help us delimit the range of possible consequences to be considered in any rational decision process. If we had an independent idea about what such things might look like, then the hypothesis would be an interesting claim—perhaps a proposal to identify emotions with this antecedently discovered class of mechanisms. However, the sad fact is that we have *no idea* how such mechanisms might work. Despite over forty years of hard work, researchers in artificial intelligence are still incapable of designing mechanisms that can delimit, in advance, the range of consequences to be considered in such a way that decisions can be both rapid and rational. There are, it is true, a number of interesting proposals about specific heuristics that can make rapid, rational decisions *in a given domain*, but this merely pushes the explanatory burden back one stage, to the question of how a given real-world problem is mapped onto one of the system's domains. And nobody has any idea about how such mappings can be achieved in a rapid and rational way. Invoking 'heuristics' in response to the search problem is just passing the buck. But, then, so is invoking 'emotions'. Since we have no idea about how to solve the search problem, then to claim that emotions are what help us solve it is simply to exchange one mystery for another. What purports to be an explication of the concept of emotion turns out to be just an obfuscation.

I noted previously that the search hypothesis can be construed either as a claim about what emotions are, or as a claim about what emotions do.

The objection just raised shows that, as a claim about what emotions are, the search hypothesis is vacuous. But this objection is not fatal to the search hypothesis; after all, it is not the task of every hypothesis about emotion to tell us what emotions are. Some accounts of emotion purport to answer a rather different question; namely, how do emotions interact with reason? Perhaps the search hypothesis is better construed, then, as a claim about what emotions do.

This reading seems much more promising, though with one major caveat; construed as a claim about what emotions typically *do*, the search hypothesis remains vacuous unless we have some independent notion of what emotions *are*. Only then would the claim that emotions help us solve the search problem avoid substituting one mystery for another. In other words, the search hypothesis can only properly be evaluated in the context of a specific theory of emotion. We can ask, for example, whether the search hypothesis provides a good account of what emotions *do* in the context of Antonio Damasio's theory of what emotions *are*, or of Ronald de Sousa's account. But we cannot ask whether the search hypothesis provides a good account of what emotions do in the absence of such a theory. It is to their credit, then, that both of these authors have advocated the search hypothesis only in the context of their original accounts of what emotions are.

Damasio, for example, argues that emotions—or at least the qualitative, conscious experience of emotions that some philosophers prefer to call 'feelings'—are 'somatic markers'. That is, they are bodily sensations, whether of a visceral or nonvisceral kind, that are summoned up by particular thoughts or mental images. When the search hypothesis is advanced in the context of this particular theory of emotion, the following account of how emotions help rational decision-making emerges. When one starts thinking about the possible consequences of a decision, gut feelings may be triggered by particular images associated with certain consequences. If negative, the gut feeling 'forces attention on the negative outcome to which a given action may lead, and functions as an automated alarm signal which says: Beware of danger ahead if you choose the option which leads to this outcome' (Damasio 1994, 173). The signal may lead one to reject this option straight away, without the need for consideration of further consequences, and thus allow one to choose from among fewer alternatives.

Damasio backs up his claims with empirical data drawn from patients with various kinds of frontal lobe damage. These patients are strangely Hamlet-like. When confronted with a decision of even the most trivial nature, they may lose themselves in endless musings about the consequences of each possible action, with the result that the decision itself is postponed indefinitely.

After one consultation, for example, with a patient with frontal lobe damage, Damasio asked him when he would like to arrange his next appointment:

> I suggested two alternative dates, both in the coming month and just a few days apart from each other. The patient pulled out his appointment book and began consulting the calendar. The behaviour that ensued, which was witnessed by several investigators, was remarkable. For the better part of a half-hour, the patient enumerated reasons for and against each of the two dates: previous engagements, proximity to other engagements, possible meteorological conditions, virtually anything that one could reasonably think about concerning a simple date. ... he was now walking us through a tiresome cost-benefit analysis, an endless outlining and fruitless comparison of options and possible consequences. It took enormous discipline to listen to all of this without pounding on the table and telling him to stop, but finally we did tell him, quietly, that he should come on the second of the alternative dates. His response was equally calm and prompt. He simply said: 'That's fine'. Back the appointment book went into his pocket, and then he was off. (Damasio 1994, 193-94)

When these clinical data are combined with Damasio's claim that patients with frontal lobe damage are *emotionally* impaired, this lends some *prima facie* support to the claim that most of us are able to avoid analysis paralysis only because we are emotionally intact, and thus support the search hypothesis *when read in conjunction with* Damasio's theory of emotions as somatic markers.

Damasio's account leaves many questions unanswered. What, for example, is the patient really failing to do? Suppose, for the sake of argument, that Damasio's patient begins to construct a search tree in the typical manner. First, he starts by expanding the initial node of the tree into two states; go on Monday, and go on Tuesday. How he then goes about building the tree up from there depends on his search strategy. Most of us would soon stop the search, having found some particular node that 'tips the balance' towards one or other of the initial two nodes. The patient does not stop; but *why* not? According to Damasio's theory, he does not stop because he does not generate an appropriate somatic marker. But the theory does not say exactly why this failure occurs.

There are a number of possible answers. Perhaps the patient is simply failing to apply any test to each new node of the search tree as he generates it. Or perhaps he is applying a test, but not the right one. A third possibility is that he is applying the right test, but something is malfunctioning in the test mechanism. The somatic marker theory of emotion is consistent with all of these possibilities. Does the emotional deficit of Damasio's patient involve a failure to call up a test to be applied to each new node of the search tree as it is generated, so that no test is applied at all? Or does the patient simply apply the wrong test, so that no appropriate somatic marker can be generated? Or, as a third possibility, might the patient be applying the right test, but the test mechanism fails to trigger any somatic marker? Of course, this ambiguity is hardly grounds for dismissing Damasio's theory altogether. It simply means that Damasio's theory is couched at a certain level of generality, and is consistent with a number of more detailed specifications. It does, nevertheless, provide at least a general way of fleshing out the search hypothesis and turning it into a testable theory of the relation between reason and emotion.

Two final remarks

Before concluding, I wish to make two final remarks. The first concerns the fact that there is, at present, no consensus about what emotions are. Indeed, many philosophers now doubt that there is any good single definition of emotion. A consensus is emerging to the effect that the very diversity of phenomena referred to as 'emotions' precludes any single definition of the term. Paul Griffiths, for example, argues that 'the general category of emotion subsumes three different kinds of psychological state', and concludes that 'the general concept of emotion has no role in any future psychology' (1997, 245, 247). Jon Elster concurs. After suggesting that the emotions 'may not be a coherent and theoretically useful concept', he goes on to speculate that 'the unruly category of "the emotions" encompasses several, internally homogeneous classes of phenomena' (1999, 241). In a similar vein, Aaron Ben-Ze'ev (2000, 3) states that 'No single essence is necessary and sufficient for all emotions', and Ronald de Sousa (1994, 270) makes similar gloomy remarks about 'the sheer variety of phenomena covered by the word "emotion"'.

  The very heterogeneity of the emotions might seem to pose a further problem for the search hypothesis, construed as a claim about what emotions typically do. For if it is true that the term 'emotion' refers to a variety of natural kinds rather than a single kind, construing the search hypothesis as a claim about what emotions do may appear to reduce the hypothesis to the trite claim that a heterogeneous variety of mechanisms help us to solve the search problem. Once again, however, this is only a problem for the search hypothesis when it is considered in isolation from the context of any specific theory of emotion, or—more pertinently, if no single theory of emotion is to be found—any specific theory of a particular *class* of emotions. The search hypothesis is not necessarily committed to the view there is some single definition of emotion; all that it requires is that, if such a definition can be found, then whatever that definition turns out to be, it cannot be (on pain of circularity) that emotions are things that help us solve the search problem.

My second final remark concerns the relationship between the search hypothesis and the computational theory of mind. From the discussion so far, it may appear as if the search hypothesis, however it is read, is predicated on the assumption that humans make decisions in a way that closely resembles the way that current systems in artificial intelligence do. Only if the decision-making process in humans consists of gradually exploring a search space, is it possible to claim that emotions help humans to avoid doing so indefinitely. This, in turn, seems to pre-suppose the computational theory of mind. Indeed, part of the appeal of the search hypothesis of emotion for some may be that it promises a coherent computational account of emotion—something that many cognitive scientists are increasingly concerned to provide.

Despite these appearances, the search hypothesis is not committed to the computational theory of mind. Although the metaphor of 'exploring a search space' by 'expanding the search tree one node at a time' is couched unambiguously in the jargon of artificial intelligence, one can still think of it as a useful way of describing certain thought processes without being a fully paid-up, card-carrying computationalist. Damasio's account of the search hypothesis is a case in point. From his account of the role that somatic markers play in certain decision-making processes, it is clear that he construes some decision-making at least as consisting of something very similar to the search process described. It is also clear, however, that he takes this as a *phenomenological* description; it is meant as an account of the verbal thoughts and mental images that pass through the subject's *conscious awareness*. As such, it is agnostic about the precise nature of the unconscious processes that support this conscious superstructure. This unconscious substrate may well consist of rule-governed transformations of syntactic representations, as the computational theory of mind has it, but then again it may not. The fact that Damasio can make use of the search hypothesis without committing himself to the computational theory of mind, and do so coherently, is enough to refute the view that the search hypothesis stands or falls with computationalism.

Conclusion

The search hypothesis of emotion is the claim that emotions enable humans to solve the search problem. In other words, emotions prevent us from getting lost in endless explorations of potentially infinite search spaces by providing us with both the right kind of test and the right kind of search strategy for each kind of problem we must solve. The search hypothesis thus offers an account of the relationship between emotions and reason, according to which emotions play a positive role in aiding reason to make good decisions. However, the hypothesis is vacuous unless we have some independent account of emotion to flesh it out. It can only be assessed, then, in the context of some particular theory or other about what emotions are.

Acknowledgements

I would like to thank Nicholas Humphrey and two anonymous referees for their invaluable comments on an earlier version of this paper.

References

Ben-Ze'ev, A. (2000). *The subtlety of emotions*, MIT Press, Cambridge, MA.

Damasio, A. R. (1994). *Descartes' error: emotion, reason and the human brain*. Papermac, London.

de Sousa, R. (1987). *The rationality of emotion*, MIT Press, Cambridge, MA.

de Sousa, R. (1994). Emotion. In *A Companion to the philosophy of mind* (ed. S. Guttenplan), pp. 270–6. Blackwell, Oxford.

Elster, J. (1999). *Alchemies of the mind: rationality and the emotions*. Cambridge University Press, Cambridge.

Evans, D. (2001). *Emotion: the science of sentiment*. Oxford University Press, Oxford.

Fodor, J. A. (1983). *The modularity of mind: an essay on faculty psychology*, MIT Press, Cambridge, MA and London.

Fodor, J. A. (1987). Modules, frames, fridgeons, sleeping dogs, and the music of the spheres. In *The robot's dilemma: the frame problem in artificial intelligence* (ed. Z. W. Pylyshyn), pp. 139–49. Ablex, Norwood, NJ.

Ford, K. M. and Pylyshyn, Z. W. (ed.) (1996). *The robot's dilemma revisited: the frame problem in artificial intelligence*, Ablex, Norwood, NJ.

Frank, R. H. (1988). *Passions within reason: the strategic role of the emotions*. Norton, New York.

Griffiths, P. E. (1997). *What emotions really are: the problem of psychological categories*. University of Chicago Press, Chicago & London.

Hayes, P. (1987). What the frame problem is and isn't. in *The robot's dilemma: the frame problem in artificial intelligence* (ed. Z. W. Pylyshyn), pp. 123–37. Ablex, Norwood, NJ.

Ketelaar, T. and Todd, P. M. (2000). Framing our thoughts: ecological rationality as evolutionary psychology's answer to the frame problem. In *The evolution of minds: psychological and philosophical perspective* (ed. S. P. Davies and H. R. Holcomb), Kluvier, Dordrecht.

McCarthy, J. and Hayes, P. J. (1969). Some philosophical problems from the standpoint of artificial intelligence. In *Machine Intelligence 4* (ed. B. Meltzer and D. Michie), pp. 463–502. Edinburgh University Press, Edinburgh.

Pylyshyn, Z. (ed.) (1987). *The robot's dilemma: the frame problem in artificial intelligence.* Ablex, Norwood, NJ.

Russell, S and Norvig, P. (1995). *Artificial intelligence: a modern approach,* Prentice Hall, Upper Saddle River, NJ.

Simon, H. (1955). A behavioural model of rational choice. *Quarterly Journal of Economics,* **69**, 99–118.

CHAPTER 10

ADAPTIVE ILLUSIONS: OPTIMISM, CONTROL AND HUMAN RATIONALITY

DANIEL NETTLE

Introduction

To what extent are human beings rational? Many approaches in the behavioural sciences depend heavily on the assumption that they are almost perfectly so. The models of neoclassical economics, for example, construct a 'rational economic man' who weighs costs and benefits, and schedules his preferences, in a way that may be modelled by formal logic and probability theory.

What deeper principle stipulates that *Homo sapiens* should think in this way? Here, the theory of evolution has been periodically invoked as a guarantor (see, for example Riedl 1984, Ruse 1986). According to this type of argument, the brain is an adaptation whose function is to guide behaviour to the best fitness outcome for the individual. There is no better way to guide behaviour than having beliefs about the world that are true, and making valid inferences from them. Thus rationality, or more broadly, having cognitive structures that produce true beliefs, is argued to be a fitness maximum. Natural selection would ruthlessly remove cognitive structures that led to systematic departures from true belief or valid inference, and the cognitive system we have today is optimized for gathering knowledge and guiding action.

In apparent opposition to this vision of guaranteed rationality stands research which works inductively from actual experimental evidence of human judgement (Kahneman *et al.* 1982, Kahneman and Tversky 1973, Slovic *et al.* 1976). The thrust of this work is that people, in fact, employ various simple heuristics or rules of thumb, which lead to pervasive departures from ideal rationality. A full review is beyond the scope of this chapter, but it certainly throws into question the descriptive adequacy of rational actor models as usually defined.[1]

The evolutionary response to the apparently limited nature of real human reasoning takes several forms. One is to point out that across real-world problems, many of the simple heuristics function just as well as idealized models such as Bayesian reasoning, and have a much lower computational cost (Gigerenzer and Todd 1999). Thus the human actor is still rational, but his rationality is bounded by the constraints of cognitive capacity and time. The quick and dirty heuristics that he uses are more than adequate for most tasks, but some tricky laboratory problems can lead him to error. Another response is to point out that biases and failures of reasoning most often occur when tasks are presented which fall outside the format in which we actually reason in life, or outside the domain about which we evolved to reason (Cosmides 1989, Cosmides and Tooby 1996, Gigerenzer and Hoffrage 1995). Thus humans are rational within their native ecological context, which may not, for example, include reasoning about nuclear physics or small probabilities.

Whatever the potential of such arguments, not all biases and shortcomings of rationality can be explained away using them. Examples are the many domains where solidarity, spite, jealousy, anger, love and honour cause departures from cost-benefit optimum behaviour. Frank (1988) has suggested that these anomalies make sense if we look at the rationale for behaviour through a longer lens, inspired by evolutionary theory. In life, people are not just maximising immediate utility return, but maximizing long-term reproductive success in a complex web of social relationships which contains problems of alliances, relationship commitment, cheater deterrence and so on. Apparently irrational emotionality (moralistic anger, for example, or romantic love) often serves purposes within this context which are plausibly adaptive.

---

1 It is not just in psychology that there is an opposition between a theorized rational actor and empirical evidence of someone with quite different tendencies. In economics and anthropology, behavioural experiments and ethnographic observations undermine many assumptions of individualistic rational actor theory (Anand 1993, Bell 1995, Camerer 2002, Davis and Holt 1993, Henrich, Boyd, Bowles, Camerer, Fehr, Gintis and McElreath 2001). The solution must surely be a further iteration of theorizing with more realistic models rather than a claim that humans have properties which precede all explanation (see Nettle 1997). A similar strategy is attempted here with respect to apparently irrational judgement.

In this paper, I consider another set of well-studied departures from apparent rationality; self-enhancing or optimistic biases, and illusions of control (for a seminal review see Taylor and Brown 1988). The phenomena, which seem at first consideration to be grossly irrational, are reviewed (Section 2). Set against this (Section 3), there is a long tradition of arguing that these phenomena are, in fact, a necessary part of normal, healthy human cognition. A simple model is then presented (Section 4), in which it is shown that the irrationality of the phenomena is not as self-evident as it might appear. It is hypothesized that the biases and illusions are underlain by a heuristic which is plausibly adaptive, and perhaps even optimal in solving life-problems with imperfect information. Some implications for the conceptualization of human rationality are then discussed (Section 5).

Self-enhancement, optimism, and the illusion of control

Are our views of our own effectiveness and desirability realistic? Most of us think that we are better than average drivers (Svenson 1981), so we cannot all be right, and there is evidence that this kind of misjudgement applies quite widely. Alicke (1985) asked college students to rate various trait adjectives in terms of how characteristic they were of the respondent herself, and how characteristic they were of the average person of their generation. The trait adjectives had been independently rated for desirability by a separate panel.

The students judged, on average, that the highly desirable traits were more characteristic of themselves than of the average student, whilst they judged the undesirable characteristics to be more characteristic of the average student than of themselves. A related experiment by Campbell (1986) confirms this effect and shows that people apply different, and biased, judgement criteria to themselves than to their peers.

Campbell asked students to estimate, for a large number of different abilities, the proportion of the population who were poor, fair, average, good or very good. The respondents turned out to be quite good intuitive statisticians, producing an approximately normal distribution with the average at—yes—'average'. They were then asked to rate themselves at the same abilities. Across the whole set of respondents, the average self-rating was 'good', with less than 20% of instances of people judging themselves to be below average ability. Some people are, of course, better than average on many abilities, but they could not all be right. The fact the whole set of self-judgements is inflated compared to judgements about others demonstrates the working of a *self-enhancing bias*.

Self-enhancing biases are found in judgements about events as well as about traits. Lewinsohn, Mischel, Chaplin and Barton (1980) had participants take part in a small-group interaction task. They were then asked to rate their own influence and effectiveness in the interaction. Neutral observers did the same. Non-depressed individuals systematically assessed their own performance more favourably than the neutral observers. This finding is related to well-known biases in the attribution of causality; when making judgements about events involving the self, people tend to attribute positive outcomes to their own actions, and negative ones to the circumstances (Miller and Ross 1975, Zuckerman 1979). This effect disappears when the judgements are made about events not involving the self. For example, Mirels (1980) asked people to judge the extent to which the typical good (bad) event in their (someone else's) life was due to their own actions and abilities, and the extent to which it was due to external factors such as chance and the circumstances. In domains in which they felt highly involved, the participants consistently attributed more credit to themselves for success, and took less blame for failure, than they would for another person.

Self-enhancing biases about one's performance in the present are related to misplaced optimism about the future. Weinstein (1980) showed that people rate their own chances of positive future life events (having a good job, owning their own home, being professionally successful) as higher than the chances of their peers. Similarly, subjects will rate reliably their chances of having serious health problems such as alcoholism, mental illness or physical disability lower than an average peer (Harris and Middleton 1994, Weinstein 1980, 1982). This is not general over-optimism about or under-estimation of risk; it is a difference between risk assessments for the self and those for others. The glow of optimism is centred upon the self, but spills over into the immediate surroundings: estimates for family and friends are less optimistic than for the self, but more optimistic than for an 'average' peer (Harris and Middleton 1994). In a small-group experiment in which the performance of a fictitious product had to be predicted, participants felt, on little evidential basis, that the market would grow, year on year, as would their share of it (Larwood and Whitaker 1977). Such a biased assumption has potentially significant implications for the psychology of business.

The third cognitive illusion to be discussed here is a robust tendency known as the illusion of control (Alloy and Abramson 1979, Langer 1975, Langer and Roth 1975, Presson and Benassi 1996, Vazquez 1987). Langer conducted a series of experiments in which people engaged in blatantly chance-derived games such as dice rolling, card-drawing and lotteries. From the subjects' behaviour (for example, how much money they would need to be offered to sell their lottery ticket just before the draw), it was clear that they were working on the implicit assumption that their chances of the desired outcome were greater than they actually were. This is simply an optimistic bias. However, Langer also showed that where people had to do something active like choose their numbers or ticket themselves, the over-confidence was stronger, as if the very fact of making a behavioural decision made them feel that their behaviour controlled the flow of events. This finding has been repeated using direct measures of the feeling of control, and several different laboratory paradigms (Presson and Benassi 1996). For example, the paradigm of Alloy and Abramson (1979) asks people to estimate to what extent their pressing of a key controls the onset or not of a light. Players pay attention to the instances where the light comes on following their press, but not to those where the light comes without their pressing, and thus over-estimate their control in many conditions (Rudski 2000, Vazquez 1987). Overall, quite consistently, people over-estimate the effectiveness of their own actions in controlling the flow of events.

What is the common thread in the self-enhancing bias, the optimistic bias, and the illusion of control? McKenna (1993) has argued that the first two are products of the third, so in fact we have one cognitive illusion masquerading as three. The logic of McKenna's argument is as follows: if we over-estimate our degree of control over the flow of events, we will quite naturally be over-optimistic about our present performance and future prospects, since where we control the outcome, we will get the outcome we desire. There is certainly some appeal to this view. As McKenna shows, people are more over-optimistic about, for example, their chances of having an accident where they have control (e.g. where they are driving) than where they do not (e.g. as passengers). (This finding would account for the recurring fears voiced about the safety of public transportation, where statistics show private cars to be several times more dangerous).

However, other evidence suggests that the optimistic bias operates independently of the illusion of control. People predict better health outcomes for themselves than others, without necessarily feeling more in control of their health (Harris and Middleton 1994). Optimistic prediction and the feeling of control are not always correlated and may be evoked by separate factors in the laboratory (Budescu and Bruderman 1995). It is still an open question, then, whether self-enhancing and optimistic biases and the illusion of control represent the operation of a single underlying mechanism, or two or three independent ones. For present purposes, however, this subtle question need not affect us unduly. I will argue in Section 4 that all of these phenomena can be brought under the same analytical framework in terms of game theory. Henceforth, then, the self-enhancing and optimistic biases and the illusion of control will be referred to collectively as the *positive illusions* (Taylor 1989), without taking a position on whether they consist of a unitary cognitive mechanism or a small family.

One might reasonably ask how the positive illusions bear on human rationality. Rationality must surely involve soundness of inference in both deductive and inductive situations. In probabilistic situations, and especially under uncertainty, perfectly rational procedures can lead to error. However, it cannot be strictly rational to employ procedures that lead to *systematic* falsehood in judgements of contingency and predictions of events. More particularly, it does not seem that it can be rational to take exactly the same evidence and come up with different resulting beliefs depending on whether the person involved is the self or another. Laws of sound reasoning are laws of sound reasoning, and should be unaffected by who the people involved are, or how we chose the numbers on the ticket.

The positive illusions, then, are irrational in an everyday sense. They are also thus surprising. Human beings have made huge and costly investments in brain tissue over the last several million years of evolution (Aiello and Wheeler 1995). The payoff for this investment is often held to be enhanced ability to use present information to plan for and cope with the contingencies and vicissitudes of the future. According to the social brain hypothesis (Dunbar 1998), this ability is specially related to the social domain: the complex network of alliances, coalitions and reciprocations of the hominoid world. But many of the illusions discussed above occur in the social domain. They seem to involve reasoning deficits in areas—the way others see us, the likely outcome of future behaviour—which recurred throughout our evolutionary history, and where doing the right thing would have dramatic fitness consequences. Surely the implacable hand of natural selection would weed out a brain that systematically produced erroneous models of the world in favour of one not subject to these illusions and biases. (This argument does not, by the way, depend on these biases having an innate basis. If they are learned, one has to ask what patterns of contingency would lead to a mechanism like instrumental conditioning producing them, which raises the same questions).

Psychological considerations

One solution to the paradox might be that the positive illusions are restricted to a sub-group of individuals, perhaps affected by pathology of some kind, whilst the modal position was one of relative accuracy. This would mean that the population mean would be skewed away from veridical reasoning, but most individuals would be accurate. There is some logic to this view, since it has often been argued within psychology that having an accurate grasp of reality is diagnostic of mental health, whilst an aberrant view is a pointer to psychological problems (see Taylor and Brown 1988).

However, in the case of the positive illusions, the opposite has also been argued; that the illusions, though non-veridical, are somehow a beneficial element of a healthy mind. Such a view was expressed as early as 1902 by William James. In *The Varieties of Religious Experience* (James 1902), James argued that ' ... [in] the healthy-minded temperament ... the tendency to see things optimistically is like a water of crystallization in which the individual's character is set' (127). James sees the tension between this bias and objective rationality. The bias makes human reasoning 'inadequate as a philosophical doctrine ... because the evil facts which [the optimistic bias] refuses positively to account for are a genuine portion of reality' (163). However, he argues that a reasoning system should be justified by its 'fruits for life' rather than its formal completeness, a pragmatist vision to which we return in Section 5. He speculates that there might be particular advantages for the mind in reasoning with a personal set-point adjusted a little in the upwards direction:

> for aught we know to the contrary, 103° or 104° Fahrenheit might be a more favourable temperature for truths to germinate and sprout in, than the more ordinary blood-heat of 97° or 98° (James 1902, 15)

James certainly seems to have been correct that there is a relationship between the positive illusions and mental health, a claim documented rather richly by Taylor and Brown (1988) nearly a century later. They show that having the illusions appears to be the population norm, whilst it is their absence which is diagnostic of sub-groups with pathology. The illusion of control disappears amongst the depressed or dysphoric (Alloy and Abramson 1979, Vazquez 1987). The strength of illusion of control in a person is predictive of their negative mood following task failure, their ease of discouragement in the face of challenges, and their depressive symptoms in response to life events (Alloy and Clements 1992). The correlation is an inverse one: the stronger the illusion of control, the greater the immunity to these negative effects.

Those with low self-esteem, mild depression, or both, form views of their social performance which are close to those formed by neutral observers (Lewinsohn, Mischel, Chaplin and Barton 1980), and use uniform principles for evaluating themselves and others (Brown 1986). Indeed, one metric of the effectiveness of the intervention for depression studied by Lewinsohn, Mischel, Chaplin and Barton (1980) was that the depressed group started getting more *accurate* in their evaluations of their own effectiveness. The mildly depressed are also less likely to judge positive outcomes more likely for themselves and negative outcomes less so than their peers (Alloy and Ahrens 1987). Thus it would appear that the presence of positive illusions, far from being a pathology, is related to good and robust mental health.

Thus the evidence suggests that positive illusions are normal and perfectly healthy. Furthermore, it is quite possible to produce a mind that lacks these illusions. For one thing, the depressed lack many of them, though their cognition is highly unrealistic in other ways. More importantly, we all lack positive illusions every time we think about someone other than ourselves. There is thus nothing intrinsically impossible about making unbiased assessments of control or future prospects; we just tend not to do so when making judgements about the self. The rest of this paper is devoted to a consideration of why this should be.

An evolutionary model

As discussed in Section 1, the apparently irrational may be shown to be adaptive through a longer lens in which the focus is on the consequences of behaviour in natural settings rather than a mathematically correct by ecologically irrelevant expected payoff. Here I present a simple model that attempts to do just this. The psychological literature on positive illusions generally concerns judgements and evaluations. Outside the laboratory, judgements and evaluations are usually cognitive inputs to some sort of behavioural decision.

Following much work in evolutionary and economic theory (Binmore 1990, Gintis 2000, Maynard Smith 1982), we can conceptualize almost any behavioural decision as a game. In this game, there are two outcomes—success and failure—and two courses of action—to play or not to play. For example, let us imagine that the decision is whether to apply for a job, try for a chieftanship, or make an offer of marriage. If the player plays and succeeds, he takes a benefit of success b, if he plays and fails, some cost of failure c.

If the decision is not to play, then the direct cost is 0, since nothing is ventured nor can be lost. However, if the person would have succeeded if he had played, then by doing nothing he is missing out on something he could have gained. Thus, the player's optimal response is not to play when he would fail, and to play when he would succeed. However, let us assume that success and failure are determined only probabilistically, with a probability of success p, and thus a probability of failure $(1-p)$. If the decision is to play, then the expected direct payoff to the player is given by:

$$pb-(1-p)c \tag{1}$$

It is rational to play when the expected outcome of doing so is greater than the expected outcome of not doing so, that is when:

$$pb-(1-p)c>0 \tag{2}$$

From (2), it follows by simple algebra that the minimal probability of success required to make playing rational (p_r) is:

$$p_r=c/(b+c) \tag{3}$$

where b and c are equal, then p_r is 0.5; if the odds are better than chance, then play. When b and c are not equal, however, then interesting dynamics begin to emerge. Figure 1 shows the curve of p_r for different values of b with c held constant at 1, and for different values of c with b held constant at 1. The graphs show that, if c is small, then as b increases, the probability required to play rapidly declines to the point where it is worth playing even if the probability of success is very small (in the limit, as $b/c \rightarrow \infty$, $p_r \rightarrow 0$). Similarly, if b is small, then as c increases, p_r approaches 1, so that even if the probability of success is very high, the player should not play.

The way to behave rationally is to know p, b and c and to follow equation (3). But what if knowledge is imperfect? In particular, if the exact situation has never occurred before, then p can only be estimated with some unspecified degree of error. Error means that the subjective probability p_s which the player uses to make his choice, will differ in one way or another from the actual probability p. The player will still make an optimal decision so long as p_s and p are on the same side of the curve (that is, on the same side of p_r). If $p > p_r$ but $p_s < p_r$, then the person will not play when he should, whereas if $p < p_r$ but $p_s > p_r$, then the person should not play but will.

Whether an error will, in fact, be made in any game will depend upon the size of error and how the probabilities fall out. However, we can state generally that in the area above the curves of Fig. 10.1, overestimates of p can never lead to sub-optimal behaviour, whereas underestimates may possibly do so. It is easy to see why this is the case: if the chances are good enough to play on the basis of the actual probability, then they will always seem good enough to play using an overestimate of that probability. However, they may not seem good enough if the probability is under-estimated. Conversely, and for mirror-image reasons, in the area below the curves of Fig. 10.1, an underestimate can never lead to a sub-optimal decision, whereas an overestimate could do so. The situation is summed up by Fig. 10.2; in the zone above the curve, an overestimate never matters, and in the zone below the curve, an underestimate never matters.

Where b is bigger than c, the range of probabilities over which an overestimate never matters is large. Indeed, as b/c tends to infinity, then the range over

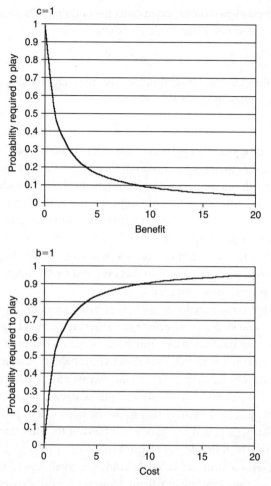

Figure 10.1 The probability required to rationally play the game, against the benefit of success with the cost of failure held constant at 1 (top), and against the cost of failure with the benefit of success held constant at 1 (bottom)

which an overestimate never matters becomes the whole range 0 to 1. As long as b is significantly bigger than c then, unless we know what the true probability is, an overestimate would be better than an underestimate, simply because the zone in which overestimation never matters is so much bigger than the zone in which underestimation never matters. In fact, if information is imperfect, an overestimate would be better than an unbiased estimate of p. This is because, using an unbiased estimate with a degree of error, some subjective probabilities would fall above the true value of p and some below. Thus, on an average, half of all subjective probabilities would be in a zone where they

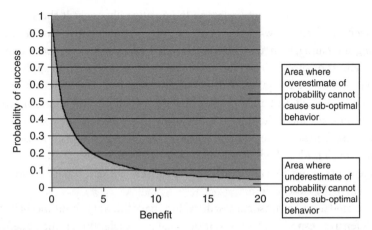

Figure 10.2 Zones in which underestimates and overestimates cannot produce sub-optimal behaviour ($c=1$).

could lead to the wrong decision. If instead of an unbiased estimate, the player forms a subjective probability which is biased by the benefit/cost ratio to a degree greater than the magnitude of uncertainty, then over most of the range of actual probabilities, he would never make the wrong decision.

Let us sum up the key generalizations from the model. The first is that if whether to play or not depends not just on the probability of success but also on the benefits and costs. Second, where the benefits of success much outweigh the costs of failure, then the probability of success required to rationally play is very small. The third is that, as the benefit/cost ratio increases, the range of circumstances over which an overestimate of the probability of success would be better than either an underestimate or an error-prone unbiased estimate gets bigger. In the limit, if something had an infinite benefit of success and a small cost of failure, you should work on the assumption that you can succeed *whatever* your true chances. Finally, where there is random error in the estimation of the probability of success, an over-estimate may actually lead to superior decisions than an unbiased estimate. With an unbiased estimate, half of all guesses will fall below the true value and half above. With a biased estimate, most or all guesses will fall on the same side of the true line. As we have seen, there is an asymmetry of outcome between guesses on the two sides of the true line; where $b > c$, overestimates lead to behaviour that is absolutely as good as perfect estimates; underestimates on the other hand can lead to error. Thus, a biased estimate could be not only as good as an unbiased one but actually superior, since once the random error is applied to the unbiased estimate, it could be pushed over into a sub-optimal decision.

How does this theorizing relate to the positive illusions? It shows that in behavioural decisions where the benefit of success much outweighs the cost of trying and failing, then, under uncertainty, it is adaptive to be optimistic about the chances of success. The crucial inequality, $b > c$, does seem to apply to the situations where the positive illusions are observed. The benefit of being perceived as intelligent and honest, of having a good job and home, of avoiding alcoholism and unhappiness is obviously huge, whereas the cost of acting as if these things can be attained when, in fact, they cannot is non-zero but much smaller. Also, the illusions disappear when the subject is asked to make judgements about a stranger, which is, precisely, the case where b and c are equal in being close to zero.

The model is also consonant with evolutionary thinking about mechanisms of defensive responses. In cases of physical and social threat, the benefit of avoiding the outcome is high, and the costs of doing so relatively small. Nesse (2001) has argued that we should thus expect threat-avoidance systems to evolve which err on the side of producing false alarms rather than the side of complacency. This indeed is what is observed in the prevalence of anxiety disorders and phobias. When it comes to self-protection, there is a 'better safe than sorry' principle, which can lead to over-estimation of threat and produce disorders of excessive defence (Gilbert 1993). The logic is also that of Pascal's famous wager, that it would be better to believe in God than not, because the benefits if He did turn out to exist would overshadow the costs of assuming he did and being disappointed (Jordan 1994).

Not all of the illusion of control findings are neatly predicted by the current model without some further consideration. For example, in the classic paradigm of Alloy and Abramson (1979), the participant has to judge the extent to which his key presses control the onset of a light. There is no reward for controlling the light. The participant gets his dollar or credit whether he controls it or not, so it would appear that $b = c$, and yet the illusion of control appears. One interpretation is that people generally find controlling the flow of events in their environment preferable to not doing so. This position has a venerable history within psychology (see Heider 1958, Lefcourt 1973); it makes *prima facie* evolutionary sense, and would mean that controlling a process in which one was involved would have an intrinsic reward greater than not controlling it. The other explanation is that participants believe that the experimenter is testing their ability to control the light. This implicitly equates to a belief that there will be some kind of social benefit in succeeding to control it, and thus brings the experiment within the framework of the current model.

The theory predicts that the positive illusions will only appear under uncertainty about the true probability of success. There is some evidence that this is correct. Koehler *et al.* (1994) show that where people play an iterated game (and hence are operating with improving data about the true probabilities), the illusion of control begins to disappear.

A Vision of Human Reason

The model suggests that under certain circumstances, being overly optimistic about one's chances/control could be adaptive, that is superior in terms of behavioural decisions to either pessimism or unbiased neutrality. The model specifies where the positive advantage applies, and the positive illusions have been observed rather precisely in the areas where the model says they should be adaptive. Thus, it is quite plausible to argue that these modes of reasoning have been acquired by human beings because they produce more successful behavioural decisions than alternative modes of reasoning.

Does this therefore make them rational? How we will answer this question depends upon our construal of rationality. There seem to be two main choices here, which may be termed *deontological* or *consequentialist* (Samuels *et al.* 2002); the Evans *et al.* 1993 distinction between rationality$_1$ and rationality$_2$ is absolutely equivalent). Under a deontological conception, then following a system of valid logical rules is constitutive of rationality. The positive illusions are therefore undeniably irrational, since they involve processes of unwarranted inference from data which systematically create false beliefs. However, the alternative, consequentialist conceptions appeal to the idea that what determines the rationality or otherwise of a process is consideration of the consequences they lead to. A process that generally leads to a person achieving his or her goal is rational in this sense, a notion that returns us to William James and his 'fruits for life'.

The model discussed in this chapter suggests strongly that positive illusions, though irrational in a deontological sense, could be said to be rational in a consequentialist sense, exactly where the benefit of success outweighs the cost of failure, and there is uncertainty about the true probability of success. This, along with other recent findings, is demanding an adjustment of our picture of *Homo sapiens*. For neoclassical economics, he was a deontological super-hero, making vastly complex rule-governed calculations of immediate utility flawlessly. For the heuristics and biases tradition of psychology, he was a poor creature, working with a few rather limited reasoning tricks that often led him into error, and 'lack[ing] the correct programs for many important judgemental tasks' (Slovic *et al.* 1976). The view of evolutionary psychology transcends both of these. An evolved mind works under limitations of capacity and time, and must solve real-world social problems. It must use heuristics, but these heuristics will be honed by natural selection to be highly effective. There is no intrinsic evolutionary advantage to deontological rationality, and such rationality should only be expected where it coincides with consequentialist considerations (which it often, but not always, does). Evolutionary psychology describes a human being who is logically quirky, but highly effective at producing the right behavioural decisions under realistic constraints of time, capacity and uncertainty, in the rich social environment in which we evolved.

Acknowledgments

I am grateful to Paul Gilbert, Tom Stoneham and the editors of this volume for their comments on this chapter. All errors and opinions are of course my own.

References

Aiello, L. C. and Wheeler, P. (1995). The expensive-tissue hypothesis: the brain and the digestive system in human and primate evolution. *Current Anthropology*, **36**,199–221.

Alicke, M. D. (1985). Global self-evaluation as defined by the desirability and controllability of trait adjectives. *Journal of Personality and Social Psychology*, **49**, 1621–30.

Alloy, L. B. and Abramson, L. Y. (1979). Judgement of contingency in depressed and non-depressed subjects: sadder but wiser? *Journal of Experimental Psychology: General*, **108**, 443–79.

Alloy, L. B. and Ahrens, A. H. (1987). Depression and pessimism for the future: biased use of statistically relevant information in predictions for self versus others. *Journal of Personality and Social Psychology*, **41**, 1129–40.

Alloy, L. B. and Clements, C. M. (1992). Illusion of control: invulnerability to negative affect and depressive symptoms after laboratory and natural stressors. *Journal of Abnormal Psychology*, **101**, 234–45.

Anand, P. (1993). *Foundations of rational choice under risk*. Oxford University Press, Oxford.

Bell, D. (1995). On the nature of sharing: beyond the range of methodological individualism. *Current Anthropology*, **36**, 826–30.

Binmore, K. (1990). *Essays on the foundations of game theory*. Blackwell, Oxford.

Brown, J. D. (1986). Evaluations of self and others: self-enhancement biases in social judgements. *Social Cognition*, **4**, 353–76.

Budescu, D. V. and Bruderman, M. (1995). The relationship between the illusion of control and the desirability bias. *Journal of Behavioural Decision Making*, **8**, 109–25.

Camerer, C. (2002). *Behavioral game theory: experiments on strategic interaction*. Princeton University Press, Princeton.

Campbell, J. D. (1986). Similarity and uniqueness: the effects of attribute type, relevance and individual differences in self-esteem and depression. *Journal of Personality and Social Psychology*, **50**, 281–94.

Cosmides, L. (1989). The logic of social exchange: has natural selection shaped how humans reason? *Cognition*, **31**, 187–276.

Cosmides, L. and Tooby, J (1996). Are humans good intuitive statisticians after all? rethinking some conclusions from the literature on judgement under uncertainty. *Cognition*, **58**, 1–73.

Davis, D. D. and Holt, C. A. (1993). *Experimental economics*. Princeton University Press, Princeton.

Dunbar, R. I. M. (1998). The social brain hypothesis. *Evolutionary Anthropology*, **6**, 178–90.

Evans, J., Over, D., and Manktelow, K. I. (1993). Reason, decision-making and rationality. *Cognition*, **49**, 165–87.

Frank, R. H. (1988). *Passions within reason: the strategic role of the emotions*. Norton, New York.

Gigerenzer, G. and Hoffrage, U. (1995). How to improve Bayesian reasoning without instruction: frequency formats. *Psychological Review*, **102**, 684–704.

Gigerenzer, G. and Todd, P. M. (1999). *Simple heuristics that make us smart*. Oxford University Press, Oxford.

Gilbert, P. (1993). Defence and safety: their function in social behaviour and psychopathology. *British Journal of Clinical Psychology*, **32**, 131–53.

Gintis, H. (2000). *Game theory evolving: a problem-centred introduction to modelling strategic behaviour*. Princeton University Press, Princeton.

Harris, P. and Middleton, W (1994). The illusion of control and optimism about health: On being less at risk but no more in control than others. *British Journal of Social Psychology*, **33**, 369–86.

Heider, F. (1958). *The psychology of interpersonal relations*. Wiley, New York.

Henrich, J., Boyd, R., Bowles, S., Camerer, C., Fehr, E., Gintis, H., and McElreath, R. (2001). In search of Homo economicus: Behavioral experiments in 15 small-scale societies. *American Economic Review*, **91**, 73–8.

James, W. (1902). *The varieties of religious experience*. Longmans, Green & Co., New York.

Jordan, J. (1994). *Gambling on god: essays on pascal's wager*. Rowman & Littlefield, London.

Kahneman, D., Slovic, P., and Tversky, A. (1982). *Judgement under uncertainty: heuristics and biases*. Cambridge University Press, Cambridge.

Kahneman, D. and Tversky, A. (1973). On the psychology of prediction. *Psychological Review*, **80**, 237–51.

Koehler, J. J., Gibbs, B. J., and Hogarth, R. M. (1994). Shattering the illusion of control: multi-shot versus single-shot gambles. *Journal of Behavioural Decision Making*, **7**, 183–91.

Langer, E. J. (1975). The illusion of control. *Journal of Personality and Social Psychology*, **32**, 311–28.

Langer, E. J. and Roth, J. (1975). Heads I win, tails it's chance: the illusion of control as a function of the sequence of outcomes in a purely chance task. *Journal of Personality and Social Psychology*, **32**, 951–55.

Larwood, L. and Whitaker, W. (1977). Managerial myopia: self-serving biases in organisational planning. *Journal of Applied Psychology*, **62**, 194–8.

Lefcourt, H. M. (1973). The functions of the illusions of control and freedom. *American Psychologist*, **28**, 417–25.

Lewinsohn, P. M., Mischel, W., Chaplin, W., and Barton, R. (1980). Social competence and depression: The role of illusory self-perceptions. *Journal of Abnormal Psychology*, **89**, 203–12.

Maynard Smith, J. (1982). *Evolution and the theory of games*. Cambridge University Press, Cambridge.

McKenna, F. (1993). It won't happen to me: unrealistic optimism or illusion of control? *British Journal of Psychology*, **84**, 39–50.

Miller, D. T. and Ross, M. (1975). Self-serving biases in attribution of causality: fact or fiction? *Psychological Bulletin*, **82**, 213–25.

Mirels, H. L. (1980). The avowal of responsibility for good and bad outcomes: the effects of generalized self-serving biases. *Personality and Social Psychology Bulletin*, **6**, 299–306.

Nesse, R. M. (2001). The smoke detector principle: natural selection and the regulation of defenses. *Annals of the New York Academy of Sciences*, **935**, 75–85.

Nettle, D. (1997). On the status of methodological individualism. *Current Anthropology*, **38**, 283–6.

Presson, P. K. and Benassi, V. A. (1996). Illusion of control: a meta-analytic review. *Journal of Social Behaviour and Personality*, **11**, 493–510.

Riedl, R. (1984). *Biology of knowledge: the evolutionary basis of reason*. Wiley, Chichester.

Rudski, J. M. (2000). Illusion of control relative to chance outcomes. *Psychological Reports*, **87**, 85–92.

Ruse, M. (1986). *Taking darwin seriously: a naturalistic approach to philosophy*. Blackwell, Oxford.

Samuels, R., Stich, S., and Faucher, L. (2002). Reason and rationality. In *Handbook of epistemology*, (ed. M. Sintonen). Kluwer, Dordrecht.

Slovic, P., Fischhoff, B., and Lichtenstein, S. (1976). Cognitive processes and societal risk taking. In *Cognition and social behaviour* (ed. J. S. Carol and J. W. Payne). Erlbaum, Hillsdale.

Svenson, O. (1981). Are we all less risky and more skillful than our fellow drivers? *Acta psychologica*, **47**, 143–8.

Taylor, S. E. (1989). *Positive illusions*. Basic Books, New York.

Taylor, S. E. and Brown, J. D. (1988). Illusion and well-being: a social psychological perspective on mental health. *Psychological Bulletin*, **103**, 193–201.

Vazquez, C. (1987). Judgement of contingency: cognitive biases in depressed and non-depressed subjects. *Journal of Personality and Social Psychology*, **52**, 419–31.

Weinstein, N. D. (1980). Unrealistic optimism about future life events. *Journal of Personality and Social Psychology*, **39**, 806–20.

Weinstein, N. D. (1982). Unrealistic optimism about susceptibility to health problems. *Journal of Behavioural Medicine*, **5**, 441–60.

Zuckerman, M. (1979). Attribution of success and failure revisited: the motivational bias is alive and well in attribution theory. *Journal of Personality*, **47**, 245–87.

CHAPTER 11

EMOTION VERSUS REASON AS A GENETIC CONFLICT

CHRISTOPHER BADCOCK

Conflict between emotion and reason is an everyday fact of life, but one that has been surprisingly little discussed in the scientific literature on emotions and/or cognition. In this short paper I suggest the possibility that such a common but scientifically unremarked observation may have an unexpected basis in genetic conflict.

Organisms can be thought of as *epigenetic agents* of their genes. In other words, genes can be seen as building bodies and brains to carry out functions on their behalf, such as real-time responses to environmental challenges that involve perception and analysis of stimuli by a nervous system in command of the organism's motility. This is something that would normally be beyond the capacity of any individual gene, but is the typical function of a brain (Badcock 2000).

However, there are now good reasons for thinking it naive to assume that all genes will agree within a multi-cellular, sexually-reproducing diploid organism (that is, one where both a father and mother contribute almost equal sets of genes to the offspring). On the contrary, as we shall now see, there are very good reasons indeed for believing that even if we ignore sex chromosomes (because of the asymmetry they introduce into an organism's genetic makeup, female mammals having two X chromosomes, but males an X and a Y), the remaining, ostensibly equal and parallel genetic endowments from the parents can occasion profound conflict.

Genomic imprinting

Although a strictly equal number of chromosomes is normally inherited from each parent, some genes have been found to be expressed when they are inherited from one parent, but not when they come from the other. This effect is known as *genomic imprinting* (Ohlsson *et al.* 1995, Reik and Surani 1997).

An imprinted gene is expressed when inherited from one parent but is not expressed when inherited from the other. A gene that is expressed only when inherited from the father is said to be *paternally-active* because it is the paternal copy only that is expressed, thanks to its maternal equivalent being imprinted. Similarly, a gene corresponding to a paternally imprinted one that is expressed only when inherited from the mother is termed *maternally-active*. In other words, the imprints on genes are reset each generation, and a gene that is maternally-imprinted in a male will be paternally-imprinted when passed on to a man's children, and vice versa. Most imprinted genes could be thought of as master control genes, which regulate many others downstream of them in the developmental cascade. For example, some produce growth factors which have effects throughout the organism and are expressed early in development, often with permanent consequences (Barlow 1995, John and Surani 1996).

IGF2 is a case in point. This gene produces insulin-like growth-factor number 2. Its effect is to stimulate the growth of the embryo. Its absence in mice results in pups that are 40 per cent smaller at birth than normal, but otherwise normally proportioned. In mice, as in most mammals, both parents tend to benefit from larger-sized offspring. In the case of human beings, larger, better-grown babies live longer, suffer less from disease, and have generally better health than smaller, less well grown ones (Barker 1994, 1996). Coronary heart disease, stroke and non-insulin dependent diabetes are particularly associated with low birthweight independent of lifestyle factors, such as smoking, obesity and socio-economic status (Barker 1998, Barker 1999). Research also suggests that taller men do better than shorter ones in many occupations and are preferred by women (Pawlowski *et al.* 2000, Barker 1999).

However, although the benefits of increased size of offspring may be similar for both parents, the costs are not. In mammals, larger offspring mean increased costs to the mother during gestation and lactation, but no necessary cost whatsoever to the father. In humans, the physical cost of a pregnancy to the mother has been estimated at about 80,000 calories (equal to 300 hamburger meals, or in energy terms, enough for a run of 800 miles). In the US at the time of writing, the going rate for egg donation was $5,000–80,000, but for sperm donation only $100. In terms of mass contributed to the newborn as a fraction of the father's only contribution (one sperm), the mother's is one hundred billion times greater (Potts and Short 1999)!

This may explain why the *IGF2* gene in humans is only active when inherited from the father. The maternal copy is imprinted. However, when the paternal *IGF2* gene is duplicated or when a mutant maternal copy is inherited that can't be silenced, the individual concerned receives a double dose of growth factor and Beckwith-Wiedemann syndrome results. The symptoms are large placenta, heavy birth weight, excessive growth during adolescence, large tongue, large liver, proliferation of insulin-producing cells and child-hood tumours—in sum, overgrowth (Reik and Surani 1997, Sun *et al.* 1997).

If a male mammal mates with several females, the situation facing a paternal allele is different from that facing a maternal one. This is because there is no necessary reason why any of that male's genes should find themselves in an offspring of the same female more than once. But maternity is certain in the sense that a fetus develops inside its mother and so is definitely hers. Any gene in the mother must have an equal chance of being in any fetus that occupies her womb. However, paternal genes do not have the same vested interest in not exploiting the mother that maternal ones have. In mating with many different females, a paternal gene that spared the mother at a cost to its own success would lose out in competition with other paternal genes that were less co-operative. If their greater demand on the mother promoted their own reproductive success as it probably would do, the more rapacious pater-nal genes would become more common than the less exploitative ones.

Considerations of this kind almost certainly explain why imprinting is not found in birds, fish or reptiles, where the mother controls the production of eggs with a fixed amount of nutrients independent of the father. However, imprinting is found in classes of organisms where offspring are nourished directly from maternal tissues, such as mammals and flowering plants, and in which paternal genes can influence the allocation of resources to the offspring. The conflict of interest between maternal and paternal genes to which this gives rise probably explains the evolution of imprinting in such cases.

Genetic conflict

Igf2r (for *Igf2* receptor) is imprinted contrariwise to *Igf2*: the mother's copy is expressed, while the father's is imprinted. *Igf2r* produces a sink for insulin-like growth factor 2, mopping it up before it can have much effect on the embryo. Its success can be gauged by the fact that mice who lack this maternal gene are on average 16 per cent larger at birth than they otherwise would be (Haig and Graham 1991). *Igf2* illustrates the tendency for paternally-active genes to make greater demands on the mother's resources, and *Igf2r* for maternally-active ones to make lesser demands on her. Paternal genes are usually associated with larger, faster-growing, or more active offspring, while maternal ones are correlated with the opposite effects. In maize, for example, paternal genes are associated with larger kernel size, while maternal genes produce smaller kernels (Domínguez 1995).

Such findings cannot be explained by the view that parental contributions are complementary because *Igf2/Igf2r* is a case of one gene sabotaging another: conflict and contradiction, not co-operation and complementarity. This is underlined by the fact that mice who lack both *Igf2* and *Igf2r* are of normal size. If co-operation between these paternal and maternal genes were essential for normal growth, knocking out both would be lethal, or at least, significant for growth and development. But if maternal and paternal genes simply counter each other in this instance, the finding that knocking out both makes little difference is exactly what you would expect (Jaenisch 1997).

A consequence of conflict between imprinted genes in mammals is that paternal genes might be expected to be particularly prominent in the placenta because it is an organ specifically designed to extract resources from the mother and transfer them to the developing fetus in her womb. The placenta is genetically part of the fetus, not of the mother, and develops out of the fertilized egg cell. In the early stages of development the placenta dominates, comprising 85 per cent of combined weight with the fetus at 8 weeks' gestation. The human placenta is the most invasive of all placentas, and in some cases can perforate the uterus, killing the mother. The fact that anemic mothers have heavier placentas than non-anemic ones despite giving birth to lower-weight babies suggests that the placenta can actively respond to deficits in the mother's provision of nutrients. The placenta is an active protagonist in pregnancy which can come under attack itself from maternal cells in the lining of the womb that resemble the natural killer cells of the immune system. Indeed, these cells may function to limit the extent of placental invasion, and thus restrict the offspring's access to maternal resources. Cells originating in the placenta appear to widen the mother's arteries that feed it by breaking down their walls and weakening them, so that they sag and distend, thereby increasing blood supply to the cavities that the placenta excavates to receive it. Fine, tree-like capillaries fill these spaces and directly absorb nutrients from the mother's blood and return wastes to it (Haig 1996).

The fact that fetal cells have direct access to the mother's circulation as a result of their invasion of her tissues means that they can attempt to influence her by releasing hormones directly into her blood-stream. If this were merely a question of communication between fetus and mother serving the common interests of both, you would predict that minimum amounts would only be necessary—a whisper, so to speak. But in reality things are not so simple, and studies show an escalation of maternal and fetal hormone production more reminiscent of a heated argument than a quiet conversation—the hormonal equivalent of a shouting match. Levels of hormones produced by the placenta in pregnancy are typically hundreds or thousands of times higher than those produced by the mother herself in the non-pregnant state (Haig 1993).

The importance of these hormones is illustrated by the role that some of them play in maintaining the pregnancy. Some estimates put the number of conceptions that never come to term as high as 75 per cent. Most of these are believed to miscarry before the twelfth week of pregnancy, and many others before the first period. Other estimates suggest that 10 to 15 per cent of fertilized eggs will never be implanted, 42 per cent will fail to halt the sexual cycle and 28 per cent of all embryos will be spontaneously aborted (Bernds and Barash 1979).

The mother's readiness to spontaneously abort a fetus in her own interests creates an incentive for the fetus to defend itself from such a threat. In order to wrest control of the pregnancy from the mother, the placenta releases large quantities of a hormone of its own (chorionic gonadotropin) into her blood. This hormone makes the mother's ovaries produce estrogens and progesterone, which stimulate growth of the womb, suppress ovulation and, in the case of progesterone, quietens it. By the seventh week of pregnancy the placenta manufactures its own estrogens and progesterone in sufficient quantities to maintain the pregnancy hormonally without the help of the mother. Progesterone output by the placenta reaches levels 20 times above those of the mother in the non-pregnant state. This in its turn may be exploited by the mother to gauge the quality of the offspring and its ability to thrive (Haig 1994).

There is also evidence that the fetus heightens maternal blood pressure in order to decrease blood flow to the mother's peripheral circulation and to increase it to the placenta. Blood pressure in mothers appears to correlate with birth weight in both directions: women with lower than normal blood pressure during pregnancy tend to have lighter babies, and those with hypertension probably have heavier ones than they would otherwise. Furthermore, women with high blood pressure tend to lose fewer babies than average (Haig 1993).

The mother's glucose level falls during early pregnancy when the demands of the fetus are small but stabilize at a new low level when its demands are rising. It seems that the mother is resetting her blood sugar level to be lower during pregnancy—in other words, providing less for herself and her baby than she does for herself alone! Genetic conflict between mother and fetus may explain these surprising findings. According to this way of looking at things, the mother reduces her glucose level in anticipation of an aggressive level of uptake by the fetus, rather as someone bidding at an auction might start off at a price much lower than the one they expected to have to pay. However, whatever the level, mother and fetus will compete for glucose after every meal. The longer the mother takes to consume her blood sugar, the more will be taken up by the fetus. Therefore the mother escalates her production of insulin so as to absorb it more quickly in late pregnancy when fetal demands are peaking. The fetus manipulates the mother's glucose economy by secreting human placental lactogen (hPL), a hormone that reduces the mother's sensitivity to her own insulin. This means that the mother's blood sugar level stays higher for longer, giving the fetus more time to consume the glucose despite the mother's best efforts to prevent this by escalating her output of insulin. The gene for hPL is paternally-active and so is yet another instance of genetic conflict between maternal and paternal genes: in other words, a case of genes in the fetus exploiting the mother because they come from the father (Haig 1993).

Imprinted genes and brain development

Prader-Willi syndrome is a developmental disorder in about 1 in 15,000 births, and is caused by the loss or silencing of paternally active genes on chromosome 15 through inheriting both copies of this chromosome from the mother, or losing part of the paternal copy (Nicholls, Saitoh et al. 1998). Significantly in view of the rule about maternal genes having a self-interest in saving the mother's resources, symptoms include lack of appetite, poor suckling ability, a weak cry, inactivity and sleepiness, high pain threshold and reduced tendency to vomit—from the mother's point of view, almost the ideal, undemanding baby (Franke et al. 1995)! Characteristic obsessive/compulsive behaviour is also sometimes listed as a symptom in Prader-Willi syndrome, and as the rule that maternal genes tend to favour smaller size would suggest, Prader-Willi children also have small stature, hands and feet (Driscoll 1994). Although there is no cure as such, the primary treatment, approved by the Food and Drug Administration in the USA, involves injections of the growth hormone Genotropin (Brody 2002).

By contrast to Prader-Willi, in Angelman syndrome only the paternal chromosome 15 is present in its entirety, and the critical maternal genes involved in Prader-Willi syndrome are missing (Nicholls et al. 1998). Symptoms include prolonged suckling, hyperactivity and frequent waking—every mother's worst fear. Although both Prader-Willi and Angelman children are retarded, Angelman retardation is usually much more severe, and speech is absent. By contrast, 'exceptional proficiency with jigsaw puzzles' has been mentioned as a diagnostic criterion in Prader-Willi cases, and speech is usually present (although articulation is often defective) (Holm *et al.* 1993). Whereas Prader-Willi patients have a high pain threshold (and often damage themselves as a result), Angelman patients have a low pleasure threshold to the extent that frequent 'paroxysms of laughter' is listed as a major diagnostic feature and the condition is sometimes known as 'happy puppet syndrome'.

Most imprinted genes will affect how much an offspring receives from its mother, at the expense of siblings. Imprinting might be expected to affect genes that influence growth, suckling, neonatal behaviour, appetite, and nutrient metabolism (Moore and Haig 1991). The hypothalamus is an important part of the limbic—or emotive—brain that is concerned with basic drives and appetites such as hunger, thirst, sex and aggression, and with emotional responses such as pleasure, pain and anxiety. Almost from the beginning, some kind of developmental defect in the hypothalamus was suspected in Prader-Willi and Angelman syndromes, in part because appetite, pain and pleasure threshold, vomiting and temperature-control are all known to be functions of the hypothalamus (Franke *et al.* 1995).

Recently, it has been possible to show that imprinted genes play a critical role in brain development, and not just the hypothalamus. Mice can be produced that are either *androgenetic chimeras* (ag, containing a diploid set of paternal genes) or *parthenogenetic chimeras* (pg, containing a diploid set of maternal genes). The resulting embryos are then implanted in receptive female mice and grown to maturity. The artificially introduced single-parent ag or pg cells can be stained so that they can be identified under a microscope. Other experiments have found that in chimeras ag cells are strongly represented in skeletal muscle but make little contribution to the brain. By contrast, pg chimeras show the opposite pattern: cells with genes exclusively from the mother contribute to brain development much more than to muscle and body growth. Indeed, pg chimeras are notably growth-retarded, while ag chimeras grow so large that they usually have to be delivered by Cæsarian section. In other words, brain growth is enhanced by maternally-expressed genes, while body growth is enhanced by paternally-expressed genes (Keverne *et al.* 1996).

pg chimera cells (those with a mother but no father) are found in large numbers in the neocortex and forebrain but very few are found in the lower, limbic brain—especially the hypothalamus. This is true both of mature, fully-grown pg chimeras but even more so of pg chimera fetuses, where there is a complete absence of pg cells from the hypothalamus. In both cases, pg chimera cells are found to be particularly clustered in the frontal lobes of the cortex. ag chimera cells, by contrast, are the exact opposite: these are found in the hypothalamus and limbic brain, but not in the neocortex. The few that are found in the forebrain tissue of embryos don't proliferate and are subsequently eliminated. However, no such difference is found in the brain-stem, which appears to be equally the work of maternal and paternal genes (Allen *et al.* 1995).

The paternal and maternal brains

The hypothalamus also regulates the production of pituitary growth hormones, which along with adrenal, thyroid and sex hormones, either directly or indirectly control growth. The pituitary is sometimes called 'the master endocrine gland' of the body, but is itself under the control of the hypothalamus, both neurologically and chemically. Neurologically, the posterior pituitary is just a part of the hypothalamus that protrudes from the brain and is not a gland in its own right (Thomson 1985). From this point of view, you could see the hypothalamus as performing a role in the body analogous to that of *Igf2* in the genome. Like *Igf2*, the hypothalamus is concerned with growth and, again like it, mammalian mothers appear to place imprints on the genes that build it, just as they do the *Igf2* gene. Presumably this is because imprinting limbic brain genes limits the growth that would result if the genes for building the limbic brain from both parents were expressed. Cells in the embryonic hypothalamus are critical for later development. The sizes of populations of cells in hypothalamic regions in the fetus could provide a prediction of the subsequent neurohormonal activity during later life (Deacon 1990).

Here another important consideration is that paternal genes have to rely on themselves alone to build and program the limbic brain so that it motivates behaviour that benefits them because the person of the father himself cannot necessarily be relied upon to be present to influence the child in the way that the mother usually can. As we have seen, the mammalian father makes no necessary contribution to the growth of the offspring in the way that the mother does during pregnancy and lactation. Although a mammalian father may be present to help nurture his offspring as many human fathers indeed are, the point is that such a presence is not biologically obligatory in the way in which the mother's is. Essentially, this is yet another expression of the fundamental principle: mother's baby—father's? maybe!

In his absence, all that a father's genes could rely on is their own, 50 per cent presence in an offspring and their innate ability to affect its growth, development and behaviour. Instinct costs less than learned behaviour, in the currency of genetic information (Williams 1966, 83), and as we have seen, fathers pay no obligatory biological cost towards their offspring beyond a single sperm. From these considerations we might deduce that the pleasure principle is likely to be more serviceable to paternal genes than to maternal ones because it epitomizes genetic, rather than environmental, influence on behaviour, as authorities from Darwin, Spencer and Freud to more recent ones such as Cabanac maintained (Spencer 1878, Cabanac 1992, Freud 1920, Platt and Glimcher 1999, Cabanac 1999). To put the same point another way, you could say that the limbic or emotional brain was primarily concerned with gratification of biological needs for growth, development and survival—just as the father's genes might be seen to prefer if we see them as playing a role comparable to that of *Igf2* and competing with those of the mother for resources favouring the growth, development and survival of his offspring.

As I have already pointed out above, the mother by contrast is the prime nurturer, bearing all the obligatory biological costs of gestation and lactation, and has an equal proportion of her genes—50 per cent—in all her children. Consequently, it is not perhaps surprising that her genes build the part of the brain that can be nurtured and exercise restraint—for example in facilitating sharing of her resources among her offspring. Here the cerebral cortex as a whole, but perhaps the frontal areas where maternally active genes are most expressed most especially, might be seen as playing a psychological role comparable to that of *Igf2r* to *Igf2*. In other words, the paternal, limbic or emotional brain may be to the maternal, cortical or cognitive brain as *Igf2* is to *Igf2r*: that is, the paternal brain makes growth-enhancing demands on the mother's resources while the maternal brain resists and counters them. If this is the case, recent findings about the human version of *Igf2r* may be relevant.

Robert Plomin and colleagues studied 51 children aged six to fifteen years with mean IQ scores of 136, and compared them with a control group of similar size and age but with a mean IQ of 103 (100 is average IQ for the population as a whole). Plomin then searched chromosome six for DNA markers that might correlate with IQ. The researchers had no particular target gene in mind, and had only chosen this chromosome because they had been advised that this would be the first to be fully sequenced by the human genome project. The gene that they found was the human form of *Igf2r* (Chorney *et al.* 1998).

As Plomin and his colleagues point out, the fact that IGF2R has been found to be statistically associated with high IQ in their sample does not mean that the gene is in fact contributing to it. What they have found may simply be a genetic marker that is close to other genes that do directly contribute to measures of IQ. To this extent, the finding may be coincidental. Nevertheless, we have already seen that *Igf2r* is a paradigmatic maternally active gene, and that it works by producing a sink for a paternally active insulin-like growth factor. Furthermore, there is recent evidence that insulin may play a role in spurring neuronal growth that contributes to learning and memory in the brain (Wickelgren 1998). This raises the question of how an *Igf2*-antagonist in mice (and presumably also in ancestral mammals) came to evolve into a gene that is linked to high IQ in some human beings.

A precedent may be found in the case the X chromosome, which is another instance of asymmetric gene expression, since female mammals carry two copies of it, but males only one. It has been known for a hundred years that mental handicap is more prevalent in males by an excess of the order of 25–50 per cent. This excess is due to genes on the X chromosome, which account for at least a quarter of all handicap in males, and possibly for 10 per cent of mild handicap in females. Studies of mental retardation have now revealed that there could be as many as 150-odd genes on the X chromosome which are directly or indirectly responsible for mental retardation. According to a recent summary, genes found in families with X chromosome-linked mental deficits indicate mutations in genes for intelligence which are distributed along the whole length of the X chromosome, and presumably code for various anatomical or functional parts of the neural substratum of IQ. There are presently no known genes, either dominant or recessive, on other chromosomes that could explain these findings (Turner 1996a, b). For example, a study of 4383 children in Orkney found that verbal IQ was definitely X-linked in normal school-age children (Goodman and Anderton 1997), and more recently still further evidence has emerged implicating the X chromosome in the inheritance of intelligence (Ananthswamy 2002).

The practical consequences of these findings is that, because males never receive an X chromosome from their father (because he gives them a Y), it is the mother who is primarily responsible for passing X chromosome genes for intelligence to her sons. And although fathers also pass an X chromosome to their daughters to complement that from the mother, it is the father's own mother's X chromosome which he transmits. A woman, by contrast, always passes on a new, unique X chromosome which is the synthesis of genes from both of those which she received from her parents.

Conclusion

Because of the mammalian mother's critical and continuing role in nurturing the offspring, her genes invested in a child can usually rely on the presence of the mother herself throughout childhood to influence and control the child's behaviour in their own interests. Consequently, it is not surprising to learn that maternal genes largely construct the cortical brain, and that it is the mother who pays for its development in terms of the resources provided by her before birth through the placenta and after it in the form of breast-milk in particular and care of the child in general. The cortical or cognitive brain has several major distinguishing characteristics from the lower, emotive centres: it is directly in contact with the senses, it can exercise reason and has linguistic competence, it is in control of voluntary thought and movement, and it can over-ride, inhibit and repress many of the more primitive responses of the emotive brain. According to a recent account,

> much of what is special about human cognition and social control of behavior seems to involve significant inhibitory components above and beyond that displayed by our close genetic relatives. We show greater voluntary control of emotions, particularly sexual behavior, than any other species; we are able to delay gratification (sometimes for years) in the quest of a goal; we can deceive others or hide our true feelings, often to our political (or simply physical) advantage. Each of these behaviours, while perhaps not unique to humans, reaches its zenith in Homo sapiens and contributes to our success as a species. Each also involves inhibition. Thus, humans' apparently increased emotional control relative to other primates is not likely due to a reduction in the role of the limbic system in human behavior; we remain highly emotional animals. A more likely cause is inhibition from the prefrontal cortex. (Bjorklund and Harnishfeger 1995).

Given that, as we have seen, the limbic system is the product of paternal genes and the cortex—and the prefrontal cortex in particular—is made by maternal genes, conflict between thought and feeling, instinct and intelligence, emotion and cognition, appears to be written into the genetic code, built into the brain long before birth and played out in life forever afterwards. Such was certainly the view of the late William Hamilton, who provides a fitting conclusion in the following extract from an autobiographical essay:

> Seemingly inescapable conflict within diploid organisms came to me both as a new agonizing challenge and at the same time a release from a personal problem I had had all my life. In life, what was it I really wanted? My own conscious and seemingly indivisible self was turning out far from what I had imagined and I need not be so ashamed of my self pity! I was an ambassador ordered abroad by some fragile coalition, a bearer of conflicting orders from the uneasy masters of a divided empire. Still baffled about the very nature of the policies I was supposed to support, I was being asked to act, and to act at once—to analyse, report on, influence the world about me. Given the realization of an eternal disquiet within, couldn't I feel better about my own inability to be consistent in what I was doing, about my indecision in matters ranging from daily trivialities up to the very nature of right and wrong? In another metaphor, I was coming to see that I simply am the two or the many quarrelling kids who are pretending to false unity for a few minutes just so that their father will withdraw his threats and take them to

the beach. As I write these words, even so as to be able to write them, I am pretending to a unity that, deep inside myself, I now know does not exist. I am fundamentally mixed, male with female, parent with offspring, warring segments of chromosomes that interlocked in strife millions of years before. (Hamilton 1996, 133–5)

Acknowledgements

Thanks to David Haig, the late Bill Hamilton, Barry Keverne, and Robert Plomin.

References

Allen, N. D., Logan, K., Lally, G., Drage, J. D., Norris, M. L., and Keverne, B., (1995). Distribution of parthenogenetic cells in the mouse brain and their influence on brain development and behavior. *Proceedings of the National Academy of Sciences, USA* 92 (11/95), 10782–6.

Ananthswamy, and Anil. (2002). X-rate brains. *New Scientist*, 25 May 2002, 26–9.

Badcock, and Christopher, R. (2000). *Evolutionary psychology: a critical introduction.* Polity Press, Cambridge.

Barker, D. J. P. (1994). Mothers, babies and disease in later life. *British Medical Journal.*

Barker, D. J. P. (1996). The unbearable lightness at birth. *Science and Public Affairs* (Spring), 33–7.

Barker, D. J. P. (1998). *Mothers, babies and health in later life*, 2nd edition. Churchill Livingstone, Edinburgh.

Barker, D. J. P. (1999). The fetal origins of coronary heart disease and stroke: evolutionary implications. In *Evolution in health and disease* (ed. S. C. Stearns). Oxford University Press, Oxford.

Barlow, D. (1995). Gametic imprinting in mammals. *Science* 270 (8 December), 1610–3.

Bernds, W. and Barash, D. (1979). Early termination of parental investment in mammals, including humans. In *Evolutionary biology and human social behavior* (ed. N. Chagnon and W. Irons). Duxbury, North Scituate, Mass.

Bjorklund, D. F. and Harnishfeger, K. K. (1995). The evolution of inhibition mechanisms and their role in human cognition and behavior. In *Interference and inhibition in cognition* (ed. F. N. Dempster and C. J. Brainerd). Academic Press, New York.

Brody, J. E. (2002). Disorder makes hunger a constant companion. *New York Times*, July 23, 2002.

Cabanac, M. (1999). Emotion and phylogeny. *Journal of Consciousness Studies*, 6, 176–90.

Cabanac, M. (1992). Pleasure: the common currency. *Journal of Theoretical Biology*, 155, 173–200.

Chorney, M. J., Chorney, K., Seese, N., Owen, M. J., Daniels, J., McGiffin, P., Thompson, L. A., Detterman, D. K., Benbow, C., Lubinski, D., Eley, T., and Plomin, R. (1998). A quantitative trait locus associated with cognitive ability in children. *Psychological Science*, 9(3), 1–7.

Deacon, T. W. (1990). Problems of ontogency and phylogeny in brain-size evolution. *International Journal of Primatology*, **11**(3), 237–82.

Domínguez, C. (1995). Genetic conflicts of interest in plants. *Trends in Ecology and Evolution*, **10** (10 October), 412–6.

Driscoll, D. J. (1994). Genomic imprinting in humans. In *Molecular medicine* (ed. T. Friedman). Academic Press, New York.

Franke, U., Kerns, J. A., and Giacalone, J., (1995). The SNRPN gene Prader-Willi syndrome. In *Genomic imprinting: causes and consequences* (ed. R. Ohlsson, K. Hall, and M. Ritzen). Cambridge University Press, Cambridge.

Freud, S. (1920). Beyond the pleasure principle. In *The standard edition of the complete psychological works of Sigmund Freud* (ed. J. Strachey, A. Freud, A. Strachey, and A. Tyson) The Hogarth Press and the Institute of Psychoanalysis, London.

Goodman, J. D. T. and Anderton, R. B. (1997). X-linkage, lyonization and a female premium in the verbal IQ results of Orkney school children, 1947–1975. *Journal of Biosocial Science*, **29**, 63–72.

Haig, D. (1993). Genetic conflicts in human pregnancy. *Quarterly Review of Biology*, **68**(4), 495–532.

Haig, D. and Graham, C. (1991). Genomic imprinting and the strange case of the insulin-like growth factor II receptor. *Cell*, **64** (March 22), 1045–6.

Haig, D. (1994). Cohabitation and pregnancy-induced hypertension. *The Lancet*, **344**, 1633–4.

Haig, D. (1996). Gestational drive and the green-bearded placenta. *Proceedings of the National Academy of Sciences of the USA*, **93**, 6547–51.

Hamilton, W. D. (1996). *Narrow roads of gene land*. 2 vols. *The collected papers of W. D. Hamilton*, Vol. 1. W. H. Freeman/Spektrum, Oxford.

Holm, V. A., Cassidy, S. B., Butler, M. G., Hanchett, J. M., Greensway, L. R., Whitman, B. Y., and Greenbergy, F. (1993). Prader-Willi syndrome: consensus diagnostic criteria. *Pediatrics*, **91**(2), 398–402.

Jaenisch, R. (1997). DNA methylation and imprinting: Why bother? *Trends in Genetics*, **13**(8), 323–9.

John, R. and Surani, M. (1996). Imprinted genes and regulation of gene expession by epigenetic inheritance. *Current Opinion in Cell Biology*, **8**, 348–53.

Keverne, E. B., Martel, F. L., and Nevison, C. M. (1996). Primate brain evolution: genetic and functional considerations. *Proceedings of the Royal Society of London B*, **262**, 689–96.

Moore, T. and Haig, D. (1991). Genomic imprinting in mammalian development: a parental tug-of-war. *Trends in Genetics*, **7**(2), 45–9.

Nicholls, R. D., Saitoh, S., and Horsthemke, B. (1998). Imprinting in Prader-Willi and Angelman syndromes. *Trends in Genetics*, **14**(5), 194–200.

Ohlsson, R., Hall, K., and Ritzen, M. (ed.) (1995). *Genomic imprinting: causes and consequences*. Cambridge University Press, Cambridge.

Pawlowski, B., Dunbar, R., and Lipowicz, A. (2000). Tall men have more reproductive success. *Nature*, **403**, 156.

Platt, M. L. and Glimcher, P. W. (1999). Neural correlates of decision variables in parietal cortex. *Nature*, **400**, 233–8.

Potts, M., and Short, R. (1999). *Ever since eve: the evolution of human sexuality*. Cambridge University Press, Cambridge.

Reik, W. and Surani, A. (1997). Genomic imprinting. In *Frontiers in molecular biology* (ed. B. D. Hames and D. M. Glover). IRL Press, Oxford.

Spencer, H. (1878). *The Principles of psychology*, 2nd edition. Williams and Norgage, London.

Sun, F.-L., Dean, W. L., Kelsey, G., Allen, N. D., and Reik, W. (1997). Transactivation of *Igf2* in a mouse model of Beckwith-Wiedemann syndrome. *Nature*, **389**, 809–15.

Thomson, R. F. (1985). *The brain: an introduction to neuroscience*. W. H. Freeman, New York.

Turner, G. (1996a). Finding genes on the X chromosome by which *Homo* may have become *sapiens*. *American Journal of Human Genetics*, **58**, 1109–10.

Turner, G. (1996b). Intelligence and the X chromosome. *Lancet*, **347**, 1814–5.

Wickelgren, I. (1998). Tracking insulin to the mind. *Science*, 24 April, 517–18.

Williams, G. C. (1966). *Adaptation and natural selection: a critique of some current evolutionary thought*. Princeton University Press, Princeton.

PART IV

PHILOSOPHICAL
PERSPECTIVES

CONSCIENCE AND CONFLICT: DARWIN, FREUD, AND THE ORIGINS OF HUMAN AGGRESSION

JIM HOPKINS

> Myself against my brother
> My brother and I against my family
> My family against the clan
> My clan against the enemy.[1]

Introduction: us and them

A striking feature of human life is the division we impose upon our psychological and social worlds between a self or *us* which we regard favourably, and an *other* or *them* which we take as correspondingly bad.[2]

   This gives rise to a series of psychological and social phenomena, ranging from transient enjoyable rivalries involving one's home town or team, through serious corporate competition, to the intractable destructive hostilities of feud, tribalism, bigotry and racism, nationalism, intolerant aggressive religious fundamentalism, individual paranoid psychosis, and disputes among schools of psychology. And however we moderns think ourselves guarded against such modes of thought, the roots remain active. The sight of a black face is still

---

1   This proverb has many versions. That quoted is Somali; the Bedouin omits clans but ends with 'All of us against the foreigner'.

2   Thus as President Bush reminded the American electorate: 'When I was coming up, with what was a dangerous world, it was us versus them, and it was clear who the them were. Today we're not so sure who they are, but we know they're out there.' Unfortunately he was right. The problem is not just the blindness of these mechanisms but also their ubiquity.

liable to distress a white amygdala, and consideration of psychoanalysis or cultural anthropology to prompt an evolutionary psychologist to spleen.[3]

Social psychologists have described the readiness with which we form such groups, and the tendency to in-group cohesion and out-group aggression which accompanies this. Also they study the serial psychological misrepresentations—including self- and group-serving biases, mirror-image perceptions, and systematic errors in psychological attribution—by which the *us* is preferred, flattered, and exalted, and the *them* correspondingly denigrated.[4] In recent times the destructive hatreds which these divisions foster have come to seem a threat to humanity itself. Hence we can appreciate the question which Einstein put to Freud:

> ... man has within him a lust for hatred and destruction. In normal times this passion exists in a latent state, it emerges only in unusual circumstances; but it is a comparatively easy task to call it into play and raise it to the power of a collective psychosis ... Is it possible to control man's mental evolution so as to make him proof against the psychoses of hate and destructiveness? (XXIII, 200-1)[5]

---

3   For unconscious racism and the amygdala see Phelps *et al.* (2000). 'Performance on indirect measures of race evaluation predicts amygdala activation'. *Journal of Cognitive Neuroscience* 12(5), 729–38; for evolutionary psychology and anthropology see Pinker's critique—as based, astonishingly, on a protocol from an anonymous graduate student— In *The language instinct*, Penguin, London. 1994 at 412 ff.

As Miller and others have observed, Pinker's version of evolutionary psychology is ill-equipped to explain the varied and expressive aspects of human culture upon which the social anthropologists Pinker caricatures have focussed. These require to be understood in terms of sexual selection and mate choice, and by implication via the symbolic values of many aspects of behaviour and culture. These latter seem to me best understood by combining psychoanalysis and recent work in conceptual metaphor. For sexual selection see Miller, G. (2000). *The mating mind*. Doubleday, New York, and 'Mental traits as fitness indicators'. *Annals of the New York Academy of Sciences*, 907, 62–74. For links between psychoanalysis and conceptual metaphor see Hopkins (2000). 'Psychoanalysis, metaphor, and the concept of mind'. In *The analytic freud* (ed. M. Levine). Routledge, London.

4   For discussions and references to empirical work on groups see for example Meyers, D. (1999). *Social psychology*, McGraw Hill, Boston. For the relation of individual and group identify see this book (41ff), and for the readiness for group formation and subsequent ingroup bias see the work by Tajfel at (353ff). For the readiness with such divisions can become violent see the experiments by Sherif and Zimbardo at (576) and (138). For the self-serving bias and the accompanying false consensus and false uniqueness effects (51ff); and for the related group-serving bias and the manipulation of the fundamental attribution error in service of it (68) and (371–3), and for the outgroup homogeneity effect and mirror-image misperceptions (365) and (529–31).

5   This reference to Einstein, and those which follow to Freud, are by volume and page (in parentheses) to *The standard edition of the complete psychological works of Sigmund Freud* (trans. and ed. J. Strachey *et al.*) Hogarth Press, London, 1958.

And we can compare this with a problem posed by William Hamilton:

> ... we would expect the genetic system ... to provide not a blank sheet for individual cultural development, but a sheet at least lightly scrawled with certain tentative outlines. The problem facing a humane civilisation may be how to complete a sketch suggesting some massive and brutal edifice—say the outlines of an Aztec pyramid—so that it reappears as a Parthenon or a Taj Mahal.[6]

Progress in these matters requires better understanding of human aggression. We can gain this by combining accounts descended from Darwin and Freud. The first concern the co-evolution of ingroup cohesion and outgroup conflict, and the second the mental processes by which individuals co-operate within groups to compete with those outside. Insofar as we can align our understanding of the forces which have shaped the overall ground-plan of the human mind with our knowledge of the depth psychology of individual motive, we can hope to triangulate more accurately on the points of connection between.

Evolution altruism and groups

Darwin suggested that altruistic moral tendencies evolved via the advantages these gave to competing groups. A tribe possessing 'a high standard of morality' would be 'victorious over most other tribes'. This would have selective force, since 'At all times throughout the world tribes have supplanted other tribes; and this would be natural selection ...'[7] Darwin's enthusiasm for morality remained unqualified by its role in perpetuating conflict; and his argument has recently been continued by Sober and Wilson[8], who dedicate their account of multilevel selection 'to altruists everywhere', while citing as favourable evidence the conquest of the Dinka by the Nuer. (Hamilton likewise emphasized 'the selective value of having a conscience', while linking the group behaviours facilitated by conscience with racism, xenophobia, and ecological disaster.)

---

6   Hamilton, W. (1995). 'Innate social aptitudes of man: an approach from evolutionary genetics'. In *The narrow roads of gene land*, p 330. Spektum and W. H. Freeman publishers, Oxford. Hamilton's reference to the social, otherwise explicit in this essay, is here conveyed via the fact that Aztec temples were used for the blood sacrifice of captives from other tribes, sometimes in large groups.

7   Charles Darwin, as quoted on p. 4 of Sober and Wilson, cited below.

8   Sober, E. and Wilson, D. S. (1998). *Unto others*. Harvard University Press. London and Cambridge Massachusetts.

Also recent work has considered the likely role of group selection on cultural as opposed to genetic variation.[9] With this has gone an emphasis on the transmission of culture within groups, and the use of cultural symbols to mark their boundaries. Thus according to Boyd and Richersen,

> ... The propensity to cooperate with sympathy-inspiring ingroup members, and to use symbolic markers to define ingroups, is like the innate principles of language. The specific markers, size of group(s), and internal structure of the group(s) to which individuals belong are culturally variable parameters that generate a specific functioning instance of the innate propensities. Like innate language structures and adult lactose absorption, the social decision-making principles most likely coevolved as adaptations to an emerging cultural environment in which cooperation within culturally marked groups was becoming important. Success in intergroup competition came to depend upon within-group cooperation; an evolutionary arms race arose. The scale of cooperation-to-compete might escalate until ecological rather than evolutionary constraints bring a halt.[10]

Such work has also focussed upon the darker side of morality and conscience. Thus Richersen and Gil-White stress the role of both punishment and moral anger.

> ... If much group competition is active rather than passive (e.g. violent combat for land), then within-group altruistic norms maintained by punishment will confer dramatic advantages. This could make the production of new altruistic groups faster than the processes which dilute altruism within the group ... The result would be a panhuman selection pressure for cognitive adaptations reducing the likelihood of 'mistakes' in order to avoid costly punishment (prosocial emotions such as duty, patriotism, moral outrage, etc. that commit us to predominant social norms even in the absence of coercion) ...

> Clearly, the other side of the coin of group cooperation is group conflict. Groups that develop norms that channel their within-group cooperation towards outward bellicosity will force other groups to develop the same (or better) or go extinct. This process selects for ever-stronger forms of within-group cooperation

---

9   This does not entail that genetic influences have played no role. Provided that genetic relatedness among members of family-composed in-groups sufficiently exceeded that among members of competing out-groups, spiteful aggression might have evolved in accord with the rules specified by Hamilton. See Hamilton, cited above, 'Spite and Price' and 'Selfish and spiteful behaviour in an evolutionary model'.

10   Richersen, P. and Boyd, R. (1998). 'The evolution of human ultra-sociality'. In *Ideology, Warfare, and Indoctrinability* (ed. I. Eibl-Eibisfeldt and F. Salter), pp. 71–96. Berghahn Books, New York.

and outward aggression and is likely an important force responsible for the creation of ever larger and more complex social human groups.[11]

Psychological mechanisms: identification and projection

How should we understand the personal motives and mechanisms which regulate ingroup co-operation and outgroup conflict? The idea above is that together with 'the propensity to co-operate with sympathy-inspiring ingroup members' there has been a co-evolution of two forms of aggression. Ingroup moral aggression, involving ingroup punishment, has evolved in the service of outgroup aggression, involving potentially violent conflict. These developments should therefore appear in the individual as two sides of the same evolutionary coinage; and if so psychological investigation should reveal connections between ingroup co-operation, cohesion, and moral anger on the one hand and outgroup violence on the other. As we shall see, these connections can be traced in detail by considering the psychoanalytic mechanisms of identification and projection, which inform the individual's images of self and other, and us and them.[12]

Identification effects 'the assimilation of one ego to another' (XXII, 63). In this it forms an image of the self as *like* an other who is worthy of emulation, so that self and other share desirable traits and perspectives.[13] This process informs many kinds of socialization and learning, including that of language. We can regard it as implemented by systems like the 'mirror neurons' which respond to observations of the behaviour of others by producing a first-person image of their activities in one's own motor system; and this goes with

---

11   Gil-White, F. and Richerson, P. (2003). 'Cooperation and conflict, large scale human'. *Encyclopaedia of cognitive science.* Macmillan, London and New York. See also Boyd and Richerson (1992). 'Punishment allows the evolution of cooperation (or anything else) in sizable groups.' *Ethology and Sociobiology*, 13, 171–95.

12   Here I am taking projection to encompass what is now called projective identification. For discussion of this see Segal, H. (1972). *Introduction to the work of Melanie Klein.* Hogarth, London.

13   Such ingroup phenomena as the group-serving bias, discussed by Meyers above, are readily related to identification, as are observations about how we like those we take to be like us (614); while others, such as mirror-image misperceptions, outgroup homogeneity, and readiness to group hostility, are likewise relatable to projection.

other tendencies to liken ourselves to those we are with.[14] Thus as Meltzoff and others report, newborn babies can imitate adults who open their mouths, stick out their tongues, etc. This indicates the early working of an ability to assume an image presented by the other, which psychoanalysis finds basic to the formation of our self-images and selves. Projection, by contrast, forms an image of the self as *unlike* another, by dissociating motives or traits from the self. It represents the self as lacking, and the other as having, the trait or aspect in question, so that the other seems different and alien.

These mechanisms work together in implementing the self- and group-serving biases and mirror-image perceptions noted above. We identify with aspects of others we regard as desirable, so identification creates images of a good self at one in purpose with good others. We tend to project aspects of our selves which we take as bad or undesirable, so projection creates images of good self opposed in purpose to bad others. Since the projected badness located in others is dissociated from the self, the good self and bad others tend to confront one another with mirroring directness. Each party's response to its own projections tends to validate those of the other, so that these mechanisms lock suspicion and hostility in step. As identification regulates co-operation between self and other, projection likewise regulates conflict.

Self-esteem and outgroup hostility

To see this better let us consider an observation from social psychology linking self-esteem and images of in- and outgroups. In several experiments, subjects are given a small setback or humiliation. After this they are probed for attitudes towards persons or groups they identify with or dissociate themselves from (members of their own or different sororities, differing national groups, etc.). People characteristically respond by feeling more favourably towards their ingroups, and less towards their outgroups, then they otherwise would.[15]

Such fluctuations in representation of *us* vs *them* are unconscious, but we can readily see how they might be effected by projection: traits regarded as bad or questionable would be unconsciously shifted from self and ingroup to

---

14   On mirror neurons see Rizzolati, Fogassi, and Gallesi (Sept 2001). 'Neurophysiological mechanisms underlying the understanding and imitation of action'. *Nature reviews neuroscience*; and Blakemore and Decity (August 2001). 'From the perception of action to the understanding of intentionality'. *Nature reviews neuroscience*. On the role of imitation see Meltzoff and others in *Intersubjective communication and emotion in early ontogeny*, Cambridge University Press, Cambridge. S. Braten, ed (1998). On other forms of assimilation of self and other see Meyers p. 158.

15   See Meyers pp. 65–6, 361.

others and outgroup, thus making the former seem better and the latter seem worse. Robert Trivers—who takes projection as one of a series of mechanisms which have evolved in the service of the unconscious deception of others— cites the example of homophobic men. Experiments indicate that hetero-sexual men who most energetically dissociate themselves from homosexuals, and who regard homosexual traits with particular discomfort and disgust— that is, heterosexuals for whom homosexuals are a bad *them*, as opposed to a good hetero *us*—are in fact more likely than others to get erections while watching homosexual pornography, and also to deny that they have done so.[16] This is consistent with the idea that in condemning homosexuality they censure in others traits dissociated from their selves.

In this case we can see how identification and projection on a single topic can create both a cohesive ingroup and a well-marked outgroup; and how the tendency to condemnation and punishment may be magnified by the identifi-cations binding the projecting group.[17] So we find group phenomena such as queer-bashing, the legal persecution of homosexuals, their organized murder by Nazis and Falangists, etc. Also it is clear that the projective defining of an outgroup need not rest on any particular internal conflict such as we find in homophobia. For since projection can always enhance the self-esteem of the projector, a group or individual marked out for hostility is liable to be targeted by a wide range of projections which have little in common besides conflict in the individuals from whom they emanate.

Conscience and the externalization of internal conflict

To understand projection in more detail we can consider the first specimen of Freud's *Interpretation of Dreams*, that of Irma's Injection (IV, 104ff). The afternoon before this dream Freud had met Otto, his family doctor, who had visited the household of Freud's former patient Irma. Freud had treated Irma for hysteria, and thought he had done enough by explaining to her the causes of her illness, which he took to include the sexual frustrations of widowhood. Otto mentioned that he had been called away to give an injection, and this reminded Freud that another patient had recently been given injections by *another* doctor, apparently with an unsterile syringe. Freud himself, as he had reflected, was always careful to keep his syringes clean.

---

16 See Trivers, 'Self-deception in the service of deceit' In *Evolution and social theory*, OUP 2002, Oxford; and Adams *et al.* (1996). 'Is homophobia associated with homosexual arousal?' *J. Abnorm. Psychol,* 105, 440–5.

17 Compare the polarizing effect of group thinking at Meyers 311 and deindividuation at 304.

Also Otto said something which impinged on Freud's self-esteem. He remarked that Irma looked 'better, but not yet well', and Freud thought this a reproof. He spent that evening writing up Irma's case history, so as to justify himself by discussing it with their senior colleague M. That night Freud dreamt that he and his wife were receiving guests, including Irma. On meeting Irma he said to her that if she still got pains, it was her own fault, for not sufficiently attending to his 'solution'. She replied that her pains were bad, and Freud, worried that he had failed to diagnose a physical illness, conducted an examination. They were joined by a number of colleagues from Freud's medical circle, including M; and it emerged that Irma indeed suffered physical illness. Otto had given her an injection of the toxic chemical *trimethylamine*. At the close of the dream Freud censured Otto, stressing that 'Injections of that kind ought not be made so thoughtlessly. And probably the syringe had not been clean.'[18]

Now this dream dealt with topics—illness of a friend and patient, misdiagnosis, malpractice by the family doctor, etc.—which were sources of anxiety to Freud. Still, by taking the context provided by Freud's memories and associations, we can see that it was wishful, in the sense that it actually represented things as Freud would partly have wished them to be. Freud had gone to sleep wanting to justify himself to M in respect of what he felt to be Otto's accusation of bad medical practice, and in the dream he received the most thorough justification, and in the presence of M and other medical colleagues. The psychotherapy about which Freud was now so enthusiastic could not be blamed for Irma's continued suffering, nor could Freud himself: for Irma had a physical illness, and this was caused by Otto's dirty toxic injection. Freud had felt guilty and privately reproached by Otto during the day; but by the end of his dream he was publicly vindicated.

Further analysis showed that Freud's favourable representation of himself as opposed to Otto also touched on guilts which were older, deeper and far more serious. For Irma was linked in his mind with another friend and another patient from years before. The patient was a woman Freud had killed, by repeatedly giving her what he took to be routine injections; and in that case, as details of the dream reminded him, he had consulted with M as well. The friend had suffered from incurable nerve pain and was addicted to the morphine he used to treat it. Freud had been an enthusiastic advocate of the medical use of cocaine, and had urged on his own experience that it was not

18   For a fuller account of this dream, and of Freud's method of analysis and the kind of support it can be taken to enjoy, see Hopkins (1999). 'Patterns of interpretation: speech, action, and dream'. In *Cultural documents: the interpretation of dreams* (ed. L. Marcus). Manchester University Press, Manchester.

addictive. This error, as he remembered, had brought 'serious reproaches down upon me'. He had persuaded his friend to use cocaine in place of morphine on this basis; and his friend became addicted and died a lingering and miserable death from cocaine injections. So by ending his dream with 'Injections of that kind ought not be made so thoughtlessly', Freud was turning towards Otto a reproach which, as he could realize on analyzing the dream, he might well have directed against himself.

Finally, the misrepresentation of Otto went further still, and in a way which touched on sexuality and the boundaries of the self and body. Freud had placed particular emphasis in the dream on the chemical trimethylamine, and noted in his associations that it was connected with sexual metabolism. (It was thought to be a decomposition product of semen.) Sexuality, as he observed, was also linked with Irma's illness, which he took to be partly due to her widowhood. But as he later confided to Abraham, further analysis of the dream revealed his own 'sexual megalomania'. The women in the dream, including Irma, were all widows, and Freud had them all. As he said, echoing a physicians' joke common at the time, 'There would be one therapy for widow-hood of course. All sorts of intimate things, naturally.'[19] Freud never seems to have acted inappropriately on sexual desire for a patient; but in the dream it was Otto rather than himself who harboured such desire, and Otto was depicted as satisfying it symbolically, by injecting Irma with a product of decomposed semen.

Taking this in relation to our present theme, we can say that Otto's remark pricked Freud's self-esteem, by reminding him of traits and actions which he was liable to condemn in himself. In waking life Freud dealt with this in an ostensibly realistic and rational way, by writing a case report which would justify his present behaviour. In his dream, by contrast, his reaction was simpler and more comprehensive. He projected the characteristics in question into Otto, and self-righteously censured them there. This use of projection thus transformed an internal and moral conflict (Freud's knowledge of his own unthinking and occasionally lethal medical practice vs. his own standards on the matter) into a social conflict concerning the conduct of another (Doctor Freud vs. Doctor Otto, as witnessed by their medical colleagues.)

---

19   For this aspect of Freud's dream see Abraham, H. and Freud, E. (ed.) (1965). *A psycho-analytic dialogue: the letters of Sigmund Freud and Karl Abraham, 1907–1926*, p 20. Hogarth Press, London. This also indicates how the dream is constructed around a pun on 'solution', which is a crossing point for a conceptual metaphor which maps mind to body. For discussion of the relation between psychoanalytic symbolism and conceptual metaphor see Hopkins (2000). 'Psychoanalysis, metaphor, and the concept of mind'. In *The analytic Freud*, (ed. M. Levine). Routledge, London.

Ingroup cohesion and outgroup hostility

We can see clearly how this way of thinking leads to an image of a good self as opposed to an other who may be censured or denigrated. Such thinking may also be co-ordinated within a group, as was that depicted in Freud's dream. Freud and Otto belonged to the same medical ingroup, whose members were identified with one another in respect of shared values relating to medical practice, and also formed an *us* with respect to local culture generally. This identificatory nexus enabled Freud to use his dream to find a satisfactory (imaginary) solution to his own internal conflict, by (imaginarily) having Irma examined in the presence of a group of his medical colleagues.

Where individuals are bound to one another by identification in this way, projection serves to balance each individual's liability to personal condemnation, guilt, shame, and loss of self-esteem, by directing moral aggression away from the self and towards others in the group, and in accord with the individual's personal version of the norms of that group. Projection thus works together with identification to create a group whose members are ready to feel guilt and shame in relation to one another, and also ready to allocate censure or punishment to one another, by reference to motives and standards which are psychologically shared as obtaining among them.

Inherent in this, however, is a tendency to represent others and outgroups as liable to condemnation by the standards which give order both to the self and the groups with which the self identifies. As Freud observed, 'It is always possible to bind together a considerable number of people in love, so long as there are other people left over to receive the manifestations of their aggressiveness.' (XXI, 114). So the family—which for most individuals constitutes their first and most basic ingroup—also appears as the first of a series of social units which, like the individual, tend to maintain an idealized and co-operative image of things within, and a corresponding denigratory and conflict-inducing image of those without. As Freud remarks,

> Every time two families become connected by marriage, each of them thinks itself superior to or of better birth than the other. Of two neighbouring towns each is the other's most jealous rival; every little canton looks down upon the others with contempt. Closely related races keep one another at arms length ... We are no longer astonished that greater differences should lead to an almost insuperable repugnance, such as the Gallic people feel for the Germans, the Aryan for the Semite, and the white races for the coloured. (XVIII, 101; cf also XVIII, 102)

And in accord with the role of projection he stresses that

> ... When once the Apostle Paul had posited universal love between men as the foundation of his Christian community, extreme intolerance on the part of Christendom towards those who remained outside it became the inevitable

consequence … Neither was it an unaccountable chance that the dream of a Germanic world-dominion called for anti-Semitism as its complement; and it is intelligible that the attempt to establish a new, communist civilisation in Russia should find its psychological support in the persecution of the bourgeois. (XXI, 114–5)

Freud developed his thinking about this only in a schematic way. He held that the cohesiveness of many groups results from their taking a particular idealized figure—such as a charismatic leader (or in the case of groups which are not led by individuals a creed or set of norms)—as representing what they regard as good (XVIII, 67ff). This identification ensures that each individual's self-esteem is regulated by reference to the idealized persons, creed, or norms which bind the group, so that aggression in service of these is a source of pride rather than guilt or shame. Individuals may also become identified by other means, such as the projection of their bad aspects—and in particular their hostile and aggressive motives—into some common locus, which therefore becomes a focus of legitimated and collective hate. In finding or creating such internal good and/or external bad objects members of a group feel at once unified, purified, and able to focus aggression which is validated by common ideals. Thus the same formations of conscience which regulate aggression within the group also provide for its unbridled expression against others outside. Even without exploring the way these ideas have been refined by Freud's successors[20], we can appreciate that they complement the evolutionary considerations noted at the beginning in interesting detail. So let us now seek to gain better focus on these matters by taking up some further aspects of Darwinian theory.

Parental investment and family conflict

The family seems the most basic of human groups which cohere to compete; and family co-operation is underlain by genetic relatedness, so that competition among families is reproductive competition as well. Parents share half their genes with each child, so that full siblings share half their genes as well. From the perspective of the genome of a parent each child constitutes an instance of reproductive success; and from that of each child the reproductive value of two siblings or four half-siblings approaches one's own. This genetic overlap provides a basis for the unity of purpose shown by members of the same family, but also underwrites divergences. These can be investigated via the notion of *parental investment*, which encompasses any benefit provided by

20   For some more recent views on this matter see Segal (1995). 'From Hiroshima to the Gulf war and after: a psychoanalytic perspective'. In *Psychoanalysis in contexts* (ed. Elliott and Frosch). Routledge, London and New York.

a parent towards the reproductive success of one offspring as opposed to that of others.[21] This includes the efforts of a mother's carrying a child in her body, those of providing food, shelter, protection, etc.—all aspects of parental care which make for the success of one child rather than another.

As Trivers has argued, parental investment is an intrinsic source of conflict within the family. For roughly, whereas parents are selected to allocate investment to a number of offspring over the course of their reproductive lives, offspring are selected to seek benefits immediately and to the full extent of their individual (genetic) interests. Accordingly each infant seeks more from its parents—particularly the mother—than they are inclined to give, and at the expense of its own siblings, whether actual or potential. These conflicts may in turn be exacerbated by those between the parents themselves, for as the modes of investment of men and women differ so do their reproductive strategies. For example it may be to the advantage of either parent to shift burdens of investment to the other, or again to reproduce elsewhere. In consequence the means by which men and women allocate parental investment seem to include not only promiscuity, infidelity, and the desertion of partners, but also abortion, infanticide, abandoning children (e.g. to foundling homes), and varieties of selective neglect.[22]

These conflicts are interwoven, and can be observed from conception in the invasion of the mother's body by the placenta. The placenta is constructed by the activity of the father's genome to extract maternal investment on behalf of the foetus, discounting other children the mother might have. The placenta thus develops as 'a ruthless parasitic organ existing solely for the maintenance and protection of the foetus, perhaps too often to the disregard of the maternal organism.'[23] So, e.g., the placenta bores into the mother's blood vessels, secreting hormones which raise her blood pressure and blood sugars in ways may injure her but benefit the foetus; her body responds by producing hormones which counteract these; and so on. Here conflict between the parents becomes conflict between mother and child; and the placenta may be

21 The term 'parental investment' was introduced by Trivers in 'Parental Investment and Sexual Selection' (1972). For this paper as well as 'Parent-Offspring Conflict' and others discussed below see Trivers (2002), *Evolution and social theory*, Oxford University Press, Oxford. Trivers also provides overviews in *Social evolution*. Benjamin/Cummings, California 1985. For recent discussion see Mock and Parker (1997), *The evolution of sibling rivalry*, Oxford University Press, Oxford.

22 For basic theory see Trivers 1972, 2002, cited above; for a wealth of related biological social and psychological detail see Hrdy (2000), *Mother nature*, Vintage, London.

23 Quoted in Hrdy, cited above, p 433. For discussion see Haig, D. (1993). 'Genetic conflicts in human pregnancy'. *Quarterly Review of Biology*, 68, 495–532.

involved in sibling rivalry more directly, as when one of a potentially multiple birth aborts others.

Conflict continues after birth, for obtaining maternal care—at whatever cost to others—is a matter of life or death for the infant. It may be in the interest of either parent to abandon a child from the start, as often happens with babies deemed defective. Feeding one child may entail neglecting another, and nursing tends to space conception, and so to delay the emergence of younger rivals, as would suit the interests of the mother as opposed to the father. So in sucking at the breast a baby may already be enforcing its own entitlements against the interests of its father and siblings; and if it stays long there it will conflict with those of its mother as well. By the time a baby is weaned its genetic interests are liable to have been opposed to those of every other member of the family, in conflict concerning the uses of the mother's body and potential rivals inside her.[24]

Infantile emotion and parental investment

We can see the emotions, in Damasio's phrase, as 'part of a multi-tiered and evolutionarily set neural mechanism aimed at maintaining organismic homeostasis'.[25] This is roughly the role which Freud assigned to what he called drives;[26] and the tiers include inbuilt capacities for distress at hunger, thirst,

---

24   These conflicts appear vividly in psychoanalytic accounts of infancy. See Klein (1974). *The psychoanalysis of children*, In *The collected works of Melanie Klein*, Hogarth, London; and Segal cited above.

25   Damasio *et al.* (October 2000). 'Cortical and sub-cortical brain activity during the feeling of self-generated emotions', *Nature Neuroscience*, 3(10), 1049.

26   This role was constant from his *Project* of 1895 onwards, and is closely related to that in terms of which Damasio and his colleagues consider emotion. As Freud described his conception,

> ... the nervous system receives stimuli from the somatic element itself— endogenous stimuli ... These have their origin in the cells of the body, and give rise to the major needs: hunger, respiration, sexuality ... They only cease subject to particular conditions, which must be realized in the external world (Cf., for instance, the need for nourishment). In order to accomplish such ... an effort is required ...' (I, 297)

The 'endogenous stimuli' of which Freud speaks can be seen as those which initiate processes for returning to equilibrium, and the 'effort' is that expended in attaining it. How Freud took this process to work and develop can be seen by considering what he says about the hunger drive in the human infant. The internal stimuli which result from a lack of nutrients constitute a departure from equilibrium, which is felt as unpleasurable; and the requisite equilibrium can normally be restored only by the satisfaction of the need.

and other forms of bodily disequilibrium, and also 'emotional command systems', which we share with other mammals, and which direct manifestations of rage and fear, sexuality, maternal (and paternal) nurturance, separation distress and social bonding, and play and social affection. These in turn integrate with a general 'seeking system', marked, as Panksepp has urged, by the mesolimbic dopamine pathway, whose nocturnal activation seems, in consilience with Freud, to be a content-specific cause of dreaming.[27]

Thus many of the subcortical basics of drive and emotion are working at birth, and prepared for expression through the baby's face, voice, and movements. These start to obtain the focus and orchestration of the complex and thought-saturated forms of emotion which we find in adult life during the first year. This seems mainly accomplished by the development, under the impact of experience, of representations of the self, the world, and others, which are realized mainly in the cerebral cortex. So while the subcortical mechanisms come with certain inbuilt relations of excitation and inhibition, they attain further co-ordination and integration as the cortex develops through critical phases of synaptic extension, myelination, and experience-dependent neural pruning; and these coincide with the infant's using its experience of relating with others—and particularly the investing mother—to build increasingly complex representations of the objects towards which its emotions are directed. This development of emotion via that of the

....

> During restoration, say by feeding, the neural pathways activated by the disequilibrating stimuli are perforce linked into a fuller network with those activated by the processes through which need is satisfied; and these include the perceptual networks active in perception of the external satisfying object, the intermediate networks involved in synthesizing information about this, and the networks for generating the motor activities of meeting the breast, sucking from it, and so on. The processes which lead to the recovery of neural equilibrium are felt as pleasurable, and strengthen neural connections throughout these networks. Thus the neural disequilibration caused by unmet need comes to cause the kind of activities through which the need is satisfied in the external world, so that such disequilibrium comes to be self-righting.

27 This particular set of designations is taken from Watt, D. (2000) 'The dialogue between psychoanalysis and neuroscience: alienation and reparation', *Neuro-Psychoanalysis*, 2(2), 187; International Universities Press. Such terms, of course, give only a very tentative and approximate indication of the nature of the neural systems in question. For a fuller account, with reference to a range of neuroscientific research, see Panksepp, J. (1998). *Affective neuroscience*, Oxford University Press, Oxford. The circuity of sexual motivation is discussed in more detail in Pfaff (1999), *Drive*, MIT Press, London and Cambridge Massachusetts. For an overview of these topics and discussion of the role of dreams see Solms and Turnbull (2002), *The brain and the inner world*, Karnac, London.

representation of its objects, in turn, seems shaped by the demands of parent–offspring conflict, and of parental investment more generally.

The infant selected for such conflict—and for later outgroup conflict as well—is dependent upon its mother's will, and so must pursue its interests by psychological means. Since mothers are selected to respond sensitively to their children's needs and condition, the infant does this by expressing and eliciting emotion. Hence this aspect of evolutionary theory leads us to expect that the infant's emotions, and the neural systems which realize them, can be understood as selected initially to extract maternal investment. Speaking very roughly, it seems that the infant has two ways of securing what it needs: co-operatively, via the elicitation of affection and love; or coercively, via the infliction of anxiety and guilt. Hence the mother is the main focus both for the new-born's affection and gratitude, and also for its uniquely arresting and motivating expressions of rage, hunger, pain, and fear. (Also this extraction may be set to proceed in a particular way. Preliminary findings suggest that the father's genome may be primarily responsible not only for the placenta but also for the subcortical basics of emotion, whereas the mother's is pivotal for the cortex, which remains to be completed by her post-natal investing attentions.[28] If so, then we can see the subcortical mechanisms of emotion as assuming at birth the egotistic extractive role of the discarded placenta, and thereafter being modified as the cortex, under the influence of the mother's care, takes forward the task of directing co-operation with the mother and other members of the family.[29])

Since nothing in the infant's life will be more important than getting what the mother has to provide, we should expect both sets of emotions to be very fully engaged. From an evolutionary perspective the distress which such expressions cause to parents are part of their efficacy as instruments of

28   For accounts of infancy which bring out the role of maternal investment vis-à-vis the cortex see Schore, A. (2001). 'Effects of a secure attachment relationship on rightbrain development, affect regulation, and infant mental health'. *Infant Mental Health Journal*, 22(1–2), 7–66; and Trevarthan, C. and Aitken, K. (2001). 'Infant intersubjectivity: research, theory, and clinical applications', *Journal of Child Psychology and Psychiatry*, Cambridge University Press. For more on intersubjectivity and the infant's sense of self see the essays by Trevarthan and others in S. Braten, ed, cited above.

29   On the mechanism responsible for this see Reik, W. and Walter, J. (January 2001). 'Genomic Imprinting: Parental Influence on the Genome' *Nature Reviews Genetics*; as regards imprinting and the cortex see Trivers, R. and Burt, A. (2000). 'Kinship and genomic imprinting', in *Genomic imprinting* (ed. R. Ohsson). Springer Verlag. This suggests that psychological conflict within the individual may be a continuation of that between maternal and paternal genes. This is discussed by Christopher Badcock in his *Evolutionary psychology: a critical introduction*, Oxford: Blackwell, 2000.

duress on the infant's behalf. Wittgenstein remarked that in an infant's cry one could discern 'terrible forces different from anything commonly assumed. Profound rage, pain and lust for destruction.'[30] But insofar as such forces have enabled their possessors to thrive by coercing mothers (or others) to provide more than they otherwise would, we should not be surprised at their existence even in the adorable baby. Also, it seems, we should not be surprised if these first engagements of emotion were guided by infantile versions of identification and projection, as we find later to be the case.

This accords with psychoanalytic hypotheses about the infantile roots of adult aggression. Freud found that the earliest and most basic of the unconscious images which drove social cohesion and conflict derived from the infant's relations with its mother. These showed a particularly radical opposition, as structured by identification and projection. The identificatory, affectionate and co-operative aspect of the relationship apparently began with satisfaction at the breast and was extended to the caring mother as a whole. This aspect was 'laid down unalterably for a whole lifetime, as the first and strongest love-object and as the prototype of all later love relations—for both sexes.' (XXIII, 188) On the other hand, there were projective images—involving, as Freud stressed, 'the earliest parental *imagoes*' (XXII, 64)—of the self as in constant conflict, either disguised or open, with a parental other who was harsh, punitive, and cruel. These images made up the most primitive aspects of the super-ego, and Freud regarded them as so suffused with 'merciless violence' (XIX, 53) as to suggest that they were formed under the influence of an innate capacity for lethal aggression, which would later show itself both in such extremeties of conscience as depression and suicide, and also in the aggressions and cruelties of warfare and conquest, as noted above.

Parental investment and emotional development

The differing positions of parent and offspring as regards parental investment also have far-reaching consequences for psychological development. The infant's role as a selfish extractor of investment is by nature preparation for a later role as an altruistic provider; and this transition is mediated by experience in a family in which parents tend to allocate benefits to children (and encourage them to act towards one another) in a way which is fairer than the infant's own genome would dictate. So we should expect psychological

---

30 Wittgenstein, L. (1977). *Remarks on culture and value.* Tr. P. Winch, Blackwell Publishers, Oxford 2e.

development overall to have an intrinsic character which psychoanalysis has long emphasized. It involves a transition, facilitated by parental care and family life, from something like infantile egotism (or narcissism) towards a capacity for non-self-regarding love (or altruism) for those with whom it is in relations of reproductive and ingroup co-operation, and also towards increasingly mature expressions of competition and aggression.

Accordingly the growth of motivation over the lifespan should show a particular kind of continuity-in-difference, which the various forms of psychology should chart. Continuity would come from the more or less constant role of the deep subcortical bases of motivation, and differences and development from the way these components were reworked and reintegrated as representations of the objects of emotion change (and with the objects themselves) over the lifespan. These changes should both reflect and drive the transition from infantile egoistic extraction of parental investment through the co-operation required for family life to the reproductive, investment-contributing, and group-competitive stances of adulthood.[31] So the kinds of love or other emotions of co-operation started in infancy with parents, siblings, and other relatives or carers, should develop, with changes in representations and objects, from early self-regarding forms towards others which are more altruistic, and in which reproduction comes to play an increasingly dominant role. And early aggressions should likewise become representationally focussed on family and later reproductive rivalries, and finally on competing outgroups.[32] Such a developmental process would enable maternal care, family life, and

---

31   This bears on the thesis of 'massive modularity' sometimes associated with evolutionary psychology. While the emotions might be regarded as modular (but not encapsulated) in their basic subcortical organization, they clearly serve a number of differing and interacting roles throughout the lifespan, as mediated by the kinds of maturation and changes in representation discussed here and below. We can clearly gain deeper understanding of emotion by studying these, as psychoanalysis, neuroscience, attachment theory, and other forms of developmental psychology aim to do. Whether further emphasis on modularity will contribute to actual research, as opposed to ideological group-marking, remains questionable.

32   Sulloway has stressed how competition among siblings within the overall co-operative structure of the family results in the allocation of individual roles or niches, which differ according to sex, order of birth, etc. This involves a dialectic between identification and differentiation similar to that discussed here, except that Sulloway concentrates on identification and ignores projection and the development of aggression. Thus he stresses that first-borns tend to be highly identified with their parents, while laterborns, having elder siblings also to identify and compete with, are less so. See F. Sulloway, *Born to rebel: birth order, family dynamics, and creative lives*, New York: Random House.

later group interactions to produce a variety of psychological types suited to local conditions.[33]

Taking this in terms of identification and projection, we should expect the infant receiving parental care to identify with the adult who provides it, thus laying down images of itself as closely associated with another whose ways of caring, relating, and loving, it can ultimately assume as its own. These basic early images should then contribute to later forms of identification and reproductive co-operation over the remainder of life. At the same time—and as we shall see in more detail below—the infant should create projective images of others which are dissociated from this early us, and are potentially bad. As this dialectic proceeds the infant can again identify with these others, and thus represent itself in a more morally and motivationally complex way. Thus the initial focus of love and affection towards the mother will be carried forward by identification into later relations of reproductive co-operation, while that of anger and aggression will be channelled by projection towards ingroup moral co-ordination in the form of guilt, shame, and readiness for punishment, and towards outgroup conflict unrestricted by identification or moral emotion, and apparently characterized by spite.[34]

Consolidation and continuity of attachment

To focus more specifically on the infantile roots of outgroup aggression we may consider the appearance of the interrelated phenomena of *separation distress*, *stranger anxiety*, and *social referencing*. As Schaffer observed:

> … crying or some other form of protest on termination of contact with an adult was apparent from the early months on … in the first half-year infants were found to cry for attention from anyone, familiar or strange, and though responsiveness to strangers tended to be less immediate and less intense than to the mother, both could quieten the infant and the departure of both could evoke protest. At the age of approximately seven months, however, a change took place. The infants still protested at the same situations, but now their protests were directed solely at certain *specific* individuals. The departure of these alone elicited crying and only their renewed attention terminated the infants' distress. Strangers, quite on the contrary, upset the infant by *approaching* him.[35]

---

33   This might be done, for example, by interactions which selectively encourage or arrest the growth of one or another emotional component, or by altering the way emotions are integrated by representations of their objects. The maintenance of conflict, or again of early or regressive forms of feeling, would thus be among the ways such variation might be produced.

34   For spite see the materials cited in footnote 9.

35   Schaffer, H. R. (1971). *The growth of sociability*, p 117, Penguin, Harmondsworth, Middx. For the cultural universality of stranger anxiety (and its relation to men with beards) see Hrdy, cited above, pp 414 ff.

At this time infants also begin to rely on their mothers as trusted sources of information about what is safe as opposed to dangerous, and hence about strangers. As Campos reports,

> ... the communication between mother and infant becomes extended to include a whole event in the environment. During this period the infant can appreciate what in the environment is the target of the other person's emotional reaction, much as the infant at this age can appreciate the referent of the mother's pointing or gaze behaviour ... Accordingly, during this period social referencing begins ... the deliberate search for emotional information in another person's face, voice, and gesture, to help disambiguate uncertainties in the environment ... a two-person communication about a third event ... [36]

These developments mark the consolidation of *attachment*, as studied in contemporary developmental psychology.[37] Their emergence just precedes the time at which infants start reliably to show the varying responses to being left alone with a stranger which are characteristic of empirically well-defined categories of secure, avoidant, ambivalent, and disorganized attachment. These responses can in turn be seen to reflect the infants' differing initial resolutions of their own internal emotional conflicts, and hence the way they project these conflicts into social life[38]; and as a wide range of empirical studies are beginning to demonstrate, they mark the inception of basic and potentially enduring patterns of relationship to others.

---

36 Campos *et al.* (1983). 'Socioemotional development'. In *Handbook of child psychology*, vol. 3 (ed. P. Mussen), p 825. John Wiley, New York.

37 For two recent surveys of empirical work on attachment which bear on the claims made in this section see Cassidy, J. and Shaver, P. R. (1999). *Handbook of attachment*, Guilford Press, New York and London, and Goldberg, S. (2002). *Attachment and development*, Hodder, London. For introduction to the Strange Situation procedure and the categories linked with it see the *Handbook* Ch 14 and the summary tables 14.1 and 14.2; for relations to teachers and childhood bullying etc. see Ch 4, and for the development of disorganization into coercion, and some examples of phantasy see Ch 23; for the adult attachment interview and correlations between adult and infant categories see Ch 19 and the summary table 19.2.; and for further discussion of attachment and evolution see Ch 6, which includes a discussion of parent-offspring conflict, and Ch 7 which both considers heritability and links attachment categories to reproductive behaviour. Goldberg's economic and thoughtful presentation covers most of the same topics, and her table 3.1 perspicuously displays some of the work on continuity of attachment patterns.

38 This claim in particular needs more explication and justification than I can provide here. Still the connection between avoidant/dismissing and conflict about the mother's significance has long been noted, and those for ambivalent/preoccupied and disorganized/unresolved are explicit in the descriptions of the categories themselves (see Chapters 14, 19, and 23 in the *Handbook* cited in the Footnote 39).

These patterns of early feeling seem to show themselves in a whole range of later transformations: in childhood phantasy and art, and relations to teachers and other children; in adolescent social behaviour, in courting, choice of reproductive strategy, and sexual partnership; in parenting; in adult patterns of grieving and other responses to abandonment and loss; and in the tendency to various kinds of psychopathology. So tracing these patterns through time enables us to track the development of emotion and relate it to early conflict. As regards aggression we can note that children who are securely attached—and therefore relatively free of emotional conflict within themselves—do not seem prone to aggressive conflict with others. When secure children play in pairs with others of any category, they neither victimize their playmates nor become victims themselves. By contrast pairs of insecurely attached children almost always fall into such patterns; and those whose initial relation to the mother is so conflicted as to be disorganized tend to become controlling and coercive as childhood unfolds.

Also the patterns pass from parent to infant. The categories of secure and insecure attachment observed for year-old babies map, among others, to counterparts discernible in the ways adults talk and think about their own childhoods. The category of an infant's attachment can be predicted with impressive regularity from the counterpart category assigned to its mother (or adoptive mother), even before the infant is born. The best explanation for this would seem to be that infants start to acquire basic patterns of emotional expression and relationship by identification with their parents, as considered above.

First representations: self and other, us and them

The correlation between the seven-month-infant's newly affectionate and communicative relation with mother on the one hand and its new fear of strangers on the other indicates that the infant has now imposed upon its experience both a form of distinction between self and other, and a related distinction between a good *us* and a potentially bad *them*. These are linked; for as the emerging *I* of the infant self is a locus of individual feeling and will, so the emerging *we* of the mother/infant pair is a locus of shared feeling and collective will, particularly in relation to threats from outside, such as strangers apparently represent. The infant's emerging distinction between self and other thus resolves out of a prior but less focussed sense of contrasting relationships, with the self already anchored in affectionate and information-gathering relations with carers, kin, and other local familiars.[39]

---

39   On the social background of the infant's sense of self see the essays in Braten (ed.), cited above.

Together with the material noted above, this strongly suggests that the innate propensity which Boyd and Richerson describe—'to cooperate with sympathy-inspiring ingroup members, and to use symbolic markers to define ingroups'—begins with relations of identification with the mother, and has its initial parameters set before the end of the first year.[40] The same applies to the other side of the coin, the infants' projective distrust of the alien. But although this development seems clearly marked in the infant's behaviour, we should note that there is something paradoxical about it. The infant distinguishes its mother from other people from birth, and by the fourth month has developed many special ways of relating to her, including elaborate and affectionate 'proto-conversations', which it conducts only with her.[41] So the question arises: if the seven-month infant already has a longstanding specific relationship with its mother, why does it now so sharply distinguish between mother (and other familiars) and strangers? And why does it so vigorously protest the departure of the one, and so readily fear the approach of the other?

The best explanation for this seems to be that the infant's prior sense of relationship includes its directing both its strongest affections and fiercest hostilities towards the mother herself, *but without yet grasping that these emotions are directed towards one and the same enduring individual, or indeed towards a person at all.* The change observable at seven months would thus result from the infant's working out that its mother was a single continuing communicating being, and thus unique and irreplaceable, so that her presence became uniquely valuable and her absence likewise threatening.

This is in effect the hypothesis advanced by Melanie Klein, in her account of the paranoid/schizoid and depressive positions of infancy.[42] From our current perspective what is most important about this development is that it represents the infant's bringing together in the representation of a single, unique and lasting *other* both identificatory and the projective images of the other

---

40 Taking this further, and in connection with the theory of conceptual metaphor, we can glimpse the possibility that markers of ethnic boundaries ultimately symbolize those of the infant's or mother's own bodies ('motherland' etc.). Again this may seem incredible, but the most basic forms of punishment and aggression are bodily, and the hypothesis under consideration is that the regulation of ingroup punishment and outgroup aggression is formative of the individual (and body-protecting) mind.

41 For description of these developments see Trevarthan and Aitken cited above, and for a fuller account see Travarthan and others in S. Braten (ed.), cited above.

42 For more detailed discussion of these see Segal, cited above, and Hopkins (1987). 'Synthesis in the imagination: psychoanalysis, infantile experience, and the concept of an object'. In *Philosophical perspectives on developmental psychology* (ed. J. Russell), Blackwell, Oxford.

which it has not previously had occasion to unify. Thus the infant's initial consolidation of an image of itself as in a co-operative (as opposed to an hostile) relation with its mother, which we see in separation distress and social referencing, has as its projective corollary the initial consolidation of an image of others who were bad and threatening, which we see in fear of strangers. The work we have considered above gives us reason to suppose that this original (and Kantian) synthesis of the object in the imagination plays a significant role in the way the infant henceforth conceives itself and others. The opposition between good us and bad them would thus lie near the core of human individuality. It would be a consequence of the interaction of identification and projection with the infant's attainment of the ability to represent itself and others as single and continuously existing.

Specific behavioural manifestations of this development may be observable in experiments conducted by Bower and Bell.[43] Bower describes

> ... A simple optical arrangement that allows one to present infants with multiple images of a single object ... If one presents the infant with multiple images of its mother—say three 'mothers'—the infant of less than five months is not disturbed at all but will in fact interact with all three 'mothers' in turn. If the setup provides one mother and two strangers, the infant will preferentially interact with its mother and still show no signs of disturbance. However, past the age of 5 months (after the co-ordination of place and movement) the sight of three 'mothers' becomes very disturbing to the infant. At this same age a setup of one mother and two strangers has no effect. I would contend that this in fact shows that the young infant (less than five months old) thinks it has a multiplicity of mothers, whereas the older infant knows it has only one.

This admits interpretation as showing that while at four months the infant takes its mother as a psychological other to whom it relates, it does not yet regard her as a single enduring person, as opposed to a potential multiplicity of presences whose spatio-temporal dimensions are as yet indeterminate. By five months, however, the baby opposes uniqueness to episodic multiplicity, and starts to view the mother (and by implication/identification its own self) as individual, continuous, and lasting.

We can also observe related changes in the infant's expressions of emotion. Thus when someone makes a four-month baby angry by impeding its movements, the baby directs its anger at the impeding hand. The four-month-old seems not to have worked out that the hand is part of, and so animated by,

---

43   See Bower, T. Development in infancy, p 217. W. H. Freeman, San Francisco; and Bell, S. 'The development of the concept of the object as related to infant-mother attachment' *Child Development*, 40, 291–311.

another person.[44] A seven-month-old, by contrast, directs its anger to the impeding agent's face. By this age the baby is capable of monitoring others' expressions and responding in complex ways to the feelings they show; and the identity of the frustrating person now apparently matters as well. The seven-month-old protests at being impeded by either its mother or a stranger; but it apparently expects its mother to comfort it after frustration by the stranger, and so is especially upset when she does not do this.[45] So by seven months the infant's anger towards its mother has been modified by the representation of itself as requiring, and her as providing, comfort and protection where strangers are concerned. Such representationally and cortically modified anger thus already differs from the newborn's initial subcortical rage.

Before the infant represents itself and its mother in these ways, however, it evidently makes her the target of anger and fear. A newborn, for example, can be provoked to rage simply by the sight of its mother's immobile face.[46] Indeed the young infant seems particularly prone to experience anger or fear whenever its mother is unresponsive or alien. (Few things are more objectively threatening to an infant than a mother who will not respond, and since mother is such an important cognitive/emotional target her familiarity would seem important also.) Carpenter describes how infants presented with their mother's face in strange circumstances 'would tense as they averted their gaze appearing to keep the target in peripheral view. From this position they would frequently take furtive glances. Sometimes they would turn ninety degrees away.' She noted that looking right away, as if trying to end the episode, was particularly frequent when infants were shown their mother's face speaking with a different voice. Again, Cohn and Tronick observed babies of just over three months, comparing the ways they related to their mothers in normal circumstances with their responses when the mother's deliberately behaved in a expressionless way. Normally the babies alternated between watching the mother, showing positive feeling, and playing interactively with her. In the abnormal circumstances, by contrast, they were fearful and suspicious, and alternated between attending warily, protesting, and turning away.[47]

---

44 This is also an instance of the psychoanalytic notion of an emotional relation to a part-object, which applies to the mother generally, including the breast.

45 See Campos *et al.*, cited above, p 824 and Sternberg et al., in Mussen (ed.), cited above, p 181.

46 Personal communication, Professor Peter Molnar.

47 Cohn, J. F. and Tronick, E. Z. (1983). 'Three-month-old infants' reaction to simulated maternal depression'. *Child Development*, 54, 185–93. Travarthan cites a number of related experiments in 'The concept and foundations of infant intersubjectivity' at p 31 of Braten (ed.), cited above.

This is how infants later act with strangers, as they consolidate their images of self and other as unique lasting beings. So these observations are consistent with the idea that strangers—and by extension members of outgroups generally—inherit the fear and rage directed at mothers who seems strange or unresponsive in the first months of life. This provides a continuity between the 'merciless violence' which Freud ascribed to the earliest parental imagoes at the basis of conscience, and the violent outgroup aggression apparently characteristic of our species life. We noted at the outset that Darwin and his successors have indicated how the formations of conscience might have evolved by binding humans in internally cohesive and externally rivalrous groups. We can now see that Freud and his successors have complemented this, by describing in detail how these same formations create a moral unity encompassing punishment within groups who co-operate via identification, and also set these groups against one another in projection-driven conflict.

If the present discussion is on the right lines, psychoanalysts also have traced these conflicts to their individual psychological roots. These lie in the infant's early pre-personal and fragmentary projective images of the other, and hence in its first confused unknowing fears, and desperate primitive extractive rage. If this is correct, then work in psychoanalysis and attachment should have particularly central place in the perspective of evolutionary psychology. For these disciplines are unique in addressing the task of moderating these emotions in infancy, overseeing their continuities in the course of development, and altering the images that channel them into destructive conflict as life unfolds.

CHAPTER 13

EMOTION, REASON, AND VIRTUE

PETER GOLDIE

Do emotions enable us to see things in their true light, as we would not be able to do if we were not capable of experiencing emotion? I think that our intuitions tend to draw us in two apparently opposing directions. On the one hand, we are inclined to say that emotional experience can sometimes tell us things about the world that reason alone will miss. That, one might think, is why we evolved as creatures capable of emotion. Yet, on the other hand, we are inclined to say that our emotions can and do profoundly distort our view of things: in anger or jealousy, for example, when the red mist comes down over the eyes, and we can feel the blood pulsing in the temples, things look other than the way they are, and, accordingly, our emotions can mislead us profoundly; literature is replete with examples.

A cheap resolution of these competing intuitions would be to say that there are cases and cases: sometimes our emotions help us to gain empirical knowledge, and sometimes they hinder us. No doubt this is true so far as it goes, but I think there is more to be said than just that. In a nutshell, what I want to argue for here is as follows. If our emotions are to yield empirical knowledge, then it is necessary for us to have the right emotional dispositions, prudential and moral, that will properly attune us to the world. Having such dispositions is part of what is involved in being prudentially and morally virtuous. If we do not have the right dispositions, then, I will suggest, our emotions can distort perception and reason so that the world seems to us other than it really is: as I will put it, the emotions *skew the epistemic landscape*. The intellectual virtues ought to help here: we ought, when (and only when) the occasion requires, to introspect, and ask ourselves what emotions we are experiencing, and whether, and in what way, those emotions are skewing the epistemic landscape, so that corrections can be made. Being appropriately disposed to do this, relying to a considerable extent of non-conscious processes, is part of what is involved in being intellectually virtuous.

Now, the epistemology of the emotions looks in two directions: introspectively, towards our own mental and physical condition; and extraspectively, towards the world beyond the bounds of our mind and bodies. It is not always possible to have reliable introspective knowledge about our own emotional condition, so, if we are less than fully virtuous prudentially and morally, we will not be in a position to know whether, and in what way, our emotions are distorting perception and reason. It is a consequence of this that we will not be able to do what we know we ought to do: we know it is part of being intellectually virtuous to check, when (and only when) the occasion requires, whether our emotions are distorting perception and reason. But we cannot reliably do this. And this leads me to two conclusions. The first conclusion is that we cannot be intellectually fully virtuous unless we are also prudentially and morally fully virtuous. The second conclusion, which is much more speculative, concerns the scope of proper accountability and blame. It is a fact that we are held accountable and blamed for our unjustified emotions, and for the way these emotions distort perception and reason, and for our ignorance that this is what is happening. Moreover, we are held accountable and blamed for the lack of virtue (prudential, moral and intellectual) which lies behind these failings. But can we be *properly* held accountable and blamed (by others and by ourselves) when these failures to comply with norms are not voluntary or within our control? I want to suggest that blame here *can* be justified, even though what we are blamed for is not voluntary: the scope of proper blame extends beyond action and omissions and whatever else is within our control.

It is a reasonable constraint on any account of empirical knowledge through emotional experience that it be pretty much continuous with empirical knowledge gained in other ways. Accordingly, I will begin with an account of how perception can be a source of knowledge in the 'ordinary' cases: that is, those cases where emotions are not involved.[1] I will not have the space here to argue for it, but I hope it will be accepted at least for the purposes of this chapter. Then I will consider those cases where emotions are involved. What will emerge, I hope, are not only the analogies but also the disanalogies between 'ordinary' perception and perception where the emotions are involved; and it is in these disanalogies that some deep epistemological difficulties arise.

---

1   The idea that there are cases where emotions are not involved will be subject later to some qualification.

Perception and reason

Empirical thinking is 'answerable to experience'[2] in the sense that perceptual experiences can themselves provide *reasons* for empirical belief and judgement. The content of our perceptions—our perceiving things to be thus and so—are, however, only *prima facie* reasons for the related empirical belief, the belief that things are indeed thus and so. A prima facie reason is a consideration that appears *at first sight* to be a reason (using the term 'reason' in the standard normative sense), but which may turn out, in fact, not to be a reason. For example, your seeing something as red or as square is a prima facie reason for believing it to be red or to be square. But if you were wearing distorting lenses that made blue things look red or rectangular things look square, then your seeing something as red or as square is not a reason (that is, not a good reason) for believing it to be so.

It is not, however, necessary that the content of each particular perceptual experience should be held in suspense pending a check on one's perceptual mechanisms or any other sort of second-order reflective endorsement. The epistemic requirement, rather, is the commonsense one that we need only consciously seek to satisfy ourselves that the deliverances of a particular perceptual experience are as they should be if there is good reason to do so on that occasion. Putting the point in terms of virtue epistemology, which I find helpful to do, there is a normative requirement to be motivated to have, and to have, the right habits and dispositions of thought, such that doubts will arise when and only when they should.[3] On particular occasions, much of our thinking will be unreflective, and not part of conscious deliberation, so we will need to rely on our habits and dispositions, at work in the background of our minds, so to speak. As Christopher Hookway puts it, 'we can be confident in our ability to reason effectively only if we are also confident that, by and large, issues enter our conscious deliberations if and only if their doing so is important for the success of our activities' (2000, 64).[4]

---

2   McDowell (1996: xix). Cf Brewer (1999).

3   For discussion of these issues in terms of virtue epistemology, see Zagzebski (1996) and Hookway (2000). Also see Brewer (1999) for what he calls a 'first-order' account of how perceptual experiences can themselves 'provide reasons for the perceiver's beliefs about the way things are in the world around him' (1999: 205)—reasons which are, however, 'always open to rational reflection and rejection' (1999: 205).

4   Hookway was concerned here with what he called 'practical rationality', and the content of perceptual experience will be part of practical rationality in the sorts of cases I have in mind. I appreciate that virtue epistemology is controversial. I will not argue for it here, but would point readers especially to Hookway's paper, where he emphasizes the parallels between the prudential and the moral virtues and the intellectual virtues, especially in respect of the importance in deliberation of what we do not consciously monitor and control, relying on the habits and dispositions which are part of the relevant virtue. There are many issues here concerning internalism and epistemic justification that I cannot go into.

Let me make one further point about 'ordinary' perception, before turning to perception and the emotions, as it will be relevant in what is to follow. I want to take here a fairly wide notion of perception under which the concepts that are deployed in perceptual receptivity—call them *perceptual* concepts—can also be, in a sense, *theoretical* concepts.[5] The point can be made most easily in relation to some sort of expertise, of the kind that is involved in playing chess or in a scientific activity. In chess, when one is first learning the skill, it is very hard, if not impossible, to see what is happening on the chessboard: that, for example, one's queen is being threatened by the bishop. One has to try to work it out through agonizing steps of reasoning, thinking through each move individually. But after experience and training, the expert will be able to *see* that his queen is threatened: the phenomenology is visual, and the judgement is spontaneous, without any sort of conscious inferential process. The perceptual capacity has become second nature for the expert. Yet, if he asks himself *why* he sees that his queen is threatened, he will be able (or at least ought to be able) to think of reasons which support his perceptual judgment. But, as we saw from the preceding paragraph in respect of practical deliberation, this question ought consciously to arise for him if and only if its doing so is important for success—in this case winning the game. Similarly, an experienced scientist will be able to *see* the photon in the cloud chamber, and again, if appropriate to his project, he will be able to think of reasons why he sees things this way. In both these examples, then, the concepts involved in the perceptual contents (that the queen is threatened; that there is a photon in the cloud chamber) will be embedded in a substantial theory. So concepts can be both perceptual and theoretical, and we can allow that the chess expert and the experienced scientist see things differently from the way their inexperienced counterparts see things. Moreover, chess experts and experienced scientists should aim to be intellectually virtuous, able to rely on their habits and dispositions of thought so that doubts and questions arise about the content of their perceptions when and only when they should.

Emotion, perception and reason

Let me begin by introducing a term: *emotion-proper property*. An emotion-proper property is the property that is proper to, or 'belongs to', a type of emotion. For example, being frightening is the emotion-proper property for fear. Other examples are being disgusting (proper to disgust), being shameful (proper to shame), being enviable (proper to envy), and being worthy of pride (proper to pride). Some emotions and emotion-proper properties will be

5   I was helped here by Blackburn (1995: 278–9) and his discussion of Churchland (1986).

(roughly) prudential, and some will be (roughly) moral, and some will be both.[6]

When we are confronted by things in the environment, and respond emotionally to them, we also, as part of the same experience, typically *perceive* those things as having the emotion-proper property. For example, if, as a caring parent, you see the out-of-control toboggan hurtling straight for your child, you feel fear, and you see the toboggan *as being frightening*. Or if you feel disgust at a maggot-infested piece of meat, you see the meat as *being disgusting*. Or if you are at a party and someone says something to you and you feel angry at the remark, you hear the remark as *being insulting*. Our ability to perceive things as having these emotion-proper properties will be more or less a matter of training and experience, depending on all sorts of factors which I need not go into here (recognizing maggot-ridden meat as disgusting takes little training or experience; recognizing the offensiveness of certain linguistic expressions or certain ways of behaving at table are things that a child has to be taught). But, drawing on the earlier discussion of perceptual and theoretical concepts, it need not be contentious that, if we do have the requisite training or experience, we can indeed *perceive* things as having such properties.

In the typical case, the experience of responding emotionally to things in the environment, combined in phenomenology with the perception of the object as having the emotion-proper property, will also involve the experience of the emotion and the perception as being *reasonable* or *justified*.[7] For example, when you feel fear, and see the out-of-control toboggan as being frightening, you take the experience to be reasonable or justified. The non-typical cases are not like this: these are the occasions where one realises *at the time* that one's emotional response is *not* reasonable or justified. For example, you feel afraid of the mouse in the corner of the room, and yet at the same time you know that your feelings are not justified. In these non-typical cases, although the object might still *seem* to have the emotion-proper property (the mouse does *seem to be* frightening), one is not inclined, as one is in the typical case, to consider one's emotional response to be justified. There is, thus, the possibility, which may, of course, not be actualized, of acknowledging, in one's own case, and at the same time as the emotional experience takes place, that things are

---

6 For the purposes of this chapter nothing hangs on distinguishing between prudential and moral emotions and emotion-proper properties; moreover, there may be other emotions and emotion-proper properties that are neither prudential nor moral—aesthetic, for example.

7 As John Skorupski puts it, 'the affective response typically carries with it a normative impulse' (2000: 125).

not really as they seem: the mouse seems frightening, but you know that it is not, for you know that your fear is not justified.

What makes an emotion reasonable or justified? Roughly, it will be justified by reasons—reasons which justify both the ascription to the object of the emotion-proper property and the emotion. For example, the ascription of the property of being disgusting to the piece of meat will be justified in part because the meat is maggot-infested, and the fact that it is maggot-infested will also justify your disgust. This relationship between (1) justified ascription of emotion-proper properties to the object of the emotion (the meat's being disgusting), (2) justified emotion (the disgust that you feel towards the meat), and (3) justifying reasons (such as the fact that the meat is maggot-infested) can be shown diagrammatically, where the lines represent justifying relations:

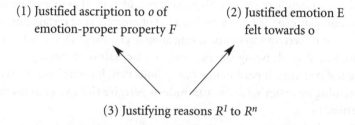

(1) Justified ascription to *o* of   (2) Justified emotion E
    emotion-proper property *F*   felt towards o

(3) Justifying reasons R^1 to R^n

More formally, the relation between (1), (2), and (3) can be put as a schema:

> An object *o* has emotion-proper property *F* iff it is possible for *o* to be the object of a justified emotion *E*; and the reasons, R^1 to R^n, that justify the ascription of *F* to *o* will be the same reasons as those that justify *E*.[8]

---

8   Each relatum is normative; at pains of falling foul of Moore's open question argument (1903), none of the relata can be explicated in non-normative terms. It is worth pointing out here that this schema ought to be equally amenable to a projectivist and to a realist (so long as one is not working with too ontologically loaded a conception of property). For a reasonable projectivist should agree that whilst one's feeling of disgust might explain why one finds the meat to be disgusting, it is not the response that makes the meat disgusting (cf Blackburn 1993: 157); and the realist will surely say the same (cf McDowell 1979 and 1987). Those emotion-proper properties that are related one-to-one to emotions will generally be at the 'thicker' end (disgusting-disgust; frightening-fear; hateful-hate; shameful-shame). Others will be much more complicated in their relations. A fully developed account will have to be able to handle the difference between two distinct uses of some of these terms for emotion-proper properties—a moralizing and a non-moralizing use (cf D'Arms and Jacobson 2000b). Consider envy. If one were to insist that envy is a vice, and that envy is never justified, then nothing is ever truly enviable. This is a moralizing use. But there is another non-moralizing use, where we would agree that it is true that my neighbour's Maserati is enviable, even though, when speaking morally, nothing is enviable. There are a number of other issues that would have to be dealt with in a fully developed account, but I will have to put these to one side here.

It can be seen that (continuing with the disgusting piece of meat as an example) the reasons that justify the ascription of disgustingness to the piece of meat (the fact that it is maggot-infested, etc.) are the *very same* reasons that make feeling disgust justified on this occasion. It is neither one's perceiving it to be disgusting that justifies one's disgust, nor is it one's feeling disgust that justifies one's perceiving it to be disgusting; the justifying route is only from the bottom up.

The epistemology of the emotions, on the other hand, often begins at the top: one often first either feels the emotion (top right in the diagram), or one perceives the object as having the emotion-proper property (top left); only later does one become conscious of the reasons that both justify one's emotion and the content of one's perception. Now, part of what lies behind the intuition that our emotions can sometimes tell us things about the world that reason alone will miss is that they can play this epistemic role: they can enable us to see things in their true light and to make correct perceptual judgements, in ways that we would not otherwise be able to do. Emotions can reveal saliences that we might not otherwise recognize with the same speed and reliability; for example, we can immediately see that something is *frightening* or *disgusting* in a way that we would not be capable of if we were not capable of feeling these emotions. Our emotional dispositions can, so to speak, *attune* us to the world around us, enabling us quickly and reliably to see things as they really are, and thus to respond as we should. In short, emotions enable us to *get things right*.[9]

Emotional mean-dispositions: being prudentially and morally virtuous

Getting things right is more than having the appropriate emotion, but also having one which is proportional to the circumstances, of the right duration, and so on. This is why it is mistaken to try, as some accounts have done, to capture this normativity with the idea that our emotional responses, at the top right of the diagram, should merely be *appropriate*.[10] An emotion being justified or reasonable is more than its being appropriate. For example, to feel grief at the death of one's much-loved pet is appropriate, but the grief could fail to be proportionate and it might last the wrong amount of time. To have an

---

9   Thus, whilst perception plays this epistemologically important role in our experience of things as having emotion-proper properties, my position does not involve a bogus intuitionism (cf McDowell 1987); justification involves reasons.

10   See, for example, Mulligan (1998), Raz (2000), and D'Arms and Jacobson (2000a).

emotional disposition that enables one to get things right is to have what Aristotle called an emotional mean-disposition. Having dispositions like this is part of what it is to be prudentially and morally virtuous; as Aristotle put it, the virtuous person will feel—that is, have emotions—and act 'at the right times, about the right things, towards the right people, and in the right way; ... this is the intermediate and best condition, and this is proper to virtue' (*Nicomachean Ethics* 1106b20).[11]

Having the emotional mean-disposition, the deployment of which is necessary to getting things right, is a profoundly normative notion. It is absurd to suggest that it is sufficient that one should check out one's emotional dispositions by comparing them to other humans or to others within one's community, and concluding that if they match up with what is typical or normal, then they are fine, if not, then they are 'wrong'. For example, it is in an important sense *normal* for humans to feel envy and sexual jealousy, but in both cases it is at least debateable whether envy and sexual jealousy are *ever* justified.[12] Moreover, in respect of an emotion towards a particular object or type of object, an entire community (or near enough entire) can be wrong, as, for example, were English people at the beginning of the First World War, who almost universally felt profound anger and disgust at all things German: Dachshunds, Wagner, and so on. We now see that as silly (or worse), and surely it is we who are right. It was certainly normal to experience what was called an 'outpouring of grief' at the death of Princess Diana, but this too has been argued to be wrong (O'Hear 1998); and here again the contrary view is not wrong simply in virtue of not being normal. In the prudential sphere, it might be normal not to fear the microwaves from mobile 'phones, but perhaps we will find out at some future date that we are wrong: we *should* be afraid. And perhaps, in people of a certain age, it has always been normal, throughout civilised time, to find modernity maddening, and to look back with yearning to times gone past.

If one is not properly attuned to the world around one, then one will be disposed to get things more or less wrong. I say 'more or less' because virtue comes in degrees, and most of us are less than fully virtuous. If, for example, you are, by disposition, an unduly timorous person, you will respond with fear to all sorts of things that are not really dangerous—or at least to things that are not as dangerous as you take them to be. And if you are disposed to be

---

11   As Simon Blackburn puts it, 'Where virtuous agents differ is in the direction of their passions, not their existence. ... They care about the right things and to the right extent' (2002: 95). See also Morton (2002).

12   Cf the discussion of envy in Footnote 8 above.

unduly indifferent to dangerous things, then you will fail to fear things as you ought. It is, of course, an over-simplification (one to which Aristotle was perhaps prone) to think in terms of there being a *single* emotional mean-disposition for fear of all sorts of things. A particular person could, for example, be both unduly indifferent in respect of the risk of being attacked by bulls in fields, and unduly timorous in respect of the risk of being attacked by muggers in dark alleyways. Another might be unduly quick to anger at critical remarks about her parents and unduly indifferent towards remarks about her sexuality. There may be explanations of these dispositions, amounting as they do to less than full virtue, that will appeal to these persons' past experiences: perhaps he was brought up in the company of an unusually friendly bull, and was also brought up by parents who were terrified of street crime, so that their timorousness in this respect rubbed off on him; and so on. Even if one has the right disposition for most situations, if one is less than fully virtuous, factors can unduly interfere with one's emotional response on an occasion, leading one to fail to get things right. I will mention two notable ones. First, one's mood can affect one's emotional response: for example, if one is in an irritable mood (perhaps through drinking too much coffee), then one is more likely to find a remark insulting and to get angry. Secondly, a recent emotional experience in relation to one thing can resonate across to some other, unrelated thing: for example, if one has just had the terrifying experience of being mugged in an alleyway, then one may be especially likely to be jumpy every time there is a knock at the door; your emotional disposition gets temporarily put 'out of tune'.[13]

I mentioned earlier, with the example of fear of the mouse, those non-typical occasions where one *realizes* that one is getting things wrong. On such occasions, where one realizes at the time that the explanation for one's emotion is not in the world, but is rather in oneself (in one's disposition, or in one's mood, or in some other factor affecting reasonable thinking and feeling), one realizes that one *ought* to stop feeling as one does. But this is, of course, a normative 'ought' and not necessarily a predictive one: one's emotions are, to a degree, cognitively impenetrable. Thus, emotions are not open to Moore's paradox in the same way as are beliefs.[14]

---

13   There are cases where being 'out of tune' on an occasion enables one, by accident, to get things right; Adam Morton suggested an example to me of someone who is especially afraid because of the scary film that he just saw, so that he notices that someone is following him, which he would not have otherwise been able to do. I appreciate that there are a number of epistemological difficulties here, but I will not address them in this chapter.

14   I discuss this in Goldie (2000: 74–8).

So now we can see what lies behind the competing intuitions over the question of whether or not the emotions enable us to see things in their true light. The answer begins to look like this: if one is of the right disposition, that is, if one has the emotional mean-disposition or virtue, and if there are no other undue influences on one's thinking, then one will see things as they really are, and one will respond in the right way. Having these dispositions can help us to find our way around the world, without our constantly having to consciously reflect on our reasons for our responses on each and every occasion; as was the case with 'ordinary' perception, having the right habits of thought and feeling (which here will be internal to the related prudential or moral virtue) will mean that doubts and questions will arise when and only when they should. But if, like most of us, one is less than fully virtuous, then there is not only a significant risk of getting things wrong. There is also a significant risk that one's emotions will *distort perception and reason* in ways that I now want to explore.

Emotions can distort perception and reason

I will explore this idea in the context of an epistemological model, which I cannot argue for here, which is essentially Neurathian and anti-foundation-alist[15], where our extraspective access to the way things are in the world, gained through our senses, is not external to what John McDowell has termed, after Wilfrid Sellars, 'the space of reasons'. This is what is at the heart of the idea that one's perceiving things to be thus and so is a *reason*—in the normative sense—for believing them to be thus and so. This model, however, should not lose sight of one's 'standing obligation', as McDowell puts it, to reflect upon, criticize, and change if necessary our way of thinking of things, although, as McDowell continues, we should accept (as an implicit part of the Neurathian model) 'that one can reflect only from the midst of the way of thinking one is reflecting about'.[16] Having a disposition to reflect in this way, *when and only when appropriate*, is part of what is involved in being intellectually virtuous.

---

15   As Otto Neurath put it, in the famous words that became Quine's motto, 'We are like sailors who have to rebuild their ship on the open sea, without ever being able to dismantle it in dry-dock and reconstruct it from the best components.' Neurath, 'Protokollsätze', *Erkenntnis* (1932–1933), repr. as 'Protocol Statements', in Otto Neurath, *Philosophical Papers* 1913–1946, ed. and tr. R. S. Cohen and M. Neurath (Dordrecht, 1983).

16   McDowell (1996: 81). He makes these remarks in the context of ethical thinking, but makes it clear that they apply equally to all empirical knowledge; cf McDowell (1987).

As I have already said, it is typical of emotional experience to consider one's emotion, and one's perception of the object of one's emotion as having the emotion-proper property, to be justified. So far so good. But what if, without your knowing it, your emotion is unjustified, and the object of your emotion does not have the emotion-proper property that it seems to have? (Perhaps you think you have the right emotional disposition but you do not; or perhaps your mind is subject to other undue influences that you are not aware of.) In such cases, one's emotions can distort perception and reason by *skewing the epistemic landscape* to make it cohere with the emotional experience: referring back to the diagram, the epistemic landscape tends to be skewed *downwards*, so to speak: we seek out and 'find' reasons—reasons which are supposed to justify what is in reality the unjustified ascription of the emotion-proper property, and which, at the same time, are also supposed to justify the emotion. The emotion, and the related perception of the object as having the emotion-proper property, tend to be *idées fixes* to which reason has to cohere. The phenomenon is a familiar one: when we are afraid, we tend unknowingly to seek out features of the object of our fear that will justify the fear—features that would otherwise (that is, if we were not already afraid) seem relatively harmless.[17] This is surely part of what is behind the commonsense intuition that our emotions can mislead us: they are *passions*, which, like *idées fixes*, we can be in the grip of.

The skewing process can be continuous whilst the emotion is in place, operating on new information as it comes in. One's emotions and emotionally held perceptual judgements *ought* to be open to be shown to be wrong by new evidence, but when new evidence does emerge, one tends not only to be insensitive to that evidence, but also, for the sake of internal coherence, to doubt the reliability of the source of that new evidence.

An extreme case is Leontes in Shakespeare's *A Winter's Tale*, who becomes jealous of his wife Hermione, and is convinced that he has been cuckolded by his boyhood friend Polixenes. Although his jealousy is not justified, everything now *seems to him* to justify his jealousy in what has suddenly become an emotionally skewed epistemic landscape: the way Hermione and Polixenes behave together; the sudden uncertainty about whether his daughter looks like him; the disappearance of his previously trusted Camillo, who is now a 'false villain'. He even rejects the evidence of the oracle of Apollo, that 'Hermione is chaste; Polixenes blameless; Camillo a true subject; Leontes a jealous tyrant;

---

17 Remember, I am not here concerned with those non-typical occasions (such as the fear of the mouse) when one knows at the time that one's emotional response is not justified, but the emotion remains; for on those occasions one's reason stands opposed to one's emotion, and one recognizes that it is one's emotion that is in error.

his innocent babe truly begotten'. Apollo, angry at having his word doubted, immediately wreaks his terrible revenge by bringing about the death of Leontes' son and wife. Only then does Leontes finally come to recognize that he has 'too much believ'd his own suspicion'; and then it is too late.

A possible objection to my position here is that there is nothing special about the emotional case: people are generally subject to all sorts of well-documented cognitive deficiencies, such as the confirmatory bias[18], and the emotional case is just an instance of this. One response to this objection, which I find independently attractive but will not pursue here, is that perhaps more of these cognitive deficiencies can be traced back to the emotions than might at first be thought. The other response, which I will put forward here, is that there *is* something special about the emotional case: emotions, and emotionally held perceptual judgements about things as having emotion-proper properties, are *more intransigent* than are their non-emotional counterparts, and thus the skewing of the epistemic landscape (for the sake of internal coherence) tends to be towards the preservation of the emotionally held *idées fixes* at the cost of the unemotional thoughts.

Now, given the generality of the normative requirement of intellectual virtue that one be disposed, when and only when appropriate, to reflect on, criticize, and if necessary change our way of thinking of things, this requirement surely ought to include a disposition to reflect critically, when and only when appropriate, on the way that one's emotions can have this skewing effect. But doing this is not so easy, largely because of the possibility that one's epistemic landscape has *already* been skewed without one's knowing it; so, like Leontes, one is not in a position, from the here and now of emotional experience, to take the dispassionate view of the evidence that the epistemic requirement demands. The problem is a very familiar one to everyday life: how to satisfy this epistemic requirement when one is in the swim of emotional experience. Consider this example. You feel in despair about your job. The job seems hopeless, and it seems to be hopeless for all sorts of reasons which seem to *justify* your feelings of despair: there are no decent prospects for promotion; most of your colleagues are people with whom you really have very little in common; you do not seem to be able to get the work done properly; the journey to and from home is a nightmare; and so on. Your friends, not in the here and now of this emotional experience, assure you that things only seem this black *because* you are feeling so despairing (you used not to be like this; perhaps some Prozac might help?). You try to stand back and see things as others do (maybe things will look a bit brighter in the morning).

18   See, for example, Nisbett and Ross (1980).

And you might succeed in doing this to some extent. But you could still think that it is your friends who are wrong: they believe these things because they do not see that things really *are* hopeless and how *right* you are to be in despair (Prozac might lift the despair, but the job will still be hopeless). The question remains: Is it you, or is it the job?

This leads me directly to a further, deeper difficulty that presses on those of us who are, prudentially or morally, less than fully virtuous. So far, my focus has been on cases where one is aware through introspection that one is experiencing a particular sort of emotion; in the example just discussed, you are aware that you are in despair. But it would be a grave mistake to think that our emotions are *always* transparent to introspection in this way. To begin with, one can sometimes not be sure what emotion it is that one is experiencing—it might be fear or it might be excitement as you approach the helter-skelter; the two emotions are phenomenologically very similar. Secondly, one can have an emotion without noticing it—one might be angry with someone and not realise it until it is drawn to your attention. (A sort of limiting case here is emotion that is repressed in the Freudian sense.) Thirdly, without one's knowledge, an emotion can, through what Jon Elster (1999) has nicely called alchemy or transmutation, be changed into a different emotion, or into some other kind of psychological state altogether. And lastly, emotions can continue to resonate in one's mental economy long after they are, as it might seem, 'over'. In all these sorts of cases (and others besides), emotion can distort reason in the ways I have been discussing. And this distorting effect can extend to judgements and beliefs that do not, in virtue of their contents, reveal themselves to be 'emotional'—that is to say, that do not themselves refer to emotion-proper properties as such. But now, one is in the worrying position of not knowing what emotions, if any, are at work, and what judgements and beliefs, if any, have been affected. One can therefore be inclined to think that one is being 'dispassionate' in one's judgment when one is not, or to think mistakenly that one sort of emotion is at work rather than another. Thus one has no way of knowing how to direct one's watchfulness. Constant checking would not only be practically paralysing; it would also be practically useless. One is in the position of having a normative requirement of intellectual virtue, which one knows of and acknowledges to be reasonable, but which one does not know how to satisfy.

Of course, if one is, in fact, fully virtuous prudentially and morally, then there will be no skewing of the epistemic landscape in this respect, and the requirement of intellectual virtue will, de facto, be met. But this is only superficially satisfactory, because, if one has, without knowing it, become *less than* fully virtuous prudentially or morally, the requirement will still *seem to be* met. And a falling away from full virtue is not always introspectively obvious. Moreover, some thoroughly *unvirtuous* prudential and moral dispositions involve, if they are deeply embedded psychologically, thinking that one is *not* in such a state; being self-righteous or being self-satisfied are perhaps examples.[19]

Let me give an example of the difficulty of knowing whether one's emotion is skewing one's epistemic landscape. A long time ago you were very angry with a colleague at work because he failed to turn up to a meeting that you were chairing, and at which his presence was essential. How *could* he do this when he *promised* to be there! You thought your anger to be thoroughly justified, on the grounds of his being so unreliable and inconsiderate. The following day, though, he came to see you with a full explanation, and was extremely apologetic. His son had been taken suddenly ill, and had to be rushed to hospital, and there was no chance of getting to a 'phone; and so on. You put your anger behind you, as you should do, realizing that your anger, although understandable at the time, was not justified, for he really had a good reason not to be there, and a good reason why he could not give you advance warning. Later still—*much* later—you are asked to provide a reference about this colleague. Without your realizing it, the content of what you say is affected by the residue of your anger, which still lies deep in the recesses of your mind. Of course, you do not go so far as to state outright that he is unreliable and inconsiderate, for your memory of the incident is at best only hazy; and anyway, as it later emerged, he was neither unreliable nor inconsiderate on that occasion. But still, unknown to you, for you think that you are being fair and dispassionate in what you say, your reference is not as favourable as it would have been if the incident had never taken place. Aware of the requirement of intellectual virtue, which is a virtue that you aspire to, you ask yourself, 'Am I emotionally involved here? Because if I am, I should be especially watchful.' But the answer comes back 'No, I am *not* emotionally involved'; moreover, you might sense a certain puzzlement as to what *sort* of emotion might be at work on this occasion. And if you were reminded of the long-past incident, you might insist that any anger that you felt all that time ago is no longer at work, distorting reason.[20]

---

19   This is echoed in Simon Blackburn's remarks, where he is drawing out the significant differences between secondary properties and 'those involved in value and obligation'. He says, 'There is no such loss [of immediately felt phenomenal quality] when we become, say, corrupt. We cannot become corrupt overnight, and usually we cannot tell when we have done so. Indeed, it would be a hallmark of many kinds of moral blindness that this is so' (1993: 159–60).

20   For some related empirical research, see Zillman and Cantor (1976).

Virtue and blame

Where are we so far? First, whilst one is in the swim of life, emotionally engaged with what is going on, one's epistemic landscape is liable, if one is less than fully virtuous, to be skewed by one's emotion and one's perception of emotion-proper properties, *idées fixes* to which reason is forced to cohere. To avoid this as much as possible, one should see oneself as subject to the requirement of intellectual virtue to reflect, as and when appropriate, on what one takes to be reasons, to make corrections where necessary, and to be disposed to be especially watchful when one is emotionally engaged. But then the further difficulty arises, that one can be emotional without knowing it, so one has no way of knowing that one's perception and reason are being distorted, or in what ways. Even if one were to accept the idea (which I am inclined to endorse) that emotions are always somewhere at work in our psyche, and thus to accept that a special watchfulness is *always* required, one will still be no wiser as to *how* to apply this normative requirement at any particular moment. This is especially troubling, as it seems that we ought to meet requirements which, if our emotions are not as they should be, we will not be able to meet: not only will our emotions be other than they ought to be; we ought to know that they are other than they ought to be. And this seems to fly in the face of the dark doctrine that 'ought' implies 'can'.

The conclusion seems to be this. If we are to be intellectually fully virtuous, we need first to be prudentially and morally fully virtuous.[21] If we fail to meet this prior condition, we will find that doubts and questions will not arise about our extraspective knowledge as and when they should, and they will not arise because we lack introspective knowledge about our emotional condition, and about how that condition is distorting perception and reason. We may be motivated to be intellectually virtuous, but we cannot actually *be* intellectually fully virtuous in this respect. And when put like that, the position is very understandable and unmysterious. Hookway, drawing a direct analogy between moral and intellectual or cognitive virtues, says 'That someone may lack the ability to display the cognitive virtues which she endorses seems a regular feature of our experience. ... Possession of intellectual virtue depends upon the possession of skills and habits whose possession is largely independent of the recognition that some state is, in fact, such a virtue' (2000, 76). And, we can now add, possession of this intellectual virtue also depends upon possession of prudential and moral virtue—that is, upon having prudential and moral emotional mean-dispositions.

---

21 Zagzebski (1996) also argues, for other reasons, that it is necessary to be morally virtuous if one is to be fully intellectually virtuous.

I want to end with some speculative remarks about accountability and blame for the failures to comply with the normative requirements that I have been discussing in this chapter. If we are prudentially and morally less than fully virtuous, are we properly to blame for our lack of virtue, for our unjustified emotions, for the distorting of perception and reason that unjustified emotions can bring about, and for our ignorance that this is what is happening? We certainly *do* ordinarily blame people, including ourselves, for these things. But the question is whether blame is appropriate here. One view is that it is not: we are only properly to blame for what is within our direct voluntary control. Thus, for example, we can be properly blamed for actions that are wrong, for these are things which are (at least typically) within our control. But we should not, according to this view, be blamed for our lack of virtue, for our unjustified emotions, or for our ignorance, for these are things which are not within our direct voluntary control.[22]

There are (at least) two possible approaches which, in contrast to this view, attempt to endorse our everyday practice of blame. On the first approach, one might, in an Aristotelian spirit, shift the focus from particular emotions and particular occasions of ignorance, which are admitted not to be in our *direct* control, and on to their sources, which are the relevant dispositional states of the person. One could then insist that these are at least within our indirect or partial control: roughly, you can be blamed for them because you did not try in the past to do things that you could have tried to do (like trying to be a nicer person), and if you had tried (and succeeded), then you would not now have the lack of virtue that you do have. Moreover, according to this view, there is no significant difference in voluntariness between intellectual virtues and prudential and moral virtues; if we can be blamed for lacking compassion, then we can equally be blamed for lacking an intellectual virtue. This would seem to be the approach of Linda Zagzebski in her very fruitful work on virtue epistemology. She says 'No one claims that our moral virtues and vices are under our complete control, but they are generally regarded as sufficiently voluntary to be the proper object of moral evaluation, including moral praise and blame' (1996, 59–60); and 'the voluntariness of intellectual virtues does not differ in any significant way from the voluntariness of the moral virtues' (1996, 60, Footnote 34).

....

22   These are familiar difficulties, and they are raised particularly in the context of virtue epistemology, given the traditional view that belief formation is involuntary. What I have in mind by the term 'voluntary control' is given by Adams (1985: 8): 'To say that something is (directly) within my voluntary control is to say that I would do it (right away) if and only if I (fully) tried or chose or meant to do so, and hence that if I did it I would do it because I tried or chose or meant to do it, and in that sense voluntarily.'

An alternative, more radical, approach is to deny that we can only be blamed for what is voluntary. I cannot argue for it here, but this position seems to me to be intuitively very attractive and well worth exploring when we consider prudential, moral and intellectual failures of the kinds that I have been considering in this chapter.[23] For it is highly intuitive that we *ought* to have the right dispositions, we *ought not* to have unjustified emotions, and ignorance of these failures is no excuse. As Robert Adams puts it, 'We ought not only to *try* to have good motives and other good states of mind rather than bad ones; we ought to *have* good ones and not bad ones.... The subject of ethics is how we ought to live; and that is not reducible to what we ought to do or try to do, and what we ought to cause or produce. It includes just as fundamentally what we should be for and against in our hearts, what and how we ought to love and hate. It matters morally what we are for and what we are against, even if we do not have the power to do much for it or against it, and even if it was not by trying that we came to be for it or against it' (1985, 12).

Consider this example. Jim lacks the emotional mean-disposition for anger, tending to become angry without what we would consider to be good reason, especially when he takes his status or moral worth to be impugned. He is like this in part because he thinks rather too highly of himself. One day, very much in character, Jim takes a harmless remark made at a meeting to be a deeply personal insult to his integrity. Now, further assume that Jim has stood back, as he should on this occasion, and asked himself if his emotion is skewing his epistemic landscape. He determines that it has not; he thinks his anger to be a fully justified righteous indignation. We blame him for being angry on this occasion, and for the lack of moral virtue which explains his being angry. We blame him for his ignorance that his epistemic landscape is being skewed, and for his lack of intellectual virtue, which lack explains his ignorance. According to this approach, blame is appropriate in all these respects, regardless of whether or not the failures were in his direct or indirect control.[24] Moreover, not only is *our* blame appropriate, Jim ought to blame himself once he comes to realise the insidious way that his anger, and his overweening self-regard, are distorting his perception and reason.

So, I hope at the end of all this we are left with a picture of the emotions that shows how they can enable us to get things right, whilst accepting that they can sometimes be deeply misleading; and I hope to have explained how

---

23 This is the position of Adams (1985).

24 Questions of punishment will need to kept separate from questions of blame; it may well be that people should not be punished in the same way for failures to meet norms where those failures are not within the person's control.

both of these are possible. Whilst we would not want other than to be creatures capable of emotion, we must not lose sight of just how messy, confusing
and difficult emotional life can be for those of us who are less than fully
virtuous.

Acknowledgements

Thanks are due to may people for their comments, including Adam Morton,
David Papineau, Carlo Penco, Finn Spicer, and the audiences at the Emotion,
Evolution and Rationality conference, The University of Genova, and the
Birkbeck Philosophical Society, where earlier versions of this chapter were
aired.

References

Adams, R. M. (1985). Involuntary Sins. *The Philosophical Review*, **94**, 3–31.

Aristotle (1985) (*NE*) *Nicomachean ethics* (trans. T. Irwin). Hackett, Indianapolis.

Blackburn, S. (1993). *Essays in Quasi-realism*. Oxford University Press, New York.

Blackburn, S. (1995). Theory, observation and drama. In *Folk Psychology* (ed. M. Davies and
T. Stone), Blackwell, Oxford, 274–90.

Blackburn, S. (2002). How emotional is the virtuous person? In *Understanding emotions:
mind and* morals (ed. P. Goldie). Ashgate Publishing, Aldershot, 2002, 81–96.

Brewer, B. (1999). *Perception and reason*. Clarendon Press, Oxford.

Churchland, P. M.(1986). Folk psychology and the explanation of human behaviour. In
Philosophical Perspectives 3. Ridgeview Publishing, Atascadero, CA, 1989.

D'Arms, J. and Jacobson, D. (2000a). Sentiment and value. *Ethics*, **110**, 722–48.

D'Arms, J. and Jacobson, D. (2000b). The moralistic fallacy. *Philosophy and Phenomenological Research.* 61, 65–90.

Elster, J. (1999). *Alchemies of the mind: rationality and the emotions*. Cambridge University
Press, Cambridge.

Goldie, P. (2000). *The emotions: a philosophical exploration*. Clarendon Press, Oxford.

Hookway, C. (2000). Epistemic norms and theoretical deliberation. In *Normativity*,
(ed. J. Dancy), Blackwell, Oxford, 60–77.

McDowell, J. (1979). Virtue and reason. *The Monist*, **62**, 331–50.

McDowell, J. (1985). Values and secondary qualities. In *Morality and objectives: a tribute to
J. L. Mackie* (ed. T. Honderich), pp. 110–29. Routledge, London.

McDowell, J. (1987). Projection and truth in ethics, Lindley Lecture at the University of
Kansas.

McDowell, J. (1996). *Mind and world*, 2nd edition. Harvard University Press, Cambridge,
Mass.

Moore, G. E.(1903). *Principia ethica*. Cambridge University Press, Cambridge.

Morton, A. (2002). Emotional truth (2). *Proceedings of the Aristotelian Society*, Supp. Vol. 76,
266–75.

Mulligan, K. (1998). From appropriate emotions to values. *The Monist*, **81**, 161–88.

Nisbett, R. E. and Ross, L. (1980). *Human inference: strategies and shortcomings of social judgement.* Prentice-Hall, Englewood Cliffs, NJ.

O'Hear, A. (1998). Diana, queen of hearts: sentimentality personified and canonised. In *Faking it: the sentimentalisation of modern society* (ed. D. Anderson and P. Mullen), pp. 181–90. Social Affairs Unit.

Raz, J. (2000). Explaining normativity: On rationality and the justification of reason. In *Normativity.* (ed. J. Dancy), pp. 34–59. Blackwell, Oxford.

Skorupski, J. (2000). Irrealist cognitivism. In *Normativity* (ed. J. Dancy), pp. 116–39. Blackwell, Oxford.

Zagzebski, L. (1996). *Virtues of the mind.* Cambridge University Press, Cambridge.

Zillman, D. and Cantor, J. (1976). Effect of timing of information about mitigating circumstances on emotional responses to provocation and retaliatory behavior. *Journal of Experimental Social Psychology,* **12**, 38–55.

INDEX

accounts of rationality 135
acrophobia 145
action affordance 99
action readiness 123–4
Adams, Robert 265
adaptive explanations 72
adaptive illusions 193–208
adaptive learning 150
adaptive plans of action 122–6
Adolphs' rating task 20–1
affect programs 35, 76, 136
affective computations 91, 94
affective primacy 90
affordance 95, 98–100
   action affordance 99
   goal-affordance 99
   happening affordance 99
aggression 28–30, 75, 225–48
   appetitive 28
   competitive 28
   offensive 28
   self-defensive 28
   self-protective 28
agrophobia 145
altruism 227–9, 241
amae (Japanese language) 75–6, 84
amok (Malay language) 75, 83, 84
amygdala 18–28
androgenetic chimeras 215
Angelman syndrome 214
anger 32–3, 75, 85, 124
   appraisal profile 112
   function of 107
   in infants 120–1
   occasions for 117–22
   other-blame as condition for 116
   real-life 119
   reasonable 113–17
   recognition of 28–30
   unreasonable 113–17
anxiety disorders 204
appetitive aggression 28
appraisal 89–92, 107–29

adaptive plans of action 122–6
   and affordance 98–100
   appraisal-emotion connections 112–13
   of different emotions 109–11
   functional appraisals 108–9
   Machiavellian 100–2
   and philosophy of emotion 92–6
   theory of 96–8
arachnophobia 145
as-if-body-loop 6, 165
attachment 242–4
attack 124
automatic appraisal mechanism 91
aversions 150
avoidances 145

basic emotions 69–87
behavior system 36
behavioral ecology 18
belief-desire theory 51–68
Ben-Ze'ev, Aaron 188
bias 142
Big Six emotions 70, 76, 84–5
biocultural model 137, 138
bizarre beliefs and desires 63
Blackburn, Simon 262
blame 263–6
   non-emotional 114
bodily changes 5, 61
bodily sensations *see* somatic markers
body loop 6, 12, 165
body-proper 6
Boyd, Robert 134
brain
   development 214–16
   frontal lobe 187
   hypothalamus 216
   maternal 216–18
   paternal 216–18
   ventromedial prefrontal cortex 167–8
brain damage 167–8, 169, 186–7
brain stem 11

Cannon, Walter 10
cat, amygdala responses in 22
causal explanation 64, 68
causative object 5
claustrophobia 145
cognitive appraisal 60
cognitive computations 91
cohesion 234–5
color perception 70
competitive aggression 28
conditioned fear 19
conflict 225–48
conformist bias 142, 152
conscience 225–48, 231–3
conscious awareness 189
consequentialist approach 134, 205
consolidation 242–4
constructionism 74–6, 78–81
content of emotion 82
continuity of attachment 242–4
control
    illusion of 195–8
    voluntary 264
convergent evolution 147
coping strategies 161
Copper Eskimos 146
core disgust system 25
core relational themes 17, 80, 89, 90, 137
cost-benefit analysis 167, 170
cultural child 141
cultural inertia 146
cultural influences 83–4, 126
cultural inheritance 141–2, 146–9
cultural parent 141
cultural variation 75, 78
cultures of honor 147–9

Damasio, Antonio 82, 132, 160, 164, 186
    somatic marker hypothesis 164–70
Darwin, Charles 227
de Sousa, Ronald 186, 188
    frame problem 182
    The Rationality of Emotion 181
decision-making 171
decoupled reflexes 109
defense systems 24
DeLancey, Craig 62
deliberation 162–3
deontological approach 134, 205
dependency 76
depression 199–200
direct bias 142
directed processes 142
disgust 71, 85, 153, 254–5
disgust recognition 24–8
disgust response 24–8
dishonor 97

display rules 18, 100
    cultural influences on 136
dissociation 23
distaste 24
dopamine 28–30
double-body 6
drives 237

ecological perception 99
ecological rationality 135, 159–78
    definition of 160
Ekman, Paul
    affect program theory 136
    automatic appraisal 91
    Big Six emotions 70, 76, 84–5
    display rules 100
Elster, John 261
embodied appraisal theory 81–3
emotion-proper property 252
emotional appraisal *see* appraisal
emotional attitudes 58
emotional behavior 51–68
emotional development 240–2
emotional feelings 164
emotional mean-dispositions 255–8
Emotional Preselection Theory of Action
    Choice 167
emotional prosody 22
Emotional Selection Theory of Action
    Choice 171
emotional states 5, 164
emotionally-competent stimulus 5, 7
emotivations 124
empirical thinking 251
environment 140
    proper 135
epigenetic agents 209
epistemic landscape 54, 62
    skewing of 54, 249, 255, 259–60
Evans, Gareth 96
evolutionary approach 30–4, 69, 133–58
evolutionary psychology 70–4, 78–81
expressive behaviors 61

facial expressions 18, 20, 23, 71, 78
    lack of relation to emotional
        response 123
facial mimicry 34
family conflict 235–7
fear 164
    auditory stimuli 22
    conscious experience of 23
    innate 145
    memories 20
    recognition 18–28
fear response 18–28, 71–2, 124

feelings 5, 55, 164
  see also somatic markers
Fessler, Daniel 96
fight or flight response 18–28, 71–2, 124
flattened affect 93
Fodor, Jerry 181, 183
folk psychology 54
folk-theory 59, 77, 90
food taboos 153–5
Foré people 78
frame problem 182–3
Frank, Robert 132
Freud, Sigmund 227, 234
  Interpretation of Dreams 231
Frijda, Nico 138
frontal lobe damage 186–7
frustration 120
functional appraisal 108–9
fureai (Japanese language) 76

gambling experiments 169
games 200–5
gape response in rodents 24–5
Garcia aversions 150
Garcia, John 150
genetic conflict 211–14
genetic inertia 144
genetic inheritance 140, 141, 209
genomic imprinting 209–11
  and brain development 214–16
Gibson, J.J. 99
Gigerenzer, Gerd 135
globus pallidus 24–8
goal-affordance 99
Goldie, Peter 54, 61
Griffiths, Paul 58, 188
group altruism 227–9
group conflict 228–9
group-serving bias 229
guilt 72, 75
  appraisal profile 112
gustatory insula 24–8
gut feelings 186

Hamlet's problem 181, 184
happening affordance 99
happiness 85
Hayes, Patrick 183
hemophobia 145
heuristics 185
Hobbes, Thomas 180
homology in emotion 15–47
homosexuality 231
Hookway, Christopher 251
Humean psychology 51–68
Huntington's disease 26

hybrid theories of emotion 55, 76–7
hypothalamus 216

idées fixes 54, 259–60, 263
identification 229–30
igf2 gene 210, 216–17
igf4 gene 211
illusion of control 195–8
imitation 141
indirect bias 142, 152
individual learning 140
infantile emotion 237–40
infidelity 73, 79
informational encapsulation 36
ingroup cohesion 234–5
inheritance 141, 209
innate fears 145
innateness 140
intention-tokening 163
intentional psychology 60, 65
intentionality 5, 53
  flexible notion of 94
intentions 163, 168
internal conflict 231–3
IQ 217
irrational emotions 143–56

James, William 3–14, 205
  criticism of 8–13
  The Varieties of Religious Experience 199
James-Lange theory of emotion 71
jealousy 73, 75, 79
joint perception 5

Ketelaar, Timothy 182
Klein, Melanie 245

Lange, Carl 4
learnability 71
learning
  adaptive 150
  individual 140
  social 140, 142
LeDoux, Joseph 91, 139
Levinson, Robert 137
limbic system 15, 30
linguistic context of emotion 75–6
locked-in syndrome 11–12
love 72–3, 79–80
luck 160

McCarthy, John 183
McDowell, John 258

McDowellean explanation 57–8
Machiavellian appraisal 100–2
Machiavellian Emotion Hypothesis 101
maladaptive value structures 143–56
marah (Malay language) 75
Mason, William 101
massive modularity 241
Millikan, Ruth 94
mirror neurons 6, 229–30
Möbius syndrome 34
monotonicity 16
moods 53
moral virtue 255–8
mother-infant interactions 73, 237,
    242–4
    see also parental investment
motivational congruence 112
motivational incongruence 112–13
multi-level appraisal 91
music, emotional response to 70

narcissism 241
natural selection 141
negative view of emotion 179
negotiation 18
Neurath, Otto 258
neurobiology of emotion 3–14
Newell, Alan 183
nomological view 56–7, 59, 64
non-intentionality 53
non-reductive view 58, 59, 60
normative moralization 155
Nussbaum, Martha 92–3

Oatley, Keith 138
obsessive compulsive disorder 26
offensive aggression 28
Ohman, Arne 90
oime (Japanese language) 76
olfaction 24
ophidophobia 145
optimism 195–8
Ortony, Andrew 138
other-accountability 111, 112
other-blame 111, 115–16, 121
    as condition for anger 116
outcomes 180–1
outgroup hostility 230–1, 234–5

PANAS scales 23
paralanguage 18
parental investment 235–7
    and emotional development 240–2
    and infantile emotion 237–40
parthenogenetic chimeras 215

passions 259
perception 251–2
    distortion of 258–62
perceptual states 57
philosophy of emotion 92–6
phobias 144–5, 204
phylogenetics 16
pituitary gland 216
placenta, invasivness of 212–14, 236–7
Plomin, Robert 217
plurality of ignorance 149
positive illusions 197–8, 204–5
postfunctional behaviors 62
practical rationality 159–78, 251
    definition of 162
Prader-Willi syndrome 214
preadaptation 25, 126–7
pregnancy 212–14
prestige bias 142, 151–2
pride, appraisal profile 112
primate studies 19–20
Prinz, Jesse 97
probability theory 200–5
projection 229–30, 234–5
projective identification 229
proper environment 135
property defense 28
prosodic fear 22
prosody 26
proto-conversations 245
prototype theory 119
prudential virtue 255–8
psychopaths 171, 174
punishment 165, 228

racism 226
rationality 64, 193–208
    accounts of 135
    approaches to 134–6
    ecological 135
reason 205–6
    distortion of 258–62
    and perception 251–2
reasonable anger 113–17
reasonable emotions 107–29, 252–5
resemblance 140
resource artefacts 15
Richerson, Peter 134
Rogers, Everett 152
rogue memes 151
romantic infidelity 79

sadness 85, 165
Scarantino, Andrea 99
Schadenfruede 84
Scherer, Klaus 90, 138

search hypothesis 179–91
　readings of 185–8
search strategy 184
self, concept of 244–8
self-accountability 112
self-blame 111
self-defensive aggression 28
self-enhancing bias 195–8
self-esteem 230–1, 232
self-protection 204
self-protective aggression 28
Sellars, Wilfred 258
separation distress 242
sexual infidelity 79
sham rage 11
shame 96
Shaw, Cliff 183
Sherrington, Charles 10
sibling rivalry 241
Simon, Herbert 183, 184
skin-conductance responses 169
Smith, Barry 51
social constructionism 74–6, 78–81
social learning 140, 142
social phobia 145
social referencing 242
socially mediated ingestive
　conditioning 155
Solomon, Robert 91
somatic markers 164–70
　reconstitution of 165
somatic state 166
spinal cord 8–10
Stein, Nancy 100
stranger anxiety 242, 246
subsumption of beliefs 69
subtraction 16
surprise 85

taboos 153–5
taste 24
taste aversion 25
teaching 140
teleosemantics 97–8
telereceptors 24
threat avoidance 204
time-slicing 173
Todd, Peter 182
Tourette's syndrome 26
toxins 24
transactional theory 111
tribalism 227–9
Trivers, Robert 231, 236

umbrella view 56, 59, 64
universal antecedents 17
universality of emotions 70
unreasonable anger 113–17
unreasonable emotions 121
Urbach-Wiethe disease 20
us and them 244–8

value structures 126, 133, 136–9
　content of 139–43
　maladaptive 143–56
ventromedial prefrontal cortex 167–8
virtue 263–6
voluntary control 264

X chromosome 218

Zagzebski, Linda 264
Zajonc, Robert 90